The New Crusades

The New Crusades

Constructing the Muslim Enemy

Edited by Emran Qureshi
and Michael A. Sells

COLUMBIA UNIVERSITY PRESS   NEW YORK

In Memory of Eqbal .

COLUMBIA UNIVERSITY PRESS

Publishers Since 1893
New York, Chichester, West Sussex

Library of Congress Cataloging-in-Publication Data

The new crusades : constructing the Muslim enemy / edited by Emran Qureshi and
Michael A. Sells.

    p. cm.
Includes bibliographical references and index.
ISBN 0–231–12666–2 (cloth : alk. paper) — ISBN 0–231–12667–0 (pbk. : alk.
paper)
    1. Islamic countries—Foreign relations—Europe. 2. Europe—Foreign rela-
tions—Islamic countries. 3. Islamic fundamentalism. 4. War—Religious aspects—
Islam. 5. Islamic countries—Foreign relations—United States. 6. United States—
Foreign relations—Islamic countries. 7. Terrorism—Religious aspects—Islam.
I. Qureshi, Emran. II. Sells, Michael Anthony.

D860.N389 2003
327.4017'671'09045—dc21

2003043768

Contents

Part II

Preface: A Tribute to Eqbal Ahmad

Emran Qureshi

This book is dedicated to the living memory of Eqbal Ahmad (1933–1999). Eqbal Ahmad nurtured this book project: guiding it, encouraging it, and contributing to it immeasurably over a five-year period. It is only fitting that his contribution be suitably acknowledged. This preface is thus intended to be a tribute to Eqbal Ahmad, a brief tribute, but one that nevertheless attempts to outline his contributions to this book project and, more important, to briefly sketch the contours of his political thought.

Eqbal Ahmad was among the most original political thinkers on the Middle East and South Asia. Eqbal Ahmad's writings consist of weekly commentaries on third world societies. Regrettably, he is known primarily as a journalist. Many of his political ideas are submerged within his journalistic writings. Within these weekly commentaries he wrote extensively on the pathologies of state and society in the Arab-Islamic world. Woven through these commentaries is a coherent set of political beliefs about third world societies and the ills that afflict them. Together, these commentaries draw a powerful, penetrating portrait of third world societies in a near permanent state of crisis.

At first blush, it is difficult to categorize the political ideas of Eqbal Ahmad. His work is evocative of the theories of Hannah Arendt and Antonio Gramsci. Like Hannah Arendt, Eqbal Ahmad examined the crucial political events of the day and, like Gramsci, he was an organically connected intellectual. He defined his politics in an interview as "socialist and democratic" and "by democratic I mean [a] genuine commitment to equality, freedom of association, to critical thought and to accountability of rulers to citizens" and noted "I took rather seriously Karl Marx's old dictum that the function of knowledge is to comprehend in order to change."[1] Eqbal Ahmad in his essays examined imperialism, revolutionary transformation, and the rise of Islamic fundamentalism, third world democracies, and the pathologies of postcolonial societies. His writings were original and subtle, complex, and interconnected, always providing clarity and insight into the pathologies afflicting third world societies, especially his native Pakistan.

Hannah Arendt once observed, "No matter how abstract our theories may appear, there are incidents and stories behind them which, at least for ourselves, contain as in a nutshell the full meaning of whatever we have to say."[2] The basic questions that animated Eqbal Ahmad's political thought sprang from his particular life experiences: the tumult and the horrors of the bloody partition of the Indian subcontinent, the struggle for Algerian independence, support for the Palestinian cause, the fight against Pakistani military dictators, and the bitter harvest of postcolonial states and societies.

It is not Eqbal Ahmad's genuinely unique insight into Arab-Islamic societies that is the primary reason for the increasing interest in his work but his steadfast independence as a public intellectual, which would not be compromised or intimidated.[3] The journalist David Barsamian asked Eqbal "What do you tell your students?" He replied, "I don't tell them anything. I think that my life and my teachings all point to two morals: think critically and take risks."[4] This anthology is, accordingly, conceived in that spirit. It is intended to critique a longstanding, dominant Western intellectual tradition that views Islam as an existential threat and to explore the consequences of viewing a religion and a culture as a threat.

Notes

1. Eqbal Ahmad, *Confronting Empire* (Cambridge: South End, 2000), p. 66.
2. Margaret Canovan, *Hannah Arendt: A Reinterpretation of Her Political Thought* (Cambridge: Cambridge University Press, 1992), p. 1.
3. See Carollee Bengelsdorf and Margaret Cerullo, eds., *The Collected Writings of Eqbal Ahmad* (New York: Columbia University Press, forthcoming).
4. Eqbal Ahmad, *Confronting Empire* (Cambridge: South End, 2000), p. 66.

Acknowledgments

For their help and support, we wish to thank Amina Adams, Amila Buturovic, David Barsamian, Annette Barone, Zahida and Akram Bhatti, Kim Elliott, Diane Fruchtman, Ayman Hassan, F. Zahra Hassan, Alia and Murray Hogben, Humera Ibrahim, Afra Jalabi, Mariam Jalabi, Alim Khan, Faiz Khan, Jabbar Khan, Rahat Kurdi, Zaineb Istrabadi, Laurie Hart, Janet Marcus, Tarek Mounib, Adnan Qayyum, Alireza Rahbar-Shamskar, Bruce Shapiro, Jeff Spurr, and Jamel Velji.

The Hogben residence in Kingston, Ontario has long been a literary salon for those keen on passionately debating and struggling for women's rights in the Islamic world over camaraderie, good cheer, and Tim Horton's coffee. Rafi Khan, Soraya Moghadam, Nelofer Pazira, and Andaleeb Qayyum have provided encouragement over many years.

The idea for this book was first discussed with the late Eqbal Ahmad, who constantly and tirelessly encouraged the project at every opportunity. It was conceived in a long series of conversations with Rabia Ali and Lawrence Lifschultz, who presciently noted that any investigation of anti-Muslim prejudice must also deal with the pathologies of Muslim societies.

Khaled Abou El Fadl, Ammiel Alcalay, Abdullah An-Na'im, Juan Cole, Susan Dayall, David Theo Goldberg, John Lotherington, John P. McCormick, Norma Claire Moruzzi, Carol Off, and Danny Postel generously answered numerous queries.

We wish to thank Roger Owen and Thomas Mullins of Harvard University's Center for Middle Eastern Studies for allowing unfettered access to the center and its affiliated libraries. As well, András Riedlmayer of the Harvard Fine Arts Library patiently, expertly, and graciously answered far too many questions.

Haverford College has supplied generous research assistance.

The editors and staff at Columbia University Press have supervised the design and production of this volume with care, insight, and patience. We owe special gratitude to Susan Pensak for her superb copyediting and responsiveness throughout the editing process.

Emran Qureshi wishes especially to thank Nader Hashemi and Ausma Khan for support above and beyond the call of friendship and offers gratitude to Zamir and Iqbal Qureshi for exemplifying a tolerant and plural view of humanity.

We wish to express our deepest appreciation to the contributors of this anthology for their tireless efforts and forbearance in bringing this project to publication.

The New Crusades

Introduction: Constructing the Muslim Enemy

Emran Qureshi and Michael A. Sells

The Clash of Civilizations

Is Islam at war with the West? A number of voices, from Harvard political scientist Samuel P. Huntington to the exiled Saudi radical Osama bin Laden have answered yes. The ruthless and deadly attack of September 11 has led to a new wave of enthusiasm in the U.S. for Huntington's claim that there is a "clash of civilizations" between Islam and the West and that Islamic civilization is, by its very nature, hostile to Western values. There is no doubt the suicide bombers hated the civilization symbolized by their targets: the World Trade Center in New York, the Pentagon, and, most probably, the Capitol or White House. The attitudes and pathologies they exhibited certainly represent a serious threat.

The association of the 9/11 attackers with Islam was reinforced by the fact that they were recruited, indoctrinated, financed, and trained by a sophisticated network of radicals scattered around the world and claiming to fight in the name of Islam. A wider circle of Muslims, while not direct supporters of the militants, have refused to take a public stand against them. Others have condemned the violence, but without clear repudiation of the ideologies of violent intolerance that encourage it, or else link any reaction to such acts to a list of grievances against Western policies.[1] Still others have expressed skepticism that the attacks occurred at all or have suggested that they were carried out by Jews, the Israeli government, or the U.S. government. Other Muslims have taken much clearer stands against extremism, but their voices have seemed less audible to the general public, a phenomenon exacerbated by the almost exclusive focus of the press and media on conflict.

It is not surprising then that the "clash of civilizations" theory has gained renewed popularity among a Western public shocked to find that what many consider to be a triumphant and benevolent civilization is not only resented but viewed by an indeterminate but seemingly large percentage of Muslims as an enemy. The breadth and depth of Muslim hostility toward many Western policies is clear. Also clear is the existence of a clash between powerful forces speaking in the name of Islam and the Western powers who still dominate much of the world in which Muslims live. What is in question is the basic premise of the clash of civilizations theory: that such a clash is not the product of particular historical circumstances that can change but that the essence of Islam as a religion is antipathetic to the fundamental core values of the West; that Islam is inherently violent in nature; and that, therefore, violent attacks against the West are inevitable and are provoked not by any particular grievances or set of circumstances but by the very existence of Western civilization.

The proclamation of such innate civilizational conflict contains a double function similar to that found within declarations of war. As a description, a declaration of war announces the objective reality that a state of hostility exists between two nation states. As a performance, it ushers in a state of formal hostility that entails certain ineluctable consequences. The proclamation by individual writers of a clash between civilizations does not have the formal performative effect of a declaration of war. Yet it is more than a description. To warn that an entire civilization and religion is, by definition, "our" enemy is to raise a call to arms. Given that the hostility is said to be rooted in the very essence of one or both of the opposed civilizations, no peace is possible, rather at best a tactical truce or cold war.

The claim of a clash of civilizations is a grave one. If indeed there do exist two bounded entities in inherent conflict—"the West" and "Islam"—such a conflict would be deeper and broader than the cold war between the capitalist West and the communist East. Islam is a religion and tradition encompassing more than a billion people spread across five continents, is growing rapidly, and is more historically rooted than the Soviet empire, which lasted less than a century and collapsed with stunning speed. The assertion of a clash of civilizations, whether or not it is valid, has become an undeniable force as a geopolitical agent. Even if it is mistaken, the hypothesis is read and believed in military and foreign policy circles both in the U.S. and internationally.[2] It was cited by Balkan nationalists in defense of their effort to create ethnoreligiously pure states in the Balkans. It is cited by radical Islamic ideologues who find in it a vindication of their own claims of essential incompatibility between Islamic and Western values. The assertion, regardless of its merits, has become an ideological agent that may help generate the conflict that it posits. The sweeping generalizations of the clash hypothesis may also strengthen and embolden those parties that do pose serious threats while at the same time making us less able to precisely locate and counter them.

The image of Islam and the West in a state of fundamental hostility is not new. As the essays in this volume demonstrate, it has emerged at various periods in Western history. The current popularity of the expression *clash of civilizations* stems from a 1990 article in the *Atlantic Monthly* by Bernard Lewis, then professor of history at Princeton University.[3] In "The Roots of Muslim Rage" Lewis traces the conflict to the "classical Islamic view" that divides the world into two opposing forces: the House of Peace (Islam) and the House of War.[4] In such a view any civilization outside Islam is, by the very fact that it is not Islamic, the enemy. The problem posed by Islamic extremists, as implied by Lewis's argument, is not that they ground their violent ideology in their own interpretation of Islam but that their interpretation is the correct one. Violent intolerance, Lewis maintains, is inscribed within the origins of Islam and is the logical, indeed necessary, result of such inscription.

Lewis's interpretation of Muhammad is particularly explicit in this regard:

> Muhammad, it will be recalled, was not only a prophet and a teacher, like the founders of other religions; he was also the head of a polity and of a community, a ruler and a soldier. Hence his struggle involved a state and its armed forces. If the fighters in the war for Islam, the holy war "in the path of God," are fighting for God, it follows that their opponents are fighting against God. And since God is in principle the sovereign, the supreme head of the Islam state—and the Prophet and, after the Prophet the caliphs are his viceregents—then God as sovereign commands the army. The army is God's army and the enemy is God's enemy. The duty of God's soldiers is to dispatch God's enemies as quickly as possible to the place where God will chastise them—that is to say, the afterlife.[5]

Lewis does not offer these assertions as the perspective of a particular school of Islamic history or a particular version of Islam. Instead, he presents them as the reflection of objective reality; it is the religious duty of Muslims to dispatch God's enemies (i.e., non-Muslims), and this duty is presented as incontestable.

The unfavorable comparison of Muhammad to the founders of other religions has a long history in missionary and colonial polemic. It may be that Islam is violent, indeed, by its very nature. But then, so, too, might Judaism and Christianity. Religion itself may be inherently violent. In order to make a claim concerning the relationship of a religion to violence we need to examine the role of sacred texts and sacred models in obligating, motivating, and justifying violence.[6] Each of the apparently obvious logical steps offered by Lewis ("hence," "it follows," "and since . . . then") slide over a number of serious questions. The Moses of the Christian and the Jewish Bible carried out divine commands to destroy God's enemies and his successors waged holy genocide against the Canaanites.[7] While the Christian Gospels contain injunctions against violence, they also contain passages that validate the promised land, threaten nonbelievers with eternal torment, blame Jews for the death of the redeemer Son of God, and envisage cosmic war against the forces of the Antichrist. All these themes have been used to generate ideologies of violence. Christianity's history of inquisition, pogrom, conquest, enslavement, and genocide offers little support for assertions that Islam's sacred text or its prophet entail a propensity for violence greater in degree or different in kind.

Judaism, Christianity, and Islam all claim the heritage and covenant of Abraham, and the three Abrahamic religions defined themselves, at least in part, against one another. Non-Abrahamic religions have revealed similar patterns of self-definition through opposition to the other. The point here is not that we should not examine carefully the way in which violence and intolerance may be inscribed into Islamic sacred texts or models. But to single out Islam and its prophet as particularly violent, without discussion of the various forms of violent logic found within religions and without the comparative framework that would allow for a comparative judgment, is to fail to give the question the serious attention it deserves.

Once the road of easy deductions is chosen, however, the logical conclusion is inevitable. If Islam is, by nature, a religion based on the obligation to "dispatch" non-Muslims, non-Muslims had better prepare themselves for assault. Even when Muslims appear peaceable, the inherent logic of their faith belies such appearance; to trust in it would be foolhardy. If Lewis's claim is false, however, the claim itself is dangerous. Those who believe it will begin preparations to defend themselves against Islam. Such defensiveness can turn a potentially friendly or neutral tradition into the enemy it was assumed to be in the first place.

Once Islam is defined as inherently violent and intolerant, modern conflicts involving Muslims can be reduced to a single cause:

> It should by now be clear that we are facing a model and a movement far transcending the level of issues and policies and the governments that pursue them. This is no less than a clash of civilizations—the perhaps irrational but surely historic reaction of an ancient rival against our Judeo-Christian heritage, our secular present, and the worldwide importance of both.[8]

"The Roots of Muslim Rage" begins by ascribing a sense of rage to Islamic militants or fundamentalists. But as the article's title suggests, the distinction between Islamic militants and Muslims as a whole is not sustained. Lewis attributes what he labels Muslim rage to the frustration felt by Muslim believers unable to dispatch the enemies of God. Lewis locates the problem in what he calls the "classical view" of Islam, where Lewis asserts an absolute divide between Muslim communities (the House of Islam) and non-Muslim societies (the House of War), with no third category. Therefore, Lewis suggests, Islam gives the right and the obligation to Muslims to plunder and dispatch those in the House of War, or, if that is not feasible, to withdraw all Muslim presence from such societies. In these claims about Islam Lewis is in agreement with many contemporary Islamic radicals. The inability of Muslims to carry out this central obligation of their faith, Lewis explains, leads to the clash of civilizations, "the perhaps irrational but surely historic reaction of an ancient rival against our Judeo-Christian heritage, our secular present, and the worldwide importance of both."[9]

Central to such assertions is the suggestion that Muslims who resist Western power are acting out of rage, that they are irrational. Others, from Samuel Huntington to Francis Fukuyama, have taken up the binary logic of opposition between the rational West and the irrational East. As Fatema Mernissi points out, the overeager adoption of clash theory "turns the world's 1.2 billion Muslims into potential enemies" and thus itself constitutes "a bellicosity smacking more of irrationality than of cold analysis."[10] These assumptions also neglect the historical evidence, the centuries of lived experience in both the "House of War" and the "House of Peace," centuries in which Muslims and non-Muslims have managed to peacefully and constructively interact in a great many places and for extended periods of time.

The popular notion that contemporary anger in the Islamic world represents a historic reaction rooted in the classical worldview is based on the assumption of another binary categorization, that between the modern world and the medieval. Many militants, however, know little of the classical Islamic tradition. The Taliban in Afghanistan, for example, grew up in the proxy war fought in Afghanistan between the West and the Soviet Union. To the extent they were educated at all, they received a political indoctrination in the fundamentalist religious schools across the border in Pakistan[11] Indeed, the Taliban set about destroying the thousand-year history of Islamic tradition in Afghanistan, the libraries, cultural artifacts, and monuments, all of which they viewed with ignorant contempt. Nor are upper- and middle-class fundamentalists necessarily more conversant with Islamic tradition; many are trained largely in technical areas (engineering, medicine, computers) and possess little knowledge of Islamic history as it has been presented either by either Islamic or Western scholarship. Contemporary Islamic fundamentalism, like its counterparts in other religions, is grounded in a rejection of tradition and the assumption that the true origins of the tradition are accessible to the fundamentalist, directly, without the mediation of history.[12]

Bernard Lewis refers to "our Judeo-Christian civilization" as self-evident fact. Yet for a thousand years, up through the Holocaust, Jews were, at best, tolerated evils in the view of dominant Christian ideologies. In *Faith After the Holocaust* Eliezer Berkovits rendered his own judgment on the West as Jews had known it: "Israel was God's question of destiny to Christendom. In its answer, the Christian world failed him tragically. Through Israel God tested Western man and found him wanting."[13]

When Lewis writes of the Judeo-Christian West, he is writing primarily of the Christian West. Jews have contributed at least as much to the civilizations ruled by Islam as they have to those ruled by Christianity. To be consistent in his language of hybrid civilizations, Lewis would have to redefine the clash of civilizations as a clash between Judeo-Christianity and Judeo-Islam. Lewis's confused terminology of Judeo-Christianity could be cleared up in part with adoption of the language put forward by Marshall Hodgson that distinguishes Islamdom and Christendom—as civilizations ruled by Christians and Muslims that frequently contained vibrant minorities of other traditions—from Islam and Christianity as religions. In Hodgson's terms, then, Sephardic and Eastern Jewry could certainly be considered part of the tradition of Islamdom, what Hodgson calls Islamicate civilization as opposed to Islam.[14]

The terminological confusion apparent in such apologetic use of the term *Judeo-Christian* points toward a profoundly tragic trend in the Middle East. As early as 1950 Hannah Arendt warned of the consequences of Israel's exclusive identification with the West. "Jews who know their own history should be aware that such a state of affairs will inevitably lead to a new wave of Jew-hatred; the antisemitism of tomorrow will assert that Jews not only profited from the presence of the foreign big powers in that region but had actually plotted it and hence are guilty of the consequences."[15] Arendt couldn't have been more prophetic. With each Israeli-Palestinian conflict the frustration in the Arab and, increasingly, the wider Islamic world has led to a proliferation of antisemitism borrowed by anti-Israeli militants directly from Europe and based upon an ideology that is within the context of classical Islam.[16] By justifying their most controversial settlement policies on the basis of Western civilizational superiority, Israeli governments risk re-creating within the Middle East the same ghetto conditions they had suffered in Europe, a Jewish ghetto this time surrounded by two hundred million Arabs and a billion Muslims. Supporters of Israeli settlement policies have warmly embraced the clash of civilizations thesis.[17] The U.S.-Israeli alliance, self-proclaimed as Western, has placed U.S. policy and power at odds with the increasingly intense support of the Palestinian cause among Muslims. It also allows rejectionist groups to argue against Israel's right to exist on the grounds that Israel is, in the words of its own leaders, a bastion of Western civilization in the Middle East. For many who have known other bastions of Western civilization, from Crusader castles to colonial rule, such a self-definition is not a confirmation of legitimacy.

Lewis depicts "our secular present" as the other target of Muslim rage. The secular nature of the post-Enlightenment West is a commonplace among those who assert Western civilization superiority over Islam. Although Christianity may have been intolerant in the past, it has achieved reform, they argue, while Islam remains trapped in medieval fanaticism. If one steps outside the present environment of moral triumphalism, the claim that post-Enlightenment Christian civilization is less violent than other traditions is breathtaking. The Enlightenment brought many benefits, including important formulations of human rights and democratic institutions. Among the children of Enlightenment and post-Enlightenment Christianity, however, are the colonial conquest and enslavement of much of the world, two world wars, a nuclear arms race that brought the world to the brink of destruction, massive environmental damage, and the Holocaust.

Some examples were more secular than others. While World War I had little overt religious motivation, the destruction of the African civilizations in South Africa, the taking of the land, and the placing of the remnant populations in shrinking reservations and ultimately state apartheid were carried out with Bibles open, by Christians executing what they viewed as their divinely ordained right and duty. The development of a powerful and rejectionist Zionist lobby among evangelical groups in the U.S., many of whom have a long history of antisemitism, has accented yet again the contradiction inherent in an allegedly secular U.S. support for a nation-state based in large part on biblical promise. And within the rhetoric of those who proclaim the superiority of Western secular society is embodied an often surprisingly explicit missionary appeal to the superiority of Jesus as a religious figure and Christianity as a religion. The following prediction of conflict between Islam and the West is a typical example of secularist Christian apologetics:

> This is why this coming conflict is indeed as momentous and as grave as the last major conflicts, against Nazism and Communism, and why it is not hyperbole to see it in those epic terms. What is at stake is yet another battle against a religion that is succumbing to the temptation Jesus refused in the desert—to rule by force. The difference is that this conflict is against a more formidable enemy than Nazism or Communism.[18]

As the case of Serb nationalism has shown, even a shallow sentimentalized religiosity, when manipulated by self-professed secular or atheist ideologues, can make room for the most classical forms of religiously motivated persecution.[19]

While Western policy is less pure of religious justifications than may seem to be the case, conflicts involving Muslims are certainly less globally grounded in classical Islam than clash theorists would like to believe. Bernard Lewis suggested that Kosovar Albanians—who at the time were engaged in nonviolent civic resistance prompted by the Milošević government's brutal imposition of an apartheid regime on Kosovo—were acting out of an age-old, Islamic, religiously inspired desire to dominate other religions and cultures. In fact, the resistance of Kosovar Albanians who include Catholics and Muslims as well as atheists was thoroughly secular, devoid of religious ideology whatsoever.[20] What would have happened if allegations of the religious, fundamentalist nature of Kosovar resistance had persuaded the international community to acquiescence in the ethnoreligious purification of Kosovo that had been the goal of Serb nationalism for more than a decade? Kosovar survivors of the killings and atrocities might have been confined in refugee camps along the unstable boundaries of the region and susceptible to the same kind of desperation and vulnerable to the same kind of fundamentalist radicalization suffered by many Palestinians who up until the 1967 war resisted Israeli policies from largely secularist platforms.

Similarly hasty assumptions of civilization clash helped facilitate the organized killings and expulsions in Bosnia-Herzegovina. Serb and Croat religious nationalists and those who wished to acquiesce in their program of violent ethnoreligious purification depicted civilizational clash in the Balkans as "age-old hatreds" and portrayed Bosnian Muslims as plotting an Islamic state in Bosnia and, eventually, the Islamization of all of Europe. From 1992–1995 Croat and Serb forces, backed by nationalist regimes in Croatia and Serbia, engaged in a campaign of "ethnic cleansing" against Bosnian Muslims, with a goal of destroying them as a people and carving up Bosnia between the two expansionist Christian nationalist states. Bosnian Muslims, poorly armed and on the brink of annihilation, were subjected to the worst organized persecution in Europe since World War II, a persecution that has been formally declared genocide by the International Criminal Tribunal for the Former Yugoslavia. Yet Samuel Huntington, apparently driven by the necessity of his vision of the "bloody borders of Islam" managed to turn victims into the perpetrators: "Muslims have fought a bloody and disastrous war with Orthodox Serbs and have engaged in other violence with Catholic Croatians."[21] Huntington's accusation was made as Serbia was descending, with the complicity of its intellectuals and Church leaders, into a mass psychology of war and hate.

The claim of Lewis and Huntington that Muslims are obligated by their religion to work for world domination reinforced the claims of extremist Serb and Croat nationalists that Muslims could never be trusted to live among them. It is not surprising, therefore, that Serb and Croat nationalists championed the Lewis and Huntington theories of civilizational clash in arguing for the inability of Muslims to be integrated into the European communities of the Balkan region. Franjo Tudjman, for example, cited Huntington in defense of his plan to violently partition and "ethnically cleanse" Bosnia-Herzegovina.[22] A prominent Serb nationalist also cited Lewis's view that Islam was based on the division of humanity between the House of War and House of Islam and the imperative to subjugate the House of War to argue that Islam is, by nature, a totalitarian religion.[23]

The Lewis and Huntington claim also reinforced the assumption by Western policy makers that nothing could be done to stop the carnage in the Balkans because that carnage was an eruption of age-old antagonisms and proposals, which continue to this day, to partition Bosnia between Croatia and Serbia and force the Bosnian Muslims into an artificially created Islamic state or ghetto. Had the policy based on these assumptions continued after the Srebrenica genocide of 1995, Serb and Croat nationalists could have achieved their complete aim. Muslim survivors would have been confined to a ghetto, the surviving Muslim population, trapped and abandoned by Christian Europe, would have remained vulnerable to the claims of militants that, indeed, Muslims cannot live in a multireligious society and to arguments by Islamic militants that the fate of Bosnian Muslims proves that Muslims will never be secure outside an Islamic state.[24]

V. S. Naipaul, laureate of the 2001 Nobel Prize in literature, offers another example of the cost of uncritical assumptions. Although Naipaul is less associated than Lewis and Huntington with the specific expression *clash of civilizations*, his view of Islam's compatibility with the West is every bit as categorical as theirs. For Naipaul also the problem lies in the very nature and definition of the religion. Islam, he declares, is by definition fundamentalist.[25] Once Islam becomes the villain, rather than particular individuals, groups, or ideologies, it is an easy slide into self-defeating generalizations. Naipaul warns us, for example, of "the Pakistani fundamentalist fanatic Fazel-ur-Rehman, himself enjoying, bizarrely, academic freedom at the University of Chicago, and sleeping safe and sound every night, protected by laws, and far away from the mischief he was visiting on his countrymen at home."[26] In fact, Fazlur Rahman, the distinguished professor of Islamic studies at the Universty of Chicago, had been forced to flee his native Pakistan when he was attacked by a mob reacting to his reformist ideas. He dedicated much of his life in exile to interreligious reconciliation and understanding and to educating a generation of scholars in both the wide diversity of Islamic thought and in his own reformist understanding of the tradition. By representing as a fundamentalist fanatic a man whose life was dedicated to an inclusive view of religion, Naipaul undermines progressives and encourages the fanaticism that drove Rahman out of Pakistan.[27] The justified fear of terrorism, combined with mistaken and irresponsible charges made by influential authors such as Naipaul, could lead to visa restrictions that would do little to keep out terrorists but would keep out the voices of reason that are most needed.

Naipaul also repays his former translator and host in Pakistan, Ahmed Rashid, by portraying him as a bourgeois revolutionary, oblivious to historical and local contexts and to life on the ground.²⁸ At the time that Naipaul was polishing his caricature, Rashid was examining the role played by Saudi fundamentalism, U.S. policy blunders, and Pakistani support in the rise of the Taliban. Rashid's 1999 book on the Taliban chillingly exposed the growing ties between Osama bin Laden and Taliban leader Mullah Muhammad Omar.²⁹ The Nobel committee biography of Naipaul lauded his "critical assessments of Muslim fundamentalism in non-Arab countries such as Indonesia, Iran, Malaysia and Pakistan."³⁰ Those reading Rashid rather than Naipaul had clear advance warning of the enormity of the danger posed by the Taliban leadership and the pathological extremism into which they had fallen. Those reading Naipaul, on the other hand, were left only with anxiety over a religious tradition "critically assessed" by Naipaul as universally and homogeneously hostile, fundamentalist, parasitic, and culturally inauthentic, a critical assessment as useful as a security alert that offers no clue as to the nature and provenance of the threat. Ultimately, those who make the assumption that Islam is by nature violently intolerant are blind to the specific ideologies within Islam that do threaten religious diversity and rational debate.

Constructing the Muslim Enemy

The end of the cold war led to a transformation in the way in which conflict is channeled, funded, and justified. With all its violence and potential for nuclear war, the cold war had the virtue (in terms of Realpolitik) of controlling the flow of violence. Western and Soviet blocs manipulated wars and revolutions from Korea to Guatemala, from Cambodia to Angola. Proxy warfare between the superpowers exacerbated the conflicts, with incalculable human cost for those in the proxy battlefields and enormous financial profit to the arms industries in both blocs. The cold war also gave the military and industrial establishments a secure place in organizing and managing such conflict. A party to conflict could always call upon one bloc for aid; the opposing side would then count on the support of the opposing geopolitical bloc. The two superpowers were spared having blood shed on their own soil even as they were able to manage the conflicts to their own benefit and profit from their role as arms merchants.

Militant religious ideology has served as a partial replacement for the cold war as a conduit for conflict. Major violence has been carried out in the name of Buddhism, Christianity, Hinduism, Islam, Judaism, and Sikhism. A significant number of these conflicts involve Muslims: in the Sudan, India, Chechnya, Kashmir, Afghanistan, Bosnia, Kosovo, Iraq, and Palestine, to mention only a few. It is a seemingly elegant and simple solution to see the conflict in terms of East-West. East-West rivalry had been used as a framework for the cold war, with the West defined as liberal capitalism and the East as communism. Rather than having to construct a new paradigm, the clash theorists could simply redefine the East of the cold war as the older Orientalist East, as Islam and/or Confucianism. The West is a relational designation; it has meaning only in contrast or opposition to an East. The self-definition of the West and its military, economic, and ideological investment in the defense against communism need not be dismantled but could be directed toward the threat of this newly configured East. The same West (defined as individualistic, enterprising, egalitarian, peaceable, and tolerant) is pitted against an East now embodied by Islam and characterized as fundamentalist, reactionary, terrorist, static, and oppressive of women. Anti-Western Muslim militants construct a similarly absolute conflict between the degenerate, repressive, soulless, hedonistic, and women-exploiting West and the justice, truth, and moral center represented by Islam.

Lewis's "The Roots of Muslim Rage" appealed strongly to Samuel Huntington, who presented his own clash-of-civilizations hypothesis in a 1993 article in *Foreign Affairs*, a journal influential among policy makers and the military establishment.[31] Huntington suggests the conflict that had been directed between the West and the Communist bloc is now being redirected through civilizations. He brands Confucian and Islamic civilizations as most inimical to Western values, but singles out Islam as the prime enemy. In his 1996 book, *The Clash of Civilizations and the Making of the New World Order*, he sharpens his view of a uniformly hostile Islam with "bloody borders."[32] Huntington illustrates his claim that Islam has bloody borders with a map showing Muslim-populated areas throughout the world ringed with blood-red boundaries.

Huntington repeats Lewis's claim that violence is inherent to Islam because of its essential distinction between the "House of Islam" and the "House of War" and because of Muhammad's role as prophet, warrior, and ruler. Like Lewis, he makes no effort to demonstrate through comparative analysis of scriptures or historical records that Islam's propensity for violence is greater than that of other religions.[33] Once the essentially violent and hostile nature of Islam has been identified and the state of clash between Islam and the presumably less violent West has been established, Huntington draws the conclusions for those concerned with national security. "We" should cooperate with those civilizations that are less inimical to us. But in the face of an inherently hostile civilization like Islam, we should adopt a posture that treats Islam as the enemy it is. We should maintain a strong defense: we should limit its military threat, maintain our own military superiority over it, and "exploit the interior differences and conflicts among Confucian and Islamic states."[34]

U.S. policy toward Iraq has offered an instructive test case for Huntington's prescription that we should exploit the interior differences and conflicts among Islamic states. During the war between Iran and Iraq, Western governments authorized major arms sales to the police-state dictatorship of Saddam Hussein, while some of them also continued weapons sales to Iran, thus helping fuel, between two majority-Muslim nations, a war of incalculable futility not seen since the trench warfare of World War I. From 1982 the U.S. provided the regime of Saddam Hussein with an average $500 million in annual subsidies. This support continued, despite the brutal nature of the Hussein regime, on through the 1988 Al-Anfal genocide campaign against Iraq's Kurdish population.[35] When Iraq turned the military machine it had developed with Western help on Kuwait, the West joined a coalition that included some Arab states and embarked on the Gulf War against Iraq. Once again, Muslim was killing Muslim with Western arms.

The formal goal of the United Nations (i.e., the Security Council dominated by the U.S., Britain, and France) was the defense of Kuwait's national sovereignty. The unofficial but clearly governing motivation of the Western powers was to protect their sources of inexpensive oil. In the U.S., however, the war was marketed as a morally mandated fight against the evil regime of Saddam Hussein, an evil that U.S. president George H.W. Bush claimed was worse in some ways than that of Hitler. Images of Saddam Hussein with a Hitler mustache appeared in the popular press. Congress devoted special evening sessions to reading human rights reports of atrocities committed by Iraqi forces. The war fervor, along with the brutal behavior of Hussein, led to the largest outbreak of anti-Muslim prejudice in the United States since the Iran hostage incident. At the same time, Hussein manipulated U.S. media to show him standing before a backdrop of Arabic script and symbols of Islam, toying with hostages and engaging in threats. These images, daily accounts of gruesome atrocities inflicted by Iraqi forces, and the constant association of Saddam Hussein with Islam had the double effect of demonizing Muslims and dehumanizing Iraqis. All Iraqis were made into little Saddams.[36] Even the bombs dropped over Iraq were covered with messages "for Saddam," though it was clear that those bombs were landing on just about anyone in Iraq except the regime leadership and its bodyguards.

U.S. president George H. W. Bush appealed to the Iraqi people to rise up and overthrow their tyrant.[37] As the U.S.-led coalition crushed the Iraqi army, Kurds in the North and Shi'ites in the South did rebel, seizing fourteen of eighteen Iraqi provinces. But U.S. generals had deliberately halted the military assault just short of the Republican Guard unit that kept Saddam Hussein in power.[38] In addition, General Normal Schwartzkopf, representing the U.S. at the Safwan cease-fire talks, authorized the Iraqi regime to use its attack helicopters. The Republican Guard was able to use its helicopter gunships to overcome the rebellion and to carry out a savage campaign of reprisal against the rebels, their families, and their entire regions. U.S. military and civilian authorities rejected repeated pleas from the rebels, not to intervene on their behalf but simply to order the regime to ground the helicopters, an order that would have been categorical given U.S. military supremacy and control of the air.[39] One reason for the abandonment of the insurrection was a deep-seated prejudice against Shi'ite Muslims who, in the generalized imagination of post-Khomeini policy makers, had become the enemy within the enemy—despite the antimilitant stand of the Iraqi Shi'ite leadership.[40]

In heeding the first Bush administration's call to revolt, the Iraqi opposition had exposed itself more effectively than it could ever have been exposed by Saddam's secret police. Once exposed, they were betrayed. As one observer put it, "The Iraqi people tried to help in toppling the regime. All parties in the conflict were rewarded except the Iraqi people who were bombed and destroyed."[41] After the insurrection was crushed, leaving firmly in power a regime that had been within days of falling, the U.S. insisted that the UN maintain economic sanctions against Iraq. As one U.S. official put it: "Iraqis will pay the price while he [Saddam Hussein] is in power. All possible sanctions will be maintained until he is gone."[42] The Iraqi people, their infrastructure destroyed by the bombing, their rebellion smashed with U.S. acquiescence, their economy ruined by years of misrule, sank further into misery. Saddam Hussein, his opposition exposed and crushed, secure in his power, began rebuilding his weapons programs and accumulating a fortune through his monopoly on embargo-breaking smuggling operations.

Even as Saddam was liquidating the remnants of his betrayed opposition, the U.S. press, public, and politicians erupted into a historic national celebration, replete with a Fifth Avenue ticker tape parade honoring the victory over Saddam Hussein. A war that ended with the exposure and annihilation of Hussein's enemies was hailed as a triumph over Hussein and his regime, and those who planned and executed the war were hailed as heroes. Meanwhile the U.S. was forced to garrison troops in Saudi Arabia to defend its oil from the threat it had supposedly defeated, a policy that led to a further radicalization of Islamic opposition across the Middle East. After the attack of September 11 the administration of George W. Bush, led by those who had decided in 1991 to leave Saddam Hussein in power, reverted to the characterization of Saddam as a Hitlerian dictator who gassed and murdered his own people as one justification for a U.S.-led invasion and occupation of Iraq.

Historians will long debate the reason behind a policy that shifted from support of Saddam Hussein prior to the Gulf War (particularly during the period he was using poison gas against his own people), expressed horror at his human rights record during the Gulf War, postwar abandonment of his opposition to savage reprisals, brutal economic sanctions that punished the country as a whole, and a final invasion amid sudden expressions of horror at Saddam's human rights record—a record that had been hideously consistent for two decades. To what extent were these shifts in policy and in rhetoric due to blundering and incompence and to what extent did they stem from a Realpolitik that attempted, whenever possible, to use the Saddam police state as a wedge against Iran, thereby exploiting interior differences among the nations of an enemy civilization? One thing is clear: for those exulting in the victory of the first Gulf war, Iraqis had been dehumanized to the point that they were now viewed as little Saddams, and thus their death, even when they opposed Saddam Hussein could be celebrated as a victory over Saddam.[46]

We might ask the Bernard Lewis question here, in reverse. Did the popular euphoria over a victory in which the enemy was not defeated and in the face of the inestimable suffering of Iraqis and the internal opponents of that enemy, followed by an illogically sudden and fervent horror at the savagery of the same regime when invasion and occupation of Iraq became more useful, not reflect "the perhaps irrational but surely historic reaction of an ancient rival" extending back through the Crusades to the origins of the Christian West itself? Or is it perhaps a moment of group psychology that may or may not endure, which tells us nothing definitive about the essence of any civilization?[44] Before we can ask if Islam and the West are in a state of fundamental clash, however, we need to ask whether they are as distinct and independent from one another as clash theory presumes.

Islam and the West

In the opening chapter of this volume Fatema Mernissi challenges the assumption that the West (defined as liberal democracy) and Islam are two distinct entities that can be viewed as either in conflict or not in conflict with one another. Her analysis of Western relations with Saudi Arabia demonstrates the interdependence and interpermeation of Islamic and Western states. Since the 1930s the Western powers have supported what Mernissi calls the "palace fundamentalism" of the Saudi regime, a regime based on the militantly intolerant ideology known as Wahhabism, after the eighteenth-century ideologue and warrior Ibn 'Abd al-Wahhab. Because of its immense wealth, Saudi-sponsored Wahhabism dominates many Islamic organizations worldwide. Saudi sources, both official and private, have funded militant Islamic and Islamist groups around the globe, including both the Taliban and the radical Islamist madrasas in Pakistan that gave birth to the Taliban.[45] Saudi groups have disseminated European-based antisemitic tracts such as *The Protocols of the Elders of Zion*. They have insisted that non-Muslims pollute the Arabian Peninsula and should be banned. Indeed, Osama bin Laden turned on his Saudi mentors only when he realized that they were breaking their own ideological commitments by allowing U.S. troops to remain after the Gulf War. After the wars in Bosnia and Kosovo, Saudi-Wahhabi aid groups pushed successfully for the destruction of mosques and shrines in Bosnia and Kosovo that had survived Serb and Croat attacks — as a way of purifying Islam from what they view as Islamic cultures polluted by contacts with other religions.[46]

Bernard Lewis admitted, after September 11, that he had not understood the danger and power of extreme Wahhabism.[47] Given Lewis's view that all of Islam is, by nature, based on a religious obligation to slay the infidel, there is no reason he or those who follow him should have been able to distinguish Wahhabi extremism from other forms of Islam. Nor is there any reason they should not have been taken by surprise that most of the suicide bombers of September 11 were Saudi; after all, according to Lewis, the obligation to slay the infidel is not the interpretation of a single small group but of Islam as a whole. Others, however, had been for years warning of precisely this danger. As early as 1988 Olivier Roy had identified both the phenomenon of Wahhabi influence and the dangers it posed in Afghanistan to Muslim and non-Muslim alike:

> The prospects for the traditional clerics are also dim. Most of the new madrasas built in Peshawar are wahhabi-sponsored. Wahhabis gener-

ally despise traditional Afghan Islamic culture, considering it to be full of ignorance and superstition. The following quote from *Arab News* (14 September 1985, p. 9) is illuminating: "The Muslim scholars in the world have a great role to play in enlightening the ignorant Afghans. Un-Islamic customs and traditions have found their way into their lives." The fact that the author makes no reference to Afghan clerics shows that he is ignorant himself; the target of his attack is really Sufism and traditional Persian literature.[48]

As Eqbal Ahmad noted in regard to U.S. support for the Afghani mujahidin: if the West wishes to counter Islamic radicalism, it could start by not supporting it.[49] The close economic dependency of the two Bush admininistrations upon Gulf oil interests make it all the less likely the second Bush administration will understand the unintended irony of its declaration that whoever supports terrorism is the enemy.

For many Muslims it is a bitter irony that the dominant stereotype of Islam is based upon the Saudi model of police-state repression, religious intolerance, oppression of women, moral hypocrisy among the male elite, and an aggressive and highly funded export of militant anti-Western ideology—and that the Saudi monarchy is kept in power by the very Western nations that display fear and loathing at that stereotype. Mernissi points out that the oil wealth of the Gulf states, rather than serving to develop the economy of the Islamic Middle East, has been ploughed back into Western economies through massive arms sales. The symbiotic relationship between Western liberal democracies and the palace fundamentalisms of the Gulf states (along with the popular street fundamentalisms they fund outside their borders) puts into question the supposition of a rational, democratic, liberal West facing an irrational and fundamentalist East. Commenting on the symbiotic relationship between U.S. oil and arms industries and the Saudi regime, Mernissi writes that "the young executives working for Boeing and McDonnell-Douglas seem more like the 'cousins' and 'brothers' of the Emirs than do young, unemployed Mustapha and Ali, strolling the streets of Cairo in humiliating uselessness."[50]

The essays by Roy Mottahedeh, Edward Said, and John Trumpbour present critical evaluations of the clash thesis, with reference both to the theory's validity and role within U.S. and Western politics. Said illuminates what we might call the "original error" of clash theory, the posing of constructed and conflictual categories as if they were descriptions of objective reality: "Thus to build a conceptual framework around the notion of us-versus-them is in effect to pretend that the principal consideration is epistemological and natural—our civilization is known and accepted, there is different and strange—whereas in fact the framework separating us from them is belligerent, constructed, and situational."

Said goes on to describe earlier manifestations of "wars of the worlds" mythologies in which two separate, self-contained civilizations engage in a cosmic clash. He also points to the way in which colonialist assertions of a "rhetoric of identity"—pitting one civilization against another or one civilization against those lacking civilization—led to a reverse rhetoric of identity among those seeking independence from colonial rule. The earlier revolutionary rhetorics of identity, from Nkrumah's Ghana to Nasser's Egypt to the India of the Congress Party, were predominantly secularist. With the failure of secular Arab and Iranian nationalist movements, the revolutionary rhetoric of identity has turned to Islamism in a struggle against continued Western domination.

Of particular importance is the contested and multiform nature of tradition itself. Said observes that a tradition like Islam is made up of numerous voices, not always in agreement, and contains its own countercultures that challenge seemingly fixed paradigms. We might add that the Islamic concept of consensus accents the situational character of Islamic. Interpretation of the meaning and boundaries of Islam is subject to the general agreement among those trained in Islamic tradition, the *ulama'*. What is orthodoxy by consensus in one generation can be replaced in the next by a perspective that had been previously marginalized. Also, what is orthodoxy in one region may be rejected by consensus in another region.[51] No human construction of Islamic belief is secure or permanent.

In the next essay John Trumpbour examines clash theory in the light of American domestic political and economic interests, from the anti-Palestinian agenda of the rejectionist wing of Zionism to the domestic attack on multiculturalism by Dinesh D'Sousa and Irving Kristol. As the cold war ended, the neoconservative movement, without an internal communist threat to combat, found a new enemy within, "multiculturalism." The shifting of immigration patterns and the articulation of U.S. culture as diverse and contested created a backlash with a reified Western, Nordic, or "Judeo-Christian" culture threatened by allegedly unassimilable emigrants from alien civilizations. In a subtle and wide-ranging exploration of the use and abuse of theories of civilizational clash in U.S. society and politics, Trumpbour holds up the construction of the Muslim enemy as a mirror of our own society's anxieties and fears.

Roy Mottahedeh then probes Huntington's assumptions and claims about Islam and the history of Islam-West interaction, assessing what Huntington labels the "bloody borders" of Islam and his treatment of conflicts from the central African state of Chad to the Russian states of Ingushetia and Ossetia, from Afghanistan to the Gulf War. Mottahedeh exposes numerous and serious errors of fact and locates the root of the error, precisely, in Huntington's inability to recognize the diversity and contestations within societies with Islamic populations. In the second part of his essay Mottahedeh examines Huntington's definitions of Islam and the West, of "us" and "them," finding such large civilizational groups far less stable, structured, and mutually exclusive than Huntington assumes. The clash thesis is revealed to be less an explanatory system than a highly schematized and empirically flawed description—and, with the suggestion that the West exploit conflicts among Muslims, a troubling prescription.

While the Lewis and Huntington versions of the clash of civilization have appealed to foreign policy, political science, and military circles, V. S. Naipaul's claim of an incompatibility between Islam and the West appeals to both elite and popular readerships. Rob Nixon examines the influence of Naipaul on the representation of Islam for academics and intellectuals in Britain and North America. He also traces Naipaul's appeal to a more popular audience, as shown by Naipaul's appearance on the cover of *Newsweek* magazine as an authority on Islam. Nixon goes on to explore Naipaul's influential depiction of Muslims as afflicted with a disease of parasitic mimicry, relying on the West for the goods of modernity while simultaneously despising and resenting the source and the civilizational gestalt that conferred these goods and their benefits upon them. As Nixon points out, these gifts of colonialism came with a legacy of disruption and continued—albeit more subtle—postcolonial domination and exploitation that is ignored by Naipaul.

Nixon then moves to Naipaul's theory that non-Arab Muslims are converts and thus inherently inauthentic in their cultural and religious identity. As for Muslim "converts," their ancestors—insofar as we accept the largely mythical notion of any religious connection not broken and complicated by multiple past conversions—converted long before their European or Latin American counterparts converted to Christianity. Extending Naipaul's logic to Christianity, only the Semitic Christians of the Middle East would escape cultural inauthenticity and the social pathology to which it allegedly must lead. As Eqbal Ahmad pointed out, the same logic would extend to other religions, to Chinese and Japanese Buddhists, for example, who would be, by definition, inauthentic Buddhist converts.[52] Naipaul's ideology of conversion proves to be hauntingly similar to Serb and Croat nationalist views of Slavic Muslims as inherently inauthentic, having "Turkified" through the conversion of their ancestors to Islam, thereby losing their Slavic identity, which is inherently Christian.[53] The similarity of Naipaul's views of Muslims as inherently inauthentic converts to Hindu nationalist claims that Indian Muslims are traitors to their essential Hindu identity is not coincidental. Naipaul has been an avid supporter of the radical Hindu nationalist movement, which he has called a "mighty creative process" and a "great historical awakening."[54]

Mujeeb Khan closes part 1 of this volume with a meditation on the Western philosophical background both of the notion of civilizational clash and of Francis Fukuyama's proclamation of the triumph of liberal democracy and the "end of history." Khan focuses in particular on the role of Alexandre Kojève's lectures in the 1930s in the development of the modern understanding of Hegel's *Phenomenology of the Spirit*. He then demonstrates the divergences in Hegelianism between the disciples of Kojeve and of Leo Strauss, with one strand of Straussian thought leading toward the neoconservative triumphalism of Irving Kristol and Allan Bloom.[55]

Khan surveys the issue of genocide from a historical perspective and in view of the Hegelian dialectic of master and slave, suggesting that history has shown itself to be very much alive, with the genocide in Bosnia following upon a long trail of precedents. He places the ideology necessary for genocide within a comparative lens, looking at the way in which European Jews, Bosnians, and most recently Muslim communities in India have been subjected to a similar process of ideological dehumanization. He concludes with a reconsideration of the possibility of a moral imperative within humanity confronting the continued outbreaks of history in the form both of genocidal ideologies and the policies that such ideologies enable and reflect.

The essays in part 2 focus upon emblematic examples of the construction of Western identities in opposition to Islam. Tomaž Mastnak examines the figure of the "the Turk" in relation to the transformation of Europe from an obscure classical myth into a self-proclaimed, culturally and religiously bounded civilization. In the medieval period the architects of the Crusades had called for the construction of peace among themselves by channeling violence against the Muslim other.[56] There is a symbiotic power of reciprocal causality in such an effort. For the preachers of the Crusade peace was the precondition for a Crusade, and, at the same time, the Crusade was the means for promoting and maintaining peace. In the sixteenth century Christendom yields to Europe and the war against Islam (now conceived of as "the Turk") becomes both the stimulus and the result of "peace" within Europe, as Mastnak shows through the construction of Europe in the works of figures such as Erasmus and the Duke of Sully, the minister to Henry IV of France and proponent of a "grand design" for peace in Europe through war with the Turk. While recognizing how often European leaders found themselves in alliances with the Ottoman Empire, Mastnak reveals a deep pattern of European identity construction as conditioned upon a civilizational and military conflict (a clash, we might call it) with those same Ottomans.[57]

While Mastnak delineates the process by which Europe constructed itself in conflictual opposition to its construction of the Turk, María Rosa Menocal explains how postmedieval Europe cleansed itself of its Jewish and Islamic heritage. This cleansing took place within the construction of the Renaissance and its myth of a pure lineage of Western heritage linking Athens to Renaissance Europe, with a period of latency during the Dark Ages. Menocal's essay reconfigures common views of both history and possibility, challenging the construction of two historically separate civilizations. She points out that the Islamic world and "us" had been intertwined throughout the medieval period and were only separated out by Renaissance and post-Renaissance philological and literary cleansing. That cleansing erased the formative role of Arabs and Muslims in the formation of what came to be viewed as European culture and substituted in its place the mythology of a medieval latency in which the unbroken chain of Western civilization extending back to Athens awaited Renaissance awakening. The significance of Arab and Islamic culture was reduced to the purely mechanical transmission of translated Greek classics. Elsewhere, Menocal details the Renaissance and post-Renaissance endeavor to cleanse Europe of its Islamic heritage.[58] The cleansing can be seen in the way in which the cultural world associated with the troubadours has been artificially severed from the world of Arab poets across the Pyrennes with which it was intimately intertwined. It is seen in the furious and ultimately failed attempt to deny the massive influence of Islamic *miraj* legends (ascent through the levels of heavens, purgatory, and hell) on Dante's *Comedia*. It is also seen in what Menocal points out is an unprecedented use of the term *occupation* to refer to a seven-hundred-year Islamicate civilization in Andalus (if after seven hundred years one is still an occupier, how many millennia would it take to become a resident?).

She ends her contribution with a meditation on the five hundredth anniversary of the year in which Europe began its project of "cleansing" itself of the Moorish and Jewish other—an eerily exact five hundred years before a similar project of cleansing of Bosnia-Herzegovina took place. There, too, those who worked to eradicate it and expel the survivors labeled the half-millennium civilization of Balkan Islam an alien "occupation" and thus a transient phase—like the Nazi occupation of World War II—rather than an integral part of the common historical experience of the peoples of the region, an era of intense interactions in which cultures were created and transformed. Menocal also points out the vital relationship between the "ethnic cleansing" exemplified by the activities of the Spanish ruling classes in 1492 (the attempted extirpation of the interior "other" through Inquisition and cultural revisionism) with conquest and domination of the exterior "other" that began in earnest with Columbus. These otherings are two sides of the same coin; expansionist aggression and interior purification are parts of the same process.

These cleansings—literary, cultural, linguistic, ethnic, and religious—however sustained and however violent—have failed to eradicate that part of "us" (Europeans, Westerners) that was and is Arab and Muslim at the historical origin of our civilization. While Menocal recognizes the oppositional logic and the violence that has occurred between Muslims and Christians, she demonstrates that even at the extremes of polarization what has been constructed and rejected as other continues to exist within us. The continued existence within cultural memory, however repressed, of this world constructed as other makes impossible any secure division between "us" and "them" in terms of Islam and Europe or Islam and the West. In looking back over Menocal's essay, we might ask whether the fury and savagery of "ethnic cleansing" is not in fact due to the knowledge that extirpating the other from ourselves is ultimately an impossible task. We might also ask if the extreme violence of some anti-Western ideologues may not be due to their inability to disentangle and cleanse from their own language and thought ideas they have inherited and appropriated from the civilizational world they wish to demonize.[59]

Through a close examination of the case of France, Neil MacMaster demonstrates both a commonality between France and the larger unit of

Europe as well as its specificity.[60] He begins by tracing the transformation of the Arab and Muslim image within France—in response to the changes in Algerian guest worker patterns, the situation in Algeria itself, French internal politics, and perceptions in France of the Khomeini revolution. Through attention to situation and context MacMaster illuminates the transmutation of biological anti-Arab racism into cultural racism that masks itself as a defense of national values against a monotonic, unassimilable, alien Islam. Popular and academic experts on Islam in France have manipulated "the activities of a highly unusual and relatively isolated minority" to represent an alleged Muslim norm. A case in point was the controversy of 1989 and 1994 over the exclusion of Muslim girls wearing scarves from French schools—on the grounds that their headscarf was a religious symbol that violated the French Republican culture and separation of church and state—despite the fact that less than 1 percent of Muslim girls of school age wore the scarf, and despite tolerance of Jews with yarmulkes and Christians with crosses. A fabricated "veiled" Muslim woman was placed on the cover of the popular news magazine *L'Express*, in the kind of full veil seldom used by French Muslims. The veiled woman, her eyes just visible through a slit, is selected as the symbol or signifier for an entire social and religious order, the immigrant/Muslim community allegedly incapable of accommodation with Republican values and universality.

Among the French experts that have arisen to explain militant Islam, Gilles Kepel has exerted the most influence. MacMaster examines Keppel's stance in the controversy over the proposal for an Islamic studies center at Strasbourg University. The center would "foster a 'home-grown' and modernizing Islam suited to the needs of the French Muslim community, an Islam *à la française* that would remove the dependency on conservative imams formed in—and attached to—the interests of a foreign state." Kepel's opposition to the proposal is a symptom of wider trend: Muslims are accused of refusing to assimilate and are presented as homogenous members of an alien culture. Yet the most vocal opposition to Muslims is generated not by the importation of Muslim religious leaders from elsewhere but rather by attempts to create an Islamic identity with local institutional, societal, and cultural structures. The local Muslim community is thereby thwarted in its attempt to be both visible and naturalized and thus forced into the sphere of outside influence to which the Islamophobic construction of Muslims is committed.

Nothing is more threatening to Islamophobic ideology than the Muslim who can acknowledge and negotiate the multiple identities, the Muslim who is simultaneously a Frenchman, for example. Bernard Lewis expressed confusion when he is confronted by a French Maghrebi: "'My father,' he said, 'was a Muslim, but I am a Parisian.' What, I wondered did he mean?" Lewis dismisses the comment as incomprehensible, presumably because it was irrational.[61] Yet, if we listen more carefully, we might understand what the man was telling us: we have multiple identities: religious, ethnic, class, family. When pressed to define ourselves, we have to choose one according to the context in which that self-definition is made. Depending upon the circumstances our choice might change. Lewis recognizes multiple identities but then defines the phenomenon as exclusively Western; by definition, then, he finds a Muslim expressing such to be a category mistake.[62] It also leads to policies that thwart the effort of Muslims and others to exist with the multiple affiliations that allows them to share a sense of community with non-Muslims.

While MacMaster reveals transformations in the construction of the enemy other in France, Norman Cigar reveals similar complexities in his meticulous examination of the role of Serbian nationalist intellectuals in motivating and justifying the elimination of the Muslim communities in the former Yugoslavia. He shows how the majority of influential writers, poets, and professors propagated the messages that there is an essential incompatibility between Islam and Europe. Those Muslims who saw themselves in terms normally viewed as European were labeled dissemblers. The Serb nationalist combination of biological, cultural, and civilizational stereotypes succeeded in dehumanizing the Muslim population in the eyes of many Serbs, to the point where their elimination was not only permissible but necessary. While Serbian nationalist stereotypes against Muslims may differ from the language of the North American theorists of civilizational clash, the fundamental categories do not. Indeed, Serbian anti-Muslim nationalist discourse forms a kind of microcosm of many aspects of the larger international debate.[63] In one of the most precise analyses of the rise of an ideology of dehumanization written in the past decades, Cigar charts the resurgence of religious nationalism in Serbia and the vital role played by both writers and clerics in intensifying that nationalism to the point that it became genocidal. Even after the fall of Slobodan Milošević, this exclusionary ideology remains hegemonic throughout Serbia, Montenegro, and the "Republika Srpska" entity in Bosnia-Herzegovina.[64]

In the final essay of this volume Michael Sells examines the tangible connections and the theoretical overlapping of three modes of Islamophobe discourse. The first mode, Serbian religious nationalism, is exemplified by the passion play remembrance of the "Serbian Golgotha," the death of the Christ-Prince Lazar at the battle of Kosovo in 1389. The power of the passion play to collapse the past (1389) into the present (1989) is shown to be the dominant symbolic force in the creation of a mass psychology of ethnic cleansing. The force of the Lazar commemoration was intensified by the collapse of World War II atrocities into the present, an ideologically polarizing history that portrays Ottoman rule as one of unremitting evil, the emotive power of false allegations of genocide in Kosovo against Serbs during the 1980s, and Serb nationalists' claim on Kosovo, their "Serbian Jerusalem." All five elements merged during the 1989 commemoration of the six hundreth anniversary of Lazar's death. Sells calls particular attention to the nineteenth-century work, *The Mountain Wreath*, that was exploited by Serb religious nationalists in the 1980s as a centerpiece in their Islamophobic ideology of nationhood. In the Kosovo revival literature generally and in *The Mountain Wreath* especially, the antipathy between Islam and Christianity is not only "age old," it is cosmic; it is an eternally decreed law, inscribed within the soul of Christianity and the Serb nation, that they cannot thrive until purified of all traces of their primordial enemy, Islam.

The second mode is represented by the work of Bat Ye'or (Giselle Litmann) and Jacques Ellul, who portray Islam, always and everywhere, as a religion of aggressive violent penetration (jihad) and parasitic absorption (dhimmitude), implying that Muslim immigrants in the West are just the latest weapon in this fundamental war of Islam against Christianity and Judaism. Like Lewis, Bat Ye'or insists that the absolute division between the House of Islam and the House of War is the essence of Islam. Like most theorists of a clash of civilization between Islam and the West, Bat Ye'or imagines a common Judeo-Christian civilization stretching back through the Holocaust into the millenium of Christian persecution of Jews.

The third mode is exemplified by Robert Kaplan's *Balkan Ghosts*, a book that presents the Balkans as a region of ancient, inevitable, civilizational clash, and by an influential article by Joseph Brodsky that forms the basis for Kaplan's portrayal of Kosovar Albanians. Sells demonstrates that, despite the journalistic conceit of first-hand, I-was-there witnessing, no Kosovar Albanian is actually given voice; rather, the irrational, violent, drunken Kosovar Albanian was spliced together in large part from the writings of Rebecca West and Joseph Brodsky. Kaplan follows Brodsky both in the imagining of the Turk and Muslim as an embodiment of filth and in the suggestion that the inherently totalitarian and brutal nature of Islam and the Ottomans was in fact the ideological basis for Stalinist despotism. While Huntington poses the Islamic East as the successor to the geopolitical East of the cold war, Brodsky and Kaplan suggest that Leninist communism was in fact a new manifestation of Muslim totalitarianism; in both cases the geopolitical cold war East has been merged with the Orientalist East.

We Have Met the Enemy

Carl Schmidt argued that peace at home is a function of defining an out-side enemy; that "what we are" is defined by what we are against.[65] There is no doubt that an outside enemy can reduce tensions within or, to put it more accurately, that various possible factions and enemies see themselves as one people once a particular faction or enemy becomes or is chosen as a threat. The essays in this volume demonstrate such a dynamic at work in North American domestic politics, in wider "Western" self-construction, in the construction of peace within Christianity, and Europe, and in the cases of France and the Balkans. Former U.S. president Ronald Reagan famously evoked this principle during the cold war, musing that if only there were an outside alien enemy the Soviet and Western blocks would unite as one peo-ple in opposing it.

In all the above cases the principle of outside-enemy/peace-within con-tains vital ambiguity. Is the principle of uniting around a common enemy descriptive or prescriptive? Does it describe the temporary alliances formed in the regrettable case of a wider war? Or does it prescribe and encourage the construction of an outside enemy in order to achieve consensus and cohesion back home? The symbiotic relationship of peace among ourselves (however we name ourselves) and the war against that which we pose as our other enhances the ambiguity: our peace makes possible the construction of the other, while the enemy other makes our peace possible.

But such a phenomenon carries a heavy price. Polarized conflict engen-ders a mimetic reduplication of violence. Each act of violence—and we should include ideological polemics within the definition of violent acts—engenders an increased homogenization with both sides.[66] Those who attempt to avoid the polarization (the Croat or Serb in Bosnia who wishes to live with the Muslim as one people, for example) become its first targets, and their numbers diminish through both physical liquidation, intimidation by one's "own," and fear of generic retaliation by the targeted group against not only its persecutors but all those in the group in whose name the persecuted is carried out. Not only are differences broken down within each of the polarized communities but the differences between self and enemy gradually collapse as well. Each act in response to that of the other brings the two sides into closer mirror imaging. In the mob interior differences break down between warring groups. In the rhetoric, body language, and logic of violence two mobs facing one another mirror one other more and more precisely as the violence continues. At such a moment the human being loses the sense of multiple identity — succumbs, in other words, to fanaticism.

Islam and the West share a history of complex interaction that has included intense and sustained conflict. As a religion Islam is a sibling and rival to the other Abrahamic traditions of Judaism and Christianity. The rivalry is reflected in the way each tradition has defined itself, at least in part, in contrast to one or both the others. The scriptural and the historical manifestations of such rivalry in the past two decades has been the subject of much needed dialogue and self-critique. As Mastnak shows, medieval Christendom and, later, Europe defined themselves in part through a categorical rejection of the Muslim or Turk other. If such identities, in the words of Edward Said, are constructed and inherently conflictual, then the claim of a clash of civilization is true, in the philosophically trivial sense of tautology: generalized identities that have been constructed in opposition to one another are in opposition to one another. Said also points out that colonization justified by conflictually constructed ideologies generated reactive, conflictually constructed politics of identity among the colonized.[67] It should be noted that two of the most influential Islamist political parties in the Arab-Islamic world, the Muslim Brotherhood in Egypt and the Jamaat-e-Islami in Pakistan, arose during the period of decolonization. The Egyptian Muslim Brotherhood achieved prominence during the period of decolonization from England. Much of its activities should be seen as a form of postcolonial identity formation, that is, demarcating a newly constructed "Islamic" Egypt against an Anglo-French colonial legacy.[68] The Jama'at-Islami in the Indian subcontinent was conceived as a response to Indian Muslim fears of Hindu dominance within a postcolonial India. Islam within this conception was first and foremost a marker of communal identity.[69] The Hamas movement came to prominence in Palestine after the defeat of secularist Arab resistance against what it views as an extension of Western colonial occupation.

Consequently these parties can be seen as having arisen in the aftermath of colonialism that was justified through a conflictual definition of the West and the alleged superiority of its values. As a result the very identity and self-definition of those movements has been conflictual with or a contestation of "Western" values. As globalization encroaches further, and "Western" values entrench within their societies, these parties and others similar to them continue to feel similarly threatened. Ironically, all three movements were supported at times by Western powers and by Western-aligned regional dictatorships in an effort to control what was seen as the graver threat of Marxist or leftist resistance to Western domination.[70]

Religiously inspired violence and intolerance in the wake of the cold war has inspired a lively debate over the definition and nature of fundamentalism and fanaticism.[71] The essays in this volume suggest that one essential aspect of fundamentalism can be defined as follows: a stubborn belief in an unchanging, essentialist, monotonic identity for both self and other that refuses to acknowledge any counter evidence, an irrational inability to see the diversity of identity in each of us. Fanaticism might be defined as the collapsing of identities into a single association. The human being carries a multiplicity of identities (religious, philosophical, political, linguistic, cultural, aesthetic, sexual, to name only a few), each of which expands into a community of others sharing that particular identity. At any given time a person may identify primarily with one identity, but without losing the others. The multiple, partially overlapping identities allow an individual a sense of multiple, overlapping communities, i.e., a sense of humanity. From the perspective of clash theories that divide the world into clearly bounded, antagonist camps based on what Huntington calls the widest group affiliation, the man who calls himself a Parisian in Paris and a Muslim in Morocco becomes incomprehensible, as do all of us who identity in different ways at different times. For a person to live in a state of perpetual jihad or crusade based upon a single association requires the collapsing of all modes of identity and affiliation into only one.

This is not a book about Islam. No claim is made concerning the peaceful or warlike character of Islam, its validity as a religion, its ultimate viability as a civilization, or its compatibility with the West. Our endeavor here is to scrutinize a mode of thinking and a mode of expression that both posits conflicting worlds, each made up of homogeneous, single identities, and, through the implications of such an assumption, helps turn its own assumption into a reality. Those who proclaim such a clash of civilizations, speaking for the West or for Islam, exhibit the characteristics of fundamentalism: the assumption of a static essence, knowable immediately, of each civilization, the ability to ignore history and tradition, and the desire to lead the ideological battle on behalf of one of the clashing civilizations. Fundamentalism grows out of conflicts and, in turn, intensifies and unites complex conflicts into overarching wars of the worlds. The problem is not that there are a few fanatics in the world, but that conflict-driven fundamentalism induces others to identify with the homogenous, monotonic "we" in which individual and group affirmation becomes possible only through the destruction of the other.

In his recent book, *What Went Wrong*, Bernard Lewis diagnoses what he sees as the fatal refusal of Islamic civilization to find anything of value or interest in Europe. Habituated to centuries of cultural, economic, and military dominance, the Muslim world was seduced by its own sense of civilizational superiority into ignoring the experiments in science and technology being undertaken by its apparently backward rivals in Christendom. Within a few centuries the backwater of Europe had become the colonial master of much of the Islamic world. For intellectuals within the Islamic world the long dominance of Islamic cultures proved the religious and civilizational entitlement of Islam to rule and blinded them both to their own deficiencies and to the scientific breakthroughs taking place just across their borders.

Many Muslim intellectuals have offered incisive critiques of some of the specific problems discussed by Lewis, but without the sweeping theory of arrogance and decline Lewis proposes.[72] What distinguishes the critiques of clash theorists such as Lewis from other critics, from within and without Islam, is the consistent inability either to find anything to criticize in the contemporary policy or attitudes of the civilization they consider their own or to find anything of interest or value in the worlds they consider to belong to the backward other, in this case the Arab and Muslim Middle East. Their civilizational triumphalism shows no awareness that the stance they take is exactly the stance Lewis argues led to an inevitable decline of Islamic civilization: a lack of genuine interest in any positive aspects of the civilization viewed as inferior.

Notes

1. Such reactions often contain the statements "Islam is against violence" or "Islam means peace." When made without any acknowledgment of the growth of ideologies of violent intolerance within Islam, these claims can become apologetic. The word *Islam* is based upon the Arabic word for "peace" (*salam*), but Islam literally means not peace but "submission" (to God). The statement "Islam means peace" could mean that Muslims are called to be vigilant in rejecting the use of Islam to justify violence and has been used in that sense by important Islamic leaders. But it could also mean that true peace resides in submission to God, that is, in Islam. Any conflicts involving Islamic and non-Islamic parties must, by definition, be the fault of the non-Muslim party to the conflict. Unless those claiming that Islam means peace specify clearly which of the two meanings they intend, the statement raises more fears than it assuages.
2. In addition to the appeal of Samuel Huntington to many policy makers, Bernard Lewis and Robert Kaplan came to exercise, in the wake of September 11, a particularly strong influence on President George W. Bush. For Kaplan's role, see Steven Mufson, "The Way Bush Sees the World," *Washington Post*, Sunday, February 17, 2002, B01.
3. Bernard Lewis, "The Roots of Muslim Rage," *Atlantic Monthly*, September 1990. In his essay in this volume, John Trumpbour explains that Lewis had used the expression *clash of civilizations* in pre-1990 writings, but it was only with the *Atlanitc Monthly* article that the expression became popular.
4. Lewis, "The Roots of Muslim Rage," 49. The accusation that contemporary Muslims are embracing the "House of Peace" and "House of War" terminology is a major component in many Islamophobe writings, including those of Giselle Litmann cited in the essay of Michael Sells in this volume. Lewis cites no examples of contemporary use of the distinction between *dār al-islam* (the House of Islam) and *dār al-harb* (The House of War). See also Bernard Lewis, *What Went Wrong: Western Impact and Middle Eastern Response* (Oxford: Oxford University Press, 2001), 36. Khaled Abou El Fadl notes that some of the citations that Lewis provides were from Islamic jurists who witnessed the expulsion of Spanish Muslims during the Reconquista and thus reflected the fears and anxieties prevalent in Muslim lands. In modern times as well as medieval times, juridical traditions have reflected prevailing social and political orthodoxies. El Fadl cites the case of Rashid Rida who was asked about the obligations of Muslims in Bosnia during the aftermath of the Austrian annexation. Rida wrote, "they are the best judges of their own affairs." See Khaled Abou El Fadl, "Legal Debates on Muslim Minorities: Between Rejection and Accommodation" *Journal of Religious Studies* 22.1 (1994): 127–162.

We might add one of the warnings prevalent in the writings of Muslims discussing the Reconquista, that Muslims under Christian rule would be forced to assimilate, was tragically vindicated by the Inquisition, but those jurists could not even imagine what would happen next. The Inquisition first required conversion (breaking previous pledges made by Catholic rulers) and then began centuries of repression on the grounds that those Muslims who converted may be tempted to retain their old religious loyalties behind a veneer of Christianity—the same suspicion that led to the savage inquistorial repression of Jewish conversos. The attempt of the Moriscos, the descendants of the Muslims of Spain who had converted yet retained some of their cultural mores, ended with their expulsion to North Africa in the seventeenth century.

5. Lewis, "The Roots of Muslim Rage," 49. For a constructive discussion of contemporary Islam and the question of violence, see Bruce Lawrence, *Shattering the Myth: Islam Beyond Violence* (Princeton: Princeton University Press, 1998).

6. A preliminary set of such functions would include the possibility that strict Abrahamic monotheism is, through its self-definition in relationship to other gods, violently intolerant, the concept of divinely commanded holy war and/or genocide, the use of purity laws as a mode of dehumanizing the other, the relationship between violence toward women and violence toward other religions (idolatry as whoredom), the Promised Land that the people favored by God are commanded to seize from those inhabiting it, the sacred place that must be seized and returned to its original (as with the Babri Masjid in the Indian town of Ayodhya, a sixteenth-century mosque allegedly built on the birthplace of the Hindu god Ram, Serb nationalist claims on Kosovo, and Catholic nationalist opposition to the rebuilding of mosques destroyed in the Bosnian war on the grounds that the mosques had been built on pre-Ottoman Catholic shrines), the manipulation or interpretation of a scriptural passion story (Jesus, Imam Husayn, Prince Lazar) to target an entire people (as classically exemplified in the Christ-killer charge based on passages from the Gospels of Matthew and John), the notion that those holding wrong beliefs will suffer eternal torment at the hands of the wrathful God and that violence meant to save people from heresy is always preferable to eternal divine violence (the logic of the Inquisition), and the apocalyptic view that there is a war to the end between the enemies of God and the friends of God, and that one is either one side or the other, with no middle ground.

7. For some of the more recent work in this area, see Regina Schwartz, *The Curse of Cain: the Violent Legacy of Monotheism* (Chicago: University of Chicago Press, 1997); Jan Assman, *Moses the Egyptian: The Memory of Egypt in Western Monotheism,* (Cambridge: Harvard University Press, 1997); Mark Juergensmeyer, *Terror in the Mind of God: The Global Rise of Religious Violence* (Berkeley: University of California Press, 2000); Omer Bartov and Phyllis Mack, eds.,

In God's Name: Genocide and Religion in the Twentieth Century (New York: Bergahn, 2001).

8. Lewis, "The Roots of Muslim Rage," 60.

9. The modern Egyptian writer Sayyid Qutb has propounded the kind of categorical distinction between the House of War and the House of Islam that Lewis claims is basic to classical Islam. Though Qutb's ideology is partially rooted in the thought of the medieval writer Ibn Taymiyya, he represents only one of many sides of Ibn Taymiyya. And Ibn Taymiyya represents only one trend within classical Islam. Both Ibn Taymiyya and, even more strongly, Sayyid Qutb, propounded conflictual views of Islam. Ibn Taymiyya warns continually against associating with Christians, Jews, and Muslims who practice popular Islam. Sayyid Qutb turns such warnings of non-association into an eternal struggle against the "age of ignorance" (*al-Jahiliyya*) usually viewed as the pre-Islamic culture of Arabia, but perceived by Qutb as a perpetual threat, renewed in his time by secular Muslim regimes, Jews, Christians, and the West. Both writers developed their conflictual understanding of Islam at a time when Islam was being conquered or colonized. See Eric Davis, "Ideology, Social Class, and Islamic Radicalism in Modern Egypt" in Said Amir Arjomand, ed., *From Nationalism to Revolutionary Islam* (Albany: SUNY Press, 1984), 134–157; and John Esposito, *Unholy War: Terror in the Name of Islam* (New York: Oxford University Press, 2002), 26–71.

The conflictual understanding of Sayyid Qutb and Ibn Taymiyya has been spread throughout the Islamic world by the Saudi government, itself based on a particularly radical version of conflictual definition of religion known as Wahhabism, and by wealthy Saudi princes and other individuals, where it is taught as the true or authentic Islam. But conflictual views of religions or civilizations are more complex than Lewis acknowledges, and in modern Islam the "House of War" language is not necessarily the central element in such definitions. A particularly illuminating example can be found in Morocco. During the French occupation of Morocco, French authorities propounded a rule forbidding non-Muslims to enter mosques. The ruling resulted from riots caused by drunken French soldiers encroaching upon mosques. After independence Morocco continues to be dominated by the effects of French occupation; many Moroccans speak French better than classical Arabic. Europe also refuses to purchase Moroccan produce, preferring to employ low-wage Moroccan workers in agricultural sweat shops in Spain, for example. Thus, while mosques in most other Islamic cultures are open to respectful non-Muslims, they are off-limits in Morocco, and the prohibition against entering mosques has been expanded to include the areas around mosques and even Sufi shrines. By maintaining and even expanding this interdiction, Moroccan Muslims are claiming some territory in their own country as uncolonized;

they have appropriated a rule imposed by French colonial authorities and used it to set up a clear demarcation of religious space. To apply the method of Lewis here, of attributing contemporary conflictual ideologies to classical or foundational religious doctrines, would be to suggest that in this instance the French-initiated prohibition in Morocco against non-Muslims entering mosques is based upon some ancient Christian need for zones of spatial religious exclusion.

10. See Fatema Mernissi's "Palace Fundamentalism and Liberal Democracy" this volume.

11. The basics of the "classical Islamic view" include Qur'an, hadith, Qur'anic exegesis (*tafsir*), classical Arab grammar, literary criticism, classical poetry, *adab* (the equivalent to belles lettres), sacred history, scholastic theology (*kalam*), Qur'an articulation and recitation (*tajwid*), the principles of law (*'usul al-fiqh*), the principles of faith (*'usul ad-din*), and often mastery not only of classical Arabic, but of classical Persian and/or Ottoman and the literary and philosophical tradition embodied within all three major language systems. Ideologues like Shaykh Omar of the Taliban know little this classical Islamic tradition.

12. See Khaled Abou Fadl, *And God Knows the Soldiers: The Authoritative and Authoritarian in Islamic Discourses* (Lanham, Md. : University Press of America, 2001).

13. Eliezer Berkovits, *Faith After the Holocaust* (New York: KTAV, 1973), 69.

14. At one point Lewis does acknowledge the existence of Judeo-Islamic civilization. He concedes that the Sephardic and Levantine population in Israel, those Jews whose traditions developed under Islamic rule, as Judeo-Islamic. Lewis, *What Went Wrong*, 155. His clash of civilization hypothesis is based, however, on the notion of a Judeo-Christian West in conflict with Islam. There is no place in the hypothesis for Eastern and Sephardic Jews. The clash hypothesis fails to acknowledge that, if there is such as thing as "Judeo-Christian" civilization, then there must be a "Judeo-Islamic" or even "Judaic-Christian-Islamic" civilization, given that Jews and Christians played key roles in the development of what is commonly called Islamic civilization. Lewis's insinuations that Islamic in contrast to Western "Judeo-Christian" civilization is not capable of learning from other religions is already assumed in his original choice of vocabulary. Similarly, the popular definition of Israel as a beacon of Western civilization erases and marginalizes eastern Jews within Israel and isolates Israel from the historical civilizations of the Middle East. And a like forgetfulness in regard to the multireligious tradition of Islamicate civilization is found among those contemporary Islamic militants whose anger at Israel leads them to reject everything connected to Judaism.

15. Hannah Arendt, *The Jew as Pariah*, ed. Ron H. Feldman (New York: Grove, 1978), 133, quoted in Richard J. Bernstein, *Hannah Arendt and the Jewish Question*, (Cambridge: MIT, 1996), 109.

16. The increased popularity of the "Christ-killer" charge among Islamic militants exemplifies this grafting of European Christian antisemitism onto militant Islam. Thus, Samiul Haq, director of the prestigious fundamentalist Haqqania madrasa in Pakistan that counts Taliban leader Mulla Muhammad Omar among its alumni, announced that it was the Jews who crucified Christ. See Jeffrey Goldberg, "Inside Jihad University: The Education of a Holy Warrior," *New York Times Magazine,* June 25, 2000, 6:32. While there are resources within classical Islam that can be turned against Jews, the Christ-killer charge is not one of them. The Qur'an emphasizes that Jesus was not crucified, but rather a likeness of him meant to fool his persecutors (Q 6:157). Cf. Ronald Nettler, *Past Trials and Present Tribulations: A Muslim Fundamentalist's View of the Jews* (Jerusalem: Pergamon, 1987).
17. The Christian right in the U.S. has recently transformed itself from its traditional antisemitism to a new support of Israel, based on its Western (i.e., Christian) values, though that support is grounded in the belief that Jews will be given one last chance to convert upon the second coming of Jesus Christ. For a perspective on the Middle East that does not efface the Sephardic and Levantine Jew, see Ammiel Alcalay, *After Jews and Arabs: Remaking Levantine Culture,* (Minneapolis: University of Minnesota, 1993); Ammiel Alcalay, *Memories of Our Future,* (San Francisco: City Lights, 1999).
18. This op-ed piece, based upon the writings of Bernard Lewis, offers a typical example of the position. See Andrew Sullivan, "This is a Religious War," *New York Times,* October 7, 2001. After this appeal to the Gospels, Sullivan reverts to the secularist pose: "For unlike Europe's religious wars, which taught Christians the futility of fighting to the death over something beyond human understanding and so immune to any definitive resolution, there has been no such educative conflict in the Muslim world." Christian apologies for violence are frequently characterized by appeals to the absolute injunction to nonviolence, to turning the other cheek, to loving thy neighbor. Thus the Inquisition, destruction of the Indians, and enslavement and conquest of Africa were commonly justified through concern and love for the eternal souls of those conquered, with the implication that the violence being committed was accidental or contrary to the Christian message. Islamic apologies rarely base their appeal on love and nonviolence but rather on the grounds that the case in question has a Qur'anic justification for the use of violence. Though this difference in self-presentation has pervaded Christian-Muslim polemics, neither tradition has achieved demonstrable advantage over the other in reducing or eliminating violence or intolerance.
19. See the essays of Norman Cigar and Michael Sells in this volume.
20. The secular nature of the Kosovar resistance followed in a long tradition of secular Albanian nationalism. See Lewis, "The Roots of Muslim Rage," 54. "But

for misbelievers to rule over true believers is blasphemous and unnatural, since it leads to the corruption of religion and morality in society, and to the flouting or even the abrogation of God's law. This may help us to understand the current troubles in such diverse places as Ethiopian Eritrea, Indian Kashmir, Chinese Sinkiang, and Yugoslav Kosovo." The charge that Kosovar Albanians were religious fundamentalists who desired to dominate or expel Serbs was raised by the Milošević regime and radical members of the Serbian Orthodox church as a rationale for the repression in Kosovo and for openly publicized plans to expel Albanians from Kosovo. The charge was exposed as a fabrication by both human rights investigators and dissident Serbian journalists. After years of nonviolent resistance and after viewing the fate of Bosnian Muslims, some Kosovars began organized, armed resistance. But even the militant Kosovo Liberation Army lacked religious ideology. The KLA contained many Catholic Albanians in its ranks and its leadership tended to be first-generation urban leftist intellectuals. Although the Kosovo problem persists, with an anti-Serb backlash from angry, returning refugees, that backlash is ethnic, not religious. The same gangs that have attacked Serbs have attacked Slavic-speaking Muslims and rival Kosovar Albanian Muslims. On the question of Kosovar nationalism, see Shkëlzen Maliqi, "Albanians between East and West," in *Kosovo-Kosova: Confrontation or Coexistence*, in Ger Duijzings, Dušan Janjić, and Shkëlzen Maliqi, eds. (Njimegen: Peace Research Centre, University of Njimegen, 1996): 15–122.

For a critique of other claims by Bernard Lewis, see C. M. Naim, "The Outrage of Bernard Lewis," *Social Text* 30 (1992): 114–120, and the earlier critiques of Edward Said during the Orientalism debate.

21. Samuel P. Huntingon, *The Clash of Civilizations and the Remaking of World Order* (New York, Simon and Schuster, 1996), 255. Independent observers and human rights organizations stress that the vast majority of violence was committed against Muslims at the hands of Serb and Croat nationalists. See, for example, the reports of Human Rights Watch, Doctors Without Borders, the Special Rapporteur on Human Rights for Bosnia, the U.N. Commission of Experts on War-Crimes in the Former Yugoslavia, eight U.S. State Department Reports, along with the Indictments and Transcripts of the International Criminal Tribunal on the Former Yugoslavia. These and other reports are available or referenced at http://www.haverford.edu/relg/sells/reports.html. In addition, in its 1998 report on the betrayal of the "Safe Area" of Srebrenica into the hands of Serb General Ratko Mladić, the United Nations renounced previous statements suggesting moral equivalence among the three sides in Bosnia, condemned its own refusal to recognize the intentions of Serb nationalists, and acknowledged that the vast majority of victims in Bosnia-Herzegovina were Muslim civilians singled out for attack because of their ethnoreligious identity.

Bernard Lewis portrays Bosnian Muslims not as victims of organized Serb and Croat nationalist persecution and genocide but of "fragmentation and internecine chaos." See Bernard Lewis, *The Middle East: A Brief History of the Last Two Thousand Years* (New York: Scribner's, 1995), 387.

22. See the essay of John Trumpbour, this volume.

23. See Alexandre Popović, *Les Musulmans yougoslaves, 1945–1989: Médiateurs et métaphores* (Lausanne: l'Age d'Homme, 1990). Popović writes (p. 9): "le 'dâr al islâm' doit s'étendre, tôt ou tard, sur l'ensemble du globe, et par conséquent le gouverner." He backs up this sweeping generalizations with a footnote (p. 9, note 2) that reads: "Cf. À ce sujet, un passages extrêmement clair chez Bernard Lewis, *Islam et laïcité*, Paris, Faryard, 1988, 288." Note that Popović makes explicit the implication in Lewis's work that even Muslims who are secular, who advocate tolerance, who seem fully committed to civic democracy (as were the vast majority of Bosnian Muslims in 1990) are guided by the alleged Islamic imperative to subjugate non-Muslims, an imperative that, according to the logic of Lewis, is essential to their very identity as Muslims. Thus Popović suggests that not only Muslim nationalists but all Muslims of Bosnia, whatever their political and social persuasion, make up a "religion totalitaire."

24. Those who tend to view the world as conflict between unchanging mono-identity traditions continue to propose the partition of Bosnia-Herzegovina along these lines, without discussing what would be done with the hundreds of thousands of refugees who have returned to areas from which the partition plan requires they be re-expelled or what would happen to the landlocked Islamic ghetto they wish to create in central Bosnia. So strong is the urge for ethnoreligious purity that it drives such proposals long after they have proven not only unworkable but catastrophic. For a discussion and critique of these proposals, see Sumantra Rose, *Bosnia After Dayton* (New York: Oxford University Press, 2002), 168–175.

25. See the *New York Times Magazine*, October 28, 2001. Adam Shatz asks Naipaul "What about non-fundamentalist Islam?" and Naipaul replies "I think it is a contradiction."

26. V. S. Naipaul, *Beyond Belief* (Boston: Little, Brown, 1998), 53. Ebrahim Moosa has written: "Fazlur Rahman was maligned and castigated by the Muslim clerical establishment, neo-revivalist political activists, and political conservatives in Pakistan and wherever their influence extended. Demagogues of both religious and political stripes, orchestrated campaigns of mass hysteria and protests against him on the pretext that they ostensibly found some of his views and interpretations offensive. The threats against him escalated to the point that there were genuine concerns for his safety and the real possibility of physical harm. In the end, he chose a self-imposed exile for the last nineteen years of his life in the United States." See Fazlur Rahman, *Revival and Reform In Islam: A*

Study of Islamic Fundamentalism, ed. Ebrahim Moosa (London: Oneworld, 1999), 4. See also Nikkie R. Keddie, review of Milton's Viorst's *Behind the Veil: In the Shadow of the Prophet* and V. S. Naipaul's *Beyond Belief: Islamic Excursions among the Converted Peoples, Los Angeles Times*, Sunday, August 2, 1998, 9. The progressive writer and scholar who taught at the University of Chicago is not be confused with Maulana Fazlur Rehman, the pro-Taliban leader of the Jamiat Ulema-i-Islam party in Pakistan.

27. Rahman was particularly concerning with training and encouraging a new generation of progressive leaders in Islam. For the important work of the Indonesian thinker Nurcholish Madjid, who completed his Ph.D. work under Rahman at the University of Chicago from 1978–1984, see Robert W. Hefner, *Civil Islam: Muslims and Democritization in Indonesia* (Princeton: Princeton University Press, 2000): 113–119.

28. For a comment on Naipaul's savage caricature of Rashid, see Eqbal Ahmad, *Against Empire* (Cambridge: South End, 2000), 110.

29. See Ahmed Rashid, *Militant Islam, Oil, and Fundamentalism in Central Asia* (New Haven: Yale University Press, 2000)

30. See http://www.nobel.se/literature/laureates/2001/naipaul-bibl.html. See the Presentation Speech of the 2001 Nobel Prize in Literature by Horace Engdahl. Engdahl, the permanent secretary of the Swedish Academy, repeated the Naipaulian mantra, noting in the 2001 Nobel Prize presentation speech, "six hundred years of Muslim imperialism that deliberately destroyed the memory of earlier civilisations and plunged the Hindus into a helplessness" and, further, "What he is really attacking in Islam is a particular trait that it has in common with all cultures that conquerors bring along, that it tends to obliterate the preceding culture." http://www.nobel.se/literature/laureates/2001/presentation-speech.html. Naipaul though, characteristically, has demurred, stating that Islam "is much, much worse in fact." See John Ezard, *Guardian*, Friday, October 12, 2001; and Fiachra Gibbons, *Guardian*, Thursday, October 4, 2001.

31. Samuel P. Huntington, "The Clash of Civilizations?" *Foreign Affairs* 72.3 (Summer 1993): 22–49.

32. Huntingon, *The Clash of Civilizations and the Remaking of World Order*, p. 254, where "Islam's Bloody Borders" is made a section heading, and p. 262: "The question remains as to why, as the twentieth century ends, Muslims are involved in far more intergroup violence than people of other civilizations."

33. Ibid, 263. Huntington puts this claim in the passive voice, "the argument is made . . . " but his uncritical adoption of Lewis's view of the nature of Islam leaves little doubt he thinks Islam is more inherently violent than other religions. Elsewhere he seems to forget his commitment to the notion that Islam is built upon a distinction between the House of War and the House of Islam and

his contention of the model of a uniquely violent prophet and, thus, a civilization that is, by nature, at war with the non-Islamic world. In a discussion of the disruption caused by high birthrates, Huntington writes as if the allegedly extraordinary contemporary propensity for violence in Islam could be a product of temporary conditions rather than something innate: "By the 2020s, however, the Muslim youth bulge will be shrinking. Conceivably, then, the age of Muslim wars could fade into history and be succeeded by a new era dominated by other forms of violence among the world's peoples."

34. Huntington, "The Clash of Civilizations," 49. Many from those civilizations deemed hostile by Huntington find such claims of Western superiority in peacefulness to be bizarre coming from a civilization that brought the world the Crusades, the Inquisition, colonial conquest, genocides and enslavements, the Holocaust, and infliction of mass terror at Dresden, Hiroshima, and Nagasaki.

35. See Samantha Power, "A Problem from Hell": America and the Age of Genocide (New York: Perseus, 2002), 171–245.

36. By the time the Gulf War began, the anti-Islamic fervor in the U.S. had reached a fever. Those who dressed in ways that seemed Islamic to the general public (including, ironically, many Hindu immigrants or traditional Hindu Americans) were harassed and began to avoid going out in public

37. The most damaging appeal was made by Bush on February 15, 1991: "There is another way for the bloodshed to stop, and that is for the Iraqi miltiary and Iraqi people to take matters into their own hands to force Saddam Hussein the dictator to step aside."

38. Colin Powell acknowledged and defended his decision to spare the key Republican Guard unit in an interview with NBC news, stating that destroying the Guard division would leave Iraq vulnerable to its "mortal enemy, Iran." General Powell justifies his decision by stating that the Republican Guard was the sole remaining defense of Iraq against its "mortal" enemy Iran. In fact, Iran showed absolutely no intention of invading Iraq, and the Iraqi Shi'ites in the South, who were assumed by the Bush administration to by sympathetic to Iran, had their own, independent, and self-consciously Arabic (as opposed or Persian) culture and loyalties. No serious study, the catastrophe of Bush administration policy notwithstanding, has shown that Iraqi Shi'ites had any intention of aiding Iran in the conquest or domination of Iraq.

Bush officials later admitted that they never did desire a popular revolution and that they viewed a militarily strong Iraqi regime as a necessary buffer against Iran. See also Lawrence Freedman and Efraim Karsh, The Gulf Conflict, 1990–1991 (Princeton: Princeton University Press, 1993), 426: "The evidence is that the Administration took a political and not a legal decision to remove any hint of support from the rebels. Saddam's calculations were eased immeasurably once he could be confident that the coalition would take a passive stance." According to Brigadier Tawfiq al-Yassari, "The Americans were indirectly responsible for igniting the uprising. They dropped thousands of leaflets and then used the media to call to the Iraqi people to rise up." According to Iraqi General Najib al-Salihi: "If the fighting had continued for another 24 hours, the Iraqi leadership would have been in difficulty. The situation would have deteriorated badly against them. If it had continued for 48 hours, the regime would have been finished." Both comments are from interviews in *The Gulf War*, videorecording, part 3 (Princeton: Films for the Humanities and Sciences, 1997).

39. Bush administration officials and General Colin Powell defend their actions by claiming that they did not wish to occupy Baghdad, but occupation was never needed or requested; instead, the forces in the area waited to see which side the U.S. would back, and when the U.S. command refused all requests to stop the Iraqi regime's use of helicopters, the message was clear. In *Waging War*, an NBC news documentary glorifying the U.S. generals, Schwartzkopf recalls with relish and a sense of triumph the meeting at Safwan on March 13, 1999. He describes how crestfallen the Iraqi military representatives were to learn of the many thousands of prisoners the U.S.-led coalition had taken. Yet he says nothing, not a word, about the crucial (and unnecessary) authorization Schwartzkopf gave to the Iraqi military to use its helicopters, the key component of its subsequent campaign to exterminate the resistance and punish the families of resisters (with heinous atrocities) and entire regions in which such resistance occurred. In an earlier interview Schwartzkopf claims that he had been "suckered" by the Iraqis at Safwan into authorizing the use of helicopters. But neither the Iraqi military nor other generals in the coalition believe that Schwartzkopf would have believed the promises of Saddam's representatives not to use the helicopters for military purposes. When it became apparent that the Republican Guards were using helicopters to annihilate its opposition—to the point of dropping burning oil on columns of refugees— Generals Schwartzkopf and Powell argued against grounding the helicopters on the grounds that it would destabilize the Iraqi regime. "It was not long before the Republican Guard was unleashed on the rebellion in the south. Eager to redeem themselves after the disgrace of the Gulf War, the Guard plunged into their new task with systematic savagery. The holy cities of Najaf and Karbala were given a particularly harsh treatment. Thousands of clerics were arrested and hundreds were summarily executed. Any turbaned or bearded man who took to the street ran the risk of being rounded up, or even executed. People were tied to tanks and used as 'human shields' while women and children were indiscriminately shot." Lawrence Freedman and Efraim Karsh, *The Gulf Conflict, 1990–1991* (Princeton: Princeton University Press, 1993), 419–420.

40. The Shi'ites of Southern Iraq are Arab and were led by Ayatollah Khoei, who condemned both the Iran-Iraq war and the Iraq invasion of Kuwait and counseled Iraqis against militarism. The Iraqi regime, sensitive to U.S. fears over Iran, played up the threat of an Iranian-backed Shi'ite revolt and U.S. officials were apparently duped, despite the fact that Iran offered no support for the rebellion.

    A major reason for U.S. abandonment of the rebels was prejudice against Shi'ite Muslims who, in popular Western stereotypes, are the enemy within the enemy. The Bush administration attempted to shift blame to the Saudis for the abandonment of the Iraqi opposition, claiming it was the Saudis who evoked fear of Iran in turning Saddam Hussein's Republican Guards loose upon the Iraqi Shi'ite population. According to Saudi officials and U.S. ambassador to Saudi Arabia Charles Freeman, the fear of an Iranian takeover of Southern Iraq emanated from Washington. The U.S. decision to offer de facto support for the Iraqi regime against the rebels was a judgment that was casually made, grounded in ignorance of the Shi'ite world and the relations between Arab and Persian Shi'ites, and calamitous in its effects. See the discussion in Andrew Cockburn and Patrick Cockburn, *Out of the Ashes: The Resurrection of Saddam Hussein* (New York: HarperCollins, 1999), 38–42. For the kind of caricature of Shi'ites upon which such decisions may have been based, see Robin Wright, *Sacred Rage* (New York: Linden, 1985), 26–45, where, among other things, the Assassins are said to have been an example of the revitalization of "the original strategy of the Shi'ite faith." Saddam Hussein arranged to have pictures of Imam Khomeini distributed in the South, as if they were being distributed by the rebels, cleverly playing on U.S. fears that the Shi'ites in Southern Iraq would align themselves with Iran. Shi'ites and Sunnis, like Muslims, were viewed as large, homogenous blocks, despite the fact that Arab Shi'ites of Iraq and Persian Shi'ites of Iran had never formed a single nation and were exceedingly unlikely to unite in a common anti-Arab cause.

41. The Kurdish leader Dr. Mahmoud Osman, interviewed in *The Gulf War*, videorecording, part 3 (Princeton: Films for the Humanities and Sciences, 1997).

42. Robert Gates, the deputy national security adviser, quoted in Cockburn and Cockburn, *Out of the Ashes*, 114; and Freedman and Karsh, *The Gulf Conflict*, 426.

43. For the role of the press and media in creating an identification of all Iraqis and Arabs with Saddam Hussein, see Malcolm Hayward, "The New World Order and the Gulf War: Rhetoric, Policy, and Politics in the United States," in Tareq Ismael and Jacqueline Ismael, eds., *The Gulf War and the New World Order* (Gainesville: University of Florida Press, 1994): 224–239.

44. In answer to the use of civilizational clash by anti-Western Muslims to explain the callousness of U.S. policy in the Gulf War, we could cite several specific contexts that would need to be considered. The "Vietnam syndrome," for

example, facilitated U.S. betrayal of the Iraqi opposition and blinded society to its consequences. The generals and the defense establishment wanted a quick, showy victory in order to exorcise the ghost of the protracted Vietnam war. The press, which had been criticized for helping demoralize the U.S. military because of its critical coverage of Vietnam, sought to regain its patriotic credentials by supporting this new, clean war and by adulation of its generals. The overthrow of Saddam by the Iraqi rebels, though clearly the only possible victory that could come out of such a war, would have entailed a longer commitment of U.S. forces, resources, and attention.

45. For the role of Saudi Arabia in bringing the Taliban to power and helping keep them in power, see Ahmad Rashid, *Taliban: Militant Islam, Oil, and Fundamentalism in Central Asia* (New Haven: Yale University Press, 2000), 44–58, 138–140. The influence of Osama bin Laden on the Taliban leadership was seen in the Taliban's move toward extremist Wahhabi positions exemplified in the dynamiting of the ancient Buddhas and the artifacts from the National Museum in Kabul that had survived centuries of Islamic culture. See also Barnett Rubin, *The Fragmentation of Afghanistan* (New Haven: Yale University Press, 1995).

46. For a report on the activities of groups such as the Saudi Joint Commission on Kosovo and Chechnya, see Saïd Zulficar, "Paper Presented to the International Symposium on Cultural Heritage and Diversity held 18–21 December 2000, Tokyo." For documentation the effort to bring authenticity to Kosovo restoration and to resist the destruction of heritage under the guise of restoration, see the Web site of Patrimoine sans Frontières, the organization founded by Saïd Zulficar after he left his position at UNESCO: http://www.axelibre.org /psf1.htm. See also Saïd Zulficar, "Alerte aux Iconoclastes," *Al-Ahram*, February 28, 2001, available online at: http://www.ahram.org.eg/Hebdo/arab/ahram/2001 /2/28/Nullo.htm.

47. Bernard Lewis, interview with Charlie Rose, PBS, January 16, 2002, transcript #3119.

48. Olivier Roy, "Modern Political Culture and Traditional Resistance," in Bo Huldt, Erland Jansson, *The Tragedy of Afghanistan: The Social, Cultural, and Political Impact of the Soviet Invasion* (Croom Helm: New York, 1988), 112

49. Eqbal Ahmed, "Jihad International," *Dawn*, February 14, 1998.

50. See Mernissi, "Liberal Democracy and Palace Fundamenalism," this volume. The arms purchased by Gulf nations as a payback to the U.S. for supporting the Gulf regimes are often too sophisticated for the Gulf-state militaries to use.

51. Thus for example, the Mu'tazilite school of theology was deemed orthodox for a period of the high orthodox caliphate of Baghdad, but later the Hanbalites, who had been persecuted by the Mu'tazilites, became accepted by Islamic consensus in Baghdad, and Hanbalite law has been adopted in several areas of

the Islamic world. Yet, in some Shi'ite regions, Mu'tazilite theology continues to be followed.

52. Eqbal Ahmad, *Confronting Empire* (Cambridge: South End, 2000), 109.

53. For Serb and Croat ideologies, see the essays in this volume of Mujeeb Khan, Norman Cigar, and Michael Sells. Khan also offers further discussion of Naipaul's connection to extremist Hindu nationalism.

54. See the *Guardian*, August 20, 1993. Naipaul made these comments after the destruction of the Babri Masjid, when bloody pogroms against Indian Muslims caused considerable loss of life. Naipaul's view of the inherent inauthenticity of Indian Muslims is remarkably similar to that of past Hindu ideologues such as V. D. Savarkar and M. K. Golwalkar who in the 1920s began codifying a new nationalist ideology. Golwalkar also wrote: "The foreign races in Hindusthan must either adopt the Hindu culture and language, must learn to respect and hold in reverence Hindu religion, must entertain no ideas but those of glorification of the Hindu race and culture ... or may stay in the country, wholly subordinated to the Hindu nation, claiming nothing, deserving no privileges, far less any preferential treatment—not even citizen's rights." See Christopher Jaffrelot, *The Hindu Nationalist Movement in India* (New York: Columbia University Press, 1996), 56. For the program to rewrite Indian textbooks to place Islam outside of Indian history as a purely alien, invading force, see Ramesh Menon, "A Saffron Tint to History?" *India Abroad*, Friday, December 7, 2001. A sample examination question from Uttar Pradesh is,"If it takes four savaks [Hindu religious workers] to demolish one mosque, how many does it take to demolish 20?" A textbook in the Hindu nationalist stronghold of Gujarat features revisionist accounts of Adolf Hitler stating that "he instilled the spirit of adventure in the common people" and makes no mention of the Holocaust. See Stephen Bates, *Guardian*, "Anger at India Textbook Bias," Thursday, February 3, 2000. The comparison of Indian Muslims to Jews remains a staple of Hindu nationalist rhetoric. Between March and April 2002 the Hindu nationalists of Naipaul's great historical awakening, with the complicity of Hindu nationalist officials in government, had burned or looted some 256 mosques and other Islamic institutions in Gujarat, burned alive an estimated 2,000 Muslims civilians, and turned more than 100,000 turned into refugees. See Celia Dugger, *New York Times*, "Discord Over Killing of India Muslims Deepens," April 29, 2002, and, for a list of burned and looted mosques and other Islamic sites, see the *Communalism Combat*, March-April 2002, at http://www.sabrang.com/cc/current/rdestruction.htm. See also the report by Human Rights Watch: *"We Have No Orders to Save You": State Participation and Complicity in Communal Violence in Gujarat*, Human Rights Watch, April 2002.

55. For an examination of Leo Strauss's unacknowledged debt to Islamic political thought see Remi Brague, "Athens, Jerusalem, Mecca: Leo Strauss's 'Muslim'

Understanding of Greek philosophy," *Poetics Today*, 19:2 (Summer 1998): 235–259. Brague argues that Leo Strauss's scholarship representing an exploration of the tension between Jerusalem and Athens is mediated through a third city, Mecca (representing the Islamic philosophical thought of al-Farabi).

56. See Tomaž Mastnak, *Crusading Peace: Christendom, the Muslim World, and Western Political Order* (Berkeley: University of California Press, 2002).

57. Turkey's application for admission into the European Union has generated strong hostility on the part of Western European leaders. In response to it Hans van Mierlo, foreign minister of the Netherlands, candidly stated, "There is a problem of a large Muslim state" and "Do we want that in Europe?" see The New York Times, *Turkey Finds European Union Door Slow to Open*, Sunday February 23, 1997, A3. Additionally, Wilfred Maartens the former Belgian Prime Minister equally bluntly squashed the idea of Turkey's admission to the EU saying "Turkey is not a candidate to become a member of the European Union, short term or long term" and "That is a European project." See The New York Times, *Brussels Meeting Dims Turkey's Bid to Join European Union*, Tuesday March 11, 1997, p. A11. Ironically it was the Greek Foreign Minister Theodoros Pangalos who criticized the EU decision, observing "I cannot accept this approach" and "Turkey is very much part of European history, and Islam is already part of Europe." See, The New York Times, *At Long Last, Greece and Turkey Tiptoe Toward Reconciliation*, July 21, 1997.

58. Menocal has offered a full critical exposition of these issues in *The Arabic Role in Western Literary History: A Forgotten Heritage* (Philadelphia: University of Pennsylvania Press, 1987), *Shards of Love: Exile and the Origins of the Lyric* (Durham, N.C.: Duke University Press), *The Ornament of the World: How Muslims, Jews, and Christians Created a Culture of Tolerance in Medieval Spain* (Boston: Little, Brown, 2002), and María Rosa Menocal, Raymond P. Scheindlin, and Michael Sells, eds., *The Cambridge History of Arabic Literature: The Literature of Al-Andalus* (Cambridge University Press, 2000).

59. For the appropriation of Enlightenment and other Western concepts by those resisting Western rule or domination, see Aziz al-Azmeh, *Islams and Modernities* (London: Verso, 1993), 39–59; and Olivier Roy, *The Failure of Political Islam* (Cambridge: Harvard University Press, 1994), 1–27. For a study showing the appropriation of modern ideas by those who see themselves or who are seen by others as rejecting modernity, see Bruce Lawrence, *Defenders of God: The Fundamentalist Revolt Against the Modern Age* (San Francisco: Harper and Row, 1989).

60. For an examination of cultural boundary construction and the negotiation of cultural boundaries see Aristide R. Zolberg, "Why Islam Is Like Spanish: Cultural Incorporation in Europe and the United States," *Politics and Society* 21.1 (March 1999): 5. For a studies of European Muslims see Jessica Jacobson, *Islam*

in Transition: Religion and Identity Among British Pakistani Youth (London: Routledge, 1998); Phillip Lewis, *Islamic Britain: Religion, Politics, and Identity Among British Muslims* (London: Tauris, 1994); and Jocelyn Cesari, *Islam in the West* (London: Palgrave, 2003).

61. Bernard Lewis and Dominique Schnapper, *Muslims in Europe* (London: Pinter, 1994), 18.

62. See Bernard Lewis's own description of his *Multiple Identities of the Middle East* (New York: Schocken, 1999). The description can be found at http://www.geocities.com/booksnewsletter/.

   Elsewhere, Lewis uses the medieval legal opinion of some jurists demanding that Muslims leave a territory ruled by a non-Muslim to argue that the Muslim immigrant or descendant of an immigrant in Europe is torn by the alleged Islamic demand that he convert Europeans, drive them away, or leave himself. As with his imputation of the medieval distinction between the "the House of Islam" and "the House of War" to contemporary Muslims, Lewis essentializes a legal issue that was important at one time and for some legal schools suggests, without evidence, that it is a defining preoccupation among contemporary Muslim populations. See Bernard Lewis, "Muslim Populations Under Non-Muslim Rule," in Lewis and Schnapper, eds., *Muslims in Europe*, 1–18.

   David Owen, who was placed in charge of European Union efforts to find a negotiated peace in Bosnia-Herzegovina, observed, in regard to his first meeting with Bosnian President Alija Izetbegović: "There was no outward and visible signs that he was a Muslim. He, his son and his daughter dressed and acted as Europeans.'" For Owen, a Muslim was, by definition, non-European and thus this Bosnian family with its European eyes and dress represented an inherent contradiction. David Owen, *Balkan Odyssey* (New York: Harcourt Brace, 1995), 39. Throughout the tragedy in Bosnia-Herzegovina Owen played an essential and persistent role in turning back proposals to lift the arms embargo that targeted mainly the Bosnian Muslims and to provide air support to save Muslims populations from the "ethnic cleansing" being leveled against them by both Croat and Serb armies. In some cases fundamentalist Saudi aid groups demonstrated in action their commitment to the same opinion, requiring starving Bosnians to adopt the aid groups' definition of Islamic dress in order to receive the donations.

63. Serb nationalists were aware of the larger debate and embraced the theories of Huntington for vindicatimg their own underappreciated efforts to deal with a force that, in Huntington's and their eyes, is essentialy incompatible with the West, with Christianity, and with Europe. Other publications dedicated to "Western" values and freedoms represent Bosnia in similar terms. In the 1997 Freedom Review from Freedom House, Bosnia was placed in the Middle East section. Geography was rearranged to conform to ideological imperatives. The author, Khalid Duran, was cognizant of the quandary when he observes,

"Although Bosnia is in Europe, it is a major factor in the Middle East." Nevertheless Croatia and Serbia managed to remain intact within Europe. See *Freedom Review* 28.1 (January/February 1997): 144.

64. Vojislav Kostunica, who succeeded Milošević as president of Serbia, is himself a religious nationalist who had supported Radovan Karadžić and Ratko Mladićin the Bosnian campaign that has now been labeled genocide by the International Criminal Tribunal for the former Yugoslavia; he has resisted all efforts to foster an open and honest discussion in Serbia of what happened under the Milosević rule. See Norman Cigar, *Vojislav Kostunica and Serbia's Future* (London: Saqi, 2001).

65. Schmitt himself has been regarded as tainted by pro-Nazi sympathies and apologetics. For a critical examination of Schmidt, see John McCormick, *Carl Schmitt's Critique of Liberalism: Against Politics as Technology* (Cambridge: Cambridge University Press, 1999).

66. René Girard, *Violence and the Sacred* (Baltimore: Johns Hopkins University Press, 1977).

67. See Edward Said's "Clash of Definitions," this volume.

68. See Christina Phelps Harris, *Nationalism and Revolution in Egypt: The Role of the Muslim Brotherhood* (The Hague: Moulton, 1964); Brynjar Lia, *The Society of the Muslim Brothers in Egypt: The Rise of an Islamic Mass Movement, 1928–1942* (London: Ithaca, 1998); and Roxanne L. Euben, *Enemy in the Mirror: Islamic Fundamentalism and the Limits of Modern Rationalism* (Princeton: Princeton University Press, 1999). See in particular Harris, *Nationalism and Revolution*, 131: "The more deeply Egypt was penetrated by westernism and by secularism, the more firmly dig Muslim reactionaries oppose westernization. They took fright, closed their ranks, and sought to protect their time-honored traditions"; and Euben, *Enemy in the Mirror*, 51: "Islamic fundamentalists such as Qutb advance essentialist versions of 'Islam' and 'the West,' yet in this context such essentialism inverts Orientalist arguments."

69. For the Pakistani Islamist party see Seyyed Vali Reza Nasr, *The Vanguard of the Islamic Revolution: The Jama'at-I Islami of Pakistan* (University of California Press: Berkeley, 1994); and Seyyed Vali Reza Nasr, *Mawdudi and the Making of Islamic Revivalism* (New York: Oxford University Press, 1996). See especially Nasr, *Vanguard*, 5: "He started with the premise that Muslims should return to a pure and unadulterated Islam to brace themselves for the struggle before them. They should reject Hindu ascendancy and continue to lay claim to the whole of India. He was especially perturbed by those Muslims who were willing to accommodate Hindus, and by supporting the Congress were acquiescing to the inevitability of the Hindu raj. His most venomous rhetoric was reserved for them. Irredentist as Mawdudi's views may have appeared they were communalist in form and content. . . . The struggle had to defend Muslim commu-

nalist interests in India and to preserve Muslim identity in the face of imminent Hindu challenges."

70. In the case of Pakistan the Jamaat-e-Islami party had a tradition of only marginal electoral successes. Prior to the fall of the Taliban regime in Afghanistan, it had, on numerous occasions, never achieved more than 5–10 percent of electoral votes and has been consistently and soundly defeated by secular political parties. However, Pakistani military dictators anxious to have the fig leaf of religious legitimacy confirmed upon them have entered into opportunistic alliances with the Jamaat-e-Islami. Thus the Pakistani dictator Zia al Haqq sought the support of the Jamaat-e-Islami when he embarked upon his anti-Soviet Jihad. In return the Jamaat-e-Islami demanded a program of Islamization that continues to haunt Pakistan and is the basis of the sectarian (Sunni-Shiite) violence that plagues the country to this day. In Egypt the Muslim Brotherhood was consciously used as a counterweight to the popularity of Egyptian leftist parties and allowed to agitate and gain power on university campuses, unlike secular parties, in the 1970s. In both cases Islamist parties have thrived when democracy was constricted. For a study of Afghanistan that highlights the implications of U.S. collaboration with the Zia al-Haqq regime, see Barnett Rubin, *The Search for Peace in Afghanistan: From Buffer State to Failed State* (New Haven: Yale University Press, 2002).

71. The term *fundamentalism* has been criticized on two grounds. First, critics argue, current religious expressions labeled fundamentalism have little to do with the original meaning of the term as a movement within Protestant Christianity to return to the roots or fundamentals of the tradition. Other critics reject the term *fundamentalism* because it has been used as a code word to brand and stereotype Muslims. But when a new meaning for a word becomes dominant among the public there is little point in attempted to push back the evolution of language. A look at any major English dictionary shows that the meaning of words is constantly evolving. And, when it is abused or used invidiously, the most adequate response is to redefine it in a way that is not abusive.

For some important discussions of fundamentalism that offer the term a definition more accurately reflecting current usage, see Lawrence, *Defenders of God*, and Mark Juergensmeyer, *The New Cold War: Religious Nationalism Confronts the Secular State* (Berkeley: University of California Press, 1993), along with the volumes of the University of Chicago Fundamentalism project. One of the most cogent theological critiques of religious intolerance and the way it inscribes itself into the very effort to speak about ultimate reality can be found in the work of the medieval Islamic mystical philosopher Muhyiddin Ibn al-'Arabi (d. 1240 C.E./638 H). See Michael Sells, *Mystical Languages of Unsaying* (Chicago: University of Chicago Press, 1994), chapters 3–4.

72. See Fatema Mernissi, *Islam and Democracy: Fear of the Modern World*, translated by Mary Jo Lakeland (Reading, Mass.: Addison-Wesley, 1992). Another form of critique is made from the perspective of a retrieval of Islamic law within a critique of the reifications of the shari'a under colonial rule. Thus Amira Sonbol, for example, has argued that "Arab and Islamic women generally had more rights in previous centuries than they enjoy today. The reason for this decline is that nineteenth-century European social mores prompted a piecemeal and Victorian-era colonial application of shari'a law which quickly became accepted and codified as the 'genuine' Arab/Islamic tradition. Muslim women's groups have shown, for example, that women had more freedom to initiate divorce before the colonial period, and that the many of repressive restrictions were added during the colonial era when state law subsumed and manipulated Islamic law." Summary of presentation by Sonbol at the Arab World 2000 conference, panel discussion on "Authority, Authoritarianism and Democracy," March 31, 2000, Center for Contemporary Arab Studies, Georgetown University. The summary is available with the conference description at http://www.ccasonline.org/symposium/panel3.htm.

Part I

Palace Fundamentalism and Liberal Democracy

Fatema Mernissi

Islamic fundamentalism is usually perceived by Western liberal democracies as something not only alien to, but also entirely incompatible with, their philosophical and ethnical foundations. Often, though, they fail to make even the elementary distinction between Islamic fundamentalism—an authoritarian ideology and political system, which sacralizes hierarchy and repudiates pluralism—and Islam as a religion and a culture. Thus the incompatibility between Islam and the West has been promoted, since the fall of the communist camp, as the principal field of conflict and lurking danger in the next century.

After making the necessary distinction between Islam as a culture and fundamentalism as a political ideology, I would like to suggest that the liberal democracies in fact have a history of promoting Islamic fundamentalism; and that, in particular, they have made extraordinary profits from Saudi fundamentalism. The internationally overwhelming role of Saudi Arabia as promoter of a kind of aggressive "petro-fundamentalism"—with its primitive messages of obedience *(Ta'a)*, intolerance, misogyny and xenophobia—is inconceivable without the liberal democracies' strategic support of conservative Islam, both as a bulwark against communism and as a tactical resource for controlling Arab oil.

Saudi Wahhabism (named after its preacher Muhammed Ibn 'Abd al-Wahhab, 1703–92) is, by the standards of many Moslems, one of the most fanatical sects of extremist Islam. It insists upon a return to the "ideal" customs of seventh-century Arab desert tribes and considers everything "added" since the prophet's time to be a foreign perversion—including all scientific and cultural achievements (with their Hellenistic and Persian components). Beginning with the alliance between the preacher Abdelwahab and the warrior Emir Muhammad Ibn Saud in 1740, Wahhabism unsuccessfully tried to invade neighboring areas. It was halted and crushed by the Ottoman Turks at the beginning of the nineteenth century.

After complete marginalization for more than a century, Wahhabism reemerged with the discovery of oil, becoming a trump card in the energy and cold war strategies of the liberal democracies. Fanatical Wahhabism proved to be an extraordinary machine for manufacturing "certainty" in world politics, since it concentrated control over one of the planet's most important sources of petroleum, and the major assets of 230 million Arab citizens, in the hands of one prince and his close court.[1]

Here we see one of the most puzzling marriages of the century: the bond between a fanatical creed and the most modern liberal states. How is this possible? How can liberal democracies oppose democratization in the Arab world? How can liberal democracies support authoritarianism and tyranny? This brings us to the almost unthinkable question: Can liberal democracies be irrational? Concern has been increasing for decades within these countries that the growth and consolidation of a very ambiguous managerial corporate power interferes with the fundamental principles of pluralism and democracy,[2] but this has not seemed to shake the average Westerner's strong belief in the pretension of the society to rationality and respect of the individual.

On the contrary, many people in the West would tend to reject as absurd the idea that their government supports Saudi palace fundamentalism, because this destabilizes the comfortable duality according to which the West is rational and progressive, and the East is a dark hole of irrationality and barbarism. Furthermore, many Westerners think it normal to believe that Islam is irrational; and when they say "Islam," they mean not only the civilization with its religions and cultural heritage and philosophical worldview, but also the entire population, regardless of class, sex, ethnic, or economic interests. Their word "Islam" refers to an indiscriminate magma of people who have the same interests and share the same fanaticism; and their unquestionable popular slogan is "Islam is Irrational." But the game becomes more interesting if we include the liberal democracies in the discussion.

Is Islam Irrational? Are the Liberal Democracies Rational?

Liberal democracies, as Francis Fukuyama describes them, leave an Arab woman bathing in dream-like envy. According to Fukuyama, they are uncompromisingly ethical and universalist: "The chief psychological imperative underlying democracy is the desire for universal and equal recognition. . . . Only liberal democracy can rationally satisfy the human desire for recognition, through the granting of elementary rights of citizenship on a universal and equal basis"[3] Many experts like Fukuyama and Samuel Huntington go on to predict that, after the fall of the communist bloc, the next challenge to universalist liberal democracies will come from authoritarian regimes in general and theocracies in particular.[4] Islam, unlike Confucianism, is singled out as the enemy most totally incompatible with liberal democracies' philosophies and interests.

The problem here is that equating Islam with irrationality immediately turns the world's 1.2 billion Muslims into potential enemies. Since creating such masses of enemies is a bellicosity smacking more of irrationality than of cold analysis, and since many Western intellectuals have produced "scientific" and "philosophical" grounds for sustaining this crusade in academic circles, while neo-fascist mobs attack Muslims in many European cities,[5] I suggest that we try to reformulate the question.

If we define irrationality as basically the intolerant behavior of a person or system believing in certainty, and therefore holding that there is only one truth and that those who think otherwise ought to be repressed, then rationality could be defined as the opposite—as what Ralf Dahrendorf has called the "ethics of uncertainty." "The ethics of uncertainty are the ethics of liberty, and the ethics of liberty are the ethics of conflict, of antagonism generated and institutionalized."[6] Within this framework, we can assume without being completely unrealistic that there must be in the Muslim world some individuals and some institutions (banks, firms, factories) that operate rationally and see their survival as vitally depending on the institutionalization of conflict. Such would certainly be the case for individuals belonging to religious and ethnic minorities (Copts in Egypt, Christians in

Sudan, Kurds in Iraq, Berbers in Algeria and Morocco, and so forth), for women who suffer from official legal discrimination, and for free thinking intellectuals, or simply for individuals who have interests that conflict with the ruling elites.[7]

We can also assume, without being too unrealistic, that some Western citizens and some institutions, although belonging to liberal democracies, might identify a despotic irrationality (as defined above) as suitable for the pursuit of their interests. We hear daily about scandalous aberrations in the ethical rules regulating the liberal market and the political systems of representative democracy. Corrective devices exist in the economic and political systems of the latter precisely because irrationality is assumed to be a possible choice for some individuals.

Assuming that citizens of liberal democracies are rational at all times and in all situations eliminates the dimension of "uncertainty" so essential to rationality and smacks of a Muslim Imam's fiat. But once we assume rationality and irrationality to be possible in both liberal democracies and Muslim countries, we can reformulate the question as follows: How can we increase the scope of rationality in the Muslim world? Of course, another question follows immediately: Who are "we"? "We" could be any individuals, regardless of culture and nationality, who are interested in nurturing the chances of rationality in the next century; and this "we" represents millions of lovers of peace and justice within and outside the Muslim world. In fact, the most difficult of all intellectual enterprises is the attempt to separate "East" from "West".

Focusing our attention on how to increase rationality in the Muslim world has at least a few advantages. The first is that it frees us of the racist bias inherent in opening a debate about which cultural group is rational and which is not. The second is that it empowers us—both "Westerns" and "Muslims"—by helping us identify key factors that can increase the chances of rational problem-solving methods and reduce violent outcomes to conflict. By focusing on the people, on the citizens' desire to exercise their free choice, we reveal the political nature of the conflict. If, to justify their budgets, some generals and arms lobbies find it appropriate to blow cultural differences into a Medieval crusade, we should not jump blindly onto their bandwagon, because we might have different interests—such as promoting dialogue, tolerance, and global responsibility, which is, at any rate, the ultimate goal of this essay.

Now let us further narrow the scope of the question to the following: How can we increase the chances for rationality in the Arab world, considering the two determinant strategic factors, which are oil and arms sales? For when one looks at the issue through the perspective of Arab oil, the landscape shifts dramatically, and strange sights begin to appear. The incompatibility between Beauty (ethical liberal democracies) and the Beast (authoritarian Islam) disappears entirely. As in *The Tales of a Thousand and One Nights*, Beauty and the Beast can then be seen entwined together, Liberal Democracies and Wahhabism in intimate embrace.

What does this mean for the livelihood of people in the Arab world, and in particular for women and minorities who are singled out as sacrificial victims by fanatics? It means repression (not only of women and minorities, but of all political dissent), support for fanatical political movements, and an irrational use of resources which could provide a decent standard of living for all people, both in the Arab world and outside it. Growing poverty and joblessness in the Arab region (and outside it) oblige us to question the way profits from oil are profligately invested in arms. They force us to ask the only question worth asking: How can we change the situation? How can we create a model of oil management that enhances dignity and well being in both West and East?

The Hijacking of Arab Jobs by the Western Arms Industry

Today, the number of unemployed in the Middle East and North Africa is estimated at ten million.[8] But a look at the national budgets of the Arab states in general, and of Saudi Arabia in particular, shows that Arab money goes to buy arms which create jobs in Los Angeles and France, rather than in Cairo and Casablanca.[9]

The Middle East is a bonanza market for arms sales—the largest in the world. While the arms purchases of developed countries represented one quarter of the world market in 1985, for example, those of the Middle East amounted to 35 percent—down from 43 percent in the two previous years. The end of the Cold War ought to have reduced arms supplies to the region. One might also have expected that the defeat of Iraq and the concentration on the peace process between Israel and its neighbors would have led to a substantial reduction in arms purchases, but his has not been so.

An overview of arms sales published in the latest report of the United States Arms Control and Disarmament Agency reveals that while these sales throughout the world are substantially decreasing, the Middle East scores higher than ever, with military expenditures representing 54 percent of public outlays and 20 percent of the GNP of these countries.[10] The only significant change since the end of the Cold War and the Gulf

War is that the United States now tops the list as the most important arms supplier for the Third World, replacing the Soviet Union. America's most greedy client is Saudi Arabia, with yearly arms purchases of 3.5 to 4 billion dollars.[11]

At a time of tragic global elimination of jobs, associated with a process of seemingly irresistible structural technological transformation, American and French presidents (as well as others from important arms-producing nations) scour the planet to secure employment for their citizens. The transformation of the heads of state of some major liberal democracies into salesmen seems neither a transient feature of current affairs nor an ethically doubtful event. On the contrary, it looks like an important shift in the role of the state in the post-modern global market. A recent issue of *Newsweek*, with a title story dedicated to "The New Diplomacy: Uncle Sam as Salesman," announces: "Now that the Cold War is over, Washington is reaffirming to the world that in foreign policy, the business of America is business." The American Secretary of State, Warren Christopher, is quoted as saying that if "for a long time Secretaries of State thought of economics as 'low policy' while they dealt only with high science like arms control, I make no apologies for putting economics at the top of our foreign policy agenda."[12] But of course American heads of state and diplomats are not the only ones helping their industries to get contracts; the leaders of other major powers do their best as well.

The arms industry lobbies have proved to be particularly influential in the global market. Not only have they successfully resisted the early post–Cold War desire for smaller arms expenditures and a less aggressive society, but they have also managed to switch the debate from peace to job creation, and thus have enlisted the help of local politicians:

> Opposition to change can come from different directions. Arms producers raise the specter of job losses, so they lobby their governments to buy more weapons, provide higher subsidies and give more support to exports. Local politicians fearing unemployment also argue against the closure of factories and military bases. And within the armed forces, officers and soldiers protest being demobilized.[13]

These interests find a loyal ally in the Saudi Arabian state. The Arab leader who sits on the world's biggest oil resources, and who claims to defend the Muslim Umma's interest, creates millions of hours of work in the Christian West. If, within a ferociously competitive global market, Saudi

Islamic fundamentalism can hijack so many potential jobs from the Arab Mediterranean to Northern Europe and the United States, should we not relinquish the idea that this fundamentalism is an anachronistic, medieval religion and start regarding it as a strategic agency to create employment in the unsettling post-modern economy of the West?

The skilful capture of jobs by liberal democracies, through the sale of arms which make the princes of undemocratic Arab states feel secure (at public expense), is one of the causes of the high rates of youth unemployment in the Middle East. It leaves states like Saudi Arabia open to the street fundamentalists' accusation that governments betray the Muslim community; and it creates a virulent internal opposition, which has gained unprecedented visibility since the Gulf War.[14]

In sum, palace fundamentalism like that of Saudi Arabia is a satanically efficient institution for supporting the global oil and arms lobbies. The young executives working for Boeing and McDonnell-Douglas seem more like the "cousins" and "brothers" of the Emirs than do young, unemployed Mustapha and Ali, strolling the streets of Cairo in humiliating uselessness. How has this come about?

The Marriage of Palace Fundamentalism with Liberal Democracies and the Attack on Arab Secularism

Wahhabism is one of a myriad fanatic reformist sects. It began in the eighteenth century in one of the most culturally marginal parts of the Arab world, the desert of Arabia. After Mohammad Ali, the sophisticated Ottoman ruler of Egypt, crushed Wahhabism, it was forgotten throughout the nineteenth century. When, in the early twentieth century, the feverishly nationalist Arab World resolutely determined to modernize, secularize and renew itself, no one would have guessed that the Saudis had any role to play on the international scene. Were it not for the discovery of oil and the systematic investment by the West in the region's Emirs from the 1930s onward, few today would know where on the map to find that kingdom.

The secularization of Arab culture and the state, promoted by a widely popular nationalist ideology, was well advanced in the 1930s and 1940s, as has been superbly documented in recent works such as Aziz Al Azmeh's, *Secularism in Modern Arab Life and Thought (al' ilmāniya)*. Al Azmeh has gathered an impressive wealth of data showing that secularism was neither a superficial nor an elitist phenomenon, but represented a profound transformation running deep at all levels of both popular mentality and state culture.[15] It is important to note that religious authorities were integrated into this intellectual renaissance; and many, like Ali Aberazik were leaders of reformist movements which produced interpretations of the Qur'an and Hadith accommodating democratization and secularization.[16]

A pertinent indicator of this advanced secularization, accompanied by the appearance of a dynamic civil society, is Egypt's strong feminist movement, animated by Huda Sha'rawi, an aristocratic beauty who, between 1923 and her death in 1947, managed to influence the ruling elite, get the attention of cultural circles and lead street demonstrations, and who, within her own lifetime, finally obtained changes in marriage law. She also managed to cast off the veil, write, have children and enjoy the unbending support of a loving husband.[17] In Egypt the famous fundamentalist brotherhood (Jama'at Ikhwan al-Muslimin) was born in the same decade (1928–36) as was Arab feminism. But they co-existed peacefully, with both feminists and fundamentalists stating their visions of the future and defending their ideas side by side. Pluralism was in place in Egypt in the 1930s. The Egyptian feminist movement deserves part of the credit for the fact that the Arab league charter of the 1940s granted women the right to vote, the right to education, and the right to work.

Unfortunately for the secular forces of the Arab world, commercially significant quantities of Saudi oil were discovered in 1938. In the following years, oil production increased at an incredible rate, from 30,000 barrels a day in 1943 to 1.2 million in 1960, 8.2 million in 1974 and 10.5 million in 1980.[18] From the beginning of this period, Saudi palace Islam was courted as a way of ensuring "certainty" in the capitalist market. But it was the Cold War that transformed the romance between the Saudi princes and the oil companies into a stable marriage between Western Liberalism and Saudi fundamentalism.

Saudi Arabia was assigned a new role in the 1950s and 1960s: to fight communism. Arab nationalism, incarnated by Nasser—proudly modernist and devoted to the idea of an *inbi'ath*, a genuine renaissance of the region as an independent actor—was perceived by the West as a dangerous potential ally of the communists.[19] Nasser became the target of Western hostility, expressed in the joint British and French attack on Egypt in 1956. Saudi money poured into the streets of Cairo, financing publishers of medieval literature as a new driving force of Arab thought. Leftist intellectuals were harassed, and many had to choose between prison and exile. It was then that the Arab world lost a substantial number of its intellectuals, who—ironically—often sought exile in the liberal democracies, where they now live and contribute to academic and intellectual life.

The current post–Cold War upsurge of street fundamentalism must be traced to this monstrous alliance between fanaticism and the oil and security policies of liberal democracies. Professor Richard Dekmejian, American Middle East expert and adviser to Presidents Reagan and Bush, provided a succinct account of this phenomenon in a recent interview published in *Al Ahram Weekly* (24–30 November 1994):

Question: How do you account for the rise of Islamist movements in the Arab region and the Middle East?

Answer: Let us start from the time of Nasser. Through Saudi Arabia, the United States provide direct support to the Muslim Brotherhood, the oldest movement in the area. The idea was to counter the rising tide of Arab nationalism and Arab unity championed by Nasser and by the Ba'ath Party in Syria and Iraq. The West became more and more convinced that Islam was the weapon to fight communism. The United States readily spent six billion dollars assisting the Afghan Mujahedin, who were resisting Soviet occupation. Israel shared similar convictions. The Likud government in the early eighties fostered the nascent Hamas to curb Fatah and the PLC.

Question: Do you believe that the Gulf War fuelled the Islamist movements?

Answer: . . . I can say with considerable certainty—since I was an advisr to both the Reagan and Bush administrations—that their policies in the region were misconceived and precipitated the war. It is well known that during his first four years in office, Reagan tried to overthrow the Libyan regime of Gaddafi and to consolidate US influence in Lebanon. Israel had failed to do so, and thus the Americans had their try. The reaction was the emergence of Hizabollah in Lebanon and a series of events: the Iran-Iraq War and the Iran-contra scandal . . . Under Bush and Baker, the United States taxpayer provided millions of dollars to support Saddam, the new Shah of the Gulf. Saddam, however, deceived all parties by invading Kuwait. Bush, who had created Saddam, had to remove him.

Here, then, we come upon that dark, totalitarian side of "rationality." Rationality can be perceived to involve creating

> the capacity for controlling future events and creating a life relatively secure from the disruptions of chance. Economic rationality indicates an ability to make reasonable predictions about returns on invest-ments, whereas legal rationality is supposed to provide protection from unpredictable political influences and from sudden changes in the social order.[20]

Western support for Islamic fundamentalism did manage to further eco-nomic "certainty" during the Cold War era. Palace fundamentalism lessens the element of chance in the market by drastically reducing the number of actors in the Arab political scene. Democratization, it seems, would have multiplied the actors and atomized decision-making by forcing leaders to submit to accountability checks. Thus democracy in the Arab world would have meant an intolerable increase in unpredictability in the oil and arms markets. The enlargement of the political theater, to allow Arab citizens to express their free will through twenty-two parliaments of Arab states, would have introduced a high level of uncertainty and posed "a barrier to rational economic behavior."[21]

But as Yehud Shenav has noted, "increased rationality increased the cer-tainty of one group, but the uncertainty of another."[22] As the liberal democ-racies' economic and political strategies tilted the balance against civil soci-ety in the Arab World, they contributed to making the life of the average Arab citizen in general, and the lives of women and minorities in particular, a terrible field of insecurity. People's incapacity to control events in their lives or to change their situation has been one of the main themes in songs, literature, and films, and lies behind the anger of young people with states that have become increasingly incapable of doing their job, which should be to defend the interest of the masses.

Interventionist States and Initiative-Deprived States

During the Cold War, then, Western liberalism perceived and approached conflict, pluralism and democratization in the Arab world as a threat to its interests. After the Cold War, things seem more ambiguous. The possibility of shifting alliances is more than probably, especially because of the viability the viability of the Middle East peace process and the security of Israel depend upon the existence of a democratic and tolerant Arab world. There is an emergent strategy to promote stability which is based on nurturing democratic Arab forces and strengthening civil society; and this gives the old lovers (Liberal Democracy and Saudi Princes) a vitally important opportunity to change their relationship. The emergence of a highly educated and sophisticated generation in the Saudi Kingdom, in particular, creates a possibility for beginning the twenty-first century on a new footing. But this possibility will be affected by the nature of the Arab state and the need for this very ambiguous entity to redesign itself in a modern form.

With the collapse of communism, debate on the nature of the state has blossomed. An excellent example was the exchange between Francis Fukuyama and Ghia Nodia on the conflict between supposedly universalistic liberalism and nationalism. The debate centers on the question, "Whose interests does the state serve? Exclusively those of its own nationals, or those of all humanity?"[23] Fukuyama argues that the liberal state is universalistic and tends to further the interests of all human beings, while nationalist states discriminate against all who do not belong to the "nation." In the debate, there are only two kinds of states, and both have the same capacities for intervention. The only difference is the number of people they intend to serve. Nationalism is inferior, according to Fukuyama, because it blocks the freedom of choice of the individual and therefore cannot win in the competition with liberal democracies:

> If, as I have argued elsewhere, liberalism is about the universal and equal recognition of every citizen's dignity as an autonomous human being, then the introduction of a national principle necessarily introduces distinctions between people. Persons who do not belong to the dominant nationality *ipso facto* have their dignity recognized in an inferior way to those who do belong—a flat contradiction of the principle of universal and equal recognition.[24]

Anything which interferes with the individual's free choice, or curtails his/her sovereign right to decide for him/herself, according to this view, is irrational and reduces the potential for creativity of a people.

I consider this position quixotic, not only because liberalism is far removed from treating all Arab citizens as human beings, but also because

the way the question is posed diverts attention from a terrifyingly dangerous polarization in the post-modern global society—a polarization
between what we would call "interventionist" states initiating planetary
strategies, on the one hand and, on the other, states executing these strategies, without having played any part in initiating them. Taking the oil and
arms nexus as an example, we could say that, during the Cold War, liberal
democratic states were able to develop planetary strategies, intervene in
the affairs of Arab states, and implement these strategies successfully;
while Arab states were unable to develop any alternative other than to execute such strategies even if they revealed themselves to be disadvantageous
to their citizens.

Indeed, one reason for the weakness of the initiative-deprived state is
the absence of a democratic base—the paralysis of civil society, which is
the only instance capable of producing strategies with a broad democratic
groundwork, allowing diverging interest groups to negotiate balanced solutions for vital problems such as employment and job creation. The more
locally focused and democratically produced the strategies, and the
broader the range of actors involved in their elaboration, the wider the
support they are likely to mobilize and the stronger the interventionist
capacity of the state.

Western liberal democracies in general, and the United States in particular, fit the description of interventionist states with planetary strategies.
Far from embodying a perfect liberal state representing universal interests
(such a state does not, in fact, exist anywhere on the planet), the American
political system is inclined toward self-interest protectionism. As the American political scientist James Kurt has pointed out, the privileged connection between the United States and international organizations (such as
the International Monetary Fund, the World Bank and the United
Nations) endows that country with "a beyond-the-nation-state interventionist capability."[25]

This distinction between interventionist and executant states helps to
explain the "conspiracy syndrome" so common among Arab citizens, who
complain that the West interferes in their affairs, and that the CIA and "the
Lobbies" are responsible for everything that happens in their lives. To say
that such conspiracy theories are imaginary is to ignore the clear discrep-
ancy between the capabilities of Western and Arab states, and to ignore the
structure of the oil and arms markets, which are far from a universal paradise
in which all human beings are treated equally.

Making Our Differences Intelligible

It is understandable that a Western intellectual who is neither an arms dealer nor a banker associated with oil monopolies could feel that his or her moral probity is being attacked, and could become defensive when an Arab intellectual complains about the tragic influence of the liberal democracies in the region during the cold War. Of course, the average citizen of liberal democracies is not responsible for the atrocities committed against progressive forces by Arab authoritarian regimes during the struggle against communism. But dismissing these emotionally charged perceptions as "paranoia" is indeed a poor response on the part of those intellectuals whose role in shaping their own countries' policies is more vital than before.

Western intellectuals are the target of complaints on the part of their colleagues from the Third World precisely because the former are perceived to be a source of hope for transforming mentalities in a dangerously consumerist and souk-like global market. Intellectuals everywhere are emerging as what Wolf Lepenies calls "translators between cultures":

> We cannot be satisfied any longer with simply trying to understand other cultures. Understanding is an attitude which involves distancing—an attitude adopted toward cultures that are only taken into account in a very indirect way, cultures with which one is willing to establish contact only in order to improve one's general knowledge. All that has changed. We are now obliged to apply ourselves to the task of rendering our cultures intelligible, because we are increasingly compelled to understand each other within the much more immediate context of living together. For all intellectuals, this is an enormous challenge.[26]

The dynamics of oil, arms and fundamentalism are not a bad place to start in rendering the relations between the peoples of the West and the Arab world intelligible. We do not live in separate worlds, but in highly interconnected ones. In the new post–Cold War world, let us rethink the entire approach to economic development and democratization in the Middle East, giving "stability" and "security" a different and more positive meaning. Western intellectuals and policy makers can make a great contribution in this regard by adopting a sense of responsibility and commitment to democracy commensurate with their great capacity to control the world's resources.

Reversing earlier policies of support for autocratic regimes and nurturing the revitalization of civil society in the Arab world would be a daring and constructive way to step into the twenty-first century.

Notes

1. This is well described in a recent *Financial Times* article on the kingdom's budgetary troubles: "Saudi Arabia's economic policymakers are busy preparing the annual January 1 budget statement, the Kingdom's main public declaration of economic policy. . . . The 'situation' is the worst slap Saudi Arabia has faced since the oil price collapse of the mid 1980's and an unprecedented tightness in public coffers—the product of the 55 billion dollar bill for the Gulf War (Desert Storm), subsequent costly military purchases, unhelpfully soft oil prices and the cumulative effects of a decade of high spending. . . . How King Fahd weighs such factors in making the budget decision—for the ultimate decision will be his—is unknowable outside his close court. . . . Only on January 1, therefore, will anyone outside the royal court know quite how serious the Saudi government believes its present economic difficulties really are." Mark Nicholson, "Saudi Budget May Have to Reflect Some Harsh Realities," *Financial Times*, November 18, 1994, 5.

2. "At the heart of the debate is an attempt to evaluate the impact of corporate power on individuals and society. On the one hand, we are afforded apocalyptic visions and dark warnings of tyranny, domination and oppression. On the other hand, we find images of utopia and promises of an organizational society without discontents. . . . On the face of it, the argument for tyranny would seem to have some merit. In its attention to the formulation and dissemination of ideology, Tech management indeed resembles Big Brother. . . . The facts seem to support the critics' claim that the modern corporation is fast becoming—if it has not already become—a monstrosity." Reinhard Bendix, *Work and Authority in Industry* (New York: Harper and Row, 1956), 339; see also Gideon Kunda, *Engineering Culture: Control and Commitment in a High-Tech Corporation* (Philadelphia: Temple University Press, 1992). Yehuda Shenhav makes a convincing argument on the authoritarian concentration of power that lies behind the concept of certainty. See Yehuda Shenhav, "Manufacturing Uncertainty and Certainty in Manufacturing: Managerial Discourse and the Rhetoric of Organizational Theory," *Science in Context* 7.2 (1994): 267–307.

3. Francis Fukuyama, "Capitalism and Democracy: The Missing Link," *Dialogue* 100.2 (1993), 6.

4. Samuel Huntington, "The Clash of Civilizations," *Foreign Affairs* 72.3 (1993).

5. Jürgen Habermas points out that "beyond the street attacks of extremists, it is their successes in parliaments which is shocking and constitutes a threat for liberal democracies' ethical foundations." Jürgen Habermas, *The Past as Future* (Omaha: University of Nebraska Press, 1994). On concerns raised by neofascist violence against Muslims in Europe, see "The Report of the Conference on Right Wing Extremism and German Democracy" (Berlin: Aspen Institute, 1994). The conference was held in Berlin, June 18–19, 1994, under the auspices of the Aspen Institute.

6. Ralf Dahrendorf, "Uncertainty, Science, and Democracy" in *Essays in the Theory of Society* (Stanford: Stanford University Press, 1965), 232–255.

7. The situations of minorities and women are probably the best indicators of secularization in Muslim states. They ought to be adopted as pertinent measures for gauging the balance between rationality and irrationality in these countries as well as for judging their achievements regarding the establishment of human rights and a civil society. Minorities, women, and slaves were the three groups that constituted a challenge and a limitation to Islam's claim to universality and equality. These three groups were the object, in the traditional Muslims state, of special legal dispositions that managed their special inferior status with the Muslim Umma while protecting them as full-fledged human beings.

   This is why most of the debate on "democracy" circles endlessly around the explosive issue of women's liberation and also why a piece of cloth like the veil is loaded with symbolism and ideological conflict, provoking constant violent clashes within and now outside Muslim territories. The heated French debate on *le foulard Islamique*, the Islamic scarf adopted by adolescent Muslims schoolgirls in Paris suburbs, shakes the Republic of France daily and splits its intellectuals and politicians, because it not only confronts France as a liberal democracy with its "unconscious," irrational, racist inconsistencies but also forces the Muslim population to discover and deal with its own inconsistencies and clashing aspirations. In this sense the foulard Islamique is far from a trivial secondary issue: it is a highly pertinent symbol upon which both supposedly universal European liberal democracies and their Muslim minorities test their claims to rationality, discovering the limits of those claims.

8. John Page Jr., "The Middle East: How Far from East Asia," note to a World Bank advisory board meeting on the Middle East and North Africa, Beirut, March 1995.

9. As items in the international press confirm: "La France va vendre à l'Arabie Saoudite deux frégates pour 19 milliards de Francs. . . . La conclusion de ce marché . . . représente 45 million d'heures de travail pour les entreprises Francaises." *Le Monde*, November 23, 1994.

10. Joe Stork, "Des arsenaux en quête de client solvable," *Le Monde Diplomatique*, January 1995, 337.

11. *Middle East Report* 24. 6 (November-December 1994).
12. Michael Hirsh and Karen Breslau, "USA, Inc," *Newsweek,* March 6, 1995, 10.
13. UNDP, *Human Development Report* (New York: Oxford University Press, 1994), 9.
14. One of the reasons for the emergence of street fundamentalism (a popular protest that expresses itself in religious form) is that palace fundamentalism raised hopes oil wealth would be equally shared between rich and poor. Massive popular support for Iraq during the Gulf War can be decoded as an expression of people's anger toward Gulf monarchies who, claiming to be saviors of the Muslim Umma, promised solidarity between rich and poor but did not deliver. Furthermore, the mistreatment of workers in the Gulf, and of Arab workers in particular, is no secret.
15. I would like to illustrate how deeply secularism ran in Arab society, and the extent to which the enlightened nationalist culture of the 1940s irreversibly changed people's lives. Arabs of my generation were taught that the reason for our humiliating military defeats, starting with Napoleon's conquest of Egypt in 1798, was the advanced state of Western science. My primary school teacher, Faqih Moulay Brahim Kettani, a religious authority and a fervent nationalist, who opened a girls' school to teach Muslim women mathematics and foreign languages, told us that when Napoleon's armada of four hundred ships appeared along the coast of Alexandria, "the most dangerous attackers were not the 36,000 soldiers, but a small group of 151 scientists, engineers and scholars, hardly noticed by anyone in the midst of the chaotic invasion of Egypt, then the jewel of the Ottoman Empire. The secret of the West's compelling superiority was that tiny group." Thus Faqih used to conclude his Friday prayer in our school mosque, which was built in the 1940s, by reminding us that "training scientific-minded Arab men and women is the best way, if not the only way, to pray to Allah and strengthen his Umma."

    Unveiling women, liberating them from seclusion, and educating them, teaching them mathematics and foreign languages, was the nationalist religious authorities' way of engaging in a jihad, or holy war, against ignorance. To serve Islam and his God, Moulay Brahim created one of the first mixed primary schools in the midst of the ninth-century medina of Fez. He imposed on us children—girls and boys alike—a tough discipline: Western sciences and the French language in the mornings, Qur'an and Arab history and poetry in the afternoon, with prayers in between. If not for petro-fundamentalism, how can we explain that now, fifty years later, educated and unveiled women and male intellectuals are targets of terrorist violence purporting to be religious?
16. Ali Abderazik's book, *Al-Islām wa Usūl al-Hukm* (Islam and the Foundations of Power) published in 1925, is still furiously attacked by fundamentalists. Abderazik stresses the secular nature of the Moslem leader: "The Caliphate or the

Big Imamat is not an institution based on religious creed nor is it a system justified by reason, and all the supposed evidence put forward to justify one or the other does not stand up to examination." The quote is taken from the 1988 edition: Ali Aberazik, *Al-Islām wa Usūl al-Hukm* (Beirut: al-mu'assasa al-'arabiyya li-dirāsat wa n-nashr, 1988).

17. See Hudá Sha'arāwī, *HaremYears: The Memoirs of an Egyptian Feminist* (1879–1924), ed. and trans, and introduced by Margot Badran (New York: Feminist Press at the City University of New York, 1987). The best source on Arab feminists is still a contribution by a man, Omar Kahhala, an Egyptian intellectual who compiled a three-volume "Who's Who" of famous women, listing hundreds of early Arab and Turkish feminists (1982).

18. George Corm, *Le Proche Orient Eclaté* (Paris: Gallimard, 1988).

19. The identification of Nasser (who was considered a hero of the Arab nationalist struggle by my generation) as a satanic enemy of the West is captured in this comment by Professor Peter Rodman: "In the Middle East, for forty years, we and our friends were in a struggle with Gamal Abdel Nasser and his heirs: military strongmen mouthing socialist slogans and backed by Soviet Weapons. This menace and this ideology are now defeated." Peter Rodman, "Arab Democracy/American Democracy," presentation at the conference "Reshaping the Agenda: U.S.-Arab Relations," hosted by the Foundation on Democratization and Political Change in the Middle East, Washington, October 1995.

20. Daniel Chirot, "The Rise of the West," *American Sociological Review* 50 (1985): 191–195.

21. Yehuda Shenav, "Manufacturing Uncertainty and Certainty in Manufacturing: Managerial Discourse and the Rhetoric of Organizational Theory," *Science in Context* 7.2 (1994): 270.

22. Ibid., 269.

23. See the special issue of the *Journal of Democracy* devoted to this debate (vol. 3, no. 4, October 1992), and, in particular, Ghia Nodia, "Nationalism and Democracy," *Journal of Democracy* 3.4 (1992): 3–22; and Francis Fukuyama, "Comments on Nationalism and Democracy," *Journal of Democracy* 3.4 (1992): 23–28.

24. Fukuyama, "Comments on Nationalism and Democracy," 24.

25. James Kurt, "Toward the Postmodern World," *Dialogue* 100.2 (1993), 13.

26. Henri de Bresson and Michel Kajman, "Un entretien avec Wolf Lepenies," *Le Monde*, May 31, 1994, 2.

The Clash of Definitions

Edward W. Said

Samuel P. Huntington's essay "The Clash of Civilizations?" appeared in *Foreign Affairs* in the summer of 1993, announcing in its first sentence that "world politics is entering a new phase."[1] By this he meant that whereas in the recent past world conflicts were between ideological camps grouping the first, second, and third worlds into warring camps, the new style of politics would entail conflicts between different and presumably clashing civilizations. "The great divisions among humankind and the dominating source of conflict will be cultural. . . . The clash of civilizations will dominate global politics." Later he explains how it is that the principal clash will be between Western and non-Western civilizations, and indeed Huntington spends most of his time in the article discussing the fundamental disagreements, potential or actual, between what he calls the West on the one hand and, on the other, the Islamic and Confucian civilizations. In terms of detail, a great deal more attention is paid to Islam than to any other civilization, including the West.

Much of the subsequent interest taken in Huntington's essay, I think, derives from its timing, rather than exclusively from what it literally says. As he himself notes, there have been several intellectual and political attempts

"The Clash of Definitions" by Edward Said. From Edward Said, *Reflections on Exile and Other Essays* (Cambridge: Harvard University Press, 2000), 569–592. Printed by permission of Edward Said.

since the end of the cold war to map the emerging world situation; this included Francis Fukuyama's the end of history and the thesis put about during the latter days of the Bush administration, the theory of the so-called New World Order. More recently Paul Kennedy, Conor Cruise O'Brien, Eric Hobsbawm—all of whom have looked at the approaching millennium—have done so with considerable attention to the causes of future conflict, which has given them all cause for alarm. The core of Huntington's vision (not really original with him) is the idea of an unceasing clash, a concept of conflict that slides somewhat effortlessly into the political space vacated by the unremitting bipolar war of ideas and values embodied in the unregretted cold war. I do not therefore think it is inaccurate to suggest that what Huntington is providing in this essay of his—especially since it is primarily addressed to the influential opinion and policy makers who subscribe to *Foreign Affairs*, the United States's leading journal of foreign policy discussion—is a recycled version of the cold war thesis, that conflicts in today's and tomorrow's world will remain not economic or social in essence but ideological, and if that is so then one ideology, the West's, is the still point or locus around which for Huntington all others turn. In effect, then, the cold war continues, but this time on many fronts, with many more serious and basic systems of values and ideas (like Islam and Confucianism) struggling for ascendancy and even dominance over the West. Not surprisingly, therefore, Huntington concludes his essay with a brief survey of what it is that the West might do to remain strong and keep its putative opponents weak and divided (it must "exploit differences and conflicts among Confucian and Islamic states; to support in other civilizations groups sympathetic to Western values and interests; to strengthen international institutions that reflect and legitimate Western interests and values and to promote the involvement of non-Western states in those institutions").[2]

So strong and insistent is Huntington's notion that other civilizations necessarily clash with the West, and so relentlessly aggressive and chauvinistic is his prescription for what the West must do to continue winning, we are forced to conclude that he is really most interested in continuing and expanding the cold war by other means rather than advancing ideas about understanding the current world scene or trying to reconcile between cultures. Little in what he says expresses the slightest doubt or skepticism. Not only will conflict continue, but, as he says on the first page, "conflict between civilizations will be the latest phase in the evolution of conflict in the modern world." It is as a very brief and rather crudely articulated manual in the art of maintaining a wartime status in the minds of Americans and others that Huntington's essay has to be understood. I would go so far as to say that it argues from the standpoint of Pentagon planners and defense industry executives who may have temporarily lost their occupations after the end of the cold war but have now discovered a new vocation for themselves. Huntington at least has the merit of underlining the cultural component in relationships between different countries, traditions, and peoples.

The sad part is that "the clash of civilizations" is useful as a way of exaggerating and making intractable various political or economic problems. It is quite easy to see how, for instance, the practice of Japan bashing in the West can be fueled by appeals to the menacing and sinister aspects of Japanese culture as employed by government spokespersons, or how the age-old appeal to the "yellow peril" might be mobilized for use in discussions of ongoing problems with Korea or China. The opposite is true in the practice throughout Asia and Africa of Occidentalism, turning "the West" into a monolithic category that is supposed to express hostility to nonwhite, non-European. and non-Christian civilizations.

Perhaps because he is more interested in policy prescription than he is either in history or the careful analysis of cultural formations, Huntington in my opinion is quite misleading in what he says and how he puts things. A great deal of his argument depends on second- and third-hand opinion that scants the enormous advances in our concrete and theoretical understanding of how cultures work, how they change, and how they can best be grasped or apprehended. A brief look at the people and opinions he quotes suggests that journalism and popular demagoguery are his main sources rather than scholarship or theory. For when you draw on tendentious publicists, scholars, and journalists like Charles Krauthammer, Sergei Stankevich, and Bernard Lewis you already prejudice the argument in favor of conflict and polemic rather than in favor of true understanding and the kind of cooperation between peoples that our planet needs. Huntington's authorities are not the cultures themselves but a small handful of authorities picked by him because in fact they emphasize the latent bellicosity in one or another statement by one or another so-called spokesman for or about that culture. The giveaway for me is the title of his essay—the clash of civilizations—which is not his phrase but Bernard Lewis's. On the last page of Lewis's essay "The Roots of Muslim Rage," which appeared in the September 1990 issue of the *Atlantic Monthly*, a journal that has on occasion run articles purporting to describe the dangerous sickness, madness, and

derangement of Arabs and Muslims, Lewis speaks about the current problem with the Islamic world: "It should by now be clear that we are facing a
mood and a movement far transcending the level of issues and policies and
the governments that pursue them. This is no less than a clash of civilizations—the perhaps irrational but surely historic reactions of an ancient rival
against our Judeo-Christian heritage, our secular present, and the worldwide
expansion of both. It is crucially important that we on our side should not be
provoked into an equally historic but also equally irrational reaction against
that rival."[3]

I do not want to spend much time discussing the lamentable features of
Lewis's screed; elsewhere I have described his methods—the lazy generalizations, the reckless distortions of history, the wholesale demotion of civilizations into categories like irrational and enraged, and so on. Few people
today with any sense would want to volunteer such sweeping characterizations as the ones advanced by Lewis about over a billion Muslims, scattered
through at least five continents, dozens of differing languages and traditions
and histories. Of them he says that they are all enraged at Western modernity, as if a billion people were but one and Western civilization were no
more complicated a matter than a simple declarative sentence. But what I
do want to stress is, first, how Huntington has picked up from Lewis the
notion that civilizations are monolithic and homogenous and, second,
how—again from Lewis—he assumes the unchanging character of the duality between "us" and "them."

In other words I think it is absolutely imperative to stress that, like
Bernard Lewis, Samuel Huntington does not write a neutral, descriptive,
and objective prose but is himself a polemicist whose rhetoric not only
depends heavily on prior arguments about a war of all against all but in
effect perpetuates them. Far from being an arbiter between civilizations,
therefore, Huntington is a partisan, an advocate of one so-called civilization
over all the others. Like Lewis, Huntington defines Islamic civilization
reductively, as if what most matters about it is its supposed anti-Westernism.
For his part Lewis tries to give a set of reasons for his definition—that Islam
has never modernized, that it never separated between church and state,
that it has been incapable of understanding other civilizations—but Huntington does not bother with them. For him Islam, Confucianism, and the
other five or six civilizations (Hindu, Japanese, Slavic-Orthodox, Latin
American, and African) that still exist are separate from each other and, consequently, potentially in a conflict that he wants to manage, not resolve. He

writes as a crisis manager, not as a student of civilization or as a reconciler between them.

At the core of his essay, and this is what has made it strike so responsive a chord among post–cold war policy makers, is this sense of cutting through a lot of unnecessary detail, of masses of scholarship and huge amounts of experience,boiling them down to a couple of catchy, easy-to-quote-and-remember ideas, which are then passed off as pragmatic, practical, sensible, and clear. But is this the best way to understand the world we live in? Is it wise as an intellectual and a scholarly expert to produce a simplified map of the world and then hand it to generals and civilian lawmakers as a prescription for first comprehending and then acting in the world? Doesn't this method in effect prolong, exacerbate, and deepen conflict? What does it do to minimize civilizational conflict? Do we *want* the clash of civilizations? Doesn't it mobilize nationalist passions and therefore nationalist murderousness? Shouldn't we ask the question Why is one doing this sort of thing? To understand or to act? To mitigate or to aggravate the likelihood of conflict?

I would want to begin to survey the world situation by commenting on how prevalent it has become for people to speak now in the name of large and, in my opinion, undesirably vague and manipulable, abstractions like the West or Japanese or Slavic culture, Islam or Confucianism, labels that collapse religions, races, and ethnicities into ideologies that are considerably more unpleasant and provocative than those of Gobineau and Renan 150 years ago. Strange as it may seem, these examples of group psychology run rampant are not new, and they are certainly not edifying at all. They occur in times of deep insecurity: that is, when peoples seem particularly close to and thrust upon each other, the result either of expansion, war, imperialism, and migration or as the effect of sudden, unprecedented change. Let me give a couple of examples to illustrate. The language of group identity makes a particularly strident appearance from the middle to the end of the nineteenth century, as the culmination of decades of international competition between the great European and American powers for territories in Africa and Asia. In the battle for the empty spaces of Africa—the dark continent—France and Britain as well as Germany and Belgium resort not only to force but to a whole slew of theories and rhetorics for justifying their plunder. Perhaps the most famous of such devices is the French concept of civilizing mission, *la mission civilisatrice*, a notion whose basic premise is that some races and cultures have a higher aim in life than others. This conclusion grants the more powerful, more developed, and more civilized the right therefore to colonize others, not in the name of brute force or raw plunder, both of which are standard components of the exercise, but in the name of a noble ideal. Joseph Conrad's most famous story, *Heart of Darkness*, is an ironic, even terrifying enactment of this thesis, that—as his narrator Marlow puts it—"the conquest of the earth, which mostly means the taking it away from those who have a different complexion or slightly flatter noses than ourselves, is not a pretty thing when you look into it too much. What redeems it is the idea only. An idea at the back of it, not a sentimental pretence but an idea; and an unselfish belief in the idea—something you can set up, and bow down before, and offer a sacrifice to."[4]

In response to this sort of logic, two things occur. One is that competing powers invent their own theory of cultural or civilizational destiny in order to justify their actions abroad. Britain had such a theory, Germany had one, Belgium had one, and, of course, in the concept of manifest destiny, the United States had one too. These redeeming ideas dignify the practice of competition and clash, whose real purpose, as Conrad quite accurately saw, was self-aggrandizement, power, conquest, treasure, and unrestrained self-pride. I would go so far as to say that what we today call the rhetoric of identity by which a member of one ethnic or religious or national or cultural group puts that group at the center of the world derives from that period of imperial competition at the end of the nineteenth century. And this in turn provokes the concept of "worlds at war" that quite obviously is at the heart of Huntington's article. It received its most frightening futuristic application in H. G. Wells's fable *The War of the Worlds*, which, one recalls, expands the concept to include a battle between this world and a distant interplanetary one. In the related fields of political economy, geography, anthropology, and historiography, the theory that each "world" is self-enclosed, has its own boundaries and special territory, is applied to the world map, to the structure of civilizations, to the notion that each race has a special destiny, psychology, ethos, etc.[5] All of these ideas, almost without exception, are based not on the harmony but on the conflict, or clash, between worlds. You see it in the works of Gustave LeBon (cf. his *The World in Revolt*) and in such relatively forgotten works as F. S. Marvin's *Western Races and the World* (1922) and in George Henry Lane-Fox Pitt Rivers's *The Clash of Culture and the Contact of Races* (1927).

The second thing that happens is that, as Huntington himself concedes, the lesser peoples, the objects of the imperial gaze, so to speak, respond by resisting their forcible manipulation and settlement. We now know that active primary resistance to the white man began the moment he set foot in places like Algeria, East Africa, India, and elsewhere. Later, primary resistance was succeeded by secondary resistance, the organization of political and cultural movements determined to achieve independence and liberation from imperial control. At precisely the moment in the nineteenth century that among the European and American powers a rhetoric of civilizational self-justification begins to be widespread, a responding rhetoric among the colonized peoples develops, one that speaks in terms of African or Asian or Arab unity, independence, self-determination. In India, for example, the Congress Party was organized in 1880 and by the turn of the century had convinced the Indian elite that only by supporting *Indian* languages, industry, and commerce could political freedom come; these are ours and ours alone, runs the argument, and only by supporting our world against *theirs* — note the us-versus-them construction — can we finally stand on our own. One finds a similar logic at work during the Meiji period in modern Japan. Something like this rhetoric of belonging is also lodged at the heart of each independence movement's nationalism, and it achieved the result shortly after World War II not only of dismantling the classical empires but also of winning independence for dozens and dozens of countries thereafter. India, Indonesia, most of the Arab countries, Indochina, Algeria, Kenya, etc.: all these states emerged on the world scene sometimes peacefully, sometimes as the effect of internal developments (as in the Japanese instance) of ugly colonial wars or of wars of national liberation.

In both the colonial and postcolonial context, therefore, rhetorics of general cultural or civilizational specificity went in two potential directions: the first, a utopian line that insisted on an overall pattern of integration and harmony between all peoples, and the second, a line that suggested all civilizations were so specific and jealous, monotheistic in effect, as to reject and war against the others. Among instances of the first are the language and institutions of the United Nations, founded in the aftermath of World War II, and the subsequent development out of that of various attempts at world government predicated on coexistence, voluntary limitations of sovereignty, integration of peoples and cultures harmoniously. Among the second are the theory and practice of the cold war and, more recently, the idea that the clash of civilizations is if not a necessity for a world of so many different parts then a certainty. According to this theory, cultures and civilizations are basically *separated* from each other. I do not want to be invidious here. In the

Islamic world there has been a resurgence of rhetorics and movements stressing the inimicability of Islam with the West, just as in Africa, Europe, Asia, and elsewhere, movements have appeared that stress the need for excluding designated others as undesirable. White apartheid in South Africa was such a movement, as is the current interest in Afrocentrism and a totally independent Western civilization to be found in the Africa and the United States respectively.

The point of this short cultural history of the idea of the clash of civilizations is that people like Huntington are products of that history, are its product, and are shaped in their writing by it. Moreover, the language describing the clash is laced with considerations of power: the powerful use it to protect what they have and what they do, the powerless or less powerful use it to achieve parity, independence, or a comparative advantage with regard to the dominant power. Thus, to build a conceptual framework around the notion of us-versus-them is in effect to pretend that the principal consideration is epistemological and natural—our civilization is known and accepted, theirs is different and strange—whereas in fact the framework separating us from them is belligerent, constructed, and situational. Within each civilizational camp, we will notice, there are official representatives of that culture or civilization who make themselves into its mouthpiece, who assign themselves the role of articulating "our" (or for that matter "their") essence. This always necessitates a fair amount of compression, reduction, and exaggeration. So on the first and most immediate level, then, statements about what "our" culture or civilization is, or ought to be, necessarily involve a contest over the definition. This is certainly true of Huntington, who writes his essay at a time in the United States when a great deal of turmoil has been occurring around the very definition of Western civilization. Recall that in the United States many college campuses have been shaken during the past couple of decades over what the canon of Western civilization is, what books should be taught, which ones read or not read, included, or otherwise given attention. Places like Stanford and Columbia debated the issue not simply as a matter of habitual academic concern but because the definition of the West and consequently of America were at stake.

Anyone who has the slightest understanding of how cultures work knows that defining that culture, saying what it is for members of the culture, is always a major and, even in undemocratic societies, a democratic contest. There are canonical authorities to be selected, and regularly revised, debated, reselected, or dismissed. There are ideas of good and evil, belonging or not belonging (the same and the different), hierarchies of value to be specified, discussed, rediscussed, and settled or not, as the case may be. Moreover, each culture defines its enemies, what stands beyond it and threatens it. For the Greeks beginning with Herodotus anyone who did not speak Greek was automatically a barbarian, an Other to be despised and fought against. An excellent recent book by the French classicist François Hartog, *The Mirror of Herodotus*, painstakingly shows how deliberately and painstakingly Herodotus sets about constructing an image of a barbarian Other in the case of the Scythians, more even than in the case of the Persians.[6]

The official culture is that of priests, academies, and the state. It provides definitions of patriotism, loyalty, boundaries, and what I have called belonging. It is this official culture that speaks in the name of the whole, that tries to express the general will, the general ethos and idea, that inclusively holds in the official past, the founding fathers and texts, the pantheon of heroes and villains, etc., and excludes what is foreign or different or undesirable in the past. From it come the definitions of what may or may not be said, those prohibitions and proscriptions that are necessary to any culture if it is to have authority.

It is also true that in addition to the mainstream, or official, or canonical, culture there are dissenting or alternative, unorthodox, heterodox cultures that contain many antiauthoritarian strains in them in competition with the official culture. These can be called the counterculture, an ensemble of practices associated with various kinds of outsiders—the poor, the immigrants, artistic bohemians, workers, rebels, artists. From the counterculture comes the critique of authority and attacks on what is official and orthodox. The great contemporary Arab poet Adonis has written a massive account of the relationship between orthodoxy and heterodoxy in Arabic culture and has shown the constant dialectic and tension between them. No culture is understandable without some sense of this ever present source of creative provocation from the unofficial to the official; to disregard this sense of restlessness within each culture, and to assume that there is complete homogeneity between culture and identity, is to miss what is vital and fecund.

In the United States the debate about what is American has gone through a large number of transformations and sometimes dramatic shifts. As I was growing up, Western films depicted the native Americans as evil devils, to be destroyed or tamed. They were called Red Indians, and insofar as they had any function in the culture at large—this was as true of films as it was of the writing of academic history—it was to be a foil to the advancing course of white civilization. Today that has changed completely. Native Americans are seen as victims, not villains, of the country's Western progress. There has even been a change in the status of Columbus. There are even more dramatic reversals in the depictions of African Americans and women. Toni Morrison has noted how it is that in classic American literature there is an obsession with whiteness, as Melville's *Moby Dick* and Poe's *Arthur Gordon Pym* so eloquently testify. Yet she says the major male and white writers of the nineteenth and twentieth centuries, men who shaped the canon of what we have known as American literature, created their works by using whiteness as a way of avoiding, curtaining off, and rendering invisible the African presence in the midst of our society. The very fact that Toni Morrison writes her novels and criticism with such success and brilliance now underscores the extent of the change from the world of Melville and Hemingway to that of Dubois, Baldwin, Langston Hughes, and Toni Morrison. Which vision is the real America, and who can lay claim to represent and define it? The question is a complex and deeply interesting one, but it cannot be settled by reducing the whole matter to a few clichés.

A recent view of the difficulties involved in cultural contests whose object is the definition of a civilization can be found in Arthur Schlesinger's little book, *The Disuniting of America*.[7] As a mainstream historian, Schlesinger is understandably troubled by the fact that emergent and immigrant groups in the United States have disputed the official, unitary fable of America as it used to be represented by the great classical historians of this country, men like Bancroft, Henry Adams, and, more recently, Richard Hofstader. The former want the writing of history to reflect not only an America that was conceived of and ruled by patricians and landowners but an America in which slaves, servants, laborers, and poor immigrants played an important but as yet unacknowledged role. The narratives of such people, silenced by the great discourses whose source was Washington, the investment banks of New York, the universities of New England, and the great industrial fortunes of the Middle West, have come to disrupt the slow progress and unruffled serenity of the official story. They ask questions, interject the experiences of social unfortunates, and make the claims of frankly lesser peoples—of women, Asian and African Americans, and various other minorities, sexual as well as ethnic. Whether or not one agrees with Schlesinger's *cri de coeur*, there is no disagreeing with his underlying thesis that the writing of history is the royal road to the definition of a country, that the identity of a society is in large part a function of historical interpretation, which is fraught with contested claims and counterclaims. The United States is in such a fraught situation today.

There is a similar debate inside the Islamic world today, which in the often hysterical outcry about the threat of Islam, Islamic fundamentalism, and terrorism that one encounters so often in the Western media is often lost sight of completely. Like any other major world culture, Islam contains within itself an astonishing variety of currents and countercurrents, most of them undiscerned by tendentious orientalist scholars for whom Islam is an object of fear and hostility or journalists who do not know any of the languages or relevant histories and are content to rely on persistent stereotypes that have lingered in the West since the tenth century. Iran today—which has become the target of a politically opportunistic attack by the United States—is in the throes of a stunningly energetic debate about law, freedom, personal responsibility, and tradition that is simply not covered by Western reporters. Charismatic lecturers and intellectuals, clerical and nonclerical alike, carry on the tradition of Shariati, challenging centers of power and orthodoxy with impunity and, it would seem, with great popular success. In Egypt two major civil cases involving intrusive religious interventions in the lives of an intellectual and a celebrated filmmaker respectively have resulted in the victory of both over orthodoxy (I refer here to the cases of Nasir Abu Zeid and Yousef Chahine). And I myself have argued in a recent book (*The Politics of Dispossession*, 1994) that far from there being a surge of Islamic fundamentalism as it is reductively described in the Western media, there is a great deal of secular opposition to it, in the form of various contests over the interpretation of *sunnah* in matters of law, personal conduct, political decision making and so on. Moreover, what is often forgotten is that movements like Hamas and Islamic Jihad are essentially protest movements that go against the capitulationist politics of the PLO and mobilize the will to resist Israeli occupation practices, expropriation of land, and the like.

I find it surprising and indeed disquieting that Huntington gives no indication anywhere in his essay that he is aware of these complex disputes or realized that the nature and identity of a civilization are never taken as unquestioned axioms by every single member of that civilization. Far from the cold war being the defining horizon of the past few decades, I would say that it is this extremely widespread attitude of questioning and skepticism toward age-old authority that characterizes the postwar world in both East and West. Nationalism and decolonization forced the issue by bringing whole populations to consider the question of nationality in the era after the white colonist had left. In Algeria, for example, today the site of a bloody contest between Islamists and an aging and discredited government, the debate has taken violent forms. But it is a real debate and a fierce contest nonetheless. Having won independence from the French in 1962, the National Front for the Liberation of Algeria declared itself to be the bearer of a newly liberated Algerian, Arab, and Muslim identity. For the first time in the modern history of the place Arabic became the language of instruction, state socialism its political creed, nonalignment its foreign affairs posture. In the process of conducting itself as a one-party embodiment of all these things the FLN grew into a massive, atrophied bureaucracy, its economy depleted, its leaders stagnating in the position of an unyielding oligarchy. Opposition arose not only from Muslim clerics and leaders but from the Berber minority, submerged in the all-purpose discourse of a supposedly single Algerian identity. The political crisis of the past several years then represents a several-sided contest for power and for the right to decide the nature of Algerian identity: what is Islamic about it, and what kind of Islam, what is national, what Arab and Berber.

To Huntington, what he calls "civilization identity" is a stable and undisturbed thing, like a roomful of furniture in the back of your house. This postulate is extremely far from the truth, not just in the Islamic world but throughout the entire surface of the globe. To emphasize the differences between cultures and civilizations (incidentally, I find his use of the words *culture* and *civilization* extremely sloppy, precisely because for him the two words represent fixed and reified objects rather than the dynamic, ceaselessly turbulent things that they in fact are) is completely to ignore the literally unending debate or contest (to use the more active and energetic of the two words) about defining the culture or civilization within those civilizations, including various "Western" ones. These debates completely undermine any idea of a fixed identity, and hence of relationships between identities, what Huntington considers to be a sort of ontological fact of political existence, to wit the clash of civilizations. You don't have to be an expert on China, Japan, Korea, and India to know that. There is first of all the American instance I mentioned earlier. Or there is the German case, in which a major debate has been taking place ever since the end of World War II about the nature of German culture, as to whether Nazism derived logically from its core or whether it was an aberration.

But there is more to the question of identity even than that. In the field of cultural and rhetorical studies a series of recent discoveries/advances have given us a much clearer insight not only into the contested, dynamic nature of cultural identity but also into the extent to which the very idea of identity itself involves fantasy, manipulation, invention, construction. During the 1970s Hayden White published an extremely influential work called *Metahistory*.[8] It is a study of several nineteenth-century historians—Marx, Michelet, and Nietzsche among them—and how it is that their reliance upon one or a series of tropes (figures of speech) determines the nature of their vision of history. Thus Marx, for instance, is committed to a particular poetics in his writing that allows him to understand the nature of progress and alienation in history according to a particular narrative model, stressing the difference in society between form and substance. The point of White's extremely rigorous and quite brilliant analysis of Marx and the other historians is that he shows us how their histories are best understood not according to criteria of "realness" but rather as to how their internal rhetorical and discursive strategies work: it is these, rather than facts, that make the visions of Toqueville or Croce or Marx actually work as a system, not any external source in the so-called real world.

The effect of White's book, as much as the effect of Michel Foucault's studies, is to draw attention away from the existence of veridic confirmations for ideas that might be provided by the natural world and focus it instead on the kind of language used, which is seen as shaping the components of a writer's vision. Rather than the idea of clash, for instance, deriving from a real clash in the world, we would then come to see it as deriving instead from the strategies of Huntington's prose, which in turn relies on what I would call a managerial poetics, a strategy for assuming the existence of stable and metaphorically defined entities called civilizations that the writer proceeds quite emotively to manipulate, as in the phrase, "the crescent-shaped Islamic bloc, from the bulge of Africa to central Asia, has bloody borders." I am not saying that Huntington's language is emotive and shouldn't be, but rather that quite revealingly it is, the way all language functions in the poetic way analyzed by Hayden White. What is evident from Huntington's language is the way he uses figurative language to accentuate the distance between "our" world—normal, acceptable, familiar, logical—and, as an especially striking example, the world of Islam, with its bloody borders, bulging contours, etc. This suggests not so much analysis on Huntington's part but a series of determinations that, as I said earlier, create the very clash he seems in his essay to be discovering and pointing to.

Too much attention paid to managing and clarifying the clash of cultures obliterates the fact of a great, often silent exchange and dialogue between them. What culture today—whether Japanese, Arab, European, Korean, Chinese, or Indian—has not had long, intimate, and extraordinarily rich contacts with other cultures? There is no exception to this exchange. One would wish that conflict managers would have paid attention to, understood the meaning of the mingling of different musics, for example, in the work of Olivier Messiaen or Toru Takemtisu? For all the power and influence of the various national schools, what is most arresting in contemporary music is that no one can draw a boundary around any of it; cultures are often most naturally themselves when they enter into partnerships with each other, as in music with its extraordinary receptivity to developments in the musics of other societies and continents. Much the same is true of literature, where readers of, for example, García Marquez, Mahfuz, and Oe exist far beyond the boundaries imposed by language and nation. In my own field of comparative literature there is an epistemological commitment to the relationships between literatures, to their reconciliation and harmony, despite the existence of powerful ideological and national barriers between them. And this sort of cooperative, collective enterprise is what one misses in the proclaimers of an undying clash between cultures: the lifelong dedication that has existed in all modern societies among scholars, artists, musicians, visionaries, and prophets to try to come to terms with the Other, with that other society or culture that seems so foreign and so distant. One thinks of Joseph Needham and his lifelong study of China or, in France, of Louis Massignon, his pilgrimage within Islam. It seems to me that unless we emphasize and maximize the spirit of cooperation and humanistic exchange—and here I do not speak simply of uninformed delight or of amateurish enthusiasm for the exotic but rather of profound existential commitment and labor on behalf of the other—we are going to end up superficially and stridently banging the drum for "our" culture in opposition to all the others.

Two other recent seminal works of cultural analysis are relevant here. In the compilation of essays entitled *The Invention of Tradition* edited by Terence Ranger and Eric Hobsbawm,[9] two of the most distinguished historians alive today, the authors argue that tradition, far from being the unshakable order of inherited wisdom and practice, is frequently a set of invented practices and beliefs used in mass societies to create a sense of identity at a time when organic solidarities—such as those of family, village, clan—have broken down. Thus the emphasis on tradition in nineteenth and twentieth cen-

turies is a way that rulers can claim to have legitimacy, even though that
legitimacy is more or less manufactured. In India, as a case in point, an
impressive array of rituals was invented to celebrate Queen Victoria's ascen-
sion to the title of Empress of India in 1872. By doing so, and by claiming
that the durbars, or grand processions, commemorating the event had a long
history in India, the British were able to give her rule a pedigree that it did
not have in fact but came to have in the form of invented traditions. In
another context sports rituals like the football game, a relatively recent practice, are regarded as the culmination of an age-old celebration of sporting
activity, whereas in fact they are a recent way of diverting large numbers of
people. The point of all this is that a great deal of what used to be thought of
as settled fact, or tradition, is revealed to be a fabrication for mass consumption in the here and now.

To people who speak solely of the clash of civilizations, there exists no
inkling of this possibility. For them cultures and civilizations may change,
develop, regress, and disappear, but they remain mysteriously fixed in their
identity, their essence graven in stone, so to speak, as if there existed a universal consensus somewhere agreeing to the six civilizations Huntington posits
at the beginning of his essay. My contention is that no such consensus exists
or, if it does, it can hardly bear the analytic scrutiny brought to bear by analyses of the kind provided by Hobsbawm and Ranger. So in reading about the
clash of civilizations we are less likely to assent to analysis of the clash than we
are to ask the following question: Why do you pinion civilizations into so
unyielding an embrace, and why then do you go on to describe their relationship as one of basic conflict, as if the borrowing and overlappings
between them were not a much more interesting and significant feature?

Finally, my third example of cultural analysis tells us a great deal about
the possibilities of actually creating a civilization retrospectively and making
that creation into a frozen definition, in spite of the evidence of great hybridity and mixture. The book is *Black Athena*; the author, the Cornell political
scientist Martin Bernal.[10] The conception most of us have today about classical Greece, Bernal says, does not at all correspond to what Greek authors
of that period say about it. Ever since the early nineteenth century Europeans and Americans have grown up with an idealized picture of Attic harmony and grace, Athens as a place where enlightened Western philosophers
like Plato and Aristotle taught their wisdom, where democracy was born,
and where, in every possible significant way, a Western mode of life completely different from that of Asia or Africa held sway. Yet to read a large

number of ancient authors accurately is to note how many of them comment on the existence of Semitic and African elements in Attic life. Bernal
takes the further step of demonstrating by the skillful use of a great many
sources that Greece was originally a colony of Africa, more particularly of
Egypt, and that Phoenician and Jewish traders, sailors, and teachers contributed most of what we know today as classical Greek culture, which he
sees as an amalgam therefore of African, Semitic, and later northern
influences.

In the most compelling part of *Black Athena*, Bernal goes on to show how
with the growth of European, and in particular German, nationalism, the
original mixed portrait of Attic Greece that obtained into the eighteenth
century was gradually expunged of all its non-Aryan elements, just as many
years later the Nazis decided to burn all books and ban all authors who were
considered non-German, non-Aryan. So from being the product of an invasion from the South (i.e., Africa), as in reality it really was, classical Greece
was progressively transformed into the product of an invasion from the
Aryan North. Purged of its troublesome non-European elements, Greece
thereafter has stood in the Western self-definition—an expedient one, to be
sure—as its *fons et origo*, its source of sweetness and light. The principle
underlined by Bernal is the extent to which pedigrees, dynasties, lineages,
predecessors are changed to suit the political needs of a later time. Of the
unfortunate results this produced in the case of a self-created white Aryan
European civilization none of us here need to be convinced.

What is even more troubling to me about proclaimers of the clash of civilization is how oblivious they seem of all we now know as historians and as
cultural analysts about the way definitions of these cultures themselves are
so contentious. Rather than accepting the incredibly naive and deliberately
reductive notion that civilizations are identical with themselves, and that is
all, we must always ask what civilizations are intended, created, and defined
by whom, and for what reason. Recent history is too full of instances where
the defense of Judeo-Christian values has been urged as a way of quelling
dissent or unpopular opinions for us passively to assume that "everyone"
knows what those values are, how they are meant to be interpreted, and how
they may or not be implemented in society.

Many Arabs would say that their civilization is really Islam, just as some
Westerners—Australians and Canadians and some Americans—might not
want to be included in so large and vaguely defined a category as Western.
And when a man like Huntington speaks of the "common objective ele-

ments" that supposedly exist in every culture he leaves the analytic and historical world altogether, preferring instead to find refuge inside large and ultimately meaningless categories.

As I have argued in several of my own books, in today's Europe and the United States what is described as "Islam" belongs to the discourse of Orientalism, a construction fabricated to whip up feelings of hostility and antipathy against a part of the world that happens to be of strategic importance for its oil, its threatening adjacence to the Christian world, its formidable history of competitiveness with the West. Yet this is a very different thing than what, to Muslims who live within its domain, Islam really is. There is a world of difference between Islam in Indonesia and Islam in Egypt. By the same token, the volatility of today's struggle over the meaning of Islam is evident in Egypt, where the secular powers of society are in conflict with various Islamic protest movements and reformers. In such circumstances the easiest, and the least accurate, thing is to say *that* is the world of Islam, and see how it is all terrorists and fundamentalists, and see also how different *they* are from us.

But the truly weakest part of the clash of civilizations thesis is the rigid separation assumed between them, despite the overwhelming evidence that today's world is in fact a world of mixtures, of migrations, of crossings over. One of the major crises affecting countries like France, Britain, and the United States has been brought about by the realization now dawning everywhere that no culture or society is purely one thing. Sizable minorities—North Africans in France, the African and Caribbean and Indian populations in Britain, Asian and African elements in the United States—dispute the idea that civilizations that prided themselves on being homogenous can continue to do so. There are no insulated cultures or civilizations. Any attempt made to separate them into the watertight compartments alleged by Huntington does damage to their variety, their diversity, their sheer complexity of elements, their radical hybridity. The more insistent we are on the separation of cultures and civilizations, the more inaccurate we are about ourselves and about others. The notion of an exclusionary civilization is, to my way of thinking, an impossible one. The real question then is whether in the end we want to work for civilizations that are separate or whether we should be taking the more integrative but perhaps more difficult path, which is to try to see them as making one vast whole whose exact contours are impossible for one person to grasp but whose certain existence we can intuit and feel. In any case, a number of political scientists, economists, and cultural analysts have for some years been speaking of an integrative world system, largely economic, it is true, but nonetheless knitted together, overriding many of the clashes spoken of so hastily and imprudently by Huntington.

What Huntington quite astonishingly overlooks is the phenomenon referred to frequently in the literature as the globalization of capital. In 1980 Willy Brandt and some associates published *North-South: A Program for Survival*.[11] In it the authors noted that the world was now divided into two vastly uneven regions: a small industrial North, comprising the major European, American, and Asian economic powers, and an enormous South, comprising the former third world plus a large number of new, extremely impoverished nations. The political problem of the future was going to be how to imagine their relationships as the North would get richer, the South poorer, and the world more interdependent. Let me quote now from an essay by the Duke political scientist Arif Dirlik that goes over much of the ground covered by Huntington in a way that is more accurate and persuasive:

> The situation created by global capitalism helps explain certain phenomena that have become apparent over the last two or three decades, but especially since the eighties: global motions of peoples (and, therefore, cultures), the weakening of boundaries (among societies, as well as among social categories), the replications in societies internally of inequalities and discrepancies once associated with colonial differences, simultaneous homogenization and fragmentation within and across societies, the interpenetration of the global and the local, and the disorganization of a world conceived in terms of three worlds or nation-states. Some of these phenomena have also contributed to an appearance of equalization of differences within and across societies, as well as of democratization within and among societies. What is ironic is that the managers of this world situation themselves concede that they (or their organizations) now have the power to appropriate the local for the global, to admit different cultures into the realm of capital (only to break them down and remake them in accordance with the requirements of production and consumption), and even to reconstitute subjectivities across national boundaries to create producers and consumers more responsive to the operations of capital. Those who do not respond, or the "basket cases" that are not essential to those operations—four-fifths of the global population by the man-

agers' count—need not be colonized; they are simply marginalized.
What the new flexible production has made possible is that it is no
longer necessary to utilize explicit coercion against labor at home or in
colonies abroad. Those peoples or places that are not responsive to the
needs (or demands) of capital, or are too far gone to respond
"efficiently," simply find themselves out of its pathways. And it is easier
even than in the heyday of colonialism or modernization theory to say
convincingly: It is their fault.[12]

In view of these depressing and even alarming actualities it does seem to
me ostrichlike to suggest that we in Europe and the U.S. should maintain
our civilization by holding all the others at bay, increasing the rifts between
peoples in order to prolong our dominance. That is, in effect, what Huntington is arguing, and one can quite easily understand why it is that his essay
was published in *Foreign Affairs*, and why so many policy makers have
drifted toward it as allowing the United States to extend the mindset of the
cold war into a different time and for a new audience. Much more productive and useful is a new global mentality that sees the dangers we face from
the standpoint of the whole human race. These dangers include the pauper-
ization of most of the globe's population; the emergence of virulent local
national, ethnic and religious sentiment, as in Bosnia, Rwanda, Lebanon,
Chechnya, and elsewhere; the decline of literacy; and onset of a new illiteracy based on electronic modes of communication, television, and the new
global information superhighway; the fragmentation and threatened disappearance of the grand narratives of emancipation and enlightenment. Our
most precious asset in the face of such a dire transformation of tradition and
of history is the emergence of a sense of community, understanding, sympathy, and hope, which is the direct opposite of what in his essay Huntington
has provoked. If I may quote some lines by the great Martinican poet Aimé
Césaire that I used in my recent book *Culture and Imperialism*:

> but the work of man is only just beginning
> and it remains to man to conquer all
> the violence entrenched in the recesses of his passion
>
> And no race possesses the monopoly of beauty,
> of intelligence, of force, and there
> is a place for all at the rendez-vous of victory.[13]

In what they imply, these sentiments prepare the way for a dissolution of cultural barriers as well as of the civilizational pride that prevents the kind of benign globalism already to be found, for instance, in the environmental movement, in scientific cooperation, in the universal concern for human rights, in concepts of global thought that stress community and sharing over racial, gender, or class dominance. It would seem to me therefore that efforts to return the community of civilizations to a primitive stage of narcissistic struggle need to be understood not as descriptions about how in fact they behave but rather as incitements to wasteful conflict and unedifying chauvinism. And that seems to be exactly what we do not need.

Notes

1. Samuel P. Huntington, "The Clash of Civilizations?" *Foreign Affairs* 72.3 (Summer, 1993): 22–50.
2. Ibid., 49.
3. Bernard Lewis, "The Roots of Muslim Rage," *Atlantic Monthly* (September 1990).
4. Joseph Conrad, *Heart of Darkness* (New York: Limited Editions Club, 1969).
5. H. G. Wells, *The War of the Worlds* (London: Heinemann, 1951).
6. François Hartog, *The Mirror of Herodotus: The Representation of the Other in the Writing of History*, trans. Janet Lloyd (Berkeley: University of California Press, 1988).
7. Arthur Schlesinger Jr., *The Disuniting of America: Reflections on a Multicultural Society* (Knoxville, Tenn.: Whittle Direct, 1991).
8. Hayden V. White, *Metahistory: The Historical Imagination in Nineteenth-century Europe* (Baltimore: Johns Hopkins University Press, 1973).
9. Eric Hobsbawm and Terence Ranger, *The Invention of Tradition* (Cambridge: Cambridge University Press, 1983).
10. Martin Bernal, *Black Athena: The Afroasiatic roots of Classical Civilization* (New Brunswick, N.J.: Rutgers University Press, 1987).
11. *North-South: A Program for Survival: Report of the Independent Commission on International Development Issues* (Cambridge: MIT Press, 1980).
12. Arif Dirlik, *Critical Inquiry* (Winter 1994), 351.
13. Aimé Césaire, *The Collected Poetry*, trans., with an introduction and notes, Clayton Eshleman and Annette Smith (Berkeley: University of California Press, 1983), 76–77. See Edward W. Said, *Culture and Imperialism* (New York: Knopf, 1993), 231.

The Clash of Civilizations: Samuel P. Huntington, Bernard Lewis, and the Remaking of Post–Cold War World Order

John Trumpbour

In the waning summer months of 1857, Alfred C. Lyall tried to explain the reasons for ongoing resistance to Britain's imperial control over the Indian subcontinent. "Of course you know by this time that the whole insurrection is a great Mahometan conspiracy," he wrote his father. He elaborated that "wherever anything horrible has been perpetrated, it has always been the act of the same fanatics." Though traumatized by the Indian Mutiny of 1857, Lyall later would emerge among the most influential nineteenth-century commentators on Asian civilizations. He clarified that "above all I can appreciate that furious hatred of all Musulmans, which is strongly shown in all the old accounts of wars with the *infidels*," who harbor toward Christians "just as fierce and bloody an enmity as in the time of El Cid." The future author of *Asiatic Societies* "could see any number of Musulmans cut to pieces without the slightest compunction." He proudly added, "we have given the Hindoos carte blanche as regards killing the Musulmans."[1]

The British army would not wait for the Hindus, as colonial troops rained vengeance on Mughal princes and heaved the corpses of leading Muslim intellectuals into the river Jumna. The renowned Urdu poet Ghalib wondered whether the agonies would ever end, "Here there is a vast ocean of blood before me, God alone knows what I shall have to behold."[2]

Seeing himself as a representative of what Macaulay had called "the greatest and most highly civilized people the world ever saw," Lyall tried to pay India his loftiest compliment by claiming that the country had "achieved a high state of European civilization"—that is to say, until the lat-

est Islamic "conspiracy" "suddenly brought" India "back to the dark ages . . .
to a state of barbarism."[3]

Surveying the thought of the leading nineteenth-century historians and
social scientists of Asia, Eric Stokes in *The Peasant and the Raj* (1978) reas-
sures contemporary scholars that virtually no one today reads Lyall.[4] They
may no longer have to, for there is a newer, more modern breed of social scientist who too finds Islam at the heart of the contemporary world's troubles.
Facing a new historical context, the end of the cold war, the West (as it likes
to call itself) had grown restless about the apparent absence of an enemy.
While the U.S. State Department is cautioning against making Islam the
new adversary, post–September 11 statecraft highlights a new triumphalism
and certainty that there are "evildoers" against whom the state must remain,
if not on a permanent war footing, in perpetual pursuit. The massacre at the
World Trade Center has divided the world into those who "are with us" and
those who are "with the terrorists," in perhaps the most famous formulation
of the early presidency of George W. Bush.

In the opening chapter of *The Clash of Civilizations and the Remaking of
World Order* (1996), Harvard political scientist and former National Security
adviser Samuel P. Huntington explains that the "grim Weltanschauung for
this new era" has been "well expressed by the Venetian nationalist demagogue in Michael Dibdin's novel *Dead Lagoon*." The *Dead Lagoon* character proclaims: "There can be no true friends without true enemies. Unless
we hate what we are not, we cannot love what we are. These are the old
truths we are painfully rediscovering after a century and more of sentimental
cant. Those who deny them deny their family, their heritage, their culture,
their birthright, their very selves! They will not be lightly forgiven."[5]

Huntington believes that the end of the cold war may have rendered the
United States less able to detect the gaseous hostility and bubbling hatreds
proliferating among the world's civilizations. Amidst "the collapse of communism," which ended up "reinforcing in the West the view that its ideology
of democratic liberalism had triumphed globally and hence was universally
valid," he judges the Western belief in the universality of its civilization to be
"arrogance." Instead Huntington sees a gulf between certain civilizations
that is unbridgeable, a chasm of peril for the new millennium. In charting
the transition from the cold war to the age of civilizational conflict, he gives
a nod to the lyrics of Peter Townshend: "The question, 'Which side are you
on?' has been replaced by the much more fundamental one, 'Who are
you?'" The national security expert exhorts "every state . . . to have an

answer," for "that answer, its cultural identity, defines the state's place in world politics, its friends, and its *enemies*" (my emphasis). Similar to the German political philosopher Carl Schmitt and the conservative émigré intellectual Leo Strauss, Huntington regards the search for enemies as crucial to achieving proper recognition of one's cultural identity. Already during thaws in the cold war and the fizzling out of East-West hostilities, he could detect whiffs of societal putrefaction. According to a Trilateral Commission report of his remarks to a plenary meeting in Kyoto, Japan (May 1975), "Huntington stressed that détente has had negative implications for the cohesion of Trilateral societies." Huntington sees the "enemy" as necessary for identity formation as well as for promoting cultural hygiene, but the cold war had put a lid on and deflected hatreds that are more deep-rooted, perhaps the very essence of many civilizations. Seeking to reconfigure the metahistorical analysis of Oswald Spengler and Arnold Toynbee for the twenty-first century, Huntington believes there are roughly eight or nine civilizations in the contemporary world: Western, Latin American, Orthodox, African, Islamic, Sinic, Hindu, Buddhist, and Japanese. In his scheme the Western, Latin American, and Eastern European Orthodox civilizations have grounds for warm collaboration in the future world order, but one grouping is prone to promote discord with the West: Muslim civilization, or what Huntington famously calls, "Islam's bloody borders."[6]

This chapter will explore three themes: first, the search for a post–cold war enemy, or whether "the Green (Muslim) menace" is likely to supplant the Red menace as the driving force of U.S. foreign policy, second, the growth of a culturalism in the social sciences wedded to what French Marxist Etienne Balibar fears is "neo-racism," more seductive for foreign policy planners and putative liberals than Anglo-Saxon traditions of discrimination based on biological definitions of inferiority, and finally, the effort to solidify ideological cohesion in Western societies, threatened by late capitalist flabbiness and liberalism's alleged surrender to the pied pipers of multiculturalism.

The Search for a Post–Cold War Enemy

Hardly before the moisture from the thawing cold war could evaporate, U.S. pundits and politicians during the 1980s and 1990s warned of a whole new assortment of threats to the American Century: the resurgence of ruthless Japanese imperialism (Theodore White), the growth of narco-terrorism in the Americas (Brian Crozier and Rachel Ehrenfeld), the expansion of Middle East terrorism (Steven Emerson), and the surge of third world immigration into the U.S. and European metropoles (Paul Kennedy and Matthew Connelly).[7]

Fears of an impending "monster shortage," to use Joseph Sobran's formulation, are a familiar part of the American political landscape.[8] In his *Notes on Democracy* (1926) H. L. Mencken wondered whether the U.S. political order sustained itself through orchestrated hatreds and the constant creation of enemies. As he explained:

> The whole history of the country has been a history of melodramatic pursuits of horrendous monsters, some of them imaginary: the redcoats, the Bank, the Catholics, Simon Legree, the Slave Power, Jeff Davis, Mormonism, Wall Street, the rum demon, John Bull, the hell hounds of plutocracy, the trusts, General Weyler, Pancho Villa, German spies, hyphenates, the Kaiser, Bolshevism. The list might be lengthened indefinitely; a complete chronicle of the Republic could be written in terms of it, and without omitting a single important episode.[9]

Mencken in *Notes on Democracy*, the muckraking financial journalist Ferdinand Lundberg in *The Treason of the People* (1954), and the most authoritative academic commentator on the phenomenon, Richard Hofstadter in *The Paranoid Style in American Politics* (1964), put a heavy stress on popular delusions as the culprit in fomenting most of these volcanic hatreds. They were generated by the religious obscurantism of the mass man, the moronism of the small town or the booboisie, and the conspiratorial populism of "the underdog forces" in U.S. society.

In contrast to their popular-plebeian explanation of enemy formation, foreign policy tends to be created by elites, and the cold war emphatically did not originate in anti-Soviet yelpings from below.[10] One of the architects of the early cold war, George Kennan, hoped that the leaders could simply bypass the U.S. public, which he likened to "one of those prehistoric monsters with a body as long as [a] room and brain the size of a pin."[11] Senator Arthur Vandenberg explained that to obtain popular support for an interventionist foreign policy President Truman would somehow have to "scare the hell out of the country."[12] Reassuring those squeamish about such tactics, Stanford historian Thomas Bailey, author of two of the century's biggest selling textbooks on U.S. history, wrote in 1948 that "because the masses are notoriously short-sighted and generally cannot see danger until it is at their throats, our statesmen are forced to deceive them into an awareness of their own long-run interests. Deception of the people may in fact become increasingly necessary, unless we are willing to give our leaders in Washington a freer hand."[13]

Indeed, Samuel P. Huntington gave such a view resounding applause in 1981, writing that "you may have to sell [intervention or other military action] in such a way as to create the misimpression that it is the Soviet Union that you are fighting. That is what the United States has done ever since the Truman Doctrine."[14] Huntington himself declares the Protestant theologian Reinhold Niebuhr to be substantially the most important influence on his own foreign policy thinking. Niebuhr, it will be recalled, spoke of "the stupidity of the average man," who thus must be supplied "necessary illusion" and "emotionally potent oversimplifications."[15]

In the contemporary historical conjuncture U.S. popular opinion has undoubtedly harbored resentments against Arabs for contributing to petroleum shortages in the 1970s, Iranians for hostage taking and indicating approval toward Hezbollah blazes of violence, and, most obviously, against Muslim extremists for the wholesale murder at the World Trade Center. Nevertheless, in the decade prior to the events of September 11, the most concerted effort at claiming an Islam-driven menace to the West came from a pair of eminent Ivy League intellectuals: Bernard Lewis, Cleveland E. Dodge Professor Emeritus of Near Eastern Studies at Princeton University, and Samuel P. Huntington, Albert J. Weatherhead III University Professor at Harvard. Members of the establishment's most elite foreign policy fraternity, the Council on Foreign Relations, they have sought to supply the intellectual ballast and conceptual universe for the geopolitics of the twenty-first century. Since September 11, according to Nicholas Lemann's extended profile of the Bush foreign policy team for the *New Yorker* (April 1, 2002), the octogenarian Lewis shares with Fouad Ajami the distinction of being the administration's favorite academic experts on the Middle East. In a cover story for *National Review* (December 17, 2001), Lewis explains that the U.S. has but two policy options: "Get tough or get out." The author of *The Arabs in History* told *U.S. News and World Report* (December 3, 2001) that in the weeks immediately following the collapse of the twin towers "I've been to Washington six times."

As early as 1964 Bernard Lewis proclaimed the clash of civilizations between Islam and the West: "The crisis in the Middle East . . . arises not from a quarrel between states but from a clash between civilizations." He elaborated the sources of anti-Western revolt in the Muslim: "His writers, his artists, his architects, even his tailors, testify by their work to the continued supremacy of Western civilization—the ancient rival, the conqueror and now the model, of the Muslim." Calling it "a deeply wounding, deeply humiliating experience," Lewis noted that "even the gadgets and garments, the tools and amenities of his everyday life are symbols of bondage to an alien and dominant culture, which he hates and admires, imitates but cannot share."[16] Lewis's idea did not achieve prominence until 1990 when the *Atlantic* ran his now famous think piece, "The Roots of Muslim Rage." With a cover illustration of a turbaned Middle Eastern figure, gasping with rage and possessing eyes permeated by American flags, Lewis's article told of centuries of Islamic humiliation at the hands of the West and of long desires to lash back against the culture responsible for the wounds of modernity. To his credit, Lewis subsequently expressed regret that the magazine's editors chose such an inflammatory depiction of an Islamic figure. Oddly, he did not think that the content of his article in any way inspired such artistic license.

Lewis's work received a major boost when one of the leading national security mandarins and grand strategic thinkers, Samuel P. Huntington, welcomed his thesis with gusto in the prestigious foreign policy journal *Foreign Affairs* (1993). *Foreign Affairs* had, previously, in Spring 1993 conducted a debate featuring Judith Miller of the *New York Times* on the question "Is Islam a Threat?" While it would be hard to imagine a similar symposium on a rival world religion, "Is Christianity a Threat?" "Is Judaism a Threat?" or "Is Buddhism a Threat?" the establishment's most influential journal did afford ample space to opponents of the Lewis-Huntington-Miller trio. Compared to the most frozen zones of the cold war, when establishment dissent centered on tactics and rarely denied the sinister machinations of global communism, the ongoing Islam debate suggests that a space still exists for alternatives to the Lewis-Huntington thesis of impending civilizational clash.

And yet Lewis and Huntington found many elites receptive to their analysis. Spy thriller novelist Richard Condon, best known for *The Manchurian Candidate*, had earlier explained that "now that the Communists have been put to sleep, we are going to have to invent another terrible threat."[17] Rhodes scholar and CIA director (1993–1995) James Woolsey also worried in a prepared statement for a U.S. Senate committee that "we have slain the dragon. But we live now in a jungle filled with a bewildering variety of poisonous snakes."[18] Leading foreign policy sages such as Henry Kissinger and Zbigniew Brzezinski thus hail Huntington for supplying the grand design lacking at the Bush and Clinton-era State Departments. According to Brzezinski, Huntington's work is "an intellectual tour de force . . . that will revolutionize our understanding of international affairs."[19] Speaking before the National Policy Conference of the Richard Nixon Center on Peace and Freedom in Washington, D.C., Kissinger spoke of a "world in which communications are instantaneous, the economy is global, but the conflicts are ethnic, civilizational . . . something for which few of our leaders have been systematically prepared."[20] Croatian President Franjo Tudjman gave this message a ringing endorsement on his nation's prime-time television by urging his compatriots to turn to "those who understand the reality—such as many representatives of American political and academic life, from Kissinger to Huntington," thinkers able to see "that the contemporary world is confronted with civilizational opposites."[21]

As Kissinger's address might indicate, the Nixon Center on Peace and Freedom regularly identifies resurgent Islam as one of grave danger to global stability. In a mildly critical review for the *Washington Post* of Benjamin Netanyahu's *How Democracies Can Defeat Domestic and International Terrorists* (1995), Peter Rodman, a former Reagan official and director of national security programs at the Nixon Center, agrees that "Islamic extremism is replacing leftist extremism as a political force motivating assaults on Western interests on many continents."[22] In February 1996 the Nixon Center sponsored a seminar on "Megaterrorism," a phenomenon spawned by the marriage of high-tech modes of devastation with religious and political fanaticism. While the conference explored non-Middle Eastern forms of megaterrorism, such as the poison gas attack on the Tokyo subway system during 1994, the program afforded Laurie Mylroie, then of the Philadelphia-based Foreign Policy Research Institute, ample opportunity to outline the advancing danger of Muslim bombing brigades and sabotage units.[23] Thus the megaterrorism school is sometimes heralded as the prophets of September 11, and they pour scorn on the political and academic castes for not properly heeding their warnings.

Nevertheless, there are a few lingering critics of the leading megaterror theoreticians. In the first place, rather than completely dozing off at the wheel, the previous Clinton-Gore national security team may have taken too much advice from the megaterrorism school. That is, the Clinton-Gore intelligence apparatus put so much emphasis on advanced high-tech, nuclear, and bioterrorist threats that they failed to see how much all-devouring ruin could result from decidedly low-tech box cutters and an old-fashioned plane hijacking. Second, again in contrast to its self-image as isolated and unheeded, the megaterrorism school feeds the preconception shared by much of the political and media elite that the grievances of peoples in the Middle East have little or no validity and should be ignored in the formulation of policy. "The United States, an overwhelmingly non-Muslim country, obviously cannot fix the problems of the Muslim world," argues scholar Daniel Pipes.[24] While pointing out that some of the most militant components of Islam are relatively affluent, he draws the lesson that efforts at promoting "broad-based economic growth" for the region are foolishly misguided: "Wealth does not resolve hatreds; a prosperous enemy may simply be one more capable of making war. Westerners and Israelis assumed that Palestinians would make broad economic growth a priority, whereas this has been a minor concern."[25] In counseling against programs for economic revitalization, Pipes appears to be little troubled by unemployment rates in the Middle East higher than any region in the world or the continued pursuit of "Washington consensus" policies of economic liberalization that have frequently failed to create jobs and instead led to dramatic leaps in poverty (i.e., a 30 percent rise in Egypt and a tripling in Jordan from 1985–90).[26] Finally, the megaterrorism school has exhibited a facile haste veering into recklessness about blaming Muslims for acts of terrorism. At the famous Nixon Center seminar on megaterrorism the leaders of this tendency exhibited no contrition for having the previous summer helped orchestrate the chorus blaming Muslims for the carnage in Oklahoma City. Laurie Mylroie's past boss, Daniel Pipes, the former director of the Foreign Policy Research Institute, had told USA Today in the explosion's aftermath of almost certain Muslim fundamentalist culpability: "People need to understand that this is just the beginning. The fundamentalists are on the upsurge, and they make it very clear that they are targeting us. They are absolutely obsessed with us." Meanwhile, terrorism "expert" Steven Emerson anticipated Pipes's analysis on the CBS Evening News: "This was done to inflict as many injuries as possible. That is a Middle Eastern trait." In his article "Camel Jockeys Killed Your Kids," James Ledbetter of the Village Voice wondered whether "someone should ask Emerson what 'trait' led the U.S. to drop atomic bombs on Japan, or Russia to devastate Chechnya." Such logic escaped both State

Department investigators and John McWethy of ABC News. The ABC correspondent appeared to parrot Emerson's wisdom: "The fact that it was such a powerful bomb immediately drew [State Department investigators] to consider deadly parallels that all have roots in the Middle East." It turned out that U.S. listeners in search of accurate news would have done much better with old reliable, Radio Teheran, which, according to a dismissive ABC News, quickly reported: "An extremist Christian group stationed in Idaho and Oklahoma state [is] suspected."[27]

While the World Trade Center bombing has once again isolated attention on Middle Eastern sources of terrorism, the *Christian Science Monitor* pointed out five years ago the limits of approaches that reflexively equate Islam with terror:

> Few Americans . . . are aware of Federal Bureau of Investigation statistics dating to 1980 showing that only two of the 170 acts of terror on U.S. soil by foreign nationals were committed by Islamists. Some 77 of the acts were by Puerto Ricans. Radical Jewish groups accounted for 16. The rest were assorted Irish, Latin American, Croatian, Russian. Only two American Muslims have ever been convicted for terrorist acts. Moreover, despite warnings, there was only one incident of Iranian terror on U.S. soil during the Ayatollah Khomeini's reign, one case of Libyan terror, and no Iraqi cases after the Gulf war.[28]

Daniel Pipes in his article "The Muslims are Coming, the Muslims are Coming . . . " argues that "Muslimphobia" has produced two major camps: first, a foreign policy school that focuses on the security danger of so-called rogue states, such as Iran and Libya, and, second, a domestic school that "fears that Muslim immigrants will subvert Western civilization from within."[29] The French new philosopher André Glucksmann, formerly a Maoist *soixant-huitarde*, articulates the latter school's anxieties when he vigorously defends efforts to ban Islamic girls from wearing the veil to school. "The Islamic scarf is a terrorist emblem," he observes, adding that several women have been assassinated in Algeria by Muslim militants after refusing "to veil themselves." For Glucksmann, "the veil is an instrument of terror," and he calls on France's government to resist "Green fascism."[30] While the vast majority of Muslim girls do not wear the veil to French schools, *citoyens* of Arab descent have wondered why Christians adorned with crosses and Jews donning yarmulkes do not meet similar public outcry.

Pipes sides more with the immigration threat camp than the foreign policy theorists who warn of Iranian, Iraqi, and Libyan jihads against the West. For Pipes Muslim fertility rates in Israel "of no fewer than 6.6 children per woman (1981 estimate)" would prove overwhelming in certain urban European settings. Moreover, "western European societies are unprepared for the massive immigration of brown-skinned peoples cooking strange foods and maintaining different standards of hygiene." He repeats the point in his latest book *Militant Islam Reaches America* (2002), saying that these societies remain "unwilling to deal with the massive immigration of brown-skinned peoples whom they perceive as cooking strange foods and not exactly maintaining Germanic standards of hygiene." He concedes that U.S. society is much better equipped to accommodate those forsaking mainstream culture, among whom he includes the Amish Mennonites of Pennsylvania and the Hasidic Jews of New York.[31]

In the end, however, the only solution, he writes, "is whether the Muslims will modernize."[32] He has claimed that "all Islamists have the same ambition, which is what they call the 'Islamization of America.' By this, they mean no less than saving the U.S. through transforming it into a Moslem country."[33] He sternly warns about the wider Muslim community: "Should they fail to modernize, their stubborn record of illiteracy, poverty, intolerance, and autocracy will continue, and perhaps worsen." Still there could be hope: "If Muslims do modernize . . . they will no longer need to train terrorists or build missiles for use against the West; to emigrate to Europe and America; or, once having moved, to resist integration in Western societies." In other words, instead of "brown-skinned peoples cooking strange foods and maintaining different standards of hygiene," they should join us in the great global shopping mall, daily deodorizing with Arid X-tra Dry, devouring their share of Chicken McNuggets and cases of fresh Coca-Cola.[34] (During 1996 Thomas Friedman, a long-time Middle East correspondent for the *New York Times*, propounded the theory that no two countries which possess a McDonald's franchise have ever gone to war against each other. Enraptured by the idyll of fast-food pacifism, this triple Pulitzer Prize-winning muse envisions the god of War, Mars, feasting on Happy Meals and thus metamorphosing into Venus, who adopts the Big Mac as the Soylent Green of the New World Order. "Would you like fries with your jihad?" is how the *Christian Science Monitor* [April 29, 1999] puts it.)

Even before the Golden Arches reign of pacifism can take hold, Thomas Friedman admits that there is some nasty business that may require the immediate attention of bomb-laden F-15s:

> The hidden hand of the market will never work without the hidden fist—McDonald's cannot flourish without McDonnell Douglas, the designer of the U.S. Air Force F-15. And the hidden fist that keeps the world safe for Silicon Valley's technologies to flourish is called the United States Army, Air Force, Navy, and Marine Corps.[35]

Elsewhere this distinguished voice of U.S. liberalism zestfully provides his preferred choreography for the carnage ahead: "Blow up a different power station in Iraq every week, so no one knows when the lights will go off or who's in charge."[36] Expressing astonishment that Friedman's steps "are recognized as war crimes under every international covenant," particularly the 1979 protocol to the Geneva Convention, the Indian commentator Sukumar Muralidharan points out:

> A power station blown up means not merely the "lights going off," but water treatment plants going out of commission, essential medicines losing their efficacy for want of refrigeration, hospitals and health care centers suspending their work, and food spoiling in storage in the killing desert heat of Iraq.[37]

Central to the thought of Friedman, Pipes, and Bernard Lewis is the notion that most of Islam cannot cope with modernity. According to Lewis's Jefferson Lecture in the Humanities, "The Roots of Muslim Rage," "This is no less than a clash of civilizations—the perhaps irrational but surely historic reaction of an ancient rival against our Judeo-Christian heritage, our secular present, and the worldwide expansion of both." He often refers to "the pent-up hate" and "the mob's anger," which is at heart arrayed "against two enemies, secularism and modernism." For Lewis, "the Muslim has suffered successive stages of defeat," the first being "his loss of domination in the world, to the advancing power of Russia and the West," and the second, "the undermining of his authority in his own country, through an invasion of foreign ideas and laws and ways of life." Finally, he concludes, "the last straw—was the challenge to his mastery in his own house, from emancipated women and rebellious children. It was too much to endure, and the outbreak of rage against these alien, infidel, and incomprehensible forces that had subverted his dominance, disrupted his society, and finally violated the sanctuary of his home was inevitable." Soon it only seemed "natural that this rage should be directed primarily against the millennial enemy and should draw its strength from ancient beliefs and loyalties."[38]

Responding to what he calls Lewis's "bizarre psycho-social analysis of the contemporary situation," C. M. Naim, professor of South Asia Studies at the University of Chicago, profoundly doubts that historians and political scientists would embrace "an exercise in analogy" were it to concern U.S. actions in the Middle East. Mimicking Lewis's very words in a dazzling display of role reversal, Naim observed (prior to the Asian economic implosion of the 1990s):

> The American has suffered successive stages of defeat. The first was his loss of domination to the advancing economic power of Japan and Germany. The second was the undermining of his authority in his own country, through the invasion of foreign ideas and ways of life brought in by waves of non-European immigrants, and the enfranchisement of the vast African-American and Mexican-American populations within the country. The third—the last straw—was the challenge to his mastery in his own house, from emancipated women and rebellious children. It was too much to endure. It was natural this rage should be directed primarily against the millennial enemy and should draw its strength from ancient beliefs and loyalties.[39]

As Naim wondered, "Dare I submit the above as a serious analysis of President Bush's recent actions in the Middle East?" Noting that the NEH Jefferson lecture is labeled "the highest honor conferred by the federal government for distinguished intellectual achievement in the humanities," Naim pauses to remark, "Sadly, the essay by Bernard Lewis is not particularly distinguished."

That has not stopped Lewis's analysis from having considerable impact. Benjamin Netanyahu's *Fighting Terrorism* holds that Arab enmity toward Israel is simply a continuation of millenarian political hatreds between Islam and Christendom. "The soldiers of militant Islam and Pan-Arabism do not hate the West because of Israel," he writes, "they hate Israel because of the West."[40] So focused on Islamic "rage" and "modernity," Lewis and his admirers have trouble accepting the possibility that many Arabs have concrete grievances against the Israeli state: i.e., hundreds of thousands of post-1948 and post-1967 refugees living in squalor, human rights abuses amply documented by Amnesty International, and several studies that have shown that twenty to thirty times more Arabs have died at the hands of the Israeli military and Jewish settlers than Israelis killed via Arab sources of terrorism. Netanyahu explains away Arab terrorism as a kind of nihilistic evil, based on the pure delight of carrying out grisly murder and fabulous destruction. "The various real or imagined reasons proffered by the terrorists to justify their actions are meaningless," he reports.[41] In this regard, Netanyahu appears to exempt Zionist "freedom-fighters," who frequently relied on home-made terrorist activities against British and Arab targets during the struggle to achieve Israeli statehood. For Bernard Lewis the early Zionists have much in common with the "American pioneers," and he hails their "more sophisticated culture" amidst "the savage oratory" of the wider Arab society.[42]

According to both Lewis and Huntington, Islam has several features rendering its followers prey to anti-Western ideologues. First, they assert there is no separation of church and state in Islam, and that its dogmas become a "whole way of life." They simply ignore historical scholarship such as that of Berkeley's Ira Lapidus, who concludes that

> the supposed Muslim norm of the integration of state and religious community actually characterized only a small segment of Middle Eastern and other populations. Undifferentiated state-religious situations were characteristic of lineage or tribal societies, as in Muhammad's Arabia, North Africa, and Morocco, early Safavid Iran, and as in the reformist period of the eighteenth and nineteenth centuries. Even in such cases the conquest of an agriculture-based, urbanized society would start a process of differentiation that broke down the integral connection of state and religion.[43]

Second, they assert that Islamic peoples divide the world into two camps: *Dar al-Islam* (the House of Islam) and *Dar al-harb* (the House of War). As far back as the earlier phases of the cold war (October 1953, specifically), Lewis explained that Islam might well advance the spread of global communism:

> The traditional Islamic division of the world into the House of Islam and the House of War, two necessarily opposed groups, of which the

first has the collective obligation of perpetual struggle against the second, also has obvious parallels in the Communist view of world affairs. There again, the content of belief is utterly different but the aggressive fanaticism of the believer is the same. . . . The call to a Communist Jihad—a new faith, but against the self-same Western Christian enemy—might well strike a responsive note.[44]

The operative concept is "aggressive fanaticism," which links Islam with the horrors of totalitarian communism. While admitting that "the Ulama of Islam are very different from the Communist Party," he then suggests "on closer examination, we find certain uncomfortable resemblances. Both groups profess a totalitarian doctrine, with complete and final answers to all questions on heaven and earth."[45] At a time when McCarthyite crusaders were routing a large corps of orientalists known as the China hands, Lewis thought it to be an opportune moment to conflate Islam with the putative Red menace. In the same year as Lewis's intervention, John T. Flynn subtitled his book on China hand and Mongolia expert Owen Lattimore "the full story of the most incredible conspiracy of our time."[46] For his insight in fighting this "incredible conspiracy," Lewis was decades later saluted by leading liberal cold warriors such as Senator Henry "Scoop" Jackson, who called Lewis's testimony on the Soviet threat to the Middle East "brilliant," an "outstanding performance" that left "all of the subcommittee . . . profoundly impressed."[47] In asserting "the aggressive fanaticism of the believer," Lewis never attempts to explore whether the average Islamic believer in the contemporary age adheres to the eighth-century idea of the House of War. But Huntington is today so certain of its validity he cites data suggesting that, with approximately 20 percent of the world's population, Islam is involved in half the world's violent ethnopolitical conflicts, hence "Islam's borders are bloody, and so are its innards." He will not allow dissent from this appraisal: "Muslim bellicosity and violence are late-twentieth century facts which neither Muslims nor non-Muslims can deny."[48] He makes the spectacular claim that in the entire corpus of Islam "a concept of nonviolence is absent from Muslim doctrine and practice."[49] Pat Robertson goes a step further: "The Koran makes it very clear. If you see an infidel, you are to kill him."[50] Huntington and the Protestant preacher are glad to overlook the various passages of the Qur'an that urge followers to practice peaceful restraint: "Know that God is with those who exercise restraint" (Qur'an 2:194), "There is no compulsion in matters of faith" (Qur'an 2:256; 10:99; 18.29), and, if unbelievers "send you guarantees of peace, know that God has not given a license [to fight them]" (Qur'an 4:90; 4:94).[51]

Other political scientists have tried to crunch the data on Islam and violence, and their results modify some of Huntington's bleaker findings. According to Jonathan Fox of Israel's Bar Ilan University, Islamic groupings have been involved in 39.6 percent of all conflicts in the post–cold war world, a high figure but substantially less than the 50 percent statistic confidently touted as irrefutable by Huntington. More significant, only 6.9 percent of all post–cold war ethnopolitical conflict involves Islam versus the West, numbers minuscule enough that Huntington himself has begun to retreat from claims of imminent intercivilizational conflagration.[52]

When Bosnian Muslims, Indian Muslims, and Palestinians protest that they are at the receiving end of much violence, Huntington is profoundly dismissive of their claims of victimhood. "Wherever one looks along the perimeter of Islam," he writes, "Muslims have problems living peaceably with their neighbors."[53] The eagerness to associate Islam with violence also conveniently absolves the West of involvement in any of the carnage found in third world regions. The U.S. long supplied arms and training to the most ferociously reactionary fighting forces in the Islamic world, including those Mujaheddin who spawned a second-generation reform movement known as the Taliban. The Taliban's slaughter of enemies and removal of women from public spaces was so extreme that Ayatollah Khomeini condemned them as a branch of *islam-i imrikai*, "American Islam."[54] Initially hailing Taliban victory "as very positive," Unocal executive vice president Chris Taggart hoped that their strong-arm tactics would expedite the building of oil pipelines from Turkmenistan through Afghanistan on to coastal Pakistan.[55] The foremost expert on extreme Islam in Central Asia, journalist Ahmed Rashid, observes that "the Clinton Administration was clearly sympathetic to the Taliban, as they were in line with Washington's anti-Iran policy and were important to the success of any southern pipeline that would avoid Iran." He also speaks of "the CIA-ISI [Interservice Intelligence, Pakistan] pipeline" that "supported the more radical Islamic parties." Moreover, "What Washington was not prepared to admit was that the Afghan jihad, with the support of the CIA, had spawned dozens of fundamentalist movements across the Muslim world which were led by militants who had grievances, not so much against the Americans, but their own corrupt, incompetent regimes."[56]

The CIA must be heartened to find journalists at the *New York Times* and biographer Peter L. Bergen in *Holy War, Inc.: Inside the Secret World of*

Osama bin Laden insisting that U.S. intelligence operatives possessed tenu-
ous and probably no connection to the Saudi-born champion of apocalyptic
showdown with the West. While it is likely that bin Laden had much cozier
ties with the ISI than the CIA itself, this should hardly give U.S. intelligence
absolution for its role in strengthening both the ISI as well as jihad international. Even bin Laden gave U.S. operatives credit for their helping hand in
constructing his Afghanistan operation, "I set up my first camp where these
volunteers were trained by Pakistani and American officers. The weapons
were supplied by the Americans, the money by the Saudis."[57] As for the Taliban and their forerunners, a "former high-ranking Pakistani civil servant,
with close ties to ISI," according to a policy brief prepared for the Kennedy
School of Government, concurred with bin Laden's version of events: "The
U.S. provided the weapons and the know-how, the Saudis provided the
funds, and we provided the training camps and operations bases for the
Islamic Legions in the early 1980s and then for the Taliban."[58] In contrast to
the tendency of Huntington's followers to see Islamic militancy as part of the
religion's own inner dynamics, Rashid carefully sketches the sequence of
events that facilitated its triumph, including the CIA-ISI nexus: "Before the
Taliban, Islamic extremism had never flourished in Afghanistan."[59] Beyond
Southwest Asia Washington has given valuable support to rightist Islamic
forces throughout the Middle East in often successful efforts to smash once
powerful socialist movements and ideologues of pan-Arabism.[60]

Huntington also blames the mass murder in East Timor on Indonesian
Muslims, but again he never mentions the substantial aid and comfort the
U.S. has supplied to this repressive regime. Meanwhile, the Middle East is
awash in arms, and Huntington sees fit to warn of dangerous Chinese arms
transfers to Iran, what he regards as a "Confucian-Islamic" alliance for the
twenty-first century. Nevertheless, among the nations of the Near and Middle East, China supplied only 1 percent of foreign arms sales from 1992 to
1995 and slightly under 5 percent from 1996 to 1999; the U.S. provided 52
percent from 1992 to 1995 and 49 percent from 1996 to 1999.[61] U.S. arms
sales to the Middle East have been so brisk that *Newsweek* (March 6, 1995)
refers to "The New Diplomacy: Uncle Sam as Salesman": "Now that the
Cold War is over, Washington is reaffirming to the world that in foreign policy, the business of America is business." The biggest beneficiary of this arms
bonanza is again one of the most reactionary representatives of Islam, the
Saudi Arabian state, which from 1992 to 1999 received $27.8 billion in U.S.
arms deliveries.[62] Sociologist Fatema Mernissi, a leading feminist in the

Islamic world, observes how liberal democracies keep jobs and defense industries humming by selling weaponry to princes, whose feelings of increased security discount the reality of heightened unemployment and discontent among the general public. The "street fundamentalists" then preach about the betrayal of the people, tapping an outrage that builds what she calls "a virulent internal opposition."[63]

According to Huntington the U.S. must continue high levels of defense spending, but, curiously, he calls on U.S. foreign policy leaders to avoid intervening in civilizational conflicts that do not involve the West. Since September 11 he has also launched a new argument that the world might witness more intracivilizational wars within Islam rather than an automatic surge of intercivilizational fights between Islam and the West. Huntington faces the accusation that he is abandoning "the clash of civilizations" thesis, just when a Washington punditry hankering for showdowns with "the axis of evil" are delighting in its heightened piquancy.[64] His stance of nonintervention has surprised some who regard him as one of the most hawkish academics in the cold war coalition, a champion of the Rapid Deployment Force in order "to deter and to defeat coups" that "could originate with either radical Marxist elements or Islamic fundamentalist elements," and an advocate of "forced urbanization" of the Vietnamese peasantry during the U.S. invasion of Southeast Asia.[65] But unlike those who spoke of "roll-back" during the early cold war or recent zealots such as Ann Coulter who dream of occupying Islamic lands and converting them to Christianity, he doubts that civilizations can transform their identity. This is reflected in his belief that Turkey should give up its twentieth-century project to secularize and Westernize, for Huntington a silly enterprise that has disabled Ankara from assuming its rightful place as the hegemonic power in the House of Islam.[66] His relative absence of interventionist fervor has caused some to wonder just how Huntington believes "the clash of civilizations" will result in "the remaking of world order."

Culture in the Remaking of the Post–Cold War Order

For a current director of the John M. Olin Institute for Strategic Studies and a former director of security planning for the National Security Council, Huntington is more preoccupied with domestic policy than the typical foreign affairs mandarin. When Daniel Pipes argued that "Muslimphobia" had spawned two wings, one that flaps about foreign policy dangers and another about the immigration threat, he might well have located Huntington among those giving priority to the latter. Suggesting that "demography is destiny" and "population movements are the motor of history," Huntington wonders if "the threat to Europe of 'Islamization' will be succeeded by that of 'Africanization.'" He adds, "While Muslims provide the immediate problem to Europe, Mexicans pose the problem for the United States."[67]

With declining fertility, Western Europe in particular is at a population crossroads. It has been estimated that the nations of the European Union will have to accept over 50 million immigrants over the next five decades just to replenish its aging labor force. Thus Europe is having to choose between two alternatives: 1. immigration growth that will allow continued funding of social welfare and generous pensions for its graying populations or 2. striving for cultural homogeneity that will require drastic fiscal austerity and likely assaults on civil liberties. Huntington somehow wishes to avert future immigration waves. But if unable to block the influx of the yellow, brown, and black hordes, he seeks to create a political and cultural environment in which the new arrivals can be prevented from transforming "Western civilization" and ushering in the end of the world as we know it.

In the 1970s Huntington contributed to a famous Trilateral Commission book, *The Crisis of Democracy*, in which he warned that the U.S. suffers from a "democratic distemper." The "excess of democracy" resulted from "previously passive or unorganized groups in the population," including "blacks, Indians, Chicanos, white ethnic groups, students, and women," who have "now embarked on concerted efforts to establish their claims to opportunities, positions, rewards, and privileges which they had not considered themselves entitled to before." These "minorities" and "special interests," who just happen to be the majority of the people, do not realize, in Huntington's words, that "the effective operation of a democratic political system usually requires some measure of apathy and noninvolvement on the part of some individuals and groups."[68] At times classified as a political Dracula for believing that power has to steer clear of sunlight, he writes in *American Politics: The Promise of Disharmony* (1981) that "the architects of power must create a force that can be felt but not seen. Power remains strong when it remains in the dark; exposed to the sunlight it begins to evaporate."[69]

Huntington's effort to curb the "excess of democracy" met popular hostility and fed paranoia about the ultimate aims of the Trilateral Commission. In his latest writings he has shifted the terrain of the debate from democracy

to culture. In his view modern liberalism has caved into multiculturalism. If
the "democratic distemper" is to be resisted, U.S. and European society
must forsake the appeals of multiculturalism now and reaffirm, in his words,
"commitment to Western civilization." For Huntington to do otherwise is to
risk cultural suicide: "If the United States is de-Westernized, the West is
reduced to Europe and a few lightly populated overseas European settler
countries. Without the United States the West becomes a minuscule and
declining part of the world's population on a small and inconsequential
peninsula at the extremity of the Eurasian land mass."[70]

U.S. capitalism may have won the ideological and economic war against
communism only to see the fruits of victory squandered by the ravenous
excesses of U.S. liberalism. At a conference celebrating the end of the cold
war, the neoconservative patriarch Irving Kristol explained that he found
opposition to communism to be obvious and too easy, that the dissident liberal Lionel Trilling had opened his eyes to a deeper reality: "to liberalism's
dirty little secret—that there was something basically rotten about its progressive metaphysics that led to an impoverishment of the imagination and
a desiccation of the spirit." Indeed, he admits, "what began to concern me
more and more were the clear signs of rot and decadence germinating
within American society—a rot and decadence that was no longer the consequence of liberalism but was the actual agenda of contemporary liberalism."[71] In language once reserved for slaying Satan and praying to God, his
friend Norman Podhoretz testifes to a life mission of "challenging the regnant leftist culture that pollutes the spiritual and cultural air we all breathe,
and to do so with all my heart and all my soul and all my might."[72] The real
enemy was always liberalism, Kristol affirms, and he relishes the opportunity
to return to this more permanent battlefield: "So far from having ended, my
Cold War has increased in intensity, as sector after sector of American life
has been ruthlessly corrupted by the liberal ethos."[73] Peregrine Worsthorne,
former columnist for the Tory *Daily Telegraph*, later added that U.S. capitalism is prone to promote narcissistic materialism, and only the cold war had
restrained these appetites. If only a new adversary could be found, would the
society return to discipline and higher purpose? He concludes that "worry-
ing about communism intellectually—as against militarily—was a gigantic
red herring, deflecting intellectual attention from liberalism, which was a
much more dangerous enemy of civilization."[74]

The cultural turn in right-wing discourse appears to be one means of
arresting the malaise, the onset of post–cold war "rot." At home Dinesh

D'Souza speaks of "civilizational differences" between blacks and whites that lead the former to prefer social mayhem and multiculturalism over civility and integration. Alleging that "most African American scholars simply refuse to acknowledge the pathology of violence in the black underclass," he scoffs at efforts to promote equal opportunity: "It seems unrealistic, bordering on the surreal, to imagine underclass blacks with their gold chains, limping walk, obscene language, and arsenal of weapons doing nine-to-five jobs at Proctor and Gamble or the State Department."[75] The notion of a permanent underclass, a staple of both neoconservative and liberal social science, shifts the emphasis from economic deprivation to a cultural poverty that is apparently intractable. Just as Huntington raises the specter of the de-Westernization of the United States, D'Souza worries that the cultural breakdown is spreading from urban minorities to the white heartland:

> The American crime rate has risen dramatically over the past few decades, and juvenile homicide has reached catastrophic proportions. Alarming numbers of high school students use drugs, get pregnant, or carry weapons to class. . . . Cultural relativism now prevents liberals from publicly asserting and enforcing civilizational standards for everyone, not just African-Americans.[76]

In an interview Huntington himself elaborates that, without an enemy, liberalism ushers in decadence. He decries "the decay of Western liberalism in the absence of a cohesive ideological challenge by a competing ideology, such as Marxism-Leninism. Fragmentation and multiculturalism are now eating away at the whole set of ideas and philosophies which have been the binding cement of American society."[77] For Kristol "Multiculturalism is as much a 'war against the West' as Nazism and Stalinism ever were."[78]

Opposition to Islam is then a means of rescuing the West from the "fragmentation" that, Huntington believes, is "now eating away at . . . the binding cement of American society." It should be recalled that the term *cold war* (*la guerra fría*) has medieval Spanish origins, referring to the struggle between Christendom and Islam. Don Juan Manuel (1282–1348) contrasted hot and cold wars: "War that is very strong and very hot ends either with death or peace, whereas Cold War neither brings peace nor gives honour to the one who makes it."[79] The millennial war against Islam is one sufficiently protracted to supply the West with a renewal of self-identity and purpose. "Now that the other 'Cold War' is over, the real Cold War has begun," proclaims

Irving Kristol in his philippic against modern liberalism. Oblivious to Don Juan Manuel's injunction that cold war "neither brings peace nor gives honour to the one who makes it," the founder of *Encounter* and publisher of the *National Interest* hails the "conflict I shall be passing on to my children and grandchildren." In a voice chillingly reminiscent of the Venetian nationalist from the *Dead Lagoon*, Kristol concludes: "But it is a far more interesting Cold War—intellectually interesting, spiritually interesting—than the war we have so recently won, and I rather envy those young enough for the opportunities they will have to participate in it."[80]

For those desiring to join Kristol's clarion call for a new cold war, they will have to come to terms with a series of fateful fissures in their movement:

Diaspora Lobbies Versus the Foreign Policy Establishment

Among the high intellectuals, Lewis, Pipes, and Huntington, the last figure in this threesome has become increasingly vocal about the dangers of "diaspora lobbies" in dominating U.S. foreign policy. If not able to restore the older Protestant stablishment to full command over foreign policy, Huntington seeks to insulate the national security apparatus from a variety of intrusive publics, among whom he includes the influential Zionist, Cuban, Asian, and Greek lobbies on Capitol Hill.[81] In contrast, neoconservatives who regularly champion Lewis and Pipes on the pages of *Commentary* spare no opportunity to enhance the prominence of pro-Israeli political action committees, what Huntington in his careful WASP code prefers to designate as "diaspora lobbies." It will not assuage Zionist partisans that much of Huntington's bile is directed at the so-called Hispanic lobby, which many mainstream political scientists blame for sabotaging restrictive immigration legislation.[82]

Demography Is Destiny: Neocons Versus Theocons

Huntington's belief that "demography is destiny" receives ratification from Pipes in his own fears of Muslim population growth and resistance to modernity; that is to say, the religion's intolerance toward inserting Western-style contraceptive devices or imbibing birth-suppressing Rexall pharmaceuticals. Again, neoconservatism's embrace of the religious right could be fraught with tension should prominent neocon sympathizers endorse international family planning and birth control measures designed to avert further detonation of the supposed Muslim population bomb.

Huntington and Pipes follow a long line of literature forecasting ominous consequences from Muslim fecundity. Shortly after World War I Lothrop Stoddard in *The New World of Islam* spoke of "the 250,000,000 followers of the Prophet from Morocco to China and from Turkestan to the Congo," who are "seething with mighty forces" and "fashioning a new Muslim world." He reflects that "the quick breeding tendencies of Oriental peoples have always been proverbial, and have been due not merely to strong sexual appetites but . . . perhaps even more to religious doctrines enjoining early marriage and the begetting of numerous sons." He adds that "the average Oriental" is "accustomed as he has been for centuries to a slipshod, easygoing existence," and "he instinctively hates things like sanitary measures and police regulations." Though "East and West can quicken each other by a mutual exchange of ideas and ideals," he concludes that "ethnic fusion . . . would result in a dreary mongrelization from which would issue nothing but degeneration and decay."[83] A Harvard Ph.D. and president of the American Birth Control League, Stoddard in 1922 wrote about the demographic threat to colonial order in *The Rising Tide of Color Against White World Supremacy*. Though Huntington is mercifully free of Stoddard's preoccupation with eugenics, both see an intimate link between the fortunes of demography and culture. Compare Huntington's cultural meditations about Muslim and Mexican population growth in Europe and the United States respectively with a statement by Stoddard from *Racial Realities in Europe*:

> The United States was founded by men of Nordic stock; its institutions, ideals, and culture are typical fruits of the Nordic spirit. These are the things which make "America." Yet only so long as America remains predominantly Nordic in blood will these things endure. History shows that as the blood of a nation changes, so does every phase of national life; it proves beyond a shadow of a doubt that if the United States should cease to be a mainly Nordic land, *our* America would pass away.[84]

Most contemporary social scientists have since driven a thick wedge between biological and culturalist explanations, the latter thought to be freer from the dual taint of racism and essentialism. But as Robert J. C. Young observes,

> Today it is common to claim that in such matters we have moved from biologism and scientism to the safety of culturalism . . . but that shift has not been so absolute for the racial was always cultural, the essential never unequivocal. . . . We may be more bound up with its categories than we like to think. Culture and race developed together, imbricated within each other. . . . The nightmare of the ideologies and categories of racism continue to repeat upon the living.[85]

Even a social scientist so prone to biological explanations of reality as Charles Murray admits that he can live with culturalist or environmental explanations of social reality if the latter have the same result: the dismantling of federal educational largesse and the liberal welfare state.[86] The legacy of Nazism has left many Western conservatives reluctant to redeploy biology; culture will have to fill in the void.

Still, on the question of population or what Foucault's followers might refer to as bio-power, culture is thought to be at stake. Huntington's claim that demography is cultural destiny echoes Britain's Royal Commission on Population (1949), which concluded that "the question" of fertility "is not merely one of military strength and security; it merges into more fundamental issues of the maintenance and extension of Western values and culture." Adding that "the drift of world affairs is giving a new emphasis to the conception of Western civilisation as an entity possessing reality and value," the report laments that "the peoples of Western civilisation" have a "rate of increase" that "has markedly declined while that of Oriental peoples has markedly accelerated."[87]

In 1974 Henry Kissinger requested National Security Study Memorandum 200, better known as NSSM 200, titled "Implications of Worldwide Population Growth for U.S. Security and National Interests." Though the memorandum put more stress on political stability and U.S. access to minerals than culture, it observes that the U.S. would have to endure a "growing power status for Brazil in Latin American and on the world scene" should this nation's population overtake that of the United States. A CIA report of February 1984 entitled "Middle East–South Asia: Population Problems and Political Stability" identifies a population bulge of young people in the fifteen- to twenty-four-year-old group as "ready recruits for opposition causes," most notably "Islamic fundamentalism which currently offers the principal ideological haven for Muslim youth." In 1991 *Foreign Affairs* adapted a report of demography expert Nicholas Eberstadt to the U.S. Army Conference on Long Range Planning. It warns that "the implications for the international political order and the balance of world power could be enormous. The population and economic-growth trends described could create an international environment even more menacing to the security prospects of the Western alliance than was the Cold War for the past generation." In the midst of such turmoil the problem will remain, says Eberstadt: "How to increase the share of the world's population living under . . . 'Western values'?" The pro-natalism of the Islamic clerics in Iran may have contributed to some of these anxieties in Western circles, yet the Iranian regime has as of late quietly sought to moderate population growth in hopes of limiting aftershocks from the Khomeini-era baby boom.

Huntington's own association of demography with cultural power may find resources for resistance from at least one community: U.S. Roman Catholics. Throughout the 1940s and 1950s Paul Blanshard wrote a series of books warning that Catholic fertility and ancestry from mostly antidemocratic nations would potentially lead to subversion of U.S. democracy. In a subchapter labeled "Conquest by Fecundity," he notes,

> Perhaps the most important factor in the penetration of Catholic power into non-Catholic territory today is a phenomenon which is almost never frankly discussed in public, the stimulated Catholic birthrate. Although it is impossible to prove by scientific statistics, it seems certain that the orthodox Catholic blocs in the Western democracies are outbreeding the non-Catholic blocs by a considerable margin.

Hailed by the *Nation*, the *New Republic*, and many liberal-left organs of opinion, Blanshard believed that the Catholic community by "outbreeding its competitors" would likely assume majority control of the American Republic. They could then remake North America in the Holy See's authoritarian cultural image, with Blanshard adding that "French Catholic Canada is winning what the French Canadians call the *la revanche des berceaux*, the revenge of the cradles." According to his conclusion, "In this type of biological penetration and conquest, the Kremlin is a very poor second to the Vatican."[88]

Multiculturalism and Homogenization:
The U.S. Versus the European New Right

In Huntington's version of history white ethnic Catholics instead conformed to Anglo-American norms because of aggressive Americanization pursued in the schools and civic life, but today multiculturalism allows the Mexicans and Muslims to revel in their alien cultures, while African Americans are, in his words, only "partially assimilated."[89] According to the book *Foundations of Sand* written by Lawrence Hafstad, with John Morse and Marianne Mele Hall, African Americans "insist on preserving their jungle freedoms, their women, their avoidance of personal responsibility and their abhorrence of the work ethic." Moreover, "blacks have inherited a different set of aptitudes, values, mores, goals and lifestyles over a period of 10,000 years." The race problem escalates "when you displace the jungle-freedom-types into the Scotland-type environment which is America."[90]

In her European commentary in *One, by One, by One: Facing the Holocaust,* Judith Miller of the *New York Times* is in accord with Huntington on the peculiar Muslim resistance to assimilation. In particular, she contrasts French Muslims unfavorably with French Jews: "The Jews, at least, had come to France seeking shelter from places from which France had never been ousted. They had also agreed to play by French rules. This is not the case for the Moslems, who are genuinely 'foreign,' who now follow France's second largest religion, and many of whom have no desire to be French."[91]

While Miller is too much of a twenty-first century liberal to cry out, "Exterminate the Brutes!" her discourse is startlingly similar to Front National descriptions of the Islamic hordes as un-French and thus ripe for deportation. For Jean-Marie LePen, commenting on Arab immigrants at the FN's congress of November 1985: "The danger resides in the presence of elements whose loyalty to the French people is a priori suspect."[92] In the current intellectual climate Miller's own remarks went unacknowledged by reviewer after reviewer. While her *New York Times* colleague William Safire hailed her work as "the nonfiction stunner of the year," Bernard Lewis salutes her for producing a "powerful book . . . that must be read." Appropriately, Miller herself says that Lewis's "work has shaped so much of my thinking about the Mideast."[93]

Miller's belief that Jews assimilate and that Muslims remain determined to be the Perpetual Other, refusing to fit in with Western societies, is not confirmed by studies of the Islamic diaspora in Europe and North America.

The Algerian-born grand mufti of Lyons notes that Front National opposition to construction of the Grand Mosque in France's third-largest city soon floundered in the mid-1990s, in part because of active Muslim efforts at reconciliation with Christian neighbors: "The protests have completely disappeared because we have shown that French Islam can be a force for moderation and integration." In Britain Dr. Hesham El-Essawy, chair of the Islamic Society for the Promotion of Religious Tolerance, points out that "the idea of separation is anathema to most Muslims. Their real grievance is that they do not find it easy to get into the mainstream of British society."[94] Meanwhile, in the United States the *Christian Science Monitor* carried out a four-part investigation into Muslim assimilation. Focusing on Cedar Rapids, Iowa, the home of Quaker Oats and the oldest mosque in the United States, they found "most Muslim families . . . today are successful and assimilated, and they prefer it that way. They play golf and shoot pool," and, on the Fourth of July, "they take the kids to McDonald's after the fireworks, where they succumb to urgent pleas for Batman cups." John Esposito, a distinguished scholar of Islam, reflects that "they are trying to do what every group has done—trying to assimilate, yet remain distinct."[95]

Huntington's own demand that Western societies should batten down the hatches on immigration has won him admiration from the European New Right. But, again, his desire that the United States strengthen ties with Europeans, against those who speak of a Pacific Rim future for U.S. capitalism, has led to surprising fissures with this same European New Right. French thinkers such as Alain de Benoist speak of ethnopluralism, a vision that calls for France to defend and protect its civilization from multicultural meltdown and the homogenizing forces of global American media. De Benoist believes that Muslims should hold on to their religion and culture, but that it rightfully belongs in North Africa. While he explicitly disavows Jean-Marie Le Pen's more vicious attacks on immigrants, and even encourages those who have arrived to guard their culture in the name of ethnopluralism, he does not think France should permit further incursions from the American model of immigration and multiculturalism. The French New Right is skeptical of Huntington's view that the United States can come closer to Europe in order to strengthen Western civilization. They have determined that America is now the Other, that the homogenizing logic of U.S. capitalism is the true threat to French and European civilization. U.S. popular culture, Coca-Colonization, and the McDonaldization so craved by foreign affairs journalist Thomas Friedman are increasingly condemned by

European New Right ideologues in the 1990s and 2000s.[96] They are thus not eager to accept Huntington's handshake of Western civilizational solidarity.

The Ceaseless Search for Enemies

Perhaps inspired by his top adviser William Kristol, U.S. vice president J. Danforth Quayle told nearly one thousand graduates from the U.S. Naval Academy: "We have been surprised this past century by the rise of communism, the rise of Nazism, and the rise of Islamic fundamentalism."[97] His analysis soon received ratification from British defense expert Clare Hollingworth: "Muslim fundamentalism is fast becoming the chief threat to global peace and security. . . . It is akin to the menace posed by Nazism and fascism in the 1930s and then by communism in the '50s."[98]

From its very inception neoconservatism has been predicated on the need for an enemy, with the movement's founding father Irving Kristol identifying liberalism as the central source of societal decay. Kristol's own intellectual hero is the émigré political philosopher Leo Strauss. The Straussians owe a substantial intellectual debt to the German philosopher Carl Schmitt, who spoke of the enemy from within and without, the adversary shaping one's core identity. As Shadia Drury in *Leo Strauss and the American Right* explains the Straussian delight with this philosophical bedfellow of European fascism:

> Like Schmitt, Strauss believes that politics is first and foremost about the distinction between WE and THEY. Strauss thinks that a political order can be stable only if it is united by an external threat; and following Machiavelli, he maintains that if no external threat exists, then one has to be manufactured. Had he lived to see the collapse of the Soviet Union, he would have been deeply troubled because the collapse of the evil empire poses a threat to America's inner stability.[99]

Though Huntington maintains that Strauss and Schmitt are not among the most important influences in his intellectual pantheon, he does agree that enemy formation, properly seized upon, can be salubrious for attaining political hygiene. As the abstract to Huntington's article for the seventy-fifth anniversary issue of *Foreign Affairs* expresses it, "Without an enemy to define itself against, America's identity has disintegrated. . . . The United States should scale back its involvement in the world until a threat reinvigorates our national purpose."[100]

Just as Huntington rails against the mushy relativism of multiculturalism, the high Straussian Allan Bloom previously called for his own jihad against this ideological scourge in his runaway best-seller *The Closing of the American Mind* (1987). Bernard Lewis termed Bloom's crusade against relativism "a fascinating and illuminating book," adding, "It should be read by every university teacher who is concerned about the nature and purpose of his vocation."[101] The waning of the cold war threatened a turning point, as the last shards of discipline could be sloughed off in favor of jungle freedoms at home and the law of the jungle abroad.

In the late nineteenth and early twentieth century elite European intellectuals embarked on a similar crusade against advancing relativism. As the literary critic Terry Eagleton expresses it, imperialism "bred an awareness of cultural relativism at precisely the point where the absolute cultural hegemony of the imperialist nations needed to be affirmed."[102] In the late nineteenth and early twentieth century many intellectuals arrested the threat of relativism by embracing Social Darwinism and eugenics. An important source of support for these ideas came from U.S. Progressives, British Fabians, and other left-leaning reformers whose scientific faith in eugenics allied them to rightist aristocrats enamored of good breeding. Banker and expansionist mastermind Cecil Rhodes gave jubilant testimony to these strange bedfellows in Britain, the mating of Tories, Liberals, and a flank of Fabian Socialists. "They are tumbling over each other, Liberals and Conservatives, to show which side are the greatest and most enthusiastic Imperialists," he told friends in southern Africa.[103] In his "Confession of Faith," he took pride that "we are the finest race in the world and that the more of the world we inhabit the better it is for the human race," if only because much of the planet is "at present inhabited by the most despicable specimens of human beings."[104] Undoubtedly, eugenics had hegemonic potency: it appealed to an enormous range of Western opinion and even permeated the thought of some anti-imperialists. As alluded to before, the carnage unleashed by European fascism would eventually discredit biological explanations for grounding social reality and proclaiming Western preeminence. Yet liberals eagerly became a bulwark in the next major ideological crusade of Western civilization, the cold war, only this time culture would supply the dominant rationalization for social hierarchy and inequalities.

This, of course, had major ramifications in domestic politics. In the mid-1960s Patrick Moynihan relied on group cultural attributes in *Beyond the Melting Pot* to explain the persistence of black poor in America, while the anthropologist Oscar Lewis spoke of a "culture of poverty," a phrasing that, despite his reformist intentions, became a metaphor for implacable resistance to progress.[105]

In international affairs culturalism soon permeated explanations for inequalities and conflicts between nations, conditions that also are regarded as intractable. According to Bernard Lewis in "The Roots of Muslim Rage" and Benjamin Netanyahu in *Fighting Terrorism*, Islam represents a culture at war with modernity. The bulk of U.S. liberals are eager to agree and, as in the cold war, can easily be enlisted in rightist campaigns against this putative menace. Agreeing with Abe Rosenthal that Israel is the symbol of "civilized democratic decency" in the Middle East, a preponderance of U.S. liberals can be mobilized when national security hawks pronounce Islamic threats to global security.[106] Still many traditional liberals are frightened that multiculturalism is invading Western liberalism, rendering the doctrine less capable of lining up behind Western civilization and Israel. Claiming that "anti-Zionism has come to play the role of a gutter multiculturalism," the 1979 Nobel laureate for Physics Steven Weinberg argues that "Zionism also represents the intrusion—by purchase and settlement rather than conquest, at least until Arab assaults made military action necessary—of a democratic, scientifically sophisticated, secular culture into a part of the world that for centuries has been despotic, technically backward, and obsessed with religion. For me, it is this essentially Western character of Zionism that gives it an attraction beyond its defensive role." Hailing "the leadership of Theodore Herzl" in the foundation of Zionism, Weinberg may be identifying with Herzl's stated goal in *The Jewish State: An Attempt at a Modern Solution of the Jewish Question* (1895): "Palestine is our ever-memorable historic home. . . . We should there form a portion of the rampart of Europe against Asia, an outpost of civilization as opposed to barbarism." Weinberg himself thus states: "There is a special pain in seeing some of my fellow Western liberals hostile to an ideal and a country I admire."[107]

To stamp out the specter of multiculturalism, the case of American Taliban John Walker Lindh has been offered regularly as an object lesson of Marin County cultural coddling and relativism run amok. On the right, syndicated columnist Ann Coulter calmly observes, "We need to execute people like John Walker in order to physically intimidate liberals, by making them realize that they can be killed too. Otherwise they will turn out to be outright traitors."[108] More generally, the leading organ of U.S. liberalism, the *New Republic*, repeatedly associates Islamic peoples with the benchmark of twentieth-century evil, Nazism. Its literary editor Leon Wieseltier elsewhere calls "the Palestinians, or many of them, and much of the Arab leadership in the 1930s and 1940s . . . Hitler's little helpers in the Middle East."[109] (The historian Peter Novick has explained how similar logic and obsession with linking Palestinians to the Holocaust led the editors of the four-volume *Encyclopedia of the Holocaust* to give the Palestinian nationalist, the mufti of Jerusalem, an improbable lead role in this historic horror: "The article on the Mufti is more than twice as long as the articles on Goebbels and Goering, longer than the articles on Himmler and Heydrich combined, longer than the article on Eichmann, of all the biographical articles, it is exceeded in length, but only slightly, by the entry for Hitler.")[110] In the *New Republic's* "Zionism at 100" issue (September 8–15, 1997) Cynthia Ozick spoke of "Arab intransigence" growing "more violent (and politically sympathetic to Nazism)," Charles Krauthammer of "a population of 3 million Palestinians bred on a hatred of Jews that beggars the imagination," and Daniel Bell of Palestinians having "sustained themselves by the emotion of race hatred against the Israelis." The Martin Peretz Professor of Yiddish Literature at Harvard, Ruth Wisse, concludes in the same issue: "The Arabs' appropriation of the United Nations as a propaganda forum proves that, although the Jewish state could defend itself militarily, it was as powerless to escape the politics of hatred as European Jews ever were under Hitler." Playing to a political culture so quick to associate Arabs with impending Auschwitz, President George Herbert Walker Bush had actually claimed that the repressive regime of Saddam Hussein surpassed the Nazi fuhrer in many measures of fiendishness: "Hitler did not stake people out against potential military targets, and he did . . . respect the legitimacy of the embassies."[111] On the subject of race hatred Ozick, Krauthammer, Bell, Wisse, and company took no notice of widespread chants of approval for Rabbi Yaacov Perrin during his eulogy for Dr. Baruch Goldstein, who had freshly massacred twenty-nine Arabs in a Hebron mosque. "One million Arabs," proclaimed Perrin, "are not worth a Jewish fingernail."[112] Concerning the rejoicing, Yuval Katz in *Yerushalaim* (March 4, 1994) observes: "It is important that according to one poll about 50 percent of Kiryat Arba inhabitants approve of the massacre. More important is another poll that showed that another 50 percent of Israeli Jews are more sympathetic to the settlers after the massacre than they were before the massacre."[113] Goldstein, incidentally, had an obsession with comparing Arabs to Nazis, as he told an Israeli radio station in the weeks before his bloodbath to glory that it was time to cut down "the Arab Nazi enemy, who strives to attack any Jew just because he is a Jew in the land of Israel."[114]

Goldstein had regularly refused medical treatment to Arabs, just one of his actions that provoked scathing commentary from the Israeli journalist Teddy Preuss:

> Compared to the giant-scale mass murderers of Auschwitz, Goldstein was certainly a petty murderer. His recorded statements and those of his comrades, however, prove that they were perfectly willing to exterminate at least two million Palestinians at an opportune moment. This makes Dr. Goldstein comparable to Dr. Mengele. . . . As their statements abundantly testify, they see the Arabs as nothing more than disease-spreading rats, lice or other loathsome creatures; this is exactly how the Nazis believed that the Aryan race alone had laudable qualities that could become polluted by sheer contact with dirty and morbid Jews. Kahane, who learned nothing from the Nuremberg Laws, had exactly the same notions about the Arabs.[115]

U.S. liberalism's own historic opportunism and complicity with politically retrograde currents, whether fin de siècle imperialism, mid-century cold warriorism, or late twentieth-century Islamophobia, poses a special problem for neoconservatism. In hoping to slay the monster of liberalism once and for all, Irving Kristol and the Straussians may not have counted on the gusto with which so many latter-day liberals would join them on the battlefield against Islam.

Alas, liberalism is a child of the Enlightenment, a philosophical movement shot through with Islamophobia. Voltaire, representing the apogee of Enlightenment reason and tolerance, told Frederick the Great, "You may still have the pleasure of seeing Muslims chased out of Europe," and Catherine the Great of his deepest desire: "I wish I had at least been able to help you kill a few Turks." Voltaire wrote, "It does not suffice to humiliate them; they should be destroyed."[116] Though Strauss wished that the Enlightenment had been strangled in the crib, he could not gainsay one reality: liberalism had long ago learned to loathe Islam.

Islam is thus not the intimate enemy ultimately sought out by neoconservatism, and even the non-Straussian Huntington has begun to concede the point in his late 1997 writing for *Foreign Affairs*. For the world's billion Muslims, it should be cold comfort to know that the very fact of a shared tradition of Islamophobia between neoconservatives and liberals may help short-circuit this current as the driving force of U.S. foreign policy. President Bush is therefore quite comfortable restating over and over that America is not at war with Islam. And yet, the relative absence of resistance to Islamophobia in Western cultures renders its practice tantalizing for demagogues of all political stripes. They should ensure that the world will revisit these nightmares, a hellish prospectus for the twenty-first century upon us.

Notes

My thanks to Eqbal Ahmad, V. G. Kiernan, Emran Qureshi, and Michael Sells for their many valuable suggestions.

1. Sir Alfred Lyall, letter of August 30, 1857, to his father, Lyall papers, MSS Eur F 132/3, India Office Library and Records. British colonialists often regarded the Muslims as a "martial race." Nevertheless, later in the nineteenth century British authorities found grounds for cooperation with Muslims against what they saw as "the better-educated, more economically active and modernizing Hindus," writes historian V. G. Kiernan in a private correspondence to the author. He adds, "this went on down to the Partition."
2. The reprisals and Ghalib response are discussed by Peter Hardy, *The Muslims of British India* (New Delhi: Foundation Books/Cambridge University Press, 2002 [1972]), 70–71. In the memories of Zahir Dihlawi, "The English soldiers began to shoot whomsoever they met upon the way . . . Mian Muhammad Amin Panjakush, an excellent writer, Moulvie Imam Bakhsh Sabhai along with his two sons. . . . were arrested. . . . shot dead and their dead bodies were thrown into the Jumna." The Governor-General, Lord Canning, soon told British troops to cool down: "The men who fought against us at Delhi were of both creeds; probably in about equal numbers . . . It was not the people of Delhi—certainly not the householders—who rebelled or abetted rebellion. . . . It would be monstrous to destroy [their property] without compensation." Canning counseled that Britain's leadership would be foolish to follow the lead of British newspapers, military men, and intellectuals who blamed the rebellion on religion, whether Muslim or Hindu. "If we destroy or desecrate Mussalman Mosques or Brahmin temples, we do exactly what is wanting to band two antagonist *races* against ourselves . . . I beg you not to ask for anything to be done against the religion of either race." Canning quoted by Hardy, 72.

3. Lyall letter, *loc. cit.* Thomas Babington Macaulay's remark comes from his essay on Thornton and is discussed in Raleigh Trevelyan, *The Golden Oriole: A 200-Year History of an English Family in India* (New York: Viking, 1987), esp. 221.

4. Eric Stokes, *The Peasant and the Raj: Studies in Agrarian Society and Peasant Rebellion in Colonial India* (Cambridge: Cambridge University Press, 1980 [1978]), 19. Stokes does explain that the waning of influence is hardly confined to Lyall: "Today few read James Mill, or Hegel, or Maine, or Lyall, or even, one suspects, Weber on India."

5. Michael Dibdin, *Dead Lagoon* quoted by Samuel P. Huntington, *The Clash of Civilizations and the Remaking of World Order* (New York: Simon & Schuster. 1996), 20.

6. For Huntington quotations, see *The Clash of Civilizations*, 125, 183, and 254. For the Trilateral Commission report, see the appendices to Michael J. Crozier, Samuel P. Huntington, and Joji Watanuki, *The Crisis of Democracy: A Report on the Governability of Democracies to the Trilateral Commission* (New York: New York University Press, 1975), 195.

7. For a representative sampling of this "threat" literature, see the following: Theodore White, "The Danger from Japan," *New York Times Magazine*, July 28, 1985; Brian Crozier, "How the Colombian Cocaine Chain Leads to Fidel Castro," *Sunday Times*, January 28, 1990; Rachel Ehrenfeld, *Narco-Terrorism* (New York: Basic, 1990); Steven Emerson, "Bush's Toothless War Against Terrorism," *U.S. News and World Report*, October 31, 1988; Steven Emerson, "A Terrorist Network in America?" *New York Times*, April 7, 1993; Paul Kennedy and Matthew Connelly, "Must It Be the Rest Against the West? Immigration and Relations Between Western and Developing Countries," *Atlantic Monthly*, December 1994. Connelly has subsequently expressed regret that the editors of *Atlantic Monthly* chopped a significant part of his historical and ideological analysis of "population threat" literature, which would have supplied context and shown the dangers of this discourse.

8. Sobran quoted by Eric Alterman, "All the World's a Stage, and Clinton and Dole merely . : . . . Pres. Clinton's and Bob Dole's Positions on Foreign Policy Issues," *Nation*, April 15, 1996.

9. H. L. Mencken, *Notes on Democracy* (New York: Knopf, 1926), 22–23.

10. Noting that "public attitudes were shaped by elite opinion," historian Melvyn P. Leffler admits that "the number of Americans saying that the United States could trust Russia declined from an all-time high of 55 percent in March 1945 to 35 percent in March 1946." Nevertheless, "most Americans were not concerned with international affairs. In October 1945 only 7 percent of the people considered foreign problems to be of vital importance. This figure rose to 21 percent in February 1946 and then fell back to 11 percent in June." Melvyn P.

Leffler, *A Preponderance of Power: National Security, the Truman Administration, and the Cold War* (Stanford: Stanford University Press, 1992), 106.

11. Kennan quoted by Lawrence F. Kaplan, "A Populist Foreign Policy?" *First Things*, March 1999, 50.

12. Vandenberg conversation with Truman recounted by Loy Henderson in Walter Isaacson and Evan Thomas, *The Wise Men: Six Friends and the World They Made* (New York: Simon and Schuster, 1986), 395. In a speech at the Nixon Center on Peace and Freedom, President William Jefferson Clinton called out, "Let us find inspiration in the great tradition of Harry Truman and Arthur Vandenberg." *U.S. Newswire*, March 2, 1995.

13. Bailey quoted by Noam Chomsky, *Necessary Illusions: Thought Control in Democratic Societies* (Boston: South End, 1989), 17–18. In their book *Hitler vs. Roosevelt: The Undeclared Naval War* (New York: Free, 1979), 272, Thomas Bailey and Paul Ryan explain that "the President, not the windy body known as Congress, is the final judge of what constitutes the national interest at a given time."

14. Samuel P. Huntington, et.al., "Vietnam Reappraised" [A roundtable discussion], *International Security*, Summer 1981, 14.

15. Huntington declared the centrality of Niebuhr to his thought in a talk at the Harvard Book Store, Cambridge, February 6, 1998, an event in which he signed copies of the then newly released paperback edition of *The Clash of Civilizations*. See also Reinhold Niebuhr, *Moral Man and Immoral Society* (New York: Scribner's, 1952 [1932]), 21, 221–223. Niebuhr's concepts are assembled in Chomsky, *Necessary Illusions*, 17, as well as in Chomsky's review essay on Niebuhr scholarship for the Winter 1987 issue of *Grand Street*.

16. Bernard Lewis, *The Middle East and the West* (Bloomington: Indiana University Press, 1964), 135 and 137.

17. Condon quoted by Daniel Pipes, "The Muslims Are Coming, the Muslims Are Coming , . . . " *National Review*, November 19, 1990, 28.

18. Woolsey testimony during confirmation hearings quoted by Jim Mann, "Woolsey Cites Dangers in Economic Espionage," *Los Angeles Times*, 3 February 1993.

19. See back jacket cover *of The Clash of Civilizations*.

20. Henry Kissinger, transcript of speech from Federal News Service, March 2,1995.

21. Tudjman (September 12, 1997 broadcast) quoted in a USIA cable from the U.S. Embassy in Zagreb, September 1997, to the U.S. secretary of state, Washington D.C. The document is numbered #4082/ 01 2650513 and is entitled "The Croatian Ascendancy of Samuel Huntington." The officials in Zagreb report that "Dr. Huntington has become something of the man of the hour in recent days in the local media, which sees him as the ideal analyst of the situation in the region."

22. Peter W. Rodman, "The Dark Shadow of Extremism," *Washington Sunday Post Book World*, October 29, 1995. For other representative samples of foreign policy expertise at this think tank, see the remarks of Dmitri Simes, president of the Nixon Center: "In Bosnia, Clinton sided with brutal wimps who demanded that the U.S. military be turned into their private air force while secretly sponsoring Iranian terrorists on their soil." Dmitri K. Simes, "Clinton Foreign Policy a Disaster—GOP Little Better," *Houston Chronicle*, March 10, 1996. See also Geoffrey Kemp, a former Middle East specialist at the State Department and director of regional strategic programs at the Nixon Center, who writes: "The United States is defending the interests of all industrial countries by its military presence in the gulf and . . . . the allies better put up or shut up." Geoffrey Kemp, "Saudi Blast also Wounds U.S. Policy," *Newsday*, June 27, 1996.

23. "Technology Leaves World Open to New Trend: Megaterrorism," Deutsche-Presse-Agentur, wire release of February 6, 1996.

24. Daniel Pipes, "Who is the Enemy?" *Commentary*, January 2002, 25.

25. Daniel Pipes, "God and Mammon: Does Poverty Cause Militant Islam?" *National Interest*, Winter 2001/02, 14–21.

26. Joel Beinin, *Workers and Peasants in the Modern Middle East* (Cambridge: Cambridge University Pres, 2001), 168.

27. Pipes, Emerson, McWethy, and Radio Teheran quoted by James Ledbetter, "Camel Jockeys Killed Your Kids," *Village Voice*, May 2, 1995, 9.

28. Robert Marquand and Lamis Andoni, "U.S. a Target? Separating the Fact from the Fiction in Islamic Extremism," *Christian Science Monitor*, February 5, 1996, 11.

29. Pipes, "The Muslims Are Coming," 28.

30. "Andre Glucksmann: 'Le foulard Islamique est un embleme terroriste,'" *Le Figaro*, October 28, 1994.

31. Pipes, "The Muslims Are Coming."

32. Ibid.

33. Daniel Pipes, "American Islamists and Lieberman," *Jerusalem Post*, August 16, 2000.

34. Pipes, "The Muslims Are Coming."

35. Thomas L. Friedman, *The Lexus and the Olive Tree* (New York: Farrar, Straus, Giroux, 1999), 373.

36. Thomas L. Friedman, "Rattling the Rattler," *New York Times*, January 19, 1999.

37. S. Muralidharan, "Arrogant Posturing," *Frontline*, 18.20, September 29–October 12, 2001.

38. Bernard Lewis, "The Roots of Muslim Rage," *Atlantic Monthly*, September 1990, 49, 59–60.

39. C. M. Naim, "The Outrage of Bernard Lewis," *Social Text*, 30, 1992, 116.

40. Benjamin Netanyahu, *Fighting Terrorism: How Democracies Can Defeat Domestic and International Terrorists* (New York: Farrar, Straus, and Giroux, 1995), 87.

41. Ibid., 21.

42. Bernard Lewis, *Semites and Anti-Semites* (New York: Norton, 1986), 177, 240.

43. Ira M. Lapidus, "State and Religion in Islamic Societies," *Past and Present*, 151, May 1996, 24.

44. Lewis's paper of October 1953, "Communism and Islam," is reprinted in Walter Laqueur, ed., *The Middle East in Transition: Studies in Contemporary History* (New York: Praeger, 1958), 321. Walter Lippmann, who is sometimes credited with popularizing the label of *cold war* for U.S.-Soviet rivalry, made reference to the *Dar al-Harb* and the *Dar al-Islam*, citing Gustave E. Von Grunebaum, *Medieval Islam* (Chicago: University of Chicago Press, 1926) in a letter to Quincy A. Wright, professor of international law at the University of Chicago. Von Grunebaum observed: "Between this 'area of warfare' and the Muslim-dominated part of the world there can be no peace." In contrast to Lewis, Lippmann found more grounds for peace both with Islam and, by analogy, with the Soviet Union: "
"After the first century of conquest the relation between Islam, the Greek empire and the western empire became fairly well stabilized for many centuries. The only point of the analogy is that the doctrine of universal conquest and conversion has never been abandoned and yet no one would think of measuring the role of Islam in the world simply by its aspirations." Elsewhere, however, Lippmann lapsed into the usual Western fears. "Our aim," he wrote Admiral Forrest P. Sherman, "should be not to encourage the unity of the Arab world and of Islam, but to keep it divided . . . a united Mohammedan world must in the end expel the western powers from all its territories . . . " See John Morton Blum, ed., *Public Philosopher: Selected Letters of Walter Lippmann* (New York: Ticknor and Fields, 1985), 505 and 508.

45. Lewis, "Communism and Islam," 320.

46. John T. Flynn, *The Lattimore Story: The Full Story of the Most Incredible Conspiracy of Our Time* (New York: Devin-Adair, 1953).

47. See Jackson's response to testimony of Bernard Lewis in Hearings before the Subcommittee on National Security and International Operations of the Committee on Government Operations United States Senate (Ninety-second Congress) (first session, part 4, March 17, 1971) (Washington, D.C.: U.S. Government Printing Office, 1971), 100–101, 114.

48. Huntington, *The Clash of Civilizations*, 258.

49. Ibid., 263.

50. "Quotes of Note," *Boston Globe*, February 23, 2002, A15.

51. See Khaled Abou El Fadl, "The Place of Tolerance in Islam," *Boston Review*, 26.6, December 2001–January 2002, 34–36.

52. Jonathan Fox, "Two Civilizations and Ethnic Conflict: Islam and the West," *Journal of Peace Research*, 38.4, July 2001, 459–472, especially the chart on 464.

53. Huntington, *The Clash of Civilizations*, 256.

54. Fred Halliday, "Kabul's Patriarchy with Guns: Fighters Armed by Pakistan Have Turned the Afghan Capital Into a No-Woman's Land," *Nation*, November 11, 1996, 20.

55. Alexander Cockburn, "Oil and the Taliban," *Nation*, November 11, 1996, 9.

56. Ahmed Rashid, *Taliban: Militant Islam, Oil, and Fundamentalism in Central Asia* (New Haven: Yale Nota Bene/ Yale University Press, 2000), 46, 84–85, 135.

57. Bin Laden quoted by Rashid, *Taliban*, 132.

58. Pakistani civil servant quoted by Nawaf E. Obaid, "Improving U.S. Intelligence Analysis on the Saudi Arabian Decision Making Process," [submitted to Ambassador Ronald Neuman, Deputy Assistant Secretary, Bureau of Near Eastern Affairs, U.S. Department of State], John F. Kennedy School of Government paper, 1998, 30. According to the author, "This document originally contained classified information and has been altered from the original in order to prepare it for public use."

59. Rashid, *Taliban*, 85.

60. For background on U.S. efforts to employ the Islamic right in hopes of slaying communism and Nasserism, see Vijay Prashad, *War Against the Planet: The Fifth Afghan War, Imperialism, and Other Assorted Fundamentalisms* (New Delhi: LeftWord, 2002), especially 69–81.

61. Data from Richard F. Grimmett, "Conventional Arms Transfers to Developing Nations, 1992–1999," Congressional Research Service/Library of Congress, August 18, 2000, especially 23 and 44. In his zeal to promote the rise of an international Islamic-Confucian alliance, Huntington is forced to minimize historic tensions between Muslims and China's rulers, including the two great Muslim uprisings that convulsed the Southwest and Northwest during the nineteenth century, as well as Beijing's contemporary conflicts with the Muslims of Sinkiang. For fifteen years, Tu Wen-hsiu, the self-proclaimed "Sultan Suleiman," ruled over a secessionist Muslim regime in nineteenth-century Yunnan Province. For PRC relations with the nation's Islamic populace, see Dru C. Gladney, *Muslim Chinese: Ethnic Nationalism in the People's Republic* (Cambridge: Council on East Asian Studies/ Harvard University Press, 1991).

62. See Grimmett, "Conventional Arms Transfers," 36 and 58. His figures for arms deliveries to Saudi Arabia are in current U.S. dollars (year 2000). Earlier the *Chicago Tribune* (March 2, 1997) pointed out that "A $6 billion order of 60 to 70 new fighter jets was on hold, at least until the oil-rich kingdom got its financial house in order. Did that upset Bethesda, Md.-based Lockheed Martin Corp., maker of the hot-selling F-16? Hardly. Its Ft. Worth factory already has a backlog of 400 jets, the biggest in history. Almost all are from overseas

orders." The article adds that "Intensive lobbying in 1995 helped the industry win a $15 billion foreign sales loan-guarantee program, championed by Sen. Christopher Dodd (D-Conn.)," one of the most liberal members of Congress. To the apparent delight of U.S. policymakers and the arms lobby, Saudi Arabia spent 14.2 percent of GDP on military expenditures in 1994, 13.8 percent in 1995, and 13 percent in 2000 , well over four times the world average of 3.0 percent (1994) and 2.8 percent (1995). Data from "Statistics, Saudi Arabia," *Britannica Online* (accessed March 2, 1998, and January 24, 1999) and *CIA World Factbook* 2001.

63. See an earlier version of her work, Fatema Mernissi, "Palace Fundamentalism and Liberal Democracy: Oil, Arms and Irrationality," *Development and Change*, 27.2, 1996, 257. The inline reference (within the body of the essay) appears on p. 104.

64. See Huntington's essay, "The Age of Muslim Wars," in the "Special Davos Edition" of *Newsweek* (December 2001—February 2002). This essay also appeared in the "Issues 2002" supplement of *Newsweek* (December 17, 2001). For a devastating critique of the shifts in Huntington's analysis after September 11, see Tariq Ali, *The Clash of Fundamentalisms: Crusades, Jihads, and Modernity* (London: Verso, 2002), 281–283.

65. Huntington's promotion of RDF interventions is quoted from S.P. Huntington, et. al., "Vietnam Revisited," *International Security*, Summer 1981, 25–26.

66. During his February 1998 talk at the Harvard Book Store, Huntington claimed to have told Turkish elites this view.

67. Huntington, *Clash of Civilizations*, 198, 204.

68. Samuel P. Huntington, "The United States" in Michael J. Crozier, Samuel P. Huntington, and Joji Watanuki, *The Crisis of Democracy: A Report on the Governability of Democracies to the Trilateral Commission* (New York: New York University Press, 1975), 61–62, 102, 113–114. The term *excess of democracy* was taken by Huntington from the historian David Donald in his writings on Jacksonian democracy.

69. Samuel P. Huntington, *American Politics: The Promise of Disharmony* (Cambridge: Harvard University Press, 1981), 75. My thanks to Noam Chomsky and David Barsamian for this reference. Barsamian employed the Dracula metaphor to explain Huntington's theory of power to his alternative radio audience.

70. Huntington, *The Clash of Civilizations*, 307.

71. Irving Kristol, "My Cold War," *The National Interest*, Spring 1993, 143–144. Kristol's article come from his remarks at a conference in 1992.

72. Norman Podhoretz, *Ex-Friends* (New York: Free, 1999), 21.

73. Kristol, "My Cold War."

74. Peregrine Worsthorne, "Liberalism Is the Real Enemy," *Sunday Telegraph*, October 18, 1992, 28.

75. Dinesh D'Souza, *The End of Racism* (New York: Free, 1995), 504. Elsewhere in
     The End of Racism D'Souza argues that "the pathologies of black culture sug-
     gest that the racists were right all along. . . . What blacks need to do is to 'act
     white,' which is to say, to abandon idiotic back-to-Africa schemes and embrace
     mainstream cultural norms so that they can effectively compete with other
     groups." Black conservative Robert Woodson described D'Souza's work as
     "Fuhrmanesque." Quoted by Amy Elizabeth Ansell, *New Right, New Racism:
     Race and Reaction in the United States and Britain* (New York: New York Uni-
     versity Press, 1997), 95.

76. Letter of Dinesh D'Souza, *Weekly Standard*, October 2, 1995. The recent mas-
     sive decline in the U.S. crime rate (for instance, murders at the lowest level in
     three decades by the end of 1998) has done little to moderate his claims that civ-
     ilizational decorum has given way to a vicious, drooling savagery.

77. "The Islamic-Confucian Connection," interview with S. P. Huntington, *New
     Perspectives Quarterly*, 10.3, June 22, 1993.

78. Irving Kristol, "The Tragedy of Multiculturalism," *Wall Street Journal*, July 31,
     1991, 15.

79. Don Juan Manuel, quoted by Fred Halliday, *The Making of the Second Cold
     War* (London: Verso, 1986), 5.

80. Kristol, "My Cold War."

81. Samuel P. Huntington, "The Erosion of American National Interests," *Foreign
     Affairs*, 76.5, September/October 1997, 28–49.

82. For a discussion of diaspora lobbies and immigration control, see Christian
     Joppke, "Why Liberal States Accept Unwanted Immigration," *World Politics*,
     50.2, 1998, 266–293.

83. Lothrop Stoddard, *The New World of Islam* (New York: Scribner's, 1923), 23–24,
     112, and 310.

84. Lothrop Stoddard, *Racial Realities in Europe* (New York: Scribner's, 1925), 239.

85. Robert J.C. Young, *Colonial Desire: Hybridity in Theory, Culture, and Race*
     (London: Routledge, 1995), 27–28.

86. See Dan Seligman and Charles Murray, "As the Bell Curves," *National
     Review*, December 8, 1997, 42–44, 60. Murray adds that "welfare reform is help-
     ing the argument along, by the way, as journalistic accounts reveal how many
     welfare mothers are not just uneducated but of conspicuously low intelligence.
     The intractability of IQ? Dick [Herrnstein] and I said that IQ was 40 to 80 per-
     cent heritable. . . . For practical purposes, the ability of public policy to affect
     IQ is probably smaller than Dick and I concluded. . . . It is not just that Dick
     and I will be proved right. We will be proved to have been—if you pardon the
     expression—conservative."

87. Royal Commission on Population Report (Cmd. 7695) (London: HMSO,
     1949), 226, paragraphs 650–651.

88. Paul Blanshard, *Communism, Democracy, and Catholic Power* (Boston: Beacon, 1951), 285–286. Blanshard's books of 1949, 1951, and 1960 deliver muscular endorsements of eugenics, as he excoriates the Roman Catholic hierarchy for opposing sterilization of the feeble-minded and other social misfits. His hearty enthusiasm for eugenic hygiene suggests that liberals may not have fully absorbed the lessons of Nazism as immediately as suggested in most mainstream accounts. Indeed the social and political movements of the 1960s may deserve some credit for curtailing eugenics, a practice that included the sterilization of habitual criminals and so-called morons.

A former associate editor of the *Nation* and its correspondent on the Holy See, Blanshard also introduces the concept of "cultural imperialism" on page 296 to describe the Vatican's international influence and educational policy. This is curious because most major studies of "cultural imperialism" trace the concept's origins to the 1960s, i.e., John Tomlinson, *Cultural Imperialism* (Baltimore: Johns Hopkins University Press, 1991).

His work follows a syllogism close to that of Bernard Lewis on the harmony between Islam and communism: "The Vatican has cultivated in millions of men that authoritarian mind which leans for support on received dogmas. That is the type of mind on which Stalin rests his vast domain, and it is not an accident that in many parts of Europe the passage of men from Catholicism to Communism has been so effortless. When the largest Communist Party outside of the Soviet Union develops in the home country of the Vatican, and captures the devotion of millions of 'Catholics,' the moral cannot be ignored" (298).

See also Paul Blanshard, *American Freedom and Catholic Power* (Boston: Beacon, 1949), and Paul Blanshard, *God and Man in Washington* (Boston: Beacon, 1960).
89. Huntington, "The Erosion of American National Interests," 29.
90. See Keith B. Richburg, "Official Worked on Book that Criticizes Blacks: Copyright Chief Disputes Association with 'Jungle' Thesis," *Washington Post*, May 1,1985, A3.
91. Judith Miller, *One, By One, By One: Facing the Holocaust* (New York: Simon and Schuster, 1990), 147.
92. LePen quoted by Diana Johnstone, "A New Vogue for the Extreme Right," *In These Times*, April 23, 1986.
93. For testimonials of Safire and Lewis, see the bookjacket of *One, by One, by One*. For Miller's debt to Lewis, see acknowledgments of this book, 306.
94. The Grand Mufti and El-Essawy quoted by John Esposito, *The Islamic Threat: Myth or Reality?* rev. ed (New York: Oxford University Press, 1995), 210–211.
95. For observations on Cedar Rapids, see *Christian Science Monitor*, January 29, 1996, 1, and Esposito quoted in edition of January 22, 1996, 9. A large social science literature indicates that the inability of immigrants to assimilate is more

often the result of the host country than the behavior and traditions of the immigrants. For instance, a study of Kwantung-province Chinese immigrants to New York and Lima, Peru found that the Lima Chinese were swiftly assimilated, spoke Peruvian Spanish, and had fluid social interaction, while in the United States the Chinese faced a heavy burden of discrimination (restrictive laws on immigration, miscegenation laws, rampant injustices in housing and employment). They found themselves confined largely to Chinatown as well as to economic enterprises without intense white labor competition; i.e., restaurants, laundries, personal service, and garment production. "All things considered, there are far fewer discriminatory immigration policies against the Chinese in Peru than in the United States," concluded Bernard Wong in his research essay, "A Comparative Study of the Assimilation of Chinese in New York City and Lima, Peru," *Comparative Studies in Society and History*, 20, 1978, 343.

96. It is worth observing that Huntington himself does not regard pop culture and Sony Walkman-type gadgetry as having deep influence. In contrast to religion, which leaves an imprint for several millennia, pop culture for him is shallow and ephemeral. Huntington may be different from Lewis who judges Western techno-superiority to be terribly wounding for Islamic peoples.

97. "World Still Dangerous, Quayle Tells Midshipmen," *Washington Post*, May 31, 1990, B3.

98. Clare Hollingworth, "Another Despotic Creed Seeks to Infiltrate the West," *International Herald Tribune*, September 9, 1993. Hollingworth's defense punditry is apparently well rewarded by the powers that be. As Peregrine Worsthorne writes in his "China Diary: In Search of Confucian China," *Sunday Telegraph*, August 6, 1995: "Wednesday morning, Hong Kong. Great welcome from Clare Hollingworth. She has been lent the chairman of Cathay Pacific's chauffeur-driven Jaguar, which wafts us to the Mandarin Hotel in great style."

99. Shadia Drury, *Leo Strauss and the American Right* (New York: St. Martin's, 1997), 23–24.

100. Huntington abstract, *Foreign Affairs*, September/October 1997, 1.

101. Lewis tribute is found on the back cover of Allan Bloom, *The Closing of the American Mind: How Higher Education Has Failed Democracy and Impoverished the Souls of Today's Students* (New York: Simon and Schuster, 1987).

102. Terry Eagleton, *Criticism and Ideology* (London: Verso, 1978 [1976]), 134–135.

103. Rhodes's description of England in 1899 quoted by William Langer, *The Diplomacy of Imperialism, 1890–1902*, 2d ed. (New York: Knopf, 1956), 79. See Vindex (pseud. John Verschoyle), *Cecil Rhodes: His Political Life and Speeches, 1881–1900* (London, 1900), 7, 642. To be fair, there were several Liberal opponents of imperialism, most notably J. A. Hobson, whose objections were some-

times marred by antisemitic outburst and Gustave LeBon-like portrayals of the masses. For a cartography of the major schools of British Liberalism, see Peter Clarke, *Liberals and Social Democrats* (Cambridge: Cambridge University Press, 1978), especially page 2, which warns against the "misleadingly right-wing image" attached to its adherents. The reasons for the rise of eugenics have been hard to establish. For an account that identifies elite fears of majority-rule democracy, see Gerald Sweeney, *"Fighting for the Good Cause": Reflections on Francis Galton's Legacy to American Heriditarian Psychology* (Philadelphia: Transactions of the American Philosophical Society, 2001), vol. 91, part 2, chapter 4.

104. Rhodes's "Confession of Faith" (1877) is quoted at length by Robert I. Rotberg, *The Founder: Cecil Rhodes and the Pursuit of Power* (New York: Oxford University Press, 1988), 100.

105. See the discussion of Moynihan and Oscar Lewis in Adolph Reed Jr., "The New Victorians: Persistence of Racist-based Theories of Public and Foreign Policy," *Progressive*, February 1994. My essay and argument about U.S. liberalism owes a substantial debt to Reed.

106. *New York Times*, May 9, 1997.

107. Steven Weinberg, *Facing Up: Science and Its Cultural Adversaries* (Cambridge: Harvard University Press, 2001), 181–183. Weinberg's essay originally appeared in the *New Republic* "Zionism at 100" issue of September 8–15, 1997. See also Theodor Herzl, *The Jewish State: An Attempt at a Modern Solution of the Jewish Question*, trans. Sylvie D'Avigdor (London: Henry Pordes, 1993 [1895]), 30. Herzl adds: "Suppose His Majesty the Sultan were to give us Palestine, we could in return undertake to regulate the whole finances of Turkey."

108. For an amusing critique of Coulter's logic, see the cartoon "This Modern World by Tom Tomorrow" in *Extra!* March/April 2002, 3.

109. Leon Wieseltier, "Palestinian Perversion of the Holocaust," *New York Times*, June 12, 1988, 4:27.

110. Peter Novick, *The Holocaust in American Life* (New York: Houghton Mifflin, 2000 [1999]), 158.

111. Bush quoted in Ann Devroy, "Bush Denies Preparing U.S. for War; President Continues to Express Outrage at Hostage Treatment," *Washington Post*, November 2, 1990.

112. Among the chants that resounded throughout the congregation: "We are all Goldsteins!" and "Arabs out of Israel!" Calling Baruch Goldstein "the greatest Jew alive," Shmuel Hacohen, a teacher in a Jerusalem college, rejoiced in the massacre: "I think it was necessary, and it's necessary to kill a lot more. . . . There are no innocent Arabs here." See Scott Kraft, "Extremists Pay Tribute to Killer of 48 at Funeral," *Los Angeles Times*, February 28, 1994, A1; and David Hoffman, "Extremists Laud Gunman as 'Hero': Hard Core of Settlers Defends Attack as Part of Anti-Arab Struggle," *Washington Post*, February 28, 1994, A1.

113. Katz quoted by Israel Shahak and Norton Mezvinsky, *Jewish Fundamentalism in Israel* (London: Pluto, 1999), 104.

114. Goldstein quoted by Fred Halliday, *Islam and the Myth of Confrontation: Religion and Politics in the Middle East* (London: Tauris, 1995), 245, n. 76.

115. Preuss quoted by Shahak and Mezvinsky, *Jewish Fundamentalism in Israel*, 106.

116. Voltaire quotations are discussed by Tomaž Mastnak, *Islam and the Creation of European Identity* (London: University of Westminster Press/ CSD Perspectives/ Centre for the Study of Democracy Research Papers, no. 4, Autumn 1994), 39–40.

The Clash of Civilizations: An Islamicist's Critique

Roy P. Mottahedeh

The twentieth century had two great prophet-philosophers of history, Spengler and Toynbee. Each of them spoke to the West about its future after a major change in circumstance and prophesied for the West on the basis of a long historical view of the destiny of civilizations, and both led careers that spanned the world of scholarship and public policy. Both of them started out as historians but came to despise their fellow professional colleagues as narrow-minded slaves of detail who made niggling objections to their larger schemes. Now, Samuel Huntington, a political scientist who has plunged into history, seems ready to join this pantheon. In his celebrated article, "The Clash of Civilizations?" published in *Foreign Affairs* and later expanded as a book, Huntington also reflects on the course of civilizations, past and, more especially, future. As a by-product he has given the United States of the 1990s what it most desires: a principle with which to make order of the post–cold war era, and a sense of purpose. It is, moreover, a testimony to the protean creativity of its highly intelligent author that he has not fallen captive to the "scientism" that has fostered so many arid debates in the discussion of foreign policy. The clash of civilizations thesis has also strengthened the reintroduction of culture into the discussion of politics; the development theories of the 1960s, which heavily discounted culture, now seem sadly naive.[1]

As a historian, I very much hope that Samuel Huntington will remain an empiricist and care about detail. Ultimately, Spengler's contempt for empiricism made him an honorable but largely irrelevant episode in twentieth-century thought. Toynbee, who maintained throughout that he was an empiricist and tried mightily to be civil to his professional detractors, could not accommodate, or even take in, the many (largely empirical) criticisms of his work; the judgment of most professional historians was summed up by the English historian John Kenyon, who wrote that "the great Toynbee Cult, which some had seen as an indirect threat to Western civilization, proved less enduring and no more significant in the long run than the similar Tolkien Cult."[2]

The heart of the Huntington thesis lies precisely in the claim, based on a trend Professor Huntington attempts to establish empirically that, in a new phase of world politics, culture will be the mainspring of the great divisions among peoples and the "dominating" source of international conflict. According to Huntington (who is strongly influenced by Toynbee's categorization of civilizations), at present the major civilizations are the Western, Confucian, Japanese, Islamic, Hindu, Slavic Orthodox, Latin American, and—possibly—African. "Western ideas of individualism, liberalism, constitutionalism, human rights, equality, liberty, the rule of law, democracy, free markets, and the separation of church and state often have little resonance in Islamic, Confucian, Japanese, Hindu, Buddhist or Orthodox cultures." (It is interesting that Buddhism appears as a fugitive category throughout the article.) The policy implications are clear: "The fault lines of civilizations are the battle lines of the future." The West must be accommodating to "alien" civilizations, if possible, but confrontational if necessary. For this purpose the United States must forge alliances with similar cultures. Whereas Huntington hopes to "incorporate" into the West societies in Eastern Europe and Latin America, there is—apparently—no such hope in the near future for the rest of the non-West. In the case of the Confucian and Islamic world the West must "limit" the expansion of their military strength by, among other measures, maintaining "military superiority in East and Southwest Asia" and by seeking "to exploit differences and conflicts among Confucian and Islamic states." But, in the final analysis, "all civilizations should learn to tolerate each other."

Huntington's thesis is arresting because it offers a broad picture of world events that seems to be supported by a wealth of examples. Yet for an Islamicist—a scholar whose primary interest touches in some way on the Islamic world—some of the examples taken from the Islamic world are far more ambiguous than they first appear, and counterexamples seem abundantly to hand. Not only is the "empirical" basis of the thesis a matter for dispute, but the theoretical structure proposed to explain the relation between "culture" and political behavior seems to the present author very much open to question. And, unfortunately, some of these examples are presented in a way that unwittingly panders to the less constructive stereotypes of the history of the non-Western world.

For example, in his capsule history of the Islamic world Huntington tells us that after "the Arab and Moorish surge west and north, the Crusaders attempted with temporary success to bring Christianity and Christian rule to the Holy Land." As Professor Huntington knows but the less informed reader of this sentence may forget, the Crusaders could not bring Christianity to the Holy land when Christianity continued to exist (and profit from Christian pilgrimage) both in the Holy Land and in the rest of the Middle East because of the principle of tolerance toward Christians (as well as Jews) in Islamic law. As often as not the indigenous Christians of the Holy Land found Crusader Christian presence a burden since the Crusaders could be extremely intolerant of the indigenous Christian groups present there.

Huntington continues his history of the relations of the Islamic world and the West by giving an accurate summary of the relations between the Arab world (with one reference to Iran) and the West. He then concludes: "This warfare between Arabs and the West culminated in 1990, when the United States sent a massive army to the Persian Gulf." (Of course, the Egyptians, the Syrians, the Saudis, and other members of the Gulf Cooperation Council, Arab nations with a collective population many times Iraq's population, also sent troops.) "This centuries-old military interaction between the West and Islam is unlikely to decline. It could become virulent." While there have been efforts to introduce democracy, "the principle beneficiaries of these openings have been Islamist movements. In the Arab world, in short, Western democracy strengthens anti-Western political forces. This may be a passing phenomenon, but it surely complicates relations between Islamic countries and the West."

Of course Professor Huntington, in spite of the alternation between "Arab" and "Islamic" in these paragraphs, knows that the categories "Arab" and "Muslim" do not even approximately overlap. At the very most one in five Muslims is an Arab. (The Arab nations claim a population of about two hundred million out of the world's approximately one billion Muslims, but this number includes several millions of Berbers and Kurds. It also, incidently, includes at least fifteen million Christian Arabs, some of whom, such as George Habash, the leader of the PFLP, are considerably less sympathetic to the West than a Muslim such as Yasir Arafat.) Therefore, a summary history of the hostilities between the Arab world and the West by itself can hardly support the conclusion that "this centuries-old military interaction between the West and Islam is unlikely to decline." In fact, even if we were to concentrate only on the Mediterranean world and disregard such peripheral matters as the British conquest of Moghul India and the Dutch conquest of Indonesia, the most important conflict between Christians and Muslims of the past five centuries of Mediterranean history would seem to be the West's struggle with the Ottoman Turks, hardly an "Arab" opponent.

Yet an important intellectual problem is raised by the conflation of Arabs and Muslims at the conclusion of this summary history: "In the Arab world, in short, Western democracy strengthens anti-Western forces. This may be a passing phenomenon, but it surely complicates relations between Islamic countries and the West." Professor Huntington's idea of civilization is such that other Muslims should behave the way Muslim Arabs behave—but they do not. In early 1996, the two non-Arab parliamentary democracies in Muslim lands led by women prime ministers—Pakistan and Bangladesh—alone had a combined population of approximately two hundred and twenty million, significantly larger than that of the Arab world. Turkey, a parliamentary democracy, also led until recently by a woman prime minister, has a population of sixty million. Is it possible that, in spite of being fellow Muslims, the Muslims of South Asia and the Muslims of Turkey have a different political culture than Arab Muslims? I believe the case that they do have such individual political cultures to be overwhelming.

Even within the Arab world the principal beneficiaries of democratic openings have not always been the Islamists: Hasan Turabi, the Islamist ideologue of the present government of the Sudan, was unable to win a parliamentary seat when that country had a democratic system. Other Islamic countries offer many parallels: in Pakistan, for example, Islamists rode high under the authoritarian rule of Zia ul-Haq but had done poorly in popular elections before his time.

Huntington, in fleshing out his theory of "the bloody borders" of Islam, tells us that in Africa the conflict between "Arab Islamic" civilization and the non-Islamic peoples to the south, in the past "epitomized in the image of the Arab slave dealers and black slaves," is now "reflected in the on-going civil war in the Sudan between Arabs and blacks, the fighting in Chad between Libyan-supported insurgents and the government, the tension between Orthodox Christians and Muslims in the Horn of Africa, and [the] conflicts between Muslims and Christians in Nigeria." But the Ethiopians, the only substantial Christian community near the Horn of Africa, are Monophysite, a variety of Christians once vigorously persecuted and still regarded as scandalously heretical by the Eastern Orthodox. In Chad Goukouni Weddeye, a Muslim, received Libyan support, while his Muslim opponent Hissein Habré was supported by Sudan, Egypt, and Saudi Arabia as well as the United States. At certain stages, Libyan-backed Goukouni Weddeye had more sympathy in the non-Muslim south than his opponent, the anti-Libyan Habré, who had to reconquer the south before he drove the Libyans from the north. As one scholar of Libyan and Chadian affairs has remarked, while feelings among Muslims were a factor in the outbreak of civil war in Chad, "Islam proved a remarkably feeble counterweight to the divisive forces of ethnicity and regionalism."[3] As for the Arabs of the Sudan (which in Arabic means "land of the blacks"), they are in majority black by the understanding of the (admittedly artificial) racial categories used in the United States and Egypt, something that only victims of stereotypes about "white" Arab slave traders would forget. The "communal violence" between Muslims and Christians in Nigeria to which Huntington refers is very real, but for years it was overshadowed by the conflict between Mashood Abiola, the Yoruba Muslim from the south who won at the polls in 1992, and the military government, dominated in part by Muslims of the north, which cancelled the result of those elections.

For the Caucasus Professor Huntington offers us two examples of the Orthodox-Muslim conflict: one is "the violence between Ossetians and Ingush, and the other the unremitting slaughter of each other by Armenians and Azeris." While including the not very important example of the Muslim Ingush and the Ossetes, who are in majority Orthodox (although with a 20 to 30 percent Muslim minority), Professor Huntington neglects many far more important counterexamples. Under Gamsakhurdia's presidency, (Orthodox) Georgia waged a bloody war against its (largely Orthodox) Ossetian minority. Since Shevardnadze assumed leadership of Georgia in 1992 there have been efforts (not altogether successful) to heal this rift; meanwhile (Orthodox) Russia has helped the (largely Muslim) Abkhazians to declare themselves independent of (Orthodox) Georgia. No surprise that Georgia has felt more sympathy to (Muslim) Azerbaijan, which has been resistant to Russian influence. No surprise, either, that Iran—the archetypal Muslim state in Western thinking—has been so careful to be neutral in the struggle between Christian Armenians and Muslim Azerbaijanis, since Iran wishes to discourage Azerbaijani separatists within its own borders and sees friendship with Russia as a key to its foreign policy. Orthodox Russia, Christian Armenia— the majority of whose population has, for over a millennium, totally rejected the authority of the Orthodox churches as normally understood—and Islamic Iran are emerging as covert allies in Caucasian affairs.[4]

Central Asia is another arena in which Muslim-Orthodox differences have a weak explanatory power. Iran joined Russia and India in strongly backing the Rabbani government in Kabul against the more "Islamist" forces of the Taliban in Afghanistan. By and large Iran did not help Muslim religious rebels in Tajikistan, where it could have great influence because of shared language, but restricted its dealings to the pro-Russian official government. To view the relations of (Orthodox) Russia with its Caucasian and Central Asian neighbors, or even to view the relations between these neighbors as primarily a Muslim-Orthodox question is a bit like viewing American relations with the Caribbean and Central America as dominated by religious questions. Russia and the United States have strong geopolitical interests in what they consider their backyards, and in sorting out conflicts in these regions, religion, more often than not, has nothing to do with the case.

So far we have been discussing civilization largely as an explanation for lines of conflict. Now we should turn to civilization as an explanation for the motives of its "members." There is a very great danger that using the term *civilization* will lead us to underestimate the variety within that designation and the rapidity with which it can change over time. There is the even greater danger that units proposed as "civilizations" but still far from being proved to be such will be treated as realities before they are shown to be such. Professor Huntington allows that civilizations have "variants" and that they are "dynamic; they rise and fall; they divide and merge." But his overall message is that civilizations are highly stable units, each internally united by a large number of characteristics: "Differences among civilizations are not only real; they are basic. Civilizations are differentiated from each other by history, language, culture, tradition and, most important, religion. The people of different civilizations have different views on relations between God and man, the individual and the group, the citizen and the state, parents and children, husband and wife, as well as differing views of the relative importance of rights and responsibilities, liberty and authority, equality and hierarchy. These differences are products of centuries. They will not soon disappear."[5]

The degree to which each civilization is closely tied to its assumed primary carriers is brought home by a paragraph in Professor Huntington's reply to his critics in a subsequent issue of *Foreign Affairs*. He notes that "the Census Bureau estimates that by 2050 the American population will be 23 percent Hispanic, 16 percent Black and 10 percent Asian-American." In the past the United States has successfully absorbed immigrants because they have "adapted to the prevailing European culture and enthusiastically embraced the American Creed of liberty, equality, individualism, democracy. Will this pattern continue to prevail as 50 percent of the population becomes Hispanic or nonwhite?" There is, he feels, a real possibility that this Hispanic and nonwhite population may not adapt to European culture and the American Creed, which would lead to "the de-Westernization of the United States" because it will have become "truly multicultural and pervaded with an internal clash of civilizations" and therefore unable to survive as a liberal democracy. In this case, "the United States as we have known it will cease to exist and will follow the other ideologically defined superpowers onto the ash heap of history."[6] Why the 16 percent black Americans of 2050, overwhelmingly descended from black Americans who arrived here long before the Slavic, Italian, and other post–civil war white immigrant groups, are considered not only not successfully absorbed but a potential source of "de-Westernization" of the United States was left unexplained in Huntington's article.

Let us, however, examine one of the global traits that Professor Huntington ascribes to Islamic civilization. When Professor Huntington tells us that, "western ideas of free markets often have little resonance in Islamic (culture)," the "often" preserves him from a totalizing description, but what are we left with? Anyone who has read premodern Islamic law knows how frequently the saying of the Prophet Muhammad "God sets prices" is quoted, and how deeply suspicious this legal tradition is of price setting. The overwhelming majority of the pre-Ottoman Islamic societies of the Middle East were free market economies. Is Professor Huntington thinking of the use of price fixing in certain periods of Ottoman history? As a student of the Islamic world, I would guess (although without great conviction) that most Muslims in most places and in most periods were free marketeers. But I do know that in the 1950s and 1960s in many Muslim countries socialist leaders such as Sukarno and Nasser insisted that Islam was inherently socialist (another totalizing assumption) and created laws accordingly. In fact, Nasser had Shaykh Makhluf, the highest religious authority in Egypt, dismissed when Makhluf rejected Nasser's contention that Islam was essentially socialistic. Therefore I know that Muslims can oppose a free market and often have enthusiastically endorsed free markets. Although perfect market economies probably exist only in the minds of Chicago economists, at present, among Islamic Middle Eastern countries alone, relatively free markets exist in Morocco, Tunisia, Turkey, Kuwait, and most of the other Arab Gulf states. Can anyone say empirically that the idea of the free (or, for that matter, the controlled) market has "little resonance" in "Islamic civilization"? And, given the vast geographical spread and long historical varieties of the experience of Muslim peoples, is the question in any way useful—or even meaningful?

Behind this assumption of the very close ties between ideas and their assumed primary carriers are several other assumptions hard to accept. One is that people are not merely influenced, sometimes shallowly, sometimes very deeply, by their cultures, but are intellectually subjugated to them. Another is that ideas live most authentically in their place of origin. Thus Professor Huntington tells us that "the very notion that there could be a 'universal civilization' is a Western idea" and, we are to understand therefore, difficult to export; it is "at odds with the particularism of most Asian societies and their emphasis on what distinguishes one people from another."[7] Even historically this claim may be questionable, as Christianity and Islam—both, incidently, Near Eastern in origin—are proselytizing monotheisms with ambitions to convert the entire world. But even granting that (on some definition of civilization) "universal civilization" may well be a "Western idea," what does this tell us? Does it tell us that "particularisms of most Asian societies and their emphasis on what distinguishes one people from another" have an iron grip on the minds of Asians and that such Asians cannot, except in some remote future, make such alien concepts as "universal civilization" their own?

To many historians claims that cultures are largely impervious and that "imported" ideas flourish less fully and authentically outside their places of origin seem strange indeed. Does the idea of casting ballots in elections flourish more authentically in its country of origin, Greece, than in Great Britain? The idea of courtly love certainly existed in early Arabic literature and probably passed from there to the West; is Chaucer's *Troilus and Criseyde* therefore less authentically English and European? Pseudo-scientific theories of race and a rigorous idea of "the color bar" are also a European invention; have they proved impossible to export?

Professor Huntington tells us that "modern democratic government originated in the West. When it has developed in non-Western societies it has usually been the product of Western colonialism or imposition." For anyone who sees a culture or "civilization" as a set of handmade Russian nesting dolls, each of which is almost certain never to fit into any other set, this view of culture, which regards "cultural grafts" as suspect a priori, will be convincing. But, of course, culture is not made of nesting dolls or precisely shaped puzzle pieces, and large elements of Western culture introduced by colonialism, imposition, or mere imitation have developed deep and authentic roots in non-Western societies, to a degree that these societies often no longer sense these elements to be alien. Nothing in the premodern Islamic tradition drives modern Muslims to give the vote to women, and many Muslim conservatives opposed the enfranchisement of women. But in countries such as Turkey, Egypt, and Iran the overwhelming majority of Islamists—advocates of the reintroduction of some measure of Islamic law—would now never raise a whisper against votes for women, who form an important part of their constituents. Even Ayatollah Khomeini, though he had been opposed to the Iranian law of 1962 that enfranchised women, never suggested that Iran's new constitution, over which he could have exercised great power, should deny women the vote. The direct electoral participation of women is an irreversible fact in the life of many Islamic countries, regardless of whether or not it is an "imposition" and/or a "product of Western colonialism." The same can be said for written constitutions and national law codes.

The history of the West itself offers many striking illustrations of the sometimes gradual, sometimes rapid circulation of ideas from one area of the West to another, the virtual "colonization" of one part of the West by another, in a way that the nesting doll or rigid puzzle piece theory of culture would consider highly unlikely. And it also offers many examples of earlier Huntingtonians. It was once commonly said, for example, that democracy could only live fully and authentically in Protestant countries. The supposedly antiliberal nature of Catholicism was a significant element in the struggle between Protestants and Catholics in nineteenth-century Germany called the Kulturkampf. The struggle took its name from the words of Rudolf Virchow, who in 1873 declared in the Prussian diet, "The contest has taken on the character of a great cultural struggle," all of which should sound enchantingly familiar to the new theorists of "the West against the rest." It was "self-evident" to many Protestants that Catholics were obedient to the pope and could not be true democratic participants in a German state; anti-Catholic sentiment was so strong that Prussia enacted a law to expel all Jesuits. Many Americans will remember the joke that the Catholic politician Alfred E. Smith, on losing his bid for the presidency in 1928, telegraphed the pope to "unpack immediately." In America this distrust of Catholicism seems only to have died with the election of John F. Kennedy as president in 1960. In 1944 the most distinguished American Protestant theologian of his time, Reinhold Niebuhr, lamented the chasm "between the presuppositions of a free society and the inflexible authoritarianism of the Catholic religion."[8] To distrust the ability of sincere Catholics to be true democrats seems as quaint and fanciful to us at the end of the twentieth century as will seem, in a generation, our present distrust of the ability of sincere Muslims to be true democrats.

This tendency to assume that a group has uniformities of attitude that originate in its religious identity, changed only with the greatest difficulty, has an earlier and dark chapter in Western Christian assessments of the Jews. In 1782 David Michaelis, a German professor of Oriental languages at the University of Göttingen and reputed to be a Christian expert on the Jews, wrote: "Does the Law of Moses make citizenship, and the full integration of the Jew into other peoples, difficult or impossible? I think it does"! Soon, this line of thought reached its full development as a theory of culture and citizenship, as when Bruno Bauer, a German Protestant theologian, wrote in 1843: "Human rights are the result of education, and they can be possessed only by those who acquire and deserve them. Can the Jew really possess them as long as he lives as a Jew in perpetual segregation from others, as long as he therefore must declare that the others are not really his fellowmen? As long as he is a Jew, his Jewishness must be stronger in him than his humanity, and keep him apart from non-Jews. He declares by his segregation that this, his Jewishness, is his true, highest nature, which has to have precedence over his humanity."[9] It should be noted that Bauer's sense of alienation from Jews was purely cultural and not racial; hence Bauer's important influence on Karl Marx, who, although of Jewish origin, agreed that Jews should strip themselves of all "Jewishness" in order to join the body politic.

One last general observation would seem to weaken the strength of the Huntington thesis: its neglect of the distinction between peoples and governments. At the 1993 World Conference on Human Rights in Vienna the majority of Chinese organizations not controlled by the Chinese government supported the Dalai Lama's right to speak, which the Chinese government unyieldingly opposed. The Dalai Lama rejected the position of China and some other Asian and African countries that human rights in less developed countries need not be as liberal as elsewhere. "I do not share this view," he said, "and I am convinced that the majority of Asian people do not support this view either."[10] Are we really supposed to believe that the Chinese Communist government is more truly Buddhist and/or Confucian than the Chinese people and/or the Dalai Lama? The United States Congress has agreed to join the over one hundred nations that have ratified the 1948 convention on genocide only with reservations that nullify its commitments. Is this a sign that the American people are less truly attuned to the values of Western civilization than most other nations in the world or that our legislative process often ties us in knots?

The sad but shocking truth is that readers less sophisticated than Professor Huntington will use his thesis to feed fantasies already too prevalent about a massive coordinated Islamic movement that sees as its primary objective the humiliation of the West. Of course, in a community of a billion souls the Muslim world contains its analogues to our homegrown organizations of bigots such as the antisemitic Christian Patriot's Defense League in the United States or the diehard fanatics in Northern Ireland. But Muslims—marvelous to say—are human beings, subject to all the pulls of economic need, local community, and other interests that influence humans everywhere, and only lavish, ignorant, and sensationalizing uses of words like *fundamentalism* have blinded us to their humanity and diversity.

There is a group of Muslims, in my opinion very distinctly a minority, who are properly called Islamists, who call for some degree of reimposition of Islamic law and tend to view the West as a more or less unified and universal "alien civilization" to be treated in the spirit of the clash of civilizations thesis—with accommodation if possible, but with "confrontation" if necessary. (I do not speak here of the very small if noisy minority of militant extremist Muslims, who should not be allowed to set anyone's agenda for anything.) I strongly believe this group will remain a distinct minority, because it disregards the large historical variation in the Islamic tradition (even in the area of law), because its followers have large areas of internal disagreement, and because it has no real answers to the problems of economic and social justice that beleaguer the majority of Muslims.

In addition to the examples from the Caucasus, Balkans, and Central Asia cited above, certain recent events have shown us the very considerable diversity of opinion on foreign policy even among this minority of Muslims who are Islamists. This diversity was dramatically illustrated by the variety of

Islamist reactions to the Gulf crisis of 1990–1991. In Egypt the Muslim Brothers were for some time unable to agree on the crisis, since Saudi Arabians had long supported them, but many members found the sight of non-Muslims sorting out a quarrel between Muslim nations unacceptable. Tunisian Islamists were similarly divided. Jordanian Islamists followed King Hussein in taking a pro-Iraqi stance. The principal Turkish Islamist party was at first favorable to Saddam, but then its leaders, after a September meeting with King Fahd of Saudi Arabia, became either neutral or somewhat critical of Saddam.[11] Professor Huntington writes, however, that, "ignoring the rivalry between Iran and Iraq, the chief Iranian religious leader, Ayatollah Ali Khamenei, called for a holy war against the West."[12] In fact, Iranian actions, such as the seizure of the Iraqi aircraft that fled the fighting to land in Iranian airports, are a far better gauge of how mindful the Iranian leadership was of its eight-year war with Iraq. It is mistaken information indeed that has persuaded Samuel Huntington to write, "Islamic fundamentalist movements universally supported Iraq rather than the Western-backed governments of Kuwait and Saudi Arabia."

Many parallel cases, in which actual policy was determined by particularistic interests over pan-Islamic interests, will suggest themselves to anyone who follows the politics of nations in which Muslims are significantly represented. For example, Khomeini, for all his fierce rhetoric about Palestine, was far more concerned with Iraq. Ali-Akbar Mohtashemi, the Iranian ambassador to Syria in the early eighties and later the hard-line minister of the interior, in an interview in *Jahan-e Islam* claimed that in 1982 Khomeini personally stopped the Revolutionary Guard of Iran from going to Lebanon to fight Israel; "the Imam explained that it was not appropriate for Iran to confront Israel from a long distance without any common border, and to do a job that the Arabs themselves should do."[13]

A major problem in discussing the validity and/or importance of a thesis such as that proposed by Samuel Huntington is the weighing of evidence. Presumably, insofar as his examples of intercivilizational conflict prove to be incorrect—as for instance in the case of Chad—the evidence for his theory becomes thinner and the theory less sustainable. And, if ideas about civilizationwide traits, such as the presumed lack of "resonance" in Islamic civilization to Western ideas, turn out to be neither historically true nor true at present, the evidence for the Huntington thesis would seem to have less weight. At this point, however, a problem arises for everyone who seeks to evaluate the Huntington thesis. Non-Western civilizations are not likely to change soon, we are told, because they have been the way they are for a long time. At the same time, much of the evidence for the nature of their long-held traits is shown in their recent behavior. Moreover, the Huntington essay is in significant part a prophecy about the future.

About the evidence that the future will provide we can (or, at least, should) agree to be silent. But if "civilizations" have proved fairly rapidly adaptive to some imported institutions, as this essay argues many Islamic societies (including the minorities of Islamists) have proven to be (in, for example, accepting the enfranchisement of women), then which long-term traits are predictive of future behavior? There is a good argument to be made that such traits can be identified in local cultures (much smaller units than the proposed "civilizations"). We must hope that in his book Samuel Huntington will provide us with a theory that will explain why there is this significant variation in local adaptability to change within each civilization. Such an explanation would advance social theory immeasurably.

If, however, only very recent events count as evidence for such a theory, then how are we to weigh examples against counterexamples? Is the supposedly intercivilizational conflict between the Ossetes and the Ingush more or less important than the intracivilizational conflict between the Ossetes and the Georgians (and so on and so forth)? Of course, the world system was partly frozen in place by the cold war, and now is in motion again with an attendant number of small wars. But is this motion a new trend, or is it back to history all over again? The nineteenth century saw the expansion of some empires on the basis of (conflictingly described) civilizational missions, as well as the contraction of others, such as the Ottomans, who energetically (but, in the end, futilely) evoked a pan-Islamic and then a pan-Turkic civilizational claim. First, the case has to be made that long existing noncivilizational causes, such as the mutual distrust of Caucasian peoples, do not satisfactorily account for the conflicts brought forward as civilizational conflicts. Second, the truly abysmal record of civilizationwide movements, from pan-Slavism and pan-Islam in the nineteenth century to the international Islamic organizations of today, to deliver effective backing for political action will have to be accounted for.

Pan-Islamic movements have often loomed unaccountably large in the mind of the West. In 1916 a supposed expert on the Middle East, the American Samuel M. Zwemer, wrote in *Muhammad or Christ*: "The coming struggle will not be solely religious, but an educational, industrial, social, and political upheaval in which religion plays a chief part. It is a struggle between two civilizations; between the ideals of the Moslem world and those of Christendom."[14] In the First World War the opposing sides in Europe nurtured hopes that they could arouse Islamic holy wars led by the (pro-German) Ottomans or the (pro-British) Hashemites. These hopes aroused the Western European imagination far more than they aroused the Middle Eastern Islamic imagination. Huntington, who has been a pioneer in developing mathematical expression of political trends, will have to give us some basis on which to weigh the comparative importance of examples and to demonstrate that the examples he cites do, in fact, show a strong new trend and are not a miscellany that could be matched in the 1890s or 1910s.

One argument implicit in Huntington's proposal—namely, that his "civilizational approach" should be accepted because it has no plausible competitors that explain contemporary international politics—seems to me to be a complete nonstarter. In his reply to his critics Huntington tells us: "When people think seriously, they think abstractly; they conjure up simplified pictures of reality called concepts, theories, models and paradigms. Without such intellectual constructs, there is, William James said, only 'a bloomin' buzzin' confusion.'"[15] William James uses this phrase in only two places I know of, and in neither does he use it in the same sense as Huntington.[16] James seems to be arguing for the need for such basic concepts as "sea" or "grass" in order for us, in his terminology, to "disassociate" discrete elements from the continuum of perception—the blooming, buzzing reality he assumes that babies feel. He goes on to say that our desire to harmonize these concepts leads to "explanatory systems." If people fail to find an explanatory system, however, it does not mean that they have regressed to seeing the world as a "blooming, buzzing confusion." When Locke saw states living in a world of unregulated competition and wrote that "the whole community is one body in the state of nature in respect to all other states," he had not with that remark entered his second infancy.[17]

Even if we were to assume that our perception of international relations would be a "blooming, buzzing confusion" without an "explanatory system," however, we need not follow Huntington's claim that his theory is better than others because "intellectual and scientific advance, as Thomas Kuhn showed, consists of the displacement of one paradigm, which has become increasingly incapable of explaining new or newly discovered facts, by a new paradigm that accounts for those facts in a more satisfactory fashion." Margaret Masterman, in an essay Kuhn has largely endorsed, has shown that Kuhn uses *paradigm* in a number of different ways, but only rarely as a hypothesis, pure and simple, although this understanding of *paradigm* seems to be the only one that has entered popular usage (which is one of several reasons that Professor Kuhn in his later years no longer used the term). What Kuhn is talking about, as he repeatedly says, is "normal science," so well accepted that experimenters who find results that contradict the paradigms of normal science blame themselves rather than "normal science."[18] For Kuhn a paradigm is never an individual possession but is constitutive of a group. No one doubts Huntington's enormous, perhaps unmatched, distinction among political scientists. But would even he, in the unlikely event that his modesty should fail him, claim that he has created a "normal" political science of international relations, in the face of which other political scientists discredit contrary examples?

A large number of international relations specialists continue to argue vigorously that Realism, the school of international relations that claims states act largely to protect their interests and are the predominant players in world politics, explains more events than any other. Against this theory Huntington has fielded some interesting possible counterexamples. Kuhn believes most of the social sciences to be in the preparadigm stage, in which examples and counterexamples are adduced and competing theories easily coexist. He writes: "In the physical sciences disagreement about fundamentals is, like the search for basic innovations, reserved for periods of chaos. It is, however, by no means equally clear that a consensus of anything like similar strength and scope ordinarily characterizes the social sciences." It is not clear that by Kuhn's standards either history or international relations will ever emerge from the preparadigm phase, but he offers historians like myself and other social scientists the wise advice: "As in individual development, so in the scientific group, maturity comes most surely to those who know how to wait."[19]

Yet does the clash of civilizations hypothesis actually offer us a theory, in William James's sense of an "explanatory system"? It seems to me far more a description (and prescription) than an explanatory system. It offers a long list of things that the West is—the bearer of individualism, liberalism, democracy, free markets, and the like—but, by and large, just tells us that the non-Western, in the great American language of the multiple choice test, is "none of the above." There are a few tantalizing hints, as when Huntington says that the Western notion of universal civilization is "at odds with the particularism of most Asian societies and their emphasis on what distinguishes one people from another." But even if we were to grant that particularism is nonexistent in the West or far weaker than in some unit transcivilizationally or geographically defined as "Asian," we are left with very little in the way of explanation as to why others act differently from the West, insofar as they do act differently. Huntington tells us that "civilizations are differentiated from each other by history, language, culture, tradition and, most important, religion." Is it, then, religion as a set of beliefs that determines social, economic, and political attitudes, and if so, are these beliefs really stable, determining the behavior of those who hold them, and clearly different from the list of beliefs Huntington ascribes to the West?

As an Islamicist, I believe that the result of our examination of the assumption about free markets given above could be multiplied manyfold. Islam exists as a normative set of beliefs chiefly at the level of Islamic law, which, as I have said, is very largely in favor of free markets. But I would not a priori expect this normative legal system actually to influence social and governmental behavior. If I did, I would be led into a set of totally mistaken assumptions about the behavior of Muslim societies in various times and places, past and present. As an Islamicist, it seems to me that to assume a set of normative beliefs over a vast area, such as a Huntingtonian civilization, is an extraordinarily difficult task even for the Islamic world, which supposedly had a normative system of law. This distinct variety among the cultures of Muslims was even true before the mid-nineteenth century, up to which time there was some limited uniformity in the training of legal experts in much of the Islamic world, a small but important "class" of bearers of this normative law. And, as a social historian, it seems to me an extraordinary assumption, even if we were to identify a large and clear set of normative beliefs for one of these civilizations, that these beliefs should easily determine the behavior of those who formally ascribe to them.[20] As someone born into an American Christian milieu and a product of twelve happy years of Quaker education, in order for me to believe that Christians when abused are supposed to turn the other cheek I must forget the example of almost all the Christians I have ever met.

If we set aside the problem of what beliefs shape a civilization and how they do so, we are still left with Huntington's definition of a civilization as the largest "identity"; the civilization is "the broadest level of identification with which he [i.e., one of its members] intensely identifies." If we disregard the question of intensity, this statement gives us a functional definition of civilization, and one that probably has more significance for Muslims than for most other groups identified by Huntington. But let us examine what this means for a specific people who are overwhelmingly Muslim: the Iranians. Why is one of the best known and most frequently quoted lines of Persian verse, "The sons of Adam are limbs of each other"? Is it possible that Iranians identify not only with Muslims but also, like the rest of us, with the human race? Over twenty years have passed since the "Islamic revolution" in Iran; if you asked Iranians individually, "Who are you?" I would guess that the first answer would be, "an Iranian," their identity, therefore, of greatest intensity. I would also guess that the great majority of Iranians would agree that, after twenty years of searching for an Islamic identity, the contents of such an identity (including the content of an Islamic foreign policy) is far less clear to them now than it has ever been.

Columbus died thinking that he had discovered the easternmost parts of Asia; his discovery is no less considerable for his mistake. Huntington has discussed the revival of identity politics, even if this identity is usually (though not always) felt "intensely" in units far smaller than his "civilizations." The social and economic revolutions of recent history have swept aside traditional elites in many parts of the world, and the revolution in communications and education has persuaded peoples all over the globe to assert themselves directly in a wider political world, and not through the intermediacy of elites. At first, many of these new political actors will form groups based on a variety of identities. In some cases such an identity will take its name from a religious group, as in Bosnia, where membership in the category Muslim has nothing to do with actual religious belief. (In Bosnia, many so-called Muslims are agnostics or atheists.) In other places, as in the Caucasus, identity seems overwhelmingly to correspond to language, so that a group such as the Ossetes, in majority Christian and in minority Muslim, nevertheless feel a strong ethnic identity and have, by and large, worked in concert. Overlapping identities are a feature of all societies and asking questions appropriate to these identities will yield different answers. Mexico, considered as a state that belongs to NAFTA, to Latin America, to the successor states of the Aztecs, to the Catholic world, and so on and so forth, will yield different explanations for its conduct in its international relations as each of those identities is considered; is it really evident that any of these identities has clear primacy for all major questions? Might not NAFTA, in some respects a weak identity, still be the central identity for a discussion of economic foreign policy?

Some identities are, indeed, transnational, and hence, to use Huntington's felicitous phrase, transnational "resonances" exist. They have some (though, more often than not, secondary) importance in explaining political behavior. Orthodox Russia feels a certain sympathy for Orthodox Serbia, Catholic Europe for Catholic Croatia, and the Muslim world for Muslim Bosnia, although invoking these three civilizational ties would lead us only a very limited way toward understanding outside reaction to the tragedy that unfolded in the former Yugoslavia. Yet in Bosnia, where the United States proved the decisive outside actor, as in Northern Ireland and so many other places, these animosities based on identity seem only to flourish when they are cultivated by desperate leaders. Many observers believe that, without Milosevic's use of "Serbian" identity, Yugoslavia might well not have unraveled. Not the least contribution of Professor Huntington is that he has increased our ability to see that appeals by leaders to the defense of "cultural" values may be increasingly used by politicians (as seems to be the case in the United States). Politicians, like writers of panegyrics, tend to be maximizers, who use every claim possible to achieve some minimal credibility. Perhaps we are reentering a period in which claims that are in some loose sense "cultural" have become more frequent. Necessarily, such a contention is hard to quantify, but if demonstrated, it offers an important insight into contemporary politics.

It would, however, be a very great mistake to buy into the cultural claims of these desperate leaders and to construct policy on their claims. As for the policy recommendation that we should seek "to exploit differences and conflicts among Confucian and Islamic states," we hope that Professor Huntington is only thinking of the pan-Asiatic games. Some of us, perhaps including Professor Huntington, actually believe that the United States has higher interests than seeking the exploitation of harmful conflicts. If we were to discover a secret memorandum circulated among the Chinese leadership that claimed a policy interest in exploiting "differences and conflicts" between Catholics and Protestants in Northern Ireland, or between the races in the United States, we would want further explanation as to what was intended. Professor Huntington, whose intentions are surely benign, should not be surprised that this aspect of his recommendations for policy has aroused great suspicion in the parts of the world he characterizes as "Confucian" and "Islamic."

By early August 1990 Saddam Hussein's initial rationale for the invasion of Kuwait—that he had come at the invitation of a "Free Kuwaiti Interim Government"—had collapsed because no Kuwaiti collaborators could be found. On August 10 Saddam decided to play the "civilizational card," as

Huntingtonian theory would have predicted, and called for an Islamic "holy war" against "aggressive invaders" and their "collaborators." He based his call in part on the linkage he claimed to have established between his withdrawal from Kuwait and Israeli withdrawal from the occupied territories. Saddam had a long record as a secularist who advocated the complete divorce of religion from politics, and he was nobody's model of a pious Muslim. Yet he found a certain, though decidedly limited (and ultimately ineffectual), response among Muslims to his call for a holy war. It has taken one of our most perceptive political scientists to show us that, for some political leaders at the end of the twentieth century, civilizationalism, and not nationalism, has become the last refuge of scoundrels.

It is, perhaps, appropriate in our conclusion to return to our two prophet-philosophers of history. Spengler believed that each culture has its unique "soul" and, hence, sought to define that soul; he also believed decline to be the result of the betrayal of that soul. (Strangely, in the German context he saw parliamentary democracy as the great betrayal.) Toynbee, like Spengler, was driven to his civilizational analysis by the shock of the First World War. But, unlike Spengler, who was a deep pessimist, Toynbee was optimistic about the coming of a successor civilization to the West. Toynbee, who struggled mightily—but not always successfully—to avoid ethnocentrism, believed that alien elements in the West such as "Negro rhythms" were evidence of its decline. (The spirit of jazz might have done a lot for Toynbee's impressive—but ultimately exhausting—stately prose style.) Since Toynbee saw many civilizations as emanating from religious and/or cultural bases, he had to classify the more ancient minority religions still living as "fossilized relics." These fossils of earlier civilizations included "the Monophysite Christians of Armenia, Mesopotamia, Egypt, and Abyssinia and the Nestorian Christians of Kurdistan and Malabar, as well as the Jews and Parsees," to which he subsequently added "the Lamaistic Mahayana Buddhists of Ceylon, Burma, and Siam, as well as the Jains in India."[21] This somewhat strange list (are Armenians and Jews really so unlike the peoples surrounding them as to be described as "fossilized relics"?) shows that even an extremely learned would-be empiricist such as Toynbee could be led astray by a mania for order. Such manias, alas, have all too often led theorists like Toynbee to strain the evidence in order to discover lists of traits that "essentially" characterize the units they call "civilizations." (In this respect Toynbee came in the end to resemble Spengler, as a discoverer of the "souls" of civilizations, an approach he claimed to dislike.)

Samuel Huntington has raised the challenge for us to define in a really empirical fashion large transnational cultural entities, to explain to what degree their systems of belief affect their behavior, and to explain why various traits of these civilizations migrate, sometimes quickly, sometimes slowly, and sometimes not at all, between these entities. Only when this challenge has been met can there be any meaningful discussion on an academic level about the nature of the "West" and its relation with "the rest." But even if (as I very much doubt) it is empirically established that the "West" is a well-defined area that is the sole bearer of many beliefs, beliefs that will not for some time be adopted by other "civilizations," do we want to construct a policy of pessimism on this finding? If we were to discover growing racism in America, we would feel a sense of urgency to strive against it. Similarly, if there really is growing alienation between civilizations we should not limit ourselves to an austere policy that only in passing mentions accommodation when possible to "alien" civilizations. My reading of the American tradition is that we should seek to create such possibilities even if at first they seem impossible. We are too great a people to do anything less.

Notes

1. Samuel P. Huntington. "The Clash of Civilizations?" in *Foreign Affairs* 72.3 (1993). The author would like to thank several Harvard colleagues, Professors Edward Keenan, Roger Owen, Roderick MacFarquhar, and Thomas Scanlon, for their extremely useful comment on this paper. I would also like to thank the late Professor Thomas S. Kuhn of MIT. All opinions expressed here are, of course, entirely my own. Although I am a historian of the medieval Middle East, my interest in the comparative study of Islamic societies dates back to a conversation in 1961 in Afghanistan with Vartan Gregorian, to whom I dedicate this paper.

   This essay was composed in response to Samuel Huntington's 1993 *Foreign Policy* article "The Clash of Civilizations?" The editors have kindly provided reference to his later book. The essay in no way whatsoever attempts to discuss the book itself.

2. John Kenyon, *The History Men* (London, 1983), 282.

3. René Lemarchand, "Chad," in the *Oxford Encyclopedia of the Modern Islamic World* (New York, 1995), 1:276.

4. See the excellent article by Mohiaddin Mesbahi, "Russian Foreign Policy Security in Central Asia and the Caucasus," *Central Asian Survey* 12.2 (1993): 181–215.

5. Huntington, "The Clash of Civilizations?" 24–25.

6. Samuel P. Huntington, "If Not Civilizations, What?" in *Foreign Affairs* 72.5 (1993): 190.

7. Huntington, "The Clash of Civilizations?" 41.

8. Reinhold Niebuhr, *The Children of Light and the Children of Darkness: A Vindication of Democracy and a Critique of Its Traditional Defense* (New York, 1944), 319. I owe this quote to John T. McGreevy's forthcoming paper, "Thinking on One's Own."

9. Paul R. Mendes-Flohr and Jehuda Reinharz, eds., *The Jew in the Modern World: A Documentary History* (New York, 1980), 37 (Michaelis) and 263 (Bauer). These remarks are not meant to suggest that Professor Huntington's name can by any stretch of the imagination be associated with antisemitism or racism of any kind.

10. Associated Press report by Alexander G. Higgins, Vienna, June 15, 1993.

11. See François Burgat, "Islamists and the Gulf Crisis," in Dan Tschirgi, ed., *The Arab World Today* (Boulder, 1994), 205–211, and Roy P. Mottahedeh, "The Islamic Movement: The Case for Democratic Inclusion," in *Contention* 4.3 (1995): 107–127.

12. Huntington, "Clash of Civilizations?" 35.

13. Quoted by William Scott Harrop, "Iran's Revolutionary Paradox," *Mind and Human Interaction* 6.1 (February 1995): 26.

14. Samuel M. Zwemer, *Muhammad or Christ* (London, 1916), 121, 124. I am grateful to the ever learned Yvonne Haddad for calling these quotations to my attention.

15. Huntington, "If Not Civilizations, What?" 186.

16. William James, *Principles of Psychology*, vol. 1 (Cambridge: , 1981), 461, and *Some Problems in Philosophy* (Cambridge, 1979), 32.

17. John Locke, *The Second Treatise of Government*, chapter 12, paragraph 145. I had wrongly ascribed this quotation to Hobbes and thank my extremely kind friend, Professor Charles Miller, for correcting that assumption.

18. Margaret Masterman, "The Nature of a Paradigm," 59–89, and Thomas S. Kuhn, "Reflections on My Critics," 231–78, in *Growth of Knowledge* (Cambridge, 1970).

19. Thomas S. Kuhn, *The Essential Tension* (Chicago, 1977), 221–222.

20. One of the greatest anthropologists of our time, in comparing Morocco and Indonesia, discussed the extraordinary difficulty in identifying features of a society as Islamic; see Clifford Geertz, *Islam Observed* (New Haven: Yale University Press, 1968).

21. A. J. Toynbee, *A Study of History* (Oxford: Oxford University Press, 1934), 1:35.

Among the Mimics and the Parasites: V. S. Naipaul's Islam

Rob Nixon

Over a period of about two decades—from the early sixties until the late eighties—V. S. Naipaul accumulated a distinctive authority as a high cultural commentator on the shortcomings of the third world. His prestige as a novelist assisted him in sustaining his visibility as an interpreter of decolonizing and neocolonial societies during that era. However, by venturing into travel writing and journalism he garnered a reputation of a different order, one that went beyond the conventionally literary to the point where—in those border regions where British and American belles lettres meet popularized political thought—he was treated as a mandarin possessing a penetrating, analytic understanding of the third world. In short, he graduated into an "expert."

Thus a British reviewer of one of Naipaul's Indian books could credit him with defining "problems quicker and more effectively than a team of economists and other experts from the World Bank."[1] At a 1986 *Salmagundi* forum on "The Intellectual in the Post-Colonial World" (where Naipaul quickly became the obsessive topic), the impassioned exchanges centered on his authority as a political analyst rather than on the merits of his fiction.[2] So, too, when David Hare staged a theatrical debate of the international politics

This essay adapts and extends sections of my book, *London Calling: V. S. Naipaul, Post-colonial Mandarin* (New York: Oxford University Press, 1992). I wish to thank Emran Qureshi for inviting me to write this essay and for his very insightful suggestions.

of poverty between a reactionary Indian mandarin and a young, idealistic Britisher, Naipaul served as a direct model for the intellectual style of the play's conservative character.[3]

But it was in the wake of the Iran hostage crisis that Naipaul achieved his highest—and most dubious—authority. The hostage crisis, the appearance of Naipaul's anti-Islamic diatribe, *Among the Believers*, and his accumulative reputation as one of "them" who can think like one of "us," together propelled Naipaul onto the cover of *Newsweek*. From that moment onward he was constructed and invoked not just as a third world expert but as an expert Islamicist.

In many ways Naipaul has mellowed over the past decade. Moreover, in a post–cold war milieu that is virtually postcommunist, post-anticommunist, and postsocialist, the political positions that brought Naipaul fame and notoriety do not have the resonance they did fifteen or twenty years ago. The notable exception is his Islamaphobia, for Naipaul has periodically resurfaced in the role of expert Islamicist. He did so, for instance, during the Gulf War and again during the rise of Hindu religious fascism in the guise of the Bharatiya Janta Party (BJP) in the India of the 1990s.[4] On such occasions Naipaul's hostility toward a hugely generalized Islam remains basically unchanged.

Among the Believers appeared early in the Reagan era, when Islamaphobia was beginning to supplement anticommunism as the great animating hostility of American political life. Naipaul deployed the routine opposition between civilization and barbarism, to which he added from his own rhetorical repertoire the crucial notions of mimicry and parasitism. Mimicry, in Naipaul's usage, wavers between an explanation and an accusation. Through its protean appearances in *Among the Believers* and elsewhere in his writing, the term accrues some elaborate associations. Naipaul deploys the word primarily to characterize a condition of insecurity that he considers endemic to third world societies. On this account the fundamental insecurity of such societies derives from a weak sense of history, the shock of partial modernization, habits of dependent idleness inculcated during the colonial era, and grandiose dreams. The bewilderment and lack of resources in such societies prompt them to plunder the West for cultural and material values, political languages, and social institutions, all of which are appropriated in incongruous, denatured, and therefore risible forms.

In his various accounts of these processes, Naipaul studiously avoids introducing notions of imperialism or neocolonialism. If the concept of neocolonialism on its own could never wholly explain the many forms of

malaise in the third world, by the same token no adequate account of that
cold war malaise could be formulated without recourse to it. Neocolonial
theorizing often became reductive. However, there is much to be said for
Kwame Nkrumah's cryptic definition of the process: "The essence of neo-
colonialism is that the state which is subject to it is, in theory, independent
and has all the outward trappings of international sovereignty. In reality its
economic system and thus its political policy is directed from outside."[5]
Hence, in Nkrumah's aphorism, "for those who practise neo-colonialism, it
means power without responsibility, and for those who suffer from it, it
means exploitation without redress."[6] Naipaul, however, has shown scant
interest in the relations between power, responsibility, and exploitation—
not least in his failure to see the historic roots of the Iranian revolution in
precisely such relations.

In tracing the dubious influence of Western values on societies too weak
either to resist or fully to absorb them, Naipaul has ever taken only a slender,
subsidiary interest in the persistence of imperialism and the forms of economic coercion that perpetuate and, conversely, are perpetuated by imbal-
ances in cultural power. Where other prominent third world writers of the
cold war era—writers like Ngugi wa Thiong'o, Sembene Ousmane, Chinua
Achebe, Frantz Fanon, George Lamming, and Edward Kamu Braithwaite—
have all anatomized the workings of neocolonialism, Naipaul's contrasting
concern is to characterize fragile third world societies as witlessly derivative
and given to grandiloquent, self-delusory, and ultimately self-destructive fantasies. At times Naipaul writes of mimicry as if it were a form of colonialism
from below, that is, as if the world's peripheral societies were imposing upon
and parasitically bleeding the global core.

If Naipaul's one-sided emphasis on the psychological issue of mimicry
distances him from theorists who emphasize questions of economic dependency, it draws him, by the same token, toward a tradition of thought about
colonial dependency that includes the psychologists Albert Memmi and
Dominique Mannoni. In Mannoni's words, "Wherever Europeans have
founded colonies of the type we are considering, it can safely be said that
their coming was unconsciously expected—even desired—by the future
subject peoples."[7] Frantz Fanon and Aimé Césaire have both challenged
Mannoni on this score, arguing that to portray a state of colonial or imperial
dependency as inevitable and psychologically attractive is to erase the economic motives behind colonial domination and to offer colonists and imperialists backdoor absolution.[8]

Naipaul lays himself open to precisely such criticisms when he, too, blames the victim by intimating that subjugated people courted their subjection. "I always try to understand," he has remarked, "why certain countries have invited conquest."[9] This utterance is of a piece with Naipaul's vision of colonial dependency as a self-subverting condition.

In Naipaul's writings on Islam the notions of mimicry, parasitism, and dependency acquire a particularly pernicious twist. Here the focus of Naipaul's dismissals and his rage is the bad faith exhibited by his generalized Islam. Islamic societies, he argues, are guilty of "technological parasitism": they depend, in his eyes, on Western creativity and generosity while rejecting the Western ideologies that gave birth to these qualities.

Naipaul's disparagement of what he reads as Islamic parasitism and mimicry has to be seen in terms of his autobiographical trajectory. He has often portrayed his own emigration from Trinidad as a bid for a level of self-sufficiency unattainable in that or any other "mimic" society. In Naipaul's early personal conception of the mortifying threat of dependency lie the roots of his later insistence that he has never been anybody's hireling or imitator.[10] One recognizes, then, a personal and rhetorical affinity between his representation of the inhabitants of former colonies as mimic dependents and his projection of himself as an independent, self-made man. It is as if his image of himself as a writer has become predicated on a contempt for those whom he feels have capitulated to a parasitic or imitative life of the sort that he is confident he has eluded. Yet, ironically, the special animus that Naipaul reserves for cultural and racial hybrids, far from securing his literary autonomy, binds him to a tradition of pathological colonial anxiety toward the *evolue*. Naipaul's response to a lecturer at Uganda's Makerere University reeks of precisely that attitude: "Those are the ones that frighten me. . . . He's carrying a book. The ones that carry books scare the hell out of me, man."[11]

No discussion of Naipaul's vision of mimicry is complete without a consideration of the allied concept of parasitism. Naipaul discovers parasites almost everywhere he travels: in Zaire, Mauritius, Argentine, Uruguay, Trinidad, Iran, and Pakistan. But the image features with unique persistence in *Among the Believers*, the record of his 1979 journey through four non-Arabic Islamic countries: Iran, Pakistan, Malaysia, and Indonesia.

It is perhaps not coincidental that Naipaul feels most at liberty to apply the term *parasite* to Islamic individuals and cultures. For of all his major journeys the trip through Iran, Indonesia, Malaysia, and Pakistan finds him most stranded linguistically and most blatantly out of sympathy with the

people he encounters. Whatever his partialities in writing about the Caribbean, Britain, India, and the U.S.A., he could claim a measure of connection to those societies. In *Among the Believers* the sense of disconnection
becomes acute. As Naipaul spoke none of the relevant languages, his interlocutors had to convey their ideas and their personalities through English or,
at times, through the mediations of an interpreter. In the most literal sense
Naipaul found the cultures indecipherable, for he could not transliterate the
Arabic alphabet.

If his outrage at Islamic "parasitism" bears the imprint of his distance
from such cultures, it is marked, too, by a suspicion of Islamic communities
that dates from inter-religious tensions transmitted to him in childhood. As
he recalls in *Among the Believers*:

> Muslims were part of the small Indian community of Trinidad into
> which I was born; it could be said that I had known Muslims all my
> life. I knew little of their religion. My own background was Hindu,
> and I grew up with the knowledge that Muslims, though ancestrally of
> India and therefore like ourselves in many ways, were different....
> The difference was more a matter of group feeling, and mysterious:
> the animosities our Hindu and Muslim grandfathers had brought
> from India had softened into a kind of folk-wisdom about the unrelia-
> bility and treachery of the other side.[12]

Naipaul had written about these formative animosities before. Some two
decades earlier he had described, in *An Area of Darkness*, his childhood
education in the need to be mistrustful of Muslims, telling how a particular
graybeard Muslim came to embody "every sort of threat."[13]

As Sudhai Rai has observed, there is, in Naipaul's first Indian travel book,
An Area of Darkness, a diametrical opposition between his empathy for
Brahmanical Hindus and his representation of Muslims as suspicious,
treacherous, and opaque. Naipaul recounts how a ritualistic meal with a
Brahman family "dislodged[d] a childhood memory" and pleasantly "awak-
ened a superseded consciousness."[14] Conversely, his encounters with Muslims on his Indian and his Islamic ventures are suffused with a sense of
youthful bigotries stirring. For the six months of Naipaul's first sojourn in
India, he employed a Muslim, Aziz, as his personal servant, but he never
grew to trust or like the man. His relationships with Muslims in Iran had a
similarly inauspicious beginning: on the first page of *Among the Believers* we

are introduced to his first interpreter, Sadeq, who is full of the "sneering pride" and the apolitical "resentments" that, for Naipaul, summarize the revolution.[15]

When Naipaul writes and talks about Islam, *parasitic* and *barbarous* become routine epithets. To a *Newsweek* query about how much Islamic literature he had read before setting off, Naipaul responded:

> Not too much. I wanted an open mind. There's an awful lot missionary stuff being passed off as scholarship by people who lie, who won't call a parasite a parasite, a barbarian a barbarian. Who say, "Poor little wog, poor little cannibal, he hasn't had his fresh meat today."[16]

One notes, first, the timing of this comment: it was made in 1981, when the Iran hostage crisis had made the civilization-barbarism opposition a touchstone for American media discussions of Islamic cultures. Here, Naipaul, as is his wont, purports to be adopting a difficult, unpopular position, while parroting the media clichés of the day. One perceives in addition the confluence of Naipaul's conceptions of open-mindedness and prejudgment: he does not immerse himself in the complex variety of Islamic literatures in case it cramps his freedom to call a barbarian a barbarian. He thus responds to the societies he visits with an attitude of open-minded ignorance that, under the joint pressure of his own childhood prejudices and the Western simplifications of Islam, soon slides toward bigotry.

From the outset of his Islamic voyage, Naipaul is obsessed with the doublethink of the parasite. The idea for the trip came to him one evening while watching television in Connecticut. An Iranian was vaunting the revolution, yet he seemed, in his tweed jacket, intent to project a sophisticated image of himself at odds with his utterances. From this and similar incidents Naipaul determined that the revolutionaries felt an unadmitted attraction to the West, an attraction that manifested itself as a concoction of "dandyism, mimicry, boasting, and rejection."[17] The trip ensued, and the book it produced brought his obsession with the various styles of third world hypocrisy to a head.

But the Islamic form of hypocrisy, as he formulates it, differs in its specifics from the varieties of mimicry he had denounced in books like *The Middle Passage*, *An Area of Darkness*, and *The Return of Eva Peron*. If third world socialists and advocates of Black Power denounced the West while depending on the West for the phrasing of their denunciations, Islamic revivalists exhibited an inverse mimicry—they possessed an endemic language of revolt but remained reliant on Western technologies and goods to a degree that compromised their principled hostility. Hence, the *mauvaise foi* of the parasites: they take, but they do not give, and they pretend, all the while, that they are above taking. As Naipaul explains:

> The West, or the universal civilization it leads, is emotionally rejected. It undermines; it threatens. But at the same time it is needed, for its machines, goods, medicines, warplanes, the remittances from the emigrants, the hospitals that might have a cure for calcium deficiency, the universities that will provide master's degrees in mass media. All the rejection of the West is contained within the assumption that there will always exist out there a living, creative civilization, oddly neutral, open to all to appeal to. Rejection, therefore, is not absolute rejection. It is also, for the community as a whole, a way of ceasing to strive intellectually. It is to be parasitic: parasitism is one of the unacknowledged fruits of fundamentalism.[18]

Naipaul discerns this particular style of bad faith in all four of the nations he visits.

He does succeed, on occasion, in exposing the worthlessness of quests for purity in their more rarefied form. He rightly debunks the myth of the precise return, the dream of restoring an Islamic order scoured of inauthenticities. The conundrum he poses is this: how does a faith remain firm—ideologically unaccommodating—yet devise institutions and technologies adequate to the modern world? Time and again Naipaul impales his (almost uniformly middle-class) interlocutors on the horns of this dilemma by stressing the gap between their ideological rigor and their continued reliance on appropriated or at best renovated Western products. And so, in the course of his travels, he develops a bloodhound's nose for the telephone, the electric typewriter, the air-conditioning unit, the photocopying machine, and the Western university degree.

Yet there remains something too clean, too zealously simplistic about Naipaul's Manichaeanism. On the one side he places the creative, living, generous "universal civilization," on the other, the destructive, inert, resentful cultures of Islam. Islam shares that far side with all sterile cultures—with those of Zaire, for instance, where "the visitor" [a.k.a. the colonialist] introduced ideas of "responsibility, the state and creativity."[19]

When discussing the "universal civilization," Naipaul is fond of making smug allusions to "the visitor" and the "oddly neutral" "living, creative civilization." In so doing he soft-pedals any suggestion that such universality might often be imperial in its expansiveness. Seen against this backdrop, his quarrel with Muslims (of all persuasions) is straightforward: their relationship to the "universal civilization" will remain contradictory and self-destructive as long as they continue to utilize the "visitor's" technologies while denouncing Western ideologies. That is, as long as they refuse to recognize those technologies as the fruit of the disparaged ideologies.

Naipaul leaves no doubt that this dissociation is widespread and, in many instances, damaging. Yet in choosing Islamic bad faith as the high theme of his book, he assumes, without question, the good faith of the West in its dealing with his four Islamic societies. The West is consistently portrayed as exploited by lesser societies resentful of its benign or, at worst, neutral, creativity. But one has only to think of the monumental profits that the American, British, and French economies have gleaned from the sale of military hardware to Islamic societies to explode any such notion of long-suffering exploitation or creative neutrality.

Naipaul is so decided in his distribution of moral and cultural worth between the cultures of anarchic rage and the universal civilization that he ends up demonizing a homogenized Islam almost as routinely as the most brittle-minded of his Islamic interlocutors demonize the West. At one point he castigates a Malaysian acquaintance (introduced simply as Shafti): "I think that because you travelled to America with a fixed idea you might have missed some things."[20] The tone of this rebuke discloses Naipaul's considerable lack of self-awareness, as if his own responses on his Islamic travels were untouched by fixed preconceptions.

American responses to *Among the Believers* suggest how the author's unmodulated binary thinking helped fuel the anti-Islamic racism of the early eighties and encouraged the drawing of self-satisfied equations between Western technological inventiveness and human worth. Hugh Trevor-Roper, writing in the *New York Review of Books*, described Naipaul as having encountered "complacent parasitism on the material achievements of the West and on the unearned wealth which Western technology has bestowed upon its passive critics."[21] Here one observes how, once the image of the ungrateful parasite is in place, a quick figurative crossing can be made to assumptions about the unappreciated host's forbearance and philanthropy. Indeed, that "unearned wealth" captures precisely the underlying sense in Naipaul's book that Islamic "parasitism" is a form of theft.

Eugene Goodheart, glossing a remark by Naipaul to the effect that only select societies sustain the concept of human quality (Trinidad and Pakistan, for instance, do not), concludes that "the societies in which the quality of people is held to be important are advanced technological societies. If technology does not humanize, it creates the conditions for a society in which the quality of people is valued.[22] This raises interesting questions. Was apartheid South Africa, by far the most technologically advanced society in Africa, a nation where conditions were generated most suitable for the respect of human worth? Goodheart asks none of the necessary questions: Who controls the technology? Is it disproportionately military? What percentages of the extracted surplus are invested internally and abroad? Internally, is wealth concentrated within a narrow elite or broadly distributed? Does the advent of technology tighten or loosen the knots of dependency? Many third world politicians and activists have favored a redistribution of technological resources, but many of them are also alert to the workings of the "global assembly line," whereby industrial misery is concentrated in so-called offshore installations in developing nations.

One can be broadly—if always circumstantially—in favor of technology without assuming, like Naipaul and Goodheart, that it will perforce generate an increased respect for human quality. Goodheart makes the familiar error (à la modernization theory) of assuming that underdevelopment is an original rather than a substantially induced condition. He makes the accompanying mistake of assuming that technology (stripped of political trappings) will automatically play a redemptive role: that it is—to recall Naipaul's phrase—"oddly neutral." Though Goodheart's approach may seem extraordinary, it is easy, in returning to the figurative matrix of *Among the Believers*, to see how the book encouraged his conclusions.

An insistent literary figure is more than decorative, more than the tinsel of ideas; rather, it is symptomatic and constitutive of the patterns of thought. There are in *Among the Believers* two primary figures expressive of Naipaul's paradoxical poles of the exploitative yet weaker societies and the exploited powerful ones. If the central figure for the former is the parasite, for the latter it is the stereotypical image of the bazaar. Naipaul's Muslims covet modern goods but fail to recognize them as products of Western creativity and industry, treating them instead "as the stock of some great universal bazaar."[23] Migrant workers are described returning to Pakistan laden with modern effects, "names of the new universal bazaar, where goods were not associated with a particular kind of learning, effort, or civilization, but were just goods, part of the world's natural bounty."[24] What Naipaul has done is take an image descriptive of a precapitalist institution and apply it to the workings of international capitalism in its monopoly phase. Clearly, he himself does not see Western products as bazaar goods; the choice of image represents an attempt to see those commodities through Islamic eyes, that is, to capture the kind of "simpler vision" that overlooks the effort behind Western production and thereby does Western societies an injustice. Yet even if one accepted this as a pervasive Muslim view of Western products, Naipaul would remain guilty of countersimplifying, for his perception of the West as a fount of pure, unappreciated creativity is as limited as his projected Islamic perception of it as an open bazaar.

Naipaul uses the figure of the bazaar to expose Islamic naïveté or bad faith. But this trope is also inapposite for reasons that he does not wish to bring into play. Specifically, the difference in scale between the local bazaar and international capitalist operations is also a difference in a peripheral society's vulnerability to outside domination through the inculcation of foreign tastes for foreign advantage—economic, cultural, and political. Prolix on the subject of Western inventiveness, Naipaul has little to say on questions of hegemony and intervention.

The consequences of this silence are felt most directly in his treatment of Iran, the nation that serves as the centerpiece of his narrative. The timing of *Among the Believers* to coincide with the height of American-Iranian tensions boosted its success and propelled Naipaul onto the cover of *Newsweek*. And it was in Iran that the relation between Islamic revivalism and a recent history of Western domination ought to have been most transparent.

In the late seventies, not long before Naipaul was to undertake his Islamic journey, Reza Baraheni, an Iranian poet who had been incarcerated by the shah and tortured by his secret police, published a book entitled, *The Crowned Cannibals: Writings on Repression in Iran*. In describing the consequences of the shah's notions of Westernization, Baraheni invokes an updated version of Naipaul's figure of the bazaar to point out some of the drawbacks of that ambiguous category "modernity," at least as it manifests itself in a client culture:

> This Woolworth mentality has been aptly summed up by one of the great intellectuals of the country, Jalal Al-ahmad, as "Westomania." The worst taste in architecture is complemented by a sickening dosage of cheap Western goods and commodities. . . . To witness the collective dispossession of the nurtured tradition and way of life in an

entire nation, travel to Iran. The people of the country are being alienated from their cultural and ethnic roots and thus from their identity.
They have been denied all that is of merit in the West while their own
values are corroded.[25]

Baraheni continues by outlining the creation of the American client regime:
how in 1953 a democratically elected government was terminated by a CIA-
sponsored coup that installed the shah, and how SAVAK, his secret police,
was trained and equipped by the CIA and tortured political prisoners so routinely (whose numbers ranged from twenty-five to one hundred thousand)
that, in the late seventies, the secretary-general of Amnesty International
declared Iran to have the worst record of human rights in the world—worse
than both South Africa and the Soviet Union.[26]

Naipaul sidesteps this history. The shah is alluded to only twice in *Among
the Believers*: once when the author skims a magazine in Qom that "raged
about the Shah" and again when he recalls having seen graffiti in London
and other Western cities "about the torture by the Shah's secret police; about
the 'fascism' of the Shah."[27] Otherwise, on that score, Naipaul maintains a
studied silence. (His brother, Shiva, who traveled to Iran as the shah's reign
was ending, goes further, justifying his ambitions and trivializing his atrocities.)[28] V. S. Naipaul neither accuses nor excuses the shah. Instead, he simply declines him a presence in the narrative, knowing, perhaps, that to do so
would jeopardize his Manichaean analysis. What the brothers Naipaul share
is a perception of the Islamic revivals as breaking with rationality where
rationality, and hence comprehensibility, are proportionate to the degree of
Westernization. However, neither Naipaul reflects on the degree to which a
dictatorial marionette like the shah was one of the more sinister products of
Western "creativity."

When V. S. declares categorically that "political Islam is rage, anarchy,"
one realizes that his personal experience of Islamic cultures as opaque has
mutated from a relationship to a set of cultural characterizations. As a foreign observer with a longstanding animosity toward Islamic cultures, V. S.
Naipaul's difficulties with the societies he observes are transmuted into a
supposedly objective set of defining cultural attributes: irrationality, anarchy,
opacity, and incomprehensibility. This kind of transference—a stock in
trade of travel writers—might have been obviated had Naipaul shown more
interest in internal accounts (such as Baraheni's) of Islamic societies' recent
experiences with the Western powers.

Modernity, civilization, technology: when read in the context of America's hegemony over Iran during the two-and-a-half decades prior to Naipaul's visit the terms begin to blur, losing the precise, wholly positive connotations that Naipaul and, following him, Goodheart assume for them. In such circumstances can one separate *modernity* from the tawdry tyranny of a kept kleptocracy? Or *civilization* from the shah's rhetoric about delivering his country to the portals of "The Great Civilization?"[29] Or *technology* from the rift between the advanced technologies of torture and repression and the technological impoverishment of other sectors of the nation?

To pose these question is not to vindicate, for an instant, the Khomeini regime's even more disastrous record on human rights. One needs, however, to ask for a more complex account than Naipaul's tale of monolithic Muslim passion, rage, anarchy, resentment, idleness, and parasitism. And one needs, as well, to label as amnesiac his affirmation that "the life that had come to Islam had not come from within. It had come from outside events and circumstances, the spread of the universal civilization."[30] But those life-giving contacts were death-dealing ones as well. By holding his hand over the recent history of modernity's entanglements with imperialism, Naipaul ignores the quandaries of people who wish to maintain selective access to modernity without being thrust more deeply into clientship. Naipaul has a quick eye for the excesses of renunciation and its attendant hypocrisies. But he might have rendered them less inscrutable, and been less pious about the universal civilization, had he acknowledged those excesses, as, in large part, responses to the historic violence of imperial imposition.

Eqbal Ahmad has written insightfully on the importance—and difficulty—of integrating a critique of Western orientalist discourses into a critique of the forms of authoritarianism that continue to flourish in many Islamic societies. Reflecting on the continuing crises in such societies, Ahmad argues for the necessity of recognizing the joint roles of colonialism and modernization in bringing about "the erosion of economic, social, and political relationships which had been the bases of traditional Muslim order for more than a thousand years."[31]

Among the Believers is a classic instance of how not to undertake the difficult endeavor that Ahmed has urged upon us. Naipaul's Manichaean oppositions—between a parasitic Islam and an open, generous universal civilization, between idle dependence and industrious productivity, between irrationality and rationality—foreclose some crucial questions, not least the question of how crises of modernization intersect with memories of Western imperial powers and their subjugation of Islamic societies.

We saw the erasure of that history repeat itself in American media analyses of the crisis leading up to the Gulf War—a war purportedly fought in defense of (a nonexistent) democracy. In the quest for underlying factors contributing to Saddam's decision to invade Kuwait, rarely did the media investigate the collusion of Western powers in inventing and sustaining the undemocratic mini–Gulf states. There was almost no mention of Britain's historic role, while carving up the region, in ensuring that Iraqi power would be contained by denying it a port. Instead, the media preferred to explain the invasion by resurrecting, as sole cause, the specter of the Islamic terrorist-madman run amok.

In the midst of the Gulf crisis Naipaul was revived as an Islamic expert. He rehashed his theory of a global showdown between Islamic irrationality and "Our Universal Civilization" in the New York Times and elsewhere.[32] A decade earlier, during the Iran hostage crisis, Naipaul had contributed to the popularization of an orientalist opposition between a generous "civilization" and an ingrate, parasitic "barbarism." The volatile climate of 1990 saw Naipaul reappear clutching, in unadjusted mode, his theory of the innate incompatibility of an overgeneralized West and an overgeneralized Islam.

During the 1990s Naipaul's pontifications on Islam were occasioned principally by the tumult in India. His response to the 1992 desecration and demolition of the Ayodhya mosque verged on exuberance. The demolition was part, Naipaul asserted, of "a mighty creative process," a signal that Hindu India was no longer prostrate, was starting to throw off the fatalism that had left it historically vulnerable to subjugation.[33] Two years later, Naipaul viewed the Shiv Sena–BJP victory in Maharashtra with similar equanimity, as a salutory manifestation of the flowering of grassroots democracy. "It is a good sign," he pronounced, "it is not a cause for anxiety. All the things that allowed India to be conquered in the past are now working in a democratic manner."[34]

In his response to the rise of violent communalism in India, Naipaul appears unperturbed by the threats that have become the subject of extensive, urgent, and fraught intellectual questioning. What is the fate of the residual, secular commitments of the Indian state? What are the implications of the Hindu right for the vision of India as a multireligious and culturally plural society? What are the consequences of BJP and Shiv Sena leaders appropriating to themselves the right to speak for all Hindus and their attempt thereby to homogenize both Hinduism and the "Islamic invader"?

Naipaul continues to recapitulates the myth of Hindu revivalism as a long-delayed and salutory display of vengeance by a people subjugated by a monolithic Islamic conquest. That simplified account of Hindu-Islamic relations cannot withstand historical scrutiny.[35] Moreover, Naipaul reiterates his view that Islam, wherever it appears, is singlemindedly uncompromising: "You cannot appeal to Muslim intellectuals. Islam is a religion of revelation. The Prophet's revelations are final. The laws have all been issued."[36] Following from this, Naipaul assumes that it is feasible for someone of Hindu ancestry like himself to maintain a secular, cultural Hinduism in a way that is unthinkable for any Muslim.[37] This move is crucial: his Islam is static and inflexible, incapable of significant political diversity or reform. Such is the absolute distinction that marks Naipaul's Islam as irreducibly different from both Hinduism and Christianity.

These problems resurface in Naipaul's sequel to *Among the Believers*, *Beyond Belief: Islamic Excursions Among the Converted Peoples*.[38] To research this book Naipaul spent five months in 1995 retracing the journey through Pakistan, Iran, Malaysia, and Indonesia that he had undertaken almost two decades earlier. This second Islamic book has not had the popular impact of *Among the Believers* in America and Europe—it lacked the earlier volume's momentous sense of historical timing. Nonetheless, *Beyond Belief* has been received as a major statement on the innate problems of a broadly generalized non-Arabic Islamic world.

This book continues Naipaul's four-decade-old quarrel with third world hybrid cultures as mimic and inauthentic, a quarrel first articulated in his 1962 West Indian travel book, *The Middle Passage*. However, in the late eighties Naipaul's antagonism toward cultural syncretism acquired a new dimension, as it became inflected with an acute personal sense of spiritual loss. This shift toward an elegiac spirituality has profound consequences for the anti-Islamic animus that marks *Beyond Belief*.

The newly numinous Naipaul appears prominently in *A Turn in the South, India: A Million Mutinies Now*, and *Beyond Belief*, but this shift in focus was first signaled by the closing pages of *The Enigma of Arrival*, in which he recounts his return to Trinidad to attend his sister's Hindu funeral rites. The occasion provokes in him a meditation on the violent disjoining of belief from place:

Our sacred world—the sanctities that had been handed down to us as children by our families, the sacred places of our childhood, sacred because we had seen them as children and had filled them with wonder, places doubly and trebly sacred to me because far away in England I had lived in them imaginatively over many books and had in my fantasy set in those places the very beginning of things, had constructed out of them a fantasy of home. . . . Though I was to learn that the ground was bloody, that there had been aboriginal people there once, who had been killed or made to die away—our sacred world had vanished.[39]

A descendant of Hindus indentured to the New World, Naipaul mourns the integral relationship between spirituality and place that his displaced people were denied. In *Beyond Belief* he turns this personal sense of having been spiritually denied against non-Arabic Islamic people en masse by railing against Islam's destruction of local beliefs. As he pronounces in the prologue to *Beyond Belief*: "Everyone not an Arab who is a Muslim is a convert. . . . His holy places are in Arab lands; his sacred language is Arabic. . . . He rejects his own; he becomes, whether he likes it or not, a part of the Arab story."[40] In such places as Pakistan, Iran, Indonesia, and Malaysia, Naipaul goes on to argue, Islam is inauthentic, an imperial religion whose migrations and impositions have sundered the older, sustaining bonds between spirituality and place. Naipaul has often been portrayed as a disenchanted observer. But in *Beyond Belief* he traces (in the full, anthropological meaning of the term) the disenchantment of place at the hands of an alien religion.

Naipaul's argument for spiritual nativism, however, is underpinned by several varieties of bad faith. First, what are we now to make of his past dismissals of more rooted systems of belief as primitive, backward, and risibly superstitious, most notably in his African writings? Given this track record, it is a little much to find him now defending indigenous animisms against alien Islam. The second, related problem is this: Naipaul assumes that there is something inherently humanizing, even civilizing, about continuities between belief and location. Yet the evidence is far from persuasive: from Nazis and Stalinists to Zionists and extremists in India's BJP, some of history's worst violence has been perpetrated in the name of the spiritual integrity of place.

The third problem stems from Naipaul's crude distinction between the authentic, original Muslims of the Arab world and later inauthentic converts in the societies to the East, converts who betrayed their spiritual roots. However, some of these supposed latecomers converted to Islam a millennium or more ago. By this standard, how many believers on the planet would qualify as authentic? Eqbal Ahmad has put his finger on the problem:

Who is not a convert? By the definition he is giving, if Iranians are converted Muslims, Americans are converted Christians, the Japanese and large numbers of Chinese are converted Buddhists. Everybody is converted because every great religious system has had only a few followers at the beginning. Given that, Christianity, Islam, Buddhism, Judaism, especially all the prophetic religions, developed through conversion and have produced an entirely distorted humanity. In that sense, his organizing thesis should not exclude anyone.[41]

To dramatize Naipaul's bad faith on the question of conversion, one need only revisit his American travel book, A Turn in the South.[42] The spiritual denouement of the journey that book circumscribes occurs during a series of encounters with James Applewhite, a Carolina tobacco country poet. Naipaul is deeply moved—almost overawed—by the numinous sense of place that Applewhite voices through his poetry and his familial history. Here is a man who carries forward the past as religion by refusing dislocation, by committing himself reverentially to an ancestral place.

By white American standards Applewhite may seem deeply located. However, had Naipaul judged him by the nativist criteria with which he judges the Muslims whom he meets, Applewhite would be seen as a descendant of shallow transplants and recent converts. Yet, peculiarly, the issue of Christianity as alien religion never arises in Naipaul's meditations on the place of belief in the American South. Nor does his obsession with conversion as amnesiac decay. Conversion, it seems, is a selective problem that mutilates Islamic societies, scarring them with inauthenticities while leaving white Americans' spiritual integrity intact.

In U.S. and NATO foreign policy Islam has taken up much of the slack that has resulted from a postcommunist enemy deficit. Naipaul, in this milieu, has used his high culture stature to insist on an insurmountable, innate incompatibility between Islam and the West. His brittle, utterly other Islam is orientalized in the most dangerously hackneyed terms. While critics have represented Naipaul as mellowing with age, his demonization of an overgeneralized Islam—encompassing almost a billion people in scores of nation-states—remains intact. He continues to advance the politically catastrophic cycles of simplification and countersimplification that have produced such damaged and paranoid relations between a whole range of Islamic and Western cultures.

Notes

1. Louis Heren, quoted on the cover of *India: A Wounded Civilization* (Harmondsworth: Penguin, 1977).

2. "The Post-Colonial Intellectual: A Discussion with Conor Cruise O'Brien, Edward Said, and John Lukas," *Salmagundi* 70-71 (Spring-Summer 1986): 65-81.

3. David Hare, *A Map of the World* (London: Faber and Faber, 1982).

4. V. S. Naipaul, "Our Universal Civilization," *New York Times*, November 5, 1990, A21. See L. K. Sharma, "Indians Have Never Talked About India in This Way Before: V. S. Naipaul," *Times of India*, December 5, 1993, 12–13; "The Hindu Awakening: An Interview with V. S. Naipaul," *New Perspective Quarterly* 10.4 (Fall 1993): 60-62; "V. S. Naipaul and the BJP-SS Victory," *Indian Express*, April 2, 1995, 9.

5. Kwame Nkrumah, *Neo-Colonialism* (New York: International, 1965), ix.

6. Ibid., xi.

7. Albert Memmi, *The Colonizer and the Colonized*, trans. Howard Greenfeld (Boston: Beacon, 1967) and *Dependence: A Sketch for a Portrait of the Dependent*, trans. Philip A. Facey (Boston: Beacon, 1984); O. Dominique Mannoni, *Prospero and Caliban: The Psychology of Colonization*, trans. Pamela Powesland (New York: Praeger, 1964).

8. See Frantz Fanon, *Black Skins. White Masks*, trans. Charles Lam Markman (New York: Grove, 1967), 83-108; Aimé Césaire, *Discourse on Colonialism*, trans. Joan Pinkham (New York: Monthly Review, 1972), 39-43.

9. Curt Suplee, "Voyager with a Dark and Comic Vision—Through the World of Islam and Beyond, with V. S. Naipaul," *Washington Post*, November 19, 1981, C-17. Naipaul's choice of phrase carries similar implications when he observes, regarding India, that "no other country was more fitted to welcome a conqueror" and, again, that it "invited conquest." See V. S. Naipaul, *An Area of Darkness* (London: Deutsch, 1964; New York: Vintage, 1981), 222, 213.

10. See, for example, Naipaul's remarks quoted in Paul Theroux, "V. S. Naipaul," *Modern Fiction Studies*, 30 (Autumn 1984): 454.

11. Ibid., 448.

12. Naipaul, *Among the Believers: An Islamic Journey* (New York: Vintage, 1982 [1981]), 111.

13. Naipaul, *An Area of Darkness*, 47.

14. Sudhai Rai, *V. S. Naipaul: A Study in Expatriate Sensibility* (New Delhi: Arnold-Heinemann, 1982), 16.

15. Naipaul, *Among the Believers*, 3.

16. Charles Michener, "The Dark Visions of V. S. Naipaul," *Newsweek*, November 16, 1981, 110.

17. Naipaul, *Among the Believers*, 12-13.

18. Ibid, 168. For related assertions, see ibid., 15, 82, 121, 167, 234.

19. Naipaul, "A New King for the Congo," in *The Return of Eva Peron* (New York: Knopf, 1980), 218.

20. Naipaul, *Among the Believers*, 375.

21. Hugh Trevor-Roper, "Born Again," *New York Review of Books*, November 5, 1981, 11.

22. Eugene Goodheart, "Naipaul's Mandarin Sensibility," *Partisan Review* 50 (1983): 254. Naipaul's remark appears in *Among the Believers*, 289.

23. Naipaul, *Among the Believers*, 33.

24. Ibid., 81. The image is used similarly on p. 38.

25. Reza Baraheni, *The Crowned Cannibals: Writings on Repression in Iran* (New York: Vintage, 1977), 5.

26. The estimates of political prisoners are for 1975. For further discussion, see Noam Chomsky and Edward S. Herman, *The Washington Connection and Third World Fascism* (Boston: South End, 1979).

27. Naipaul, *Among the Believers*, 32, 9-10.

28. Shiva Naipaul, "The Illusion of the Third World," in *An Unfinished Journey* (New York: Viking, 1987), 36-37.

29. Baraheni, *The Crowned Cannibals*, 4.

30. Naipaul, *Among the Believers*, 429.

31. Eqbal Ahmad, "Islam and Politics," in Mohammed Asghar Khan, ed., *Islam, Politics, and the State: The Pakistan Experience* (London: Zed, 1985), 19.

32. Naipaul, "Our Universal Civilization," *New York Times*, November 5, 1990, A21.

33. Cited in "Naipaul's Comments on BJP-SS Victory in Maharashtra," *Indian Express*, April 2, 1995.

34. Ibid.

35. See especially Tapan Basu et al., *Khaki Shorts and Saffron Flags: A Critique of the Hindu Right* (New Delhi: Orient Longman, 1993).

36. V. S. Naipaul, quoted in Sharma, "Indians Have Never Talked."

37. Ibid.

38. V. S. Naipaul, *Beyond Belief: Islamic Excursions Among the Converted Peoples* (New York: Little, Brown, 1998).

39. V. S. Naipaul, *The Enigma of Arrival* (New York: Knopf, 1987), 327

40. Ibid, 1.

41. Eqbal Ahmad, *Confronting Empire: Interviews with David Darsamian* (Cambridge: South End, 1999), 109.

42. V. S. Naipaul, *A Turn in the South* (New York: Vintage, 1990).

The Islamic and Western Worlds: "End of History" or the "Clash of Civilizations"?

Mujeeb R. Khan

Francis Fukuyama in his essay "The End of History?" drew upon Hegel to argue that the fall of the Berlin Wall would inevitably lead to the universal triumph of liberal democracy and capitalist consumerism. A few years later, in the wake of the first post-Holocaust genocide against a European religious-cultural minority in Bosnia-Herzegovina, Samuel Huntington opposed Fukuyama's thesis with one positing an inevitable "Clash of Civilizations" drawing upon particularity and difference.[1]

Intellectual commentators on these two popular paradigms have, however, failed to fully appreciate the philosophical basis of this discussion in a trialogue between three leading and controversial philosophers of the twentieth century; Alexandre Kojève, Leo Strauss, and Carl Schmitt. This philosophical trialogue, which in many ways was initiated and mediated by Strauss, continues to be of great relevance in addressing the symbiotic and yet vexed relationship between the Jewish, Christian, and Muslim worlds, on one level, and the antinomies between the universal and the particular in terms of identities, interests, and values in global affairs more generally.

Fukuyama's essay drew directly on the Strauss-Kojève dialogue, recently republished as part of Strauss's classic broader work on Xenophon's *Hieron*, and was inspired by his teacher the late Allan Bloom who had studied under both Strauss and Kojève in Chicago and Paris respectively. Fukuyama's essay essentially presented in a popularized form Kojève's thesis in his *Introduction à la lecture de Hegel*, that the dialectical trajectory of history was fast approaching terminus with the abolishment of essential human and ideological differences in a globalized "universal and homogeneous state," which for Fukuyama was represented by the model of Western liberal democracy and late capitalism. Huntington's essay less overtly echoed the more profound work of the right-wing German legal theorist Carl Schmitt, who gained notoriety by counterposing the primacy of particularity and conflict to that of the universal triumph of liberalism and constitutional democracy in his magnum opus *The Concept of the Political.* Strauss's philosophical mediation of these twin poles somewhere midpoint, by contrast, has been generally unaddressed.

Kojève: "The End of History and the Universal and Homogeneous State"

The Russian émigré philosopher Alexandre Kojève (1902–1968) was among the first to systematically introduce Hegel into French higher thought. In a series of remarkable lectures delivered at the *École Pratique des Haute Etudes* between 1933 and 1939, Kojève directly influenced the leading intellectuals of postwar France, many of whom repeatedly audited his lectures, from Jean Paul-Sartre, Georges Battaille, and Maurice Merleau-Ponty on the left to Raymond Aron, Gaston Fessard, and Jean Wahl on the right. Kojève's lectures were published with the assistance of Raymond Queneau under the title *Introduction à la lecture de Hegel.*[2] In his lectures Kojève presented a vision of History achieving telos in a universal and homogeneous state based upon his own highly original reading of Hegel's *Phenomenology of Spirit.*

Hegel's *Phenomenology* and, in particular, the renowned sections on "the master-slave dialectic," actually present one of the most powerful theoretical accounts of identity formation and even the potential for genocide resulting from "the struggle for recognition." The phenomena of genocide as the *summum malum* of which humans are capable has yet to be adequately theoretically addressed in scholarly literature. This, of course, continues to be hauntingly relevant with the resurrection of this evil in the last decade in Bosnia-Herzegovina and Rwanda as well as more specifically in the contentious relationship between the Western and Islamic worlds that historically determined both the Jewish and the "Eastern" or Muslim questions in Europe. The present antagonisms involving these historically driven "questions" of identity, particularity, and difference in the Balkan, Israeli-Palestinian, and Persian Gulf/Afghanistan conflicts vividly demonstrates their continued relevance. For Hegel human consciousness and identity first emerge when one becomes aware of the existence of another human being and desire recognition (*annerkenung*) from them. Paradoxically, the "Other" is essential for the awareness of the "Self," but as an independent and alterior reality it must be overcome and sublimated in this process of seeking recognition in order to assert one's own consciousness and autonomy. At first humans seek exclusive recognition from those they define as "Other," leading to a struggle for recognition between two distinct beings or collectivities that Hegel characterizes as a "struggle to the death." This struggle in History between opposed beings or collectivities may stem from perceived differences drawing upon ethnicity, religion, class, ideology, or even gender and dialectically constitute social identity itself.

The annihilation of the "Other," however, leads to a loss of recognition on the part of the victor, while the vanquished realizes that one can escape slavery only at the cost of one's physical negation in battle. Hegel thus writes that this struggle is most likely to end in the subjugation of the vanquished by the victor. This dilemma is resolved by the enslavement of the "Other" and the establishment in History of hierarchical relationships between lords and bondsmen. This relationship, for Hegel, constitutes the beginning of human history. As Kojève notes in his lectures, "Man was born and History began with the first fight that ended in the appearance of a master and slave."[3]

This "master-slave dialectic," for Hegel, continues but reaches an existential impasse when the master realizes that recognition from a slave is unsatisfactory because it is obtained not from a willing subject but rather from a being reduced to an object. Thus, for Hegel, the dialectic continues and History is the history of the working slave who through a process of labor and alienation transforms nature and creates the material world. Unlike the idle Master, the Slave by sublimating his or her desires lays the foundation for civilization in the conquest of nature, both his or her own and that of the external world. This concept, borrowed from Hegel, was to be central to the oeuvre of both Karl Marx and of Sigmund Freud. Humanity is completed through work and the transformation of given nature, which invariably also leads to the transformation of human nature by fostering equality and replacing the realm of necessity (*reich der notwendigkeit*) with the realm of freedom (*reich der freiheit*). "History stops at the moment when the difference, the opposition, between Master and Slave disappears."[4]

Fukuyama's deployment of Hegel-Kojève in announcing the "End of History" in response to the collapse of the Berlin Wall was clearly premature. In fact, the Hegelian "Master-Slave dialectic" provides us with an unsurpassed model for comprehending the still unchanged nature of identity formation and conflict at both the individual and collective levels. This model will be presented in this essay in the context of the modern resiliency of the Jewish and Muslim "questions" in Europe, demonstrating how those defined historically as "Other" are particularly vulnerable when they are perceived as transgressing definitional boundaries between "Self" and "Other" and thus must be expelled to a distance where practical and, all too often, exterminated when not. The creation of the State of Israel in parallel with the full flowering of Western liberal democracy enshrined in "equal citizenship" before the law constituted the most obvious attempt to solve such "questions" of particularity. As Leo Strauss foresaw, rather than providing a permanent solution these two endeavors fostered new permutations of what he felt was the insoluble tension between the universal and the particular in human affairs. Such an insight need not lead to nihilistic pessimism and despair, however, for it also illuminates a path to human coexistence and solidarity beyond the shackles of history and violent political struggles for recognition and identity.

The "Jewish Question" and the Problem of Particularity

In accounting for genocide in the Western world, one must address the fact that it has been precisely those religious and ethnic minorities that have been historically presented as alien in a Christianized European body politic that have been persistently vulnerable to this ultimate evil. In this sense Jews, Romas, and the Muslims of Iberia, the Balkans, Sicily, the Caucasus, and Crimea have been recurrent victims over the *longue durée* of programs of assimilation, expulsion, and/or extermination. In particular, the "Jewish Question" in Europe has been central for much of the continent's early modern history and for the intellectual inception of the Enlightenment and modernity and their eventual disillusionment in the death camps of the Second World War. Along with Niccolo Machiavelli and Thomas Hobbes, Benedict *né* Baruch Spinoza was one of the leading philosophic progenitors of this European Enlightenment and modernity. Spinoza's pointed assault against the verities of revealed religion (slyly couched in an attack on Jewish tradition, which just as easily applied to Christianity or Islam) sought to depose a theologically centered universe with one that worshipped faith in human reason and its ostensible ability to solve the most vexing problems of the human condition. His writings, which were even more brazen in their "anti-theological ire" than those of his contemporary Hobbes, who *"durst not write so boldly,"* highlights the theological-political predicament that has remained unresolved in the age of postmodernity and come to be best exemplified by this "Jewish Question." In hopes of resolving this "question," Spinoza was also the first to allude to a form of secular proto-Zionism that eventually gave birth to the State of Israel.[5]

For both French philosophes and the German thinkers of the early Enlightenment the inherent tension between the universal and the particular in human affairs was most vividly exemplified by this "Jewish Question" and the need to abolish difference, tradition, and superstition that divided societies along numerous fault lines. Gradually, the Enlightenment, and the modern state fully emerging alongside in the course of the nineteenth century, saw the attainment of societal harmony in the abolishment of substantial legal and ascriptive differences among citizens through the universalizing and homogenizing progress of capitalism, science, and positive rationality. Thus, Karl Marx in his controversial essay "On the Jewish Question" saw the solution to traditional antisemitism as being the assimilation of Jews and all other social particularities into a classless and postreligious society of equals.[6] This "solution," first hinted at by Spinoza, was also central to the French Revolutionary decree of Jewish emancipation.

The universalizing mission of the Enlightenment, it naive failure to consider the instrumental and potentially ruthless aspects of human reasoning aside, obviously could not solve for everyone the contradiction between universal ideals and particular identities and interests. The deflation of Enlightenment optimism in the Dreyfus affair led Theodore Herzl, Otto Pinsker, and other Jewish intellectuals to advocate the particular in the form of Jewish nationalism and political Zionism—a "solution" that itself spawned a chasm between the secular worship of the "nation" and traditional Jewish faith, on the one hand, and what would eventually become the moral dilemma of the perennial victims' victimization of the native Palestinian inhabitants of the yearned for "Zion," on the other. It was in this contentious early twentieth-century European Jewish milieu in which the German-Jewish philosopher Leo Strauss (1899–1973) courted and distanced himself from the alternatives posed by the Orthodox upbringing of his childhood, the flirtation with the militant Jabotinskyite Zionism of his teenage years, and the neo-Kantian optimism in progress and Enlightenment associated with the philosopher Herman Cohen that still dominated his Weimar university years. For someone who was to become a rather retiring and deeply scholastic professor of political philosophy at the University of Chicago, Strauss in recent years has garnered the undeserved reputation of having been a sinister ideological guru to some of the right-wing crusaders in the cultural wars, including Dinesh D'Souza, Norman Podhoretz, and Jeffrey Hart. Contemporary conservative devotees and liberal critics alike have often misconstrued Strauss's partisanship on behalf of classical political philosophy and his insistence on its timeless relevance. Strauss's personal confrontation with the "theological-political predicament" and the *Juden Frage*, or Jewish Question, in Weimar Germany led to a critical confrontation with Spinoza and some of the conceits of Enlightenment modernity. It also led to Strauss's critical engagement midpoint between the universalizing neo-Hegelian philosophy of Alexandre Kojève and the celebration of particularity and the primacy of the political by the archconservative German theorist Carl Schmitt.

The History and Practice of Genocide in Europe

The tragic persistence of the Jewish and Eastern or Muslim questions in Europe has of course most horrifically manifested itself in twentieth-century attempts at mass expulsion and extermination. "Ethnic cleansing" (from *etnicko ciscenje* in Serbo-Croat) was also a metaphor widely employed by the Nazis in their campaign against European Jewry. They spoke of the extermination of the Jews as being *Gesundung* (the healing of Europe), *Selbsttreinigung* (self-cleansing), and *Judensauberung* (the cleansing of Jews). Fundamentally, the *Juden Frage* was, in the words of one German foreign office press chief, "*eine Frage der politischen Hygiene.*"[7]

The Nazi administration of the *Endlosung*, or "Final Solution," was also heavily influenced by the practical exigencies of the larger war against the Allies in what has been termed by the historian Karl Schleunes "the twisted road to Auschwitz."[8] One might refer here to the ongoing historiographical debate on the Holocaust comprising "intentionalist" and "functionalist" camps. The traditional intentionalist view of the Holocaust emphasized its origins in the premeditated desire of Hitler to make Europe *Juden-rein* as witnessed by his early writings of the 1920s. The decision to target the Jews certainly had its origins in Hitler's antisemitic writings going back to the 1920s, however, functionalist scholars correctly point out that the decision to embark upon a full-blown extermination campaign and its particular implementation was also heavily influenced by the course of World War II. From the September 1939 invasion of Poland to the fall of France in the summer of 1940, the Germans planned to solve their "Jewish problem" through the traditional means of mass expulsion. Setbacks and massive casualties for the *Wehrmacht* in Operation Barbarossa made such plans unfeasible, leading to a decision to launch the "Final Solution" around the fall of 1941.

The genocide against Bosnian Muslims, and the attempted one against largely Muslim Kosovars, also followed a "twisted path" with the fomenting of anti-Islamic bigotry in Belgrade, and derivatively in Zagreb, by demagogues lusting for power. This orchestrated campaign not only drew upon a long history of anti-Islamic prejudice in the Balkans as a way of affirming a Christian European identity, it also dovetailed to a considerable degree with the resurrection of the "Green peril" in significant political sectors in Israel, Western Europe, and the United States. This contemporary phenomenon of a rearticulated Western anti-Islamic prejudice resulted from the Iranian Islamic Revolution, local challenges to Anglo-American and Israeli subjugation of the Middle East, and also large postwar Muslim immigration to the West.

The sociologist Zygmunt Bauman, in his book *Modernity and the Holocaust*, not only stresses the discontinuity between the Holocaust and earlier forms of genocide, but also with the whole previous European tradition of antisemitism as well. Bauman's fallacy here, like that of many other theorists who have followed in his footsteps, might be referred to as "the conceit of modernity" stemming from historicist or genealogical approaches that seek to posit the emergence of human phenomena at particular historical junctures. While he convincingly demonstrates how technology wedded to modern forms of bureaucratic rationality contributed to the Nazi death camps, he fails to explain why Jews above all had historically been singled out for persecution throughout Europe and why this led to repeated attempts at their expulsion and extermination in these same countries. Technology, industry, and modern ideologies of mass mobilization have certainly broadened the scale of mass killings well beyond what existed previously. However, as the low-tech Rwandan genocide—carried out at a killing rate more intense than that of the Nazis, with machetes—demonstrated, this was a change in style but not really substance from earlier extermination campaigns. The roots of this evil trail back to the emergence of history and the refusal to recognize the fellow humanity of those perceived as "Other."

In a separate work Bauman does succeed in demonstrating a significant paradox at the heart of modernity. In contradistinction to the aspirations of the Enlightenment, as the leveling process of modernity blurred historic cultural and religious distinctions it undermined the certainty of "Self" held by many in the dominant group and spurred still greater efforts at redrawing definitional boundaries to contain this "insidious infiltration." The process of modernity recast traditional roles and identifications and thus spawned a modern antisemitism, born not necessarily from the threat of great differences but from the threat of the absence of barriers between "Self" and "Other." As Bauman argues in discussing the modern Jewish Question, "In short, they undermined the very difference between hosts and guests, the native and the foreign. And as nationhood became the paramount basis of group self-constitution, they came to undermine the most basic of differences: the difference between 'us' and 'them.'"[9] By transgressing imagined national boundaries, to their deep chagrin, European Muslims and Jews in this century discovered that they embodied an existential problem that persistently for many could only be solved through expulsion where practical and extermination when not.

The Legacy of European Anti-Islamism

The path to genocide in Southeastern Europe is illuminated when one realizes that the southern and eastern Mediterranean has long served as Europe's consummate "Other." From the early medieval period to today, this "Other" has yet to be genuinely incorporated into Europe because it has been an essential antinomy in the European construction of "Self." Indeed, the renowned thesis of the Belgian historian Henri Pirenne was that the very notions of Latin Christendom and "the West" first emerged from the ruins of classical civilization with the Carolingian Holy Roman Empire's crusades against northern pagans and southern Muslim infidels.[10] It is an often overlooked fact that the early Islamic presence in Europe was actually coterminous with the forcible establishment of the Christian faith in large areas of the British Isles, Northern Europe, and the Balkans. While pagan Celts, Saxons, and Wends were Christianized and incorporated into the Germano-Latin cultural framework, monotheistic Muslims and Jews could not easily be converted and faced the constant threat of expulsion or extermination from Europe proper.[11] This pattern began during the Crusades in Central Europe and Norman Sicily in the thirteenth century and continued through Iberia and the Balkans today.

For five centuries the Ottoman Empire was one of the world's paramount powers with its center of gravity in the quarter of the European continent that it controlled. One would have expected that this long European presence would have accorded the Ottomans formal recognition as members of the European society of states. Yet the reality is that the term *European* has always had an overriding cultural and religious connotation rather than a purely geographical or even racial one. "The logical conclusion [drawn from geography] ought to be that the Ottoman Empire was, empirically, a European state. The paradox is that it was not. Even though a significant part of the Empire was based in Europe, it could not be said to have been of Europe."[12] This "question of otherness" is very much alive today in relation to Turkey's erstwhile attempts at joining the European Union. While Kemalist Turkey still falls considerably short of the democratic pluralistic standard reasonably expected of aspiring members, repeated statements by Christian Democratic leaders in a number of EU countries makes it clear that, in their eyes at least, Turkey's Ottoman-Islamic heritage also renders it an irredeemable outsider.[13]

The seminal nineteenth-century Phil-Hellenic campaign for upholding the norms of European civilization underscored the enormous task of bridging the chasm between the universal and the particular when addressing issues of human rights at a global level. Western powers forced "reforms" on the Ottoman state to benefit Christian populations through whom they controlled a huge part of the empire's trade. Needless to say, these reforms were never considered appropriate for the Muslims of Central Asia, India, the Malay Archipelago, and North Africa languishing under harsh Western imperial rule. Even today, many non-Westerners note that the U.S. pushed for human rights and democracy in China, once it became a "strategic competitor," while it studiously avoided promoting such values in the case of many Muslim "client regimes."

The Ottoman Empire was certainly less draconian in its administrative practices than its giant Russian rival to the north. Nonetheless, the issue of human rights and self-determination of solely the Christian populations was successfully used by Russia to launch an aggressive war in 1877 against the remaining Ottoman territories in the Balkans. The British prime minister

Benjamin Disraeli clearly viewed this as a challenge to longstanding British "balance of power" interests in the region. However, he was unable to offer effective support to the *Sublime Porte* because of the wildly popular moralistic crusade launched by his devoutly Evangelical rival, William Ewart Gladstone. Gladstone was reacting to the "Turkish Horrors" in Bulgaria where harsh Ottoman reprisals led to two notable massacres of Bulgarian Christians and the overall deaths of two thousand people in intercommunal fighting between local Muslims and Christians. Disraeli was immediately suspect in the eyes of his opponents because of his Jewish ancestry and pronounced Islamophilia (he enjoyed cavorting in the silk robes of an Ottoman Pasha—a fashion rather ironically initiated by Lord Byron following his visit to the rebellious Ali Pasha of Janinna). Gladstone and his acolytes were quick to employ innuendo in suggesting that this accounted for "Dizzy's" dearth of passion for "the Christian cause." Gladstone remarked to his wife that he "may be willing to risk his government for his Judaic feeling."[14] The Russians used the fighting as a pretext to launch a long prepared campaign to seize Constantinople and the Turkish straits and "cleanse" the region of its Muslim population. The definitive demographic study of the late Ottoman Empire estimates that Muslims made up nearly half of the population of this part of Europe by 1870.[15] During and after the 1877–1878 Russo-Ottoman War nearly three hundred thousand Muslims were massacred in a genocidal campaign of ethnic cleansing, while five million were ultimately forced to flee to Anatolia by the turn of the century.

Historically, the position of Muslims and Jews as the great "Others" of European Christendom rendered them de facto allies and victims. One notable study of the origins of medieval European antisemitism has linked it to the struggle with Islam and the perception that Jews were similar to and favorably inclined toward various Muslim foes.[16] Indeed, the seminal medieval massacres of Jewish communities in England and Central Germany were inextricably linked to the launching of the Crusades, as was the Spanish Inquisition to the *reconquista* against the "Moors." Another important recent study of nineteenth-century pan-Slavic antisemitism directly links it, and the subsequent launching of systematic pogroms from 1881 onward, to the Russo-Ottoman wars in the Balkans, the Black Sea, and the Caucasus (and the view that "the Jew Disraeli" was responsible for foiling Russian pan-Slavic ambitions).[17]

In terms of modern Europe, at least, ethnic-cleansing and genocide were first employed on a vast scale largely against Muslim populations in Southeastern Europe and the Caucasus by Slavic Orthodox powers. Recent prominent scholars of the Holocaust such as Zygmunt Bauman and Omer Bartov are wrong in locating the roots of modern genocide and ethnic cleansing against European civilians in the vast mechanized destruction and trench warfare of the First World War.[18] Historians have also generally failed to note that the Balkan Wars of 1912–1913, which served as a prelude to the "guns of August," were primarily conducted as extermination campaigns against European civilian populations.[19] This program of ethnic cleansing in Macedonia, Kosovo, Sandjak, and Western Thrace was first confined to Muslim populations and later extended, to a lesser degree, to the region as a whole once the victorious Christian alliance fell upon itself. This Balkan round of ethnic cleansing actually preceded and greatly influenced the similar campaign of genocide launched against the Armenians of Eastern Anatolia by Turkish secular nationalists at the beginning of World War I. With the emergence of Stalin and Hitler such genocidal policies were carried out against a whole range of "enemy populations" in Europe including Poles, Ukrainians, Kazakhs, Balts, Chechen-Ingush, Tatars, Kulaks, homosexuals, and even the mentally handicapped.

Tyranny Ancient and Modern

Nineteenth-century "primordialist" theories of national identity posited the "nation" as an ancient verity based upon common cultural, religious, and ethnolinguistic solidarities—distinct from those held by surrounding neighbors. Following this "romantic" conception of nationalism, most closely associated with Johann Gottfried Herder, nationalist theorists advocated the breakup of multinational empires and the reawakening of "dormant" national consciousness on the part of an allegedly homogeneous and cosanguiness *volkdom*. The purpose of this collective mobilization of a national "Self," which has been at the root of much modern warfare, has been to construct "nation-states" where the borders of the state are coterminous with the settlement of the "nation." The fact that very few political-territorial entities ever enjoyed homogeneous and ordered populations posed a vexing conundrum to would be "fathers of nations" who, undeterred, insisted that reality conform to ideals through "blood and iron" if necessary. Contemporary scholars of nationalism have labored to demonstrate the "invention of tradition" and the often fanciful construction of ostensibly "ancient" nations and identities. This prevailing "constructivist" paradigm in the study of nationalism draws upon, often unacknowledged, the Hegelian dialectic of "Self" and "Other" first presented in *The Phenomenology of Spirit*. The fact that "identities" are intersubjective and shaped through social intercourse does not of course make them any less "real."

Scholars of Balkan history and critics of the Western response to the Bosnian genocide have correctly refuted the "ancient hatreds" thesis frequently repeated by many Western policy makers as an excuse for inaction.[20] Genocide and ethnic cleansing are far from being a result of some spontaneous societal upwelling of suppressed tribal bloodlust. Rather, they are the product of carefully orchestrated political programs tied to the acquisition and enhancement of power by tyrannically inclined individuals or elites. This nexus between tyranny at the individual level of the "self" –i.e., a particular demagogue like Hitler or Milosevic—and its transmission to a collective national level of identity is essential for understanding the phenomenon and vitally linked to the general Hegelian dialogical theory of genocide presented in this essay. Indeed, the subject of tyranny and great political crime in many ways has been central to the very inception of political philosophy from Plato's *Republic* to Aristotle's *Politics*. A less appreciated but no less profound classical dialogue on tyranny has been the *Hieron* of Xenophon, Socrates' other historical disciple. This dialogue formed the basis for a lengthy commentary and critical debate between Leo Strauss and Alexandre Kojève on the subjects of tyranny, philosophy, and the historical process.

Much of "ancient" and "modern" political philosophy revolves around a dialectic (a "conversation" in the original ancient Greek meaning of the term) on a fixed set of themes. Hegel's "master-slave" dialectic and notion of the "struggle for recognition" as a potential "struggle to the death" was greatly influenced by the German's acknowledged debt to Thomas Hobbes and his concept of the *status naturalis* or "state of nature" presented in his works *Leviathan*, *De Cive*, and *De Homine*. The societal descent into bloodbaths such as Bosnia and Rwanda frequently recalls the Hobbesian nightmare of a "warre of alle against alle" in the state of nature—crucial also for Carl Schmitt's *Concept of the Political*. Hobbes in his calculated refutation of both religion and classical political philosophy insisted that man as the *zoon politikon*, or political animal, was motivated more by passion than reason. His memory seared by the carnage of the English Civil Wars, Hobbes felt that the ever looming danger of societal relapse into a state of nature could be held at bay only by a proper appreciation of the twin passions of "fear and the desire for eminence" that drive human political engagements and conflicts.[21] Human nature, an ever contentious *"and restlesse desire of Power after power, that ceaseth onely in Death,"*[22] could only be reconciled to the authoritarian writ of the state or *Leviathan* if it was kept in constant awareness of the *summum malum*, "a violent death."

Even prior to his traumatic experience of the English Civil Wars, this fear of the possibility of societal relapse and a violent death was deeply ingrained in Hobbes. He related to his biographer John Aubrey that his mother had suddenly given birth to him from fright in 1588, at the news of the approaching Spanish Armada. This fear in Hobbes's schema was to be crucial in keeping the other contending human passion for recognition and eminence in check. Furthermore, it necessitated Hobbes's pointed philosophical assault on religion ("the kingdom of darknesse") and classical political philosophy ("Aristotle and the schoolmen"), for "Athens and Jerusalem" both insisted that in exceptional circumstances the Leviathan could be disobeyed, while certain causes and principles were indeed worth risking life for in a violent struggle.[23] In response, Hobbes's radical "modern" relativism extended not only to denying the possibility of a God and an afterlife but also to any transcendent notion of good and evil or attendant morality beyond the individual's self-interest and the fundamental right to self-preservation.[24]

The tyrannical track of someone like Milosevic, littered with the corpses of friends, foes, and hundreds of thousands of innocents alike, hews to this classical outline. It further demonstrates the vital link between tyrannical ambition and nihilistic ruthlessness, at the individual level, and its transfusion to a collective national one resulting in genocide and ethnic cleansing. By all accounts Milosevic was a gray communist *apparatchik* with very few, if any, ideological convictions. The tinder for a catastrophic inferno in the former Yugoslavia had already accumulated in Tito's wake with a growing constitutional crisis of federalism between Belgrade and the other Yugoslav constituent ethnic groups and republics desiring greater autonomy. At a deeper structural level the fact that this crisis degenerated into a bloodbath with Yugoslav Muslims in Bosnia and Kosovo as the main victims predictably followed a well-worn European historical path. Without an arsonist like Milosevic determined to acquire absolute power, however, the Yugoslav political crisis would not have grown into a genocidal conflagration. A selective recounting of historical grievances and appeals to national myths were already underway in Yugoslavia, providing Milosevic with the fuel he needed. The central myth revolved around the *Kosovo Epic*, which was very selectively recounted and exploited to rally Serbs against their neighbors. Milosevic, who had never been a nationalist, overnight used the six hundredth anniversary of the Kosovo battle to rally Serbs against his internal and external foes.

Historical Metanarratives and the Literary Impetus for Cleansing the "Other"

The imperative for expelling or exterminating the dissonant Muslim "Other" from within has been a recurring theme of Serbian nationalist literature and vividly illustrates how our Hegelian-derived model of genocide has played out in the past. Apart from the *Kosovo Epic Cycle* itself, no work enjoys greater prestige in the Serb literary canon than *The Mountain Wreath (Gorskii Vijenac)*, by the Montenegrin bishop-prince Petar Petrovic Njegoš.[25] The poem (1847) commemorates an actual event on Christmas Eve in 1709, which was passed down in folk memory until immortalized by Njegoš as the singular event that crystalized a Montenegrin-Serb identity. The event was the carefully planned extermination of Montenegrin Muslims by their Orthodox kinsmen. *The Mountain Wreath* was required reading in Yugoslav high schools, and is a textbook representation of the need to struggle with and negate an alterior "Other" that by its very existence threatens to undermine one's own identity.

The poem is structured around a series of meetings between Bishop-Prince Danilo (1700–1735) and his noblemen where they discuss what should be done with their Montenegrin relatives who have accepted Islam. The Montenegrin Orthodox are torn between kinship ties to the Muslims and bitter opposition to their faith. For Njegoš the decision to overcome the legendary kinship solidarity of the Montenegrin tribes and exterminate, in the name of "the true faith," their "apostate" relatives represents an immense victory that gives birth to an independent Montenegrin-Serb nation. The choice is a painful one, but for Njegoš it is an essential heroic feat that allows one to choose between good and evil, sickness and health. Aware of the widespread romanticism concerning "rock ribbed" Montenegro expressed by the likes of Lord Tennyson, Njegoš proudly implies in the opening stanza of the poem that this is a choice confronted by all of Europe: "Lo to the

Devil with 7 scarlet cloaks, with two swords and with two crowns on the head, the great grandchild of the Turk with Koran! Behind him hordes of that accursed litter march to lay waste to the whole planet Earth, just as locusts devastate the green fields. If the French dike had not stood in the way, the Arab sea would have flooded it all!"[26]

Njegoš actually has a Muslim notable plead for the virtues of tolerance and coexistence among Montenegrins divided by religion but united by language and blood. Ferat Zacir Kavazbasa addresses the Orthodox leaders: "Though this country is a bit too narrow, two faiths can live together side by side, just as two soups can be cooked together in one pot. Let us live together like brothers, and we will need no additional love!"[27]

Reasonable and humane though this offer of coexistence may be, it is a temptation that must be overcome. Njegoš insists that coexistence between Muslims and Christians is not possible, for "Bairam cannot be observed with Christmas." Voivode Batrić explains why Montenegrin Christians can never recognize their Muslim relatives:

> Turkish brothers . . . not one of us can live here peacefully, what with powers that are jarring for it; for both of us there is simply no room! Accept the faith of your own forefathers! Guard the honor of our dear fatherland! The wolf needs not the cunning of the fox! Nor has the hawk the need for eyeglasses. Start tearing down your minarets and mosques. Lay the Serbian Christmas log on the fire, paint the Easter Eggs various colors, observe with care the Lent and Christmas fasts. As for the rest do what your heart desires! If you don't listen to Batric, I do swear by the faith of Obilic and by these arms in which I put trust, that both of our faiths will be swimming in blood. Better will be the one that does not sink. Bairam cannot be observed with Christmas! Is that not so, Montenegrin brothers?[28]

The poem ends with the Christmas Eve massacre of Montenegrin Muslims and the destruction of all of their mosques. Bishop Danilo celebrates the bloody Christmas, exclaiming, "You have brought me great gladness, my falcons, great joy for me. Heroic liberty! This bright morning you've been resurrected from every tomb of our forefathers."[29] *The Mountain Wreath* in striking clarity exhibits the existential problem Slavic Muslims posed for many of their Christian neighbors. The refusal of recognition and the negation of the "Other" who transgresses definitional boundaries has continued long after Njegoš in the acclaimed works of Ivo Andrić, Dobrica Ćosić, and Vuk Draskovic. *The Mountain Wreath* was required reading in all Yugoslav secondary schools. Muslim students who dared to protest were labeled fundamentalists and harshly disciplined.

Ivo Andrić, V. S. Naipaul, and the Literature of *Ressentiment*

The nexus between Serb national epics and the construction of Bosnian Muslims as an insipid and alien presence in the region is a tradition that continued unbroken during the Tito era in the works of the most prominent Yugoslav *homme de lettres*, Ivo Andrić. Andrić was the only South Slav writer to be awarded the Nobel Prize. This was largely due to his famous novel *The Bridge on the Drina*, which relates five centuries of Bosnian life as it unfolds in the town of Visegrad and around the beautiful Ottoman Bridge built by the Bosnian grand vizier Mehmet Sokolovic Pasha.[30] Andrić was born a Croat in the town of Travnik and spent his childhood in Visegrad. In many ways he embodied the unresolved tension between Yugoslav universalism and ethnoreligious particularity. During his adult life he identified with Serb nationalism because he felt that it was the core around which a Yugoslav integralism could be constructed. It would be difficult to overstate the enormous prestige and influence Andrić enjoyed in the former Yugoslavia and as its chief literary representative abroad. The Serbian Academy's 1974 bibliography of works by and on Andrić lists well over twelve hundred critical items dating from 1914 and stretching to the early seventies.[31] There has, of course, been much more written about him following his death in 1975 and the posthumous publication of his work.

Andrić, it seems, could never forgive his fellow Slavic Muslims because for him they embodied the "traitorous seed" whose very existence contributed to and prevented reconciliation between the Western and Eastern European churches he so keenly desired in the lands of the South Slavs. The parallels with *The Mountain Wreath* are direct and Andrić himself frequently cited Njegoš as his most important intellectual influence. He approvingly quotes him, "The lions turned into the tillers of the soil / the cowardly and the covetous turned into Turks." This sentiment against the "Turkish converts" is made most explicit in his doctoral dissertation written as a young diplomat in Vienna and published under the title *The Development of Spiritual Life in Bosnia Under the Influence of Turkish Rule.*[32] In an unimaginative regurgitation of the verities of early twentieth-century orientalist scholarship, Andrić is chiefly concerned with demonstrating the baleful influence of five centuries of Ottoman rule in Bosnia-Herzegovina. Bosnia should have been a bridge between the Christian West and East, were it not for the sudden intrusion of Islam. He writes,

> Having following [*sic*] to Islam, it [Bosnia] was in no position to fulfill this, its natural role, and to take part in the cultural development of Christian Europe, to which it ethnographically and geographically belonged. What is more, thanks to the domestic Islamised element, Bosnia even became a mighty bulwark against the Christian West. And in that unnatural position it was to stay for the entire duration of Turkish rule.[33]

Andrić's historical description of Bosnia is remarkably similar to his fictional ones stressing that "Bosnia was conquered by an Asiatic military people whose social institutions and customs spelled the negation of any and all Christian culture and whose religion—begotten under other skies and social circumstances and quite incapable of adaptation—shackled the life of the spirit and the mind in Bosnia, disfiguring it and moulding it into an exceptional case."[34] 's final verdict on five centuries of Islamic civilization in the Balkans is that "all researchers into Bosnia, its past be they Serbo-Croatian or foreign have felt in a position to state in concert and more or less forcefully that the effect of Turkish rule was absolutely negative."[35] As for those who point out the many outstanding accomplishments of Ottoman civilization and its unique European-Islamic synthesis in Bosnia, Andrić replies that this "can be acceptable only to the superficial observers and lovers of the picturesque and the strange."[36]

Following in Andrić's footsteps, such leading Serbian writers as Dobrica Ćosić and Vuk Draskovic have played a central role in encouraging the recent genocidal onslaught against Bosnian Muslims. It was Ćosić's inflammatory novels and his role in the circulation of the *SANU* memorandum charging a contemporary genocide against Serbs in Kosovo that directly fueled genocide in Bosnia and attempted genocide in Kosovo. Andrić, for his part, was well aware of and glaringly omits the fact that the Ottoman Bridge on the Drina was the very site of some of the worst atrocities in Yugoslavia during World War II. Hundreds of Muslims from the area were taken in August 1942 by the Chetniks of Draza Mihailovic and ritually tortured and murdered on the bridge with their bodies disposed of in the river.[37] It is therefore an unsurprising though bitter irony that thirty years after the awarding of the Nobel Prize to Andrić the Drina River under the Ottoman Bridge in Visegrad again ran red with the blood of Muslims massacred in the valley. Visegrad and the old Ottoman Bridge were the setting for some of the most nightmarish chapters in the latest genocide.[38]

Andrić's animus toward the "traitorous seed" of Bosnian Muslims uncannily foreshadows the "convert thesis" developed by the recent Nobel laureate V. S. Naipaul. In his latest book, *Beyond Belief: Islamic Excursions Among the Converted Peoples*, Naipaul argues that

> Islam is in its origins an Arab religion. Everyone not an Arab who is a Muslim is a convert. Islam is not simply a matter of conscience or private belief. It makes imperial demands. . . . His holy places are in Arab lands; his sacred language is Arabic. . . . He rejects his own; he becomes, whether he likes it or not, a part of the Arab story. The convert has to turn away from everything that is his. The disturbance for societies is immense, and even after a thousand years can remain unresolved. . . . In the Islam of converted countries there is an element of neurosis and nihilism. These countries can be easily set on the boil.[39]

Unexplained is how, if after fifteen hundred years of one of the world's dominant civilizations non-Arab Muslims are inauthentic "converts," present-day Christians and Hindus are sui generis followers of a tradition without origin and hegemony. Naipaul's opinion of Islamic civilization in India eerily echoes Andrić's verdict on Ottoman civilization, "Islam had moved on here, to this part of Greater-India, after its devastation of India proper, turning the religious-cultural light of the subcontinent, so far as this region was concerned, into the light of a dead star."[40] While Naipaul's latest effort at abstract discernment garnered the customary laudatory reviews among the *literati demimonde*, scholars of Islamic societies were quick to ridicule its less than simple-minded conclusions. However, none appreciated its basis in the thought of the fellow Brahmanical ideologue V. D. Savarkar, the founder of modern Hindu ultranationalism and its present avatar, the

RSS/BJP bloc.[41] Savarkar's obsession with "converts" and "turncoats" among India's vast non-Vedic Hindu populations is remarkably similar to that expressed by Serb ultranationalists against the "traitorous seed" of "Serb-Muslims" and "Serb-Catholics." As the father of the modern ideology of *Hindutva*, Savarkar argued that all of India's inhabitants, in order to be truly authentic "citizens," must be brought to their "original" faith. Of Muslims he writes:

> For though Hindustan to them is Fatherland as to any other Hindu, yet it is not to them a Holy Land too. Their holy-land is far off in Arabia or Palestine. Their mythology and God-men, ideas, and heroes are not the children of this soil. Consequently, their names and their outlook smacks of a foreign origin. Their love is divided. . . . They do not look upon India as their holy-land.[42]

Naipaul reveals his debt to Sarvarkar by writing:

> The fantasy still lives; and for the Muslim converts of the subcontinent it is the start of their neurosis, because in this fantasy the convert forgets who or what he is and becomes the violator. . . . There was also the Muslim convert's attitude to the land where he lives. To the convert his land is of no religious or historical importance; its relics are of no account; only the sands of Arabia are sacred. . . . There probably has been no imperialism like that of Islam and the Arabs. The Gauls, after five hundred years of Roman rule, could recover their old gods and reverences; those beliefs hadn't died; they lay just below the Roman surface. But Islam seeks as an article of faith to erase the past; the believers in the end honor Arabia alone; they have nothing to return to.[43]

Just as Serb ultranationalists were erasing five centuries of Ottoman-Islamic civilization in Bosnia, the disciples of Savarkar's ideology of *Hindutva* in the BJP-RSS were leveling the historic Mughul Baburi Mosque and instigating pogroms across Northern India that took the lives of thousands of Muslims. The same drive to transgress and "purify" later led the Taliban Islamic movement to destroy priceless treasures of Afghan Buddhist culture that had survived all manners of pillage over the centuries finally succumb to an especially virulent strain of barbarism in our lifetime. The recent examples of Orthodox, Hindu, Muslim, and Jewish ultranationalisms demonstrates how myth making and *ressentiment* play a crucial role in the politics of ethnoreligious conflict and how such movements share much more in common with one another than they do with those many more over the millennia perfectly inclined toward tolerance and coexistence.[44]

To comprehend how plum brandy–imbibing Slavic Muslim urbanites, who were often much less religiously fervent than their Catholic and Orthodox counterparts, found themselves interned en masse in rape/death camps in the heart of Europe at the end of the twentieth century, one has to consider how demagogues in Southeastern Europe so readily could employ rhetoric concerning "fundamentalism" and "terrorism" for the purpose of genocide against Muslims. Outside of Serb nationalist circles, few in Bosnia at the beginning of 1991 could have imagined that the impending Yugoslav crisis would culminate in genocide. This was despite a brazen threat in the Bosnian parliament by Radovan Karadzic that if the majority Bosnian Muslim and Croat population voted for independence it would lead to the extinction of the Bosnian Muslim people. This chilling threat directly echoed the infamous one hurled by Hitler against Jews in the Reichstag in 1938. The Bosnian president, Alija Izetbegovic, naively responded that the international community in this day and age would never allow genocide and that since the Bosnian Muslims were unarmed and refused to engage in hostilities it would be impossible for a war to break out. Izetbegovic faced the classic "security dilemma" presented by Thucydides and embellished by his most discerning student, Thomas Hobbes. To arm in defence of Serb nationalist threats would have provided Karadzic and his coterie with the ammunition concerning a "Muslim plot" they were seeking. Thus, when the Belgrade federal authorities ordered the Bosnian Territorial Defence Force to disarm, Izetbegovic hastened to comply. He repeatedly stated that by pursuing nonviolent pacifism Serb extremists would be deprived of oxygen and sidelined by "reasonable" people in Serbia and the JNA as well as in the broader international community.

Izetbegovic, a deeply spiritual and humanistic student of philosophy, would have done his people a great service by having read the most profound and disturbing critic of modern liberalism, Carl Schmitt. In his magnum opus, *The Concept of the Political* (1928), Schmitt stated that liberal attempts at avoiding bloodshed at all cost through discussion and compromise failed to appreciate that human political existence at its core was based upon the antagonism between "friend and foe."[45] The struggle between friend and foe at all times carried the potential for violent conflict, giving politics and indeed human existence its essence of utmost seriousness. For Schmitt the possibility of politics plunging into warfare was not merely the exceptional state but, in this capacity as the *Ernst fall*, or decisive case, was also the defining one to which all other spheres of existence from the cultural/aesthetic to the social/economic were subordinated in all their fragility. Echoing Hegel's theory of intersubjectivity and identity formation, Schmitt stated that the peak of politics is the moment when "the enemy is discerned, in which he is known as the negation of one's own destiny—in which and inseparably connected therewith, one's own identity is established and gains a visible figure."[46] Schmitt presented a reading of "the great sentences of the philosopher" Hegel diametrically opposed to that of Alexandre Kojève,

> Adam and Eve had two sons, Cain and Abel. That's the beginning of humanity. . . . That is the dialectical tension that keeps world history moving and world history has not yet come to its end. . . . Remember the great sentences of the philosopher: The relation of the other to oneself is true eternity. The negation of the negation, says the philosopher, is not a neutralization, but true eternity depends on it. Of course, true eternity is the basic concept of his philosophy. The enemy is the gestalt of our self-questioning.[47]

In chillingly prophetic words that have not lost their poignancy from the Warsaw ghetto to the "safe havens" of Srebrenica and Zepa, Schmitt wrote:

> It would be ludicrous to believe that a defenseless people has nothing but friends, and it would be a deranged calculation to suppose that the enemy could perhaps be touched by the absence of a resistance. No one thinks it possible that the world could, for example, be transformed into a condition of pure morality by the renunciation of every aesthetic or economic productivity. Even less can a people hope to bring about a purely moral or purely economic condition of humanity by evading every political decision. If a people no longer possesses the energy or the will to maintain itself in the sphere of politics, the latter will not thereby vanish from the world. Only a weak people will disappear.[48]

The dismal fate of the liberal Bosnians and the refusal of the West to uphold its ostensibly "higher and universal values" when they were most brazenly threatened on its doorstep would seem to vindicate aspects of Carl Schmitt's and Samuel Huntington's theories. This is born out to a certain extent but cannot be considered the final word until we consider Leo Strauss's rejoinder to both Kojève/Fukuyama and Schmitt/Huntington. The indifference of leading Western nations to genocide by a relatively minor southeast European power stemmed from a number of domestic and international factors. The circle of advisers around President Francois Mitterand and Prime Minister John Major viewed Serbia as a historic ally against a unified Germany and felt open contempt and animus toward the European Muslim population that predominated in Bosnia-Herzegovina. While the British and the French were feverishly working to shield the Serbs from air strikes during the buildup to the fall of the UN declared "safe-havens," a high ranking French diplomat indiscreetly spelled out the sentiments of leaders of his government to John Newhouse of the *New Yorker*. He explained that the Europeans

> want to prevent a wider war or the emergence of a rump Muslim state in southeastern Europe—one that might become rich, militant, and an inspiration for ethnic or communal strife elsewhere. Europeans also want to discourage a Bosnian Diaspora of the kind that was generated by the war in Palestine half a century ago. "Our interests are much closer to the Serbs than you think," a French diplomat says. "We worry more about the Muslims than about the Serbs."[49]

The American government under George Bush Sr. didn't necessarily share the same level of animus toward the Germans or Bosnian Muslims for historic reasons but was generally indifferent to the fate of this population and wanted to avoid intervention at all cost because of the upcoming general elections in November 1992. Thus, under the direction of Secretary of State Lawrence Eagleburger, the U.S. set about to deliberately cover up the emergence of Serbian genocide in the spring and summer of 1992, fearing that wide publicity would lead to irresistible pressure to intervene. Details of a program of genocide that involved the set piece massacres of thousands of civilians in places like Prijedor and Brcko and an archipelago of concentration camps were only "discovered" after exposés by Roy Gutman and after an ITN television crew talked its way into the Omerska and Trnopolje concentration camps. It immediately dawned on Gutman that such atrocities on so massive a scale could not have been occurring for months without Western intelligence agencies being aware of them and choosing to look the other way.

Gutman's theory was later confirmed by John Fox, a member of the State Department's Policy Planning Staff, who publicly accused former Secretary of State Lawrence Eagleburger of ordering a cover-up of Serb death camps.[50] After the Gutman and ITN reports in August, Eagleburger claimed that the American government had no evidence of systematic killings and tortures in the camps and knew only of "unpleasant conditions."[51] The American and Anglo-French decision to "look the other way" greatly encouraged Belgrade to expand the speed and scale of its genocidal onslaught. Serb ethnic cleansing operations in the early spring were still tentative before reaching a maddening crescendo in the early summer when it became clear that not only was the West not willing to intervene but also that it was quite willing to assist in covering up the vast crimes being committed. When the West finally acknowledged the crimes, Serb nationalist leaders mocked the pro forma nature of Western condemnation by smirking at the atrocities. Thus, shortly after the British journalist Ed Vulliamy and his American counterpart Roy Gutman had "uncovered" the death camps, they met with the Serb spokesman and Shakespearean scholar Nikola Koljević who could not resist tweaking the naïveté of the Western reporters regarding the culpability of their political establishments:

> "So you found them," he said sardonically, "congratulations!" And then, in a piquant voice that evoked his favourite Shakespearean character, Iago, he embarked on a double-edged reproach: "It took you a long time to find them didn't it? Three months! And so near Venice! All you people could think about was poor sophisticated Sarajevo, Ha-Ha!" and then, with a chill in his voice: "None of you ever had your holidays at Omarska, did you? No Olympic games in Prijedor!"[52]

The refusal by leading Western powers to halt the Bosnian genocide on the heels of their massive intervention in Operation Desert Storm led to a palpable rage not only among militants like bin Laden but also hundreds of millions of common Muslims worldwide. It also led prominent Asian intellectuals like Kishore Mahbubhani to openly ridicule Western claims of possessing a truly universal set of values. The Bosnian genocide also indirectly contributed to the subsequent one in Rwanda. which further dissipated sanctimony about human progress and international order. The Canadian general Romeo Dallaire who headed the early UN presence in Rwanda has stated that with only five thousand troops he could have halted the genocide of five hundred thousand Tutsis at the hands of the machete-wielding Hutu *Interahamwe*. The Clinton administration however, in shock over the Somalia debacle a few months earlier, determined that there would be no intervention by the U.S. or any other international force. The Somalia mission itself was undertaken as a humanitarian diversion to placate growing Muslim outrage over Bosnia. The fact that the mission was never well thought out or taken seriously resulted in the disastrous Mogadishu ambush. This fiasco in turn assured that the low-tech Rwandan genocide would occur unopposed.

Rousseau and Kant: The Tension Between the Universal and the Particular

Jean-Jacques Rousseau's most celebrated essay, *A Discourse on the Origins of Inequality*, is simultaneously a pointed critique and brilliant permutation of Hobbes's paradigm of the "state of nature." In rejecting Hobbes's solution of an authoritarian *Leviathan* demanding absolute obedience in return for protection, Rousseau also challenged the very Hobbesian conception of the *status naturalis*. Where Hobbes saw life in the state of nature as being famously "solitary, nasty, brutish, and short," Rousseau felt that it was an idyllic Eden from which man had fallen rather than escaped.[53] For Rousseau war, oppression, inequality, and misery arise in a complex civil society and the attendant division of labor and ceaseless competition for status. In passages that influenced Hegel's conception of *annerkenung* (recognition), and his "master-slave dialectic," Rousseau highlighted the centrality of greed, comparison, and envy in producing human discord. Crucial to his conception was the distinction between the *amour de soi* of natural humankind and the *amour-propre* that arises in civil society. No exact translation exists in English for these terms, but they are best translated as the "desire for self-preservation" and the "desire for eminence" respectively. In the state of nature the individual was content to slake his limited natural appetites and inclined to transgress the persons of others only on rare occasions where self-preservation warranted. By contrast, *amour-propre* and the willingness to engage in atrocious serial warfare can only arise in hierarchical civilizations where the amassing of wealth, complex division of labor, and incessant competition for dominance and recognition are made possible. In notable contradistinction to Hobbes and his modern devotee Sigmund Freud, Rousseau insisted that humans in the state of nature were filled with natural pity for the suffering of others and developed a corrupted taste for callousness and cruelty only upon leaving it for civil society.

In considering the unspeakable horrors of mass murder, rape, torture, and pillage that have defined ethnocide down the ages, Rousseau in tandem with Hobbes sheds further light on the role of distant onlookers and the ambiguous politics of humanitarian intervention. Here Hobbes's original formulation of the origins of the "natural pity" that Rousseau later expounded would seem to be more persuasive. As a philosopher who radically denied the possibility of a transcendent metaphysical order, Hobbes, in addition to rejecting traditional notions of good and evil, traced even sentiments of human compassion to selfish motives. We feel pity for the suffering of other human beings because, given the vagaries of fate, we readily can identify ourselves in their tragic circumstances. From this it stands to reason that the more one is able to identify the "self" in the suffering of "others" based upon commonalities of kinship, race, religion, and even gender,[54] the greater the likelihood of active expressions of solidarity. Here lies the basis for continuing controversies over the willingness of leading members of the international system to intervene in certain crisis zones and not in others.

To be sure, Rousseau was aware of this ambiguity and addressed it with a customary elegance far exceeding that of any contemporary pundit. In his *Discourse on Political Economy* he conceded that the sentiment of "natural pity" or compassion tended to fade the farther it radiated from the "self." "It seems that the feeling for humanity is dissipated and weakened by being extended over the whole earth, and that we cannot be moved by calamities in Tartary or Japan, as we are by those of a European people. Interest and commiseration must be limited and compressed in some way to make them active."[55] To be fair, the humanitarian nightmares in Bosnia, Kosovo, Rwanda, and East Timor did ignite global concern and much impassioned debate. However, as the year 2000 U.S. presidential debates demonstrated, with both Albert Gore and George W. Bush concurring that nonintervention in Rwanda was appropriate, there is still no consensus as to how much nations are willing to risk in order to respond to humanitarian outrages that through modern communications technology are brought from distant places to family rooms worldwide.

Immanuel Kant's two most significant late essays on international relations, *"Idea for a Universal History from a Cosmopolitan Point of View"* and *"Perpetual Peace"* drew upon the considerations of the Abbé de St. Pierre and his chief commentator, Rousseau. Kant was particularly struck by the contradiction inherent in man's escape from the state of nature through the formation of civil societies only to once again fall into a state of violence and crime in the international arena. States without any higher authority to restrain them, recast their citizenry into the *"warre of all against all"* during their frequent bouts of armed conflict. Riding the early wave of Enlightenment optimism, Kant in many ways foreshadowed some present-day globalization enthusiasts and their dreams of an international federation and normative-legal order, "Although this government at present exists only as a rough outline, nevertheless in all the members there is rising a feeling which each has for the preservation of the whole. This gives hope finally that after many reformative revolutions, a universal cosmopolitan condition, which Nature has as her ultimate purpose, will come into being."[56]

Leo Strauss: Mediating Between Particularity and Universality

The fact that the blissful universal End State remains ever elusive is not to endorse the valorization of particularity or to be pessimistically resigned to it in the manner of Schmitt-Huntington. In opposing Kojève-Fukuyama's "End of History" thesis, Strauss insisted from the position of Platonic political philosophy that particularity and the "Self" had also to be transcended with an eye to a universal standard of what would be best for humans qua humans.

In his dialogue with Kojève on Xenophon's *Hieron*, Strauss wrote, echoing Nietzsche, that such an End State of jaded "Last Men" would inevitably lead to a backlash and rekindling of recognitional struggles even if derived from purely nihilistic impulses. Strauss's relation to both Nietzsche and Schmitt has, however, been widely misinterpreted in recent writings. The young Strauss first garnered widespread attention with a brilliantly subtle review of Schmitt's *The Concept of the Political* in 1932, leading Germany's most prominent political theorist to comment, "He x-rayed me." Schmitt insisted on including the review in future editions of his magnum opus and was crucial in arranging a Rockefeller Fellowship for

Strauss to study Hobbes in France and England in May 1932, just prior to the Nazi's assumption of power. Strauss in his critical review of Schmitt noted that whereas Hobbes sought to neutralize the political as representative of the *status naturalis qua status belli*, Schmitt sought to affirm the political in a modern liberal age of "neutralization and depoliticization." Strauss discerned Schmitt's fatal flaw as being a critique of liberalism that still took place within the "horizon of liberalism" set by its modern founder, Hobbes.[57] Modern liberal critics of Strauss, such as Shadia Drury and Stephen Holmes, have woefully misinterpreted this criticism to mean that even Carl Schmitt was not antiliberal enough for Leo Strauss![58] Hobbes, as noted earlier, insisted that notions of good and evil were purely subjective and self-serving and that endless disputations over them meant that society would always be engaged in acrimony. He felt that such debates over the "good life" should be dispensed with in society in favor of safety and consumption and in effect conformity or "agreement at all cost." Lucidly comprehending that both classical political philosophy and prophetic religion insisted on posing the eternally divisive question of what is right and good, Hobbes employed his staggering genius in attacking both what he derided as "Aristotle and the schoolmen," and the "Kingdom of Darknesse."

Strauss's critique of liberalism both in its authoritarian Hobbesian conception and its later permissive and tolerant Lockean manifestation was meant to be a defence of morality and the possibility of discerning virtue and the good as transcendent ideals insisted upon by Athens as well as Jerusalem and Mecca. In response to Kojève, Strauss alludes to Schmitt's (and his own) debt to Nietzsche when he raises the issue of "the order of things" (*rank ordnung*) and states that such a depoliticized End State would mean a human existence reduced to "production and consumption," a "world of entertainment, a world of amusement, a world without *seriousness*."[59]

The key text in rendering the final verdict on Kojève's vision of the triumph of modern bourgeois liberalism in "the universal and homogeneous state" is *Thus Spoke Zarathustra*. The Prophet Zarathustra confronts the Last Men of this looming age:

"We have discovered happiness" say the Last Men and blink. . . . A little poison now and then: that produces pleasant dreams. And a lot of poison at last, for a pleasant death. . . . They still work, for work is entertainment. But they take care the entertainment does not exhaust them. . . . No herdsman and one herd. Everyone wants the same thing, everyone is the same: whoever thinks otherwise goes voluntarily into the madhouse.[60]

Strauss thus stakes a position midpoint while attempting to mediate and transcend the modern universalism of Kojève and the affirmation of particularity by Schmitt. The danger of tyranny and evil from the individual to the collective level is a problem coeval with politics and society. Accordingly for Strauss, in sharing Hobbes's moral relativism Schmitt's "affirmation of the political as such is the affirmation of fighting as such, wholly irrespective of what is being fought for. . . . The affirmation of the political as such proves to be liberalism with the opposite polarity."[61] For Strauss modern liberal relativism and the attempt at agreement at all cost can be sustained only if humans relinquish asking "the question of what is right." The rekindling of the political and the grouping of humans into friends and foes engaging in mortal combat can only be justified if one takes not agonism but the moral question of what is right seriously.

The betrayal of Bosnia has lowered the threshold of civilization across the globe and has starkly demonstrated that, pretensions of order and values aside, the nature of international relations is based upon a cultural and geopolitical hierarchy very selective in its application of international law and morality and this "new order" is still characterized by a struggle for recognition, which is a struggle to the death. In reality, the role of self and other has undergone radical permutations throughout history. Much of the worst historical bloodshed has also involved what Freud termed the "narcissism of minor differences" within groups sharing the same culture, religion, or race. Proponents of a racially and religiously charged "clash of civilizations" against the Islamic world and China would do well to keep this in mind. Both Plato and Thucydides have also left us with the pregnant example of the demise of Athenian virtue and democracy stemming from the hubris and lust for empire of tyrannically inclined elites who cloaked their unhealthy ambitions with the high-minded rhetoric of patriotism and liberation.

Notes

1. Cf. Francis Fukuyama, "The End of History?" *National Interest* 16 (Summer 1989): 3–18. Samuel Huntington, "The Clash of Civilizations?" *Foreign Affairs* 72.3 (Summer 1993).

2. Alexandre Kojève, *Introduction to the Reading of Hegel*, assembled by Raymond Queneau, ed. Allan Bloom, trans. James H. Nichols Jr. (New York: Basic, 1969).

3. Ibid., 43.

4. Ibid.

5. Benedict de Spinoza, *A Theologico-Political Treatise*, trans. R. H. M. Elwes (New York: Dover, 1951), 55–56.

6. See Karl Marx, *On the Jewish Question*, ed. David McLellan (Oxford: Oxford University Press, 2000).

7. Zygmunt Bauman, *The Holocaust and Modernity* (Ithaca: Cornell University Press, 1989), 71.

8. Karl Schleunes, *The Twisted Road to Auschwitz* (Urbana: University of Illinois Press, 1970).

9. Bauman, *The Holocaust and Modernity*, 52.

10. Henri Pirenne, *Muhammad and Charlemagne*, trans. Bernard Miall (New York: Barnes and Noble, 1955).

11. Robert Bartlett, *The Making of Europe: Conquest, Colonization, and Cultural Change, 950–1350* (Princeton: Princeton University Press, 1993).

12. Thomas Naff, "The Ottoman Empire and the European States System," in Hedley Bull and Adam Watson, eds., *The Expansion of International Society* (Oxford: Oxford University Press, 1984), 143.

13. See Mujeeb R. Khan and M. Hakan Yavuz, "Bringing Turkey Into Europe," *Current History* 102.662 (March 2003): 119–123.

14. Paul Smith, *Disraeli: A Brief Life* (Cambridge: Cambridge University Press, 1996), 189. Gladstone's recent biographer Roy Jenkins considered him to have been a "proto-Christian Democrat" who advocated a concert of Europe based upon a common faith and civilization, thus accounting for his vehement opposition to the Ottoman-Muslim presence in Southeastern Europe. Interestingly, this anti-Muslim vehemence paired with a broadminded European continentalism was shared by his iconic Liberal Party successor David Lloyd George. See Roy Jenkins, *Gladstone: A Biography* (New York: Random House, 1997).

15. See Kemal H. Karpat, *Ottoman Population 1830–1914: Demographics and Social Characteristics* (Madison: University of Wisconsin Press, 1985), 385.

16. Allan and Helen Cutler, *The Jew as Ally of Muslims: Medieval Roots of Anti-Semitism* (Notre Dame: University of Notre Dame Press, 1986).

17. John Doyle Klier writes, "The special targets were Muslims and Jews. After the third reverse at Plevna, it was reported that Jews and Tatars had taken cover or kept to the rear, helping to demoralize the beaten Russian forces." See John Doyle Klier, *Imperial Russia's Jewish Question, 1855-1881* (Cambridge: Cambridge University Press, 1995), 393.

18. See Omer Bartov, *War, Genocide, and Modern Identity* (New York: Oxford University Press, 2000).

19. Cf. *Report of the International Commission to Inquire Into the Causes and Conduct of the Balkan Wars* (Washington, D.C.: Carnegie Endowment for International Peace, 1914).

20. Lloyd and Suzanne Rudolph, "Modern Hate," *New Republic*, March 22, 1993.

21. On the ontological derivation of civil society from the mutual fear of others in a state of nature, see Hobbes, *De Cive*, 111–119. On the role played by the human penchant for envious comparision and the desire for eminence see *De Cive*, 232–33, and Thomas Hobbes, *Leviathan*, C. B. Macpherson (London: Penguin, 1981), 225–26.

22. Hobbes, *Leviathan*, 161.

23. For Hobbes's pointed assault on religion see *Leviathan*, 627–715. For his attack on classical political philosophy see *Leviathan*, 211.

24. Ibid, 215.

25. P. P. Njegoš, *The Mountain Wreath*, trans. and ed. Vasa D. Mihailovich (Irvine: Schlacks, 1986).

26. Ibid., 5.

27. Ibid., 61.

28. Ibid., 31.

29. Ibid., 95.

30. Ivo Andrić, *The Bridge on the Drina*, trans. by Lovett F. Edwards (Chicago: University of Chicago Press, 1977).

31. Cf. Henry R. Cooper Jr., "The Image of Bosnia in the Fiction of Ivo Andrić," *Serbian Studies* 3.1/2 (Fall/Spring 1984–85): 83–105.

32. Ivo Andrić, *The Development of Spiritual Life in Bosnia Under the Influence of Turkish Rule*, ed. and trans. Zelimir B. Jurici and John F. Loud (Durham: Duke University Press, 1990).

33. Ibid., 17.

34. Ibid., 16–17.

35. Ibid., 38.

36. Ibid.

37. These details were provided by the historian Smail Cekic in "History of Genocide Against the Bosniaks," unpublished paper delivered at the *International Conference on Bosnia and Bosniaks*, Sarajevo, May 1997.

38. For a rather tardy connection between Andrić's novel and the recent slaughter on the old Ottoman bridge see Chris Hedges, "The Bridge on the Drina: Trail of Pillage and Slaughter," *New York Times*, March 25, 1996.

39. V. S. Naipaul, *Beyond Belief: Islamic Excursions Among the Converted Peoples* (Boston: Little, Brown, 1998), xi.

40. Ibid., 25.

41. I am grateful to Omar Qureshi for first pointing out the source of Naipaul's "converts thesis" in the writings of V. D. Savarkar.

42. Vinayak Damodar Savarkar, *Hindutva: Who Is a Hindu?* (Bombay: Savarkar, 1969), 113.

43. Naipaul, 334.

44. For those such as the self-proclaimed "Christian humanist" committed to a "Clash of Civilizations thesis" this obvious insight is intolerable. In a book review of Mark Juergensmeyer's study of religious ultranationalism titled, *"The New Cold War?"* Christian humanist Paul Johnson took issue with the author's criticism of all forms of religious chauvinism. Instead, Johnson defends genocidal hatred when directed against Muslims as acceptable: "I think the present involvement of the United States in Bosnia is a direct consequence of the Serbs' fear that they could become victims of an Islamic Jihad." After ascertaining that the tiny Muslim population of Bosnia was a threat to all of Serbia, Johnson turned to the impoverished and marginalized Indian Muslim minority, "Even the Hindu nationalists, who are theoretically capable of taking over the Indian state, are merely reacting to what they see as a militant Muslim threat." See Paul Johnson, *New York Times Book Review*, May 9, 1993. Similarly, Daniel Pipes has recently written an article approvingly comparing the example of the RSS at Ayodhya and radical Zionist claims to the Dome of the Rock/Al-Aqsa Mosque complex. See Daniel Pipes, "India's Temple Mount," *National Post*, January 18, 2001. The use of myth and fabrication by Hindu nationalist to destroy the rich Islamic cultural presence in India is shown in a series of recent articles by the distinguished historians Romila Thapar and Richard Eaton. See "Temple Desecration in Pre-Modern India," *Frontline* 17.25 (December 9–22, 2000).

45. Carl Schmitt, *The Concept of the Political,* trans. George Schwab (Chicago: University of Chicago Press, 1996).

46. Ibid., 67.

47. Cited in Wolfgang Palaver, "A Girardian Reading of Schmitt's Political Theology," *Telos* 93 (Fall 1992): 66–67.

48. Schmitt, *The Concept of the Political,* 53.

49. Cited in Rabia Ali and Lawrence Lifschultz, eds., *Why Bosnia? Writings on the Balkan War* (Stony Creek, Conn.: Pamphleteers, 1993), xlvii.

50. Wolfgang Munchau, "Bush Team Accused of Serb Cover-up," *New York Times*, March 19, 1994, 13.

51. Gutman, 92.

52. Ed Vulliamy, "Middle Managers of Genocide." *Nation*, June 10, 1996, 13.

53. Jean-Jacques Rousseau, *A Discourse on the Origins of Inequality*, trans. Maurice Cranston (London: Penguin, 1984), 98–99.

54. Consider how the issue of mass rape in Bosnia for the first time galvanized an international feminist response on the basis of gender solidarity. This solidarity was later extended to significant opposition to the Taliban's mistreatment of Afghan women.

55. Jean-Jacques Rousseau, "Discourse on Political Economy," in *Rousseau's Political Writings*, trans. Julia Conaway Bondanella (New York: Norton), 69.

56. Immanuel Kant, "Idea for a Universal History from a Cosmopolitan Point of View, in *Philosophical Writings*, ed. Ernst Behler (New York: Continuum, 1986), 260.

57. Leo Strauss, "Notes on Carl Schmitt, The Concept of the Political," trans. Harvey Lomax, in Carl Schmitt, *The Concept of the Political* (Chicago: University of Chicago Press, 1996), 91–92.

58. See Shadia Drury, *Leo Strauss and the American Right* (New York: St. Martin's, 1997), 91–96. And Stephen Holmes, *The Anatomy of Anti-Liberalism* (Cambridge: Harvard University Press, 1993), 61–87.

59. Strauss, "Notes on Carl Schmitt," 100–101.

60. Friedrich Nietzsche, *Thus Spoke Zarathustra*, trans. R. J. Hollingdale (London: Penguin, 1961), 46.

61. Strauss, "Notes on Carl Schmitt," 105.

Part II

Europe and the Muslims: The Permanent Crusade?

Tomaž Mastnak

This essay is about Europe's attitude toward the Muslims. It does not cover the whole range of European attitudes toward the Muslim world. It deals, however, with what is most important. As such, the text that follows is a story about European animosity—not only because hostile views of the Muslims were prevalent in European history but because without that hostility there would not be *European* history in the strict sense of the word. For, without that hostility, Europe as we know it today—Europe as a political community—would not exist. Europe as a self-conscious collective entity emerged relatively late in the course of human events, and Western, Latin Christians' hostility toward the Muslims—anti-Muslim sentiments, ideas, calls for action, and action—played a key role in its formation.

The formation of Europe is a "history of the future."[1] The logic of Europe's creation was not consumed in the historical process of its creation. Rather, it has remained at work throughout the subsequent history of Europe, determining or, at least, influencing Europe's nature well into our own days. This is especially true of the animosity toward the Muslims that lies at the core of the historical constitution of Europe and the creation of European identity. In this article, however, I do not discuss the formation of Europe.[2] My story begins, rather, with the establishment of Europe as a political community. Two preliminary clarifications, however, are necessary: first, about the creation of the Muslims as the enemy of Christianity and Christendom; and second, about the role that animosity toward the Muslims played in the articulation of Europe as the historical form of Western unity that, at the end of the Middle Ages, succeeded Christendom.

Animosity Toward the Muslims and the Formation of Europe as a Political Community

Western animosity toward the Muslims has a longer history than Europe itself, yet considerably shorter than the Muslim presence on north Mediterranean soil. It did not originate with the Arab expansion in the seventh and eighth centuries.[3] The Western Christians, then, did not see the Muslims as a special threat. When they appeared in Christian lands the Muslims joined the hosts of "pagans" and "infidels" inhabiting the Western Christian imaginary world and the numerous enemies against whom the Christians fought innumerable wars. Among pagans, infidels, and enemies, however, the Muslims held no privileged place. They were not yet the chosen enemy-people. The Latin Christians' early response to the Muslims was moderate in tone,[4] and Latin Christians were, in general, indifferent to a culture and religion about which even the educated ones among them, before 1100, knew virtually nothing.[5]

At the close of the eleventh century the Latin West was coming out of a deep social transformation and redistribution of power that had taken place in an atmosphere overflowing with millenarian, eschatological, apocalyptic, and chiliastic fears and expectations and was determinedly striving for unity and peace among Christians. It was then that Muslims were made *the* enemy of Christianity and Christendom. Constructing the Muslims as the Enemy was, in fact, constitutive of the formation of Christendom—the unified Christian society that found its realization in the crusade. This new holy war, in turn, would have been impossible without the elaboration of that enemy image.[6]

The crusade was, at least at its inception, the war of Christendom against the Muslims.[7] With the Crusades, the Christian attitude toward the Muslims began to differ from Christian attitudes toward other known peoples. What distinguished the Christian attitude toward the Muslims was its fundamentally antagonistic nature.[8] Made the quintessential, "normative," enemy of Christianity and Christendom,[9] the Muslims now represented infidelity itself. They were regarded as the fundamental enemy, the personification of the very religion of Antichrist. The Muslim world became no less than "the antithetical system, the social Antichrist."[10]

As we see, this animosity toward the Muslims was not invented by Europeans, for at the time of the launching of the Crusades Europe as a political community did not yet exist. *Europe*, it is true, is a classical word—which, however, was of no great importance in the ancient Mediterranean world. The same is true of the Middle Ages, where the word was sporadically used in connection with the myth of Europa and as a vague geographical notion. Until the fifteenth century the term *Europe* did not figure as a political notion.[11] Until then it had very little general meaning, lacked integrative and mobilizing power, was not used self-descriptively by any political entity, and did not invoke a "sense of usness."[12]

This began to change in the fourteenth and especially fifteenth centuries. The word *Europe* now began to acquire distinctive emotional tones. Latin Christians began to talk of Europe as the largest community to which they saw themselves as belonging, and of themselves as Europeans. Used to rally Latin Christians for common action, the term *Europe* began to function as the bearer of Western common, collective, political consciousness.[13] This was the beginning of European history: it was then that Europe as a self-conscious collective entity emerged.

The event that crystallized this change was the capture of Constantinople by the Ottomans, in 1453. It was the Latin Christians' response to the fall of Constantinople that brought about the articulation of Europe as a political community. To that articulation animosity toward the Muslims was of central importance. While not invented by Europeans, anti-Muslim sentiments and ideas played a key role in the making of Europeans, and of Europe. This point is crucial to my understanding of the formation of Europe as a political community and thus needs to be explained more precisely.

This fundamentalist animosity toward the Muslims that was of such importance to the formation of Europe cannot be satisfactorily explained as a reaction to the Ottoman presence in some of the territories of the geographical entity called Europe. It developed, rather, when the Western Christian world was roused to the crusade. And even when it first occurred, that animosity was not a response to a Muslim threat: the Muslims gave no pretext for the crusade.[14] Formative of Christendom, that fundamentally inimical attitude toward the Muslims had not only survived the disintegration of Christendom as the medieval form of Western unity but also lent its creative potential to the formation of a new Western unity: Europe.

That animosity toward the Muslims was adopted and regenerated by Western Christians when they began their transformation into Europeans. In response to the Ottoman conquests in geographical Europe, Western Christians were able to draw on the existing hostility toward the Muslims to invoke a sense of unity and community. They capitalized on anti-Muslim ideas and sentiments they had inherited from Christendom. Specific to this new situation was the linking of animosity toward the Muslims (now represented by the symbolic figure of the "Turk"), for the first time, with the notion of Europe. The novelty was that *Europe* became the reference point for the "sense of usness" directed against the "Turk." The notion of Europe and wars against the Turks were united in an action program of "chasing the Turk out of Europe." The crusade was translated into European terms.[15]

Geographically defined with much greater exactitude than ever before, and regarded as a cultural and religious whole, Europe became both the agent and the arena of political action. Europe began to be represented as the Christians' homeland, fatherland, and native soil.[16] As the common Christian *patria* whose freedom, religion, and way of life were seen as threatened by the Turk,[17] Europe became a community fighting to cleanse its territory of the Turks. This was the "European moment." Europe emerged as a political community when Latin Christians set out to "erase the Turkish name from Europe," to "exterminate the Turk in Europe," and (which became the most frequently used formula) to "chase the Turk out of Europe."[18] Wanting to cleanse Europe of the Turk, Latin Christians transformed into Europeans. In what follows, I will show that this idea of cleansing, expressing a fundamentally inimical attitude toward the Muslims, remained—and remains—Europe's *spiritus rector*.

European Unions: The Establishment of Europe as a Political Community

Once Europe was invented some time had to pass for the new notion of the largest community of Western Christians—extending toward the Christian lands of today's Eastern Europe with quite some ambivalence[19]—to be established. Throughout this establishment process, as well as after its completion, the Europeans' hostility toward the Muslims—far from having been made obsolete—continued to play a prominent role in European politics and political imagination. Indeed, what we may call the crusading spirit— the epitome of that fundamentalist anti-Muslim attitude—appears to be still alive in our own days. I will discuss this in the next section. First, however, I will briefly turn to the establishment of Europe as a political community.

The term *Europe* coexisted, and was used interchangeably, with *Christendom* for more than two centuries after *Europe* had come to connote the largest Western body politic. A remark of the famous cartographer Ortelius, however, indicated which of the two collective nouns was coming into greater favor. The entry "Christians" in his *Synonimia geographica* from 1578 contained only the words *vide Evropaei* ("see Europeans"). Christendom was holy, *sainte crestienté*, as one of the first crusading chronicles put it. However, even before Ortelius converted Christians into Europeans, Europe itself had acquired its own "sacred" quality. Louis Le Roy, a French scholar working for the revival of the "science of politics," delivered an oration in 1559 in which he called on Christian rulers to end hostilities among themselves and to stop the Mohammedan conquests in Europe. Europe is represented, in Le Roy's plea, as "our common mother" who speaks to Christian princes with a sacred voice. To make his argument convincing, the author urged the princes, "Do but listen to the most sacred voice of Europe."[20]

Once the common mother Europe began to speak with a sacred voice, *Christendom* was doomed to become an archaic word. The "common bastion of Christianity against every outward enemy," of which Komensky wrote in his *Angelus pacis* (1667), was a bastion of "all the Christians in Europe"— and gradually became Europe itself.[21] The Peace Treaty of Utrecht (1713) was the last major diplomatic document in which the term *Christian republic* (synonymous with Christendom) was used. But while this peace treaty was being negotiated, and written in diplomats' conservative language, political publicists dealing with the same events were already using a new language. Jonathan Swift, for example, spoke about the "Balance of *Europe*" as the precondition for the "Good and Quiet of *Europe*," the "Tranquility of *Europe*," and the "Repose of *Europe*."[22] Daniel Defoe, hired by the opposite party in English politics, also wrote of the "ballance of power" in Europe as the "ground of a safe and lasting peace in Europe." He, moreover, contrasted the contemporary "affairs in Europe" to those in "Christendom before."[23] When Bolingbroke, in the 1730s, reflected on the dynastic wars concluded by the Treaty of Utrecht, he analyzed the events from the point of view of the "general history of Europe." As an actor in those events, Bolingbroke self-critically remembered how "imperfect" were his notions "of the situation of Europe in that extraordinary crisis," as a consequence of which he could only see "the true interest of my country in a half-light." What was needed to make good political decisions, and to understand politics, was "a knowledge of the true political system of Europe."[24] His was a European history in the strict sense of the word, central to which were notions like "the general system of Europe," "the general interest of Europe," "the true interest of Europe," "the common interest of Europe," "the whole constitution of Europe," "the balance of power in Europe," and "the general system of power in Europe."[25] Within this conceptual framework it was possible to analyze actions and ambitions of the "powers of Europe"—and especially of the "principal nations of Europe"—and relations among them, as well as to envisage effective pursuit, or maintenance, of security, liberties, tranquillity, and peace of Europe.[26] At an earlier stage of those wars Davenant wrote in a distinctively modern language of the "Interest of *Europe*" and argued that England's role was to "preserve *Europe*, & to maintain our Post of holding the Ballance" (which, he explained, "all *Europe*" expected from England).[27]

From the Duke of Sully at least, plans and projects for peace and unity in the West were plans and projects for specifically European unity and peace. Sully, a minister of the late Henry IV of France, wrote his "Grand Design" for peace in Europe (which he attributed to the murdered king), at the beginning of the seventeenth century. He entailed "all Europe" being "regulated and governed as one great family."[28] Political writers and statesmen, even in our own century,[29] have found inspiring Sully's idea to "divide Europe"—through a number of "different dismemberings," "cessions, exchanges, and transpositions"—"equally among a certain number of powers, in such a manner, that none of them might have cause either of envy or fear, from the possessions or power of the others."[30] Richelieu, who under Louis XIII decisively influenced domestic and foreign policies of France, gave expression to his own ideas of European unity and peace in a badly written play performed only once shortly before his death.[31] The fact that he regarded European unity and peace as a vehicle of French domination in Europe did not discredit the idea of unity and peace, for this idea is by definition an idea of supremacy.

One of the famous plans for European unity and peace was written by William Penn in 1693. In his *Essay Towards the Present and Future Peace of Europe*, Penn argued that, in the interest of peace and justice, the "sovereign princes of Europe" should agree to establish a "European Imperial Diet, Parliament, or Estates," which was to settle peacefully "all differences depending between one sovereign and another."[32] He wished heartily that the honour of proposing and effecting this "European league or confederacy," or "State of Europe," "might be owing to England, of all the countries in Europe," but he also payed homage to the "wisdom, justice, and valour of Henry the Fourth of France" (that is, to Sully), whose "Grand Design" had opened the prospect of "the peace and prosperity of Europe."[33] In 1710,another Quaker, John Bellers, published his argument for a "European State," hoping that the English queen was going "to Use Her endeavours for Uniting the Powers of *Europe* in one peaceable Settlement."[34]

The most celebrated and influential of the eighteenth-century projects for a United Europe was the endless work by Abbé de Saint-Pierre.[35] Through the establishment of a "European Republic" or "European State" Saint-Pierre wanted to make Europe an "allmighty and immortal society."[36] He published his project at the beginning of the enlightened century, when Europe came to be seen as a "kind of great republic divided into a number of states," differing among themselves in their forms of government, yet corresponding one with another because they shared the same religious ground and same principles of public law and politics, unknown in other parts of the world.[37] At the close of the century, in 1796, Edmund Burke wrote that "throughout Europe" religion, laws, and manners were, "at bottom . . . all the same," and regarded the "whole of the polity and economy of every country in Europe" as having been "derived from the same sources."[38] As such, Europe was perceived as a cultural unity, a common society, a civilization.[39] Before the term *civilization* was coined Europe was described by the word *civility*. For example, "the Pristine Barbarisme, and Incivilitie" of Asia and Africa were contrasted with the "Civilitie of Manners, and Glory of Acts and Arts" characterizing Europe.[40] As the epitome of "civility" and "civilization" Europe was regarded as a civilizing force. Daniel Defoe, for example, wrote of "civilizing the Nations where we & other *Europeans* are already settled; bringing the naked Savages to Clothe, & instructing barbarous Nations how to live."[41] But what Europeans most cherished was the "resemblance in the modes of intercourse, and in the whole form and fashion of life" throughout Europe. Because of that, Burke stated in a memorable phrase, "no citizen of Europe could be altogether an exile in any part of it."[42]

In the aftermath of the French revolution, during the romantic reaction to the Enlightenment and the reordering of Europe after the Napoleonic wars, it occasionally happened that the question of "Christendom or Europe" arose again,[43] that an offshoot of what the Enlightenment writers had seen as the common religious ground was described as the "worst enemy of Europe,"[44] and that a claim was made that Europe did not form a "constitutional body."[45] Such views might suggest that the faith in European unity was shaken. But Europe was by then an established notion. At the time of the formation of the Concert of Europe in the post-Napoleonic Congress of Vienna, a French periodical exhorted its readers to regard Europe "in its entirety and in the general system of its fundamental relations, as a society, a family, a republic of princes and peoples."[46] At about the same time, political publicists began to contemplate the United States of Europe.[47]

The Hague peace conferences at the turn of the nineteenth and twentieth centuries have often been regarded as the accomplishment of a centuries-old search for peace and unity in Europe. From this perspective the two world wars that followed were of course seen as a setback. But uncomfortable as the thought might be, the forces that gathered strength from the disaster of World War I and triggered World War II actually cultivated the idea of Europe. They did not break off the main line of ideas about Europe I have discussed here. Italian Fascists hosted an ambitious, well-attended international conference on Europe in Rome in 1932 to deal with Europe's major historical crisis and to define the "historical and spiritual unity of Europe" as the basis for the solution of the crisis.[48] The Nazis saw themselves, in their own words, as working for the "rebirth of Europe." They strove for the organic unity of Europe based on different nations (purged of "unassimilable" foreign elements) living in accordance with their own "laws of life" and conversing with each other in the spirit of "authentic chivalry." They envisaged a Europe "multifaceted within, united without."[49]

The idea of United Europe survived those trials and misfortunes undamaged and, after the war, developed into a full-fledged ideology (or, perhaps, mystique) with ever growing institutions of its own.[50] At the Hague Congress of 1948 (an important overture to the postwar unification of Europe), Churchill went back to the roots in his speech about the idea of United Europe. He praised Sully and declared that "after this long passage of time we are the servants of The Grand Design."[51] But to be a servant of Sully's *Design* is to embrace a set of apparently diverse yet closely linked and interdependent ideas. One cannot parade just those ideas agreeable to political bon ton and pass over the rest in silence. For when this happens (and it has happened all too often), silence becomes a shield that allows those ideas we do not want to discuss to accomplish their labor in peace.

Sully wanted to preserve "the peace in Europe" on the basis of an "equilibrium" of powers.[52] Peace, of course, is accepted as a universal value, while the principle of "equilibrium" represents statecraft of a particular historical period. Working for peace is universally laudable; designing a "project for an association of all the princes and states of Europe, whose interest is to diminish the power of the house of Austria" is politically wise.[53] But, when we get into Sully's ideas beyond those of peace and "equilibrium," one might feel some uneasiness. The question of whether to affiliate the countries we today call Eastern Europe to his united and peaceful Europe raised the quandary of Europe's eastern border. To this question that still besets both "European Europeans"[54] and would-be Europeans on the other side of the historical cold war divide in our own times, Sully gave the following answer: The peoples living in those lands were partly idolaters and partly schismatics and belonged "to Asia at least as much as to Europe." Almost barbarous, they and their "infidel princes who refuse to conform to any of the Christian doctrines of religion" were to be forced entirely out of Europe.[55] Any contact with the Turks and Tartars, even fighting wars against them, rendered Poles, Prussians, Livonians, Muscovites, and Transylvanians "in some manner foreign in regard to those of the Western part of Europe."[56] This articulation of European exclusivism was complemented by an exposition of Europe's dominating and aggressive attitude toward the non-European world. After it had accomplished its most noble task, the execution of the *Grand Design*,[57] a European (standing) army was to chase "strangers" from Europe and conquer "such parts of Asia as were most commodiously situated, and particularly the whole coast of Africa, which is too near to our own territories for us not to be frequently incommoded by it."[58] The dynamic establishing peace and unity in Europe, moreover, was to "convert the continual wars among its several princes, into a perpetual war against the Infidels."[59]

Sully's "perpetual war against the Infidels" was just one expression of the permanent crusade—imaginary more than real, but real, nonetheless, in its imaginary existence; an expression of the crusade kept in permanence by cultivation and circulation of anti-Muslim sentiments and ideas. In so-called practical life, it is true, alliances of a European power with Turkey (especially from the sixteenth century onward) were not uncommon, if scandalous.[60] Sometimes the balance of power within Europe was of greater concern for European princes and their counselors than was war against the Turks.[61] In polemics between Catholics and Protestants, as well as in Enlightenment attacks on the Church, a Christian adversary could be represented as worse than the Turk. But it is also true that most of the European statesmen "continued to measure the Turk by conventional standards,"[62] that Europeans kept making plans for conquest and partition of Turkey,[63] that religious divisions in Europe retreated into background before the perceived necessity of fighting the common enemy, the Turk, with joint Christian forces, and that the deep animosity toward the Muslims has remained ever present, voiced in different political languages across different historical periods and representing a ground shared by political, religious, and ideological opponents. I want to substantiate this claim by citing some examples.

Europe's Perpetual Crusade: From "Chasing the Turk Out of Europe" to "Ethnic Cleansing"

What follows may be seen as problematic on more than one account. Before I continue I want, therefore, to briefly state what I think I am doing in the coming pages. I string up names of writers, clerics, and statesmen and quote their views on the "Turkish question." The selection is arbitrary, as any selection is bound to be. I am aware of the amount of the material I could add to that presented here. Methodologically even more problematic is that the context in which the opinions I cite were uttered is scarcely indicated. That is all this limited space allows me to do. But the voices I cite actually form a specific community of discourse and a specific context of their own. It is this anti-Muslim discourse that is, almost as a rule, missing in different accounts of European history. These voices speak out that which is so often silenced in historical accounts of Europe. As such, my selection of historical material is tendentious. But so is the suppression (or, at best, marginalization) of material such as that I present here in what passes for a history of Europe.

I hope that my tendentiousness is justifiable. I am aware that the views on the "Turks" I present are unlikely to find respectable defenders in today's academic or political circles, at least in public. In fact, these views are quite embarrassing from the point of view of political culture in an age of liberal and democratic triumphalism. But my intention is not to put Europe's dirty linen on display, or to irritate colleagues by showing their intellectual heroes at their "least admirable." Nor is it my intention to debunk Christianity (for I do not discuss religion but rather its use or abuse for worldly purposes). It should be clear from what and how I write that I sympathize with neither historical hostility toward the Muslims nor our contemporary anti-Islamism. I hope, however, that I will not seem to be arguing that Europeans ought not to have hated the Muslims. The world might be a better place if they had not. But they did, as the material I present shows. We have to acknowledge and face the fact that there is a long history of deeply rooted hostility toward the Muslims in European history. I believe that this hostility is not separable from Europe's most cherished ideals of liberty, rights, justice, peace, etc. It is, rather, part and parcel of the same complex web of thought as those ideals. If the existence of anti-Muslim ideas and sentiments is not acknowledged, the complexity of what is called European thought gets lost, the ideals of liberty, peace, etc., cannot be taken seriously, and their realization, either willing or enforced, is going to keep playing havoc with the world.

Let me now go back to my narrative, turning first to Erasmus of Rotterdam. As the most influential of the so-called Christian humanists, Erasmus was able to see the Turks as men (*homines*), but as a civilized European he also regarded them as barbarians, calling them monstrous beasts, enemies of the Church, and a people contaminated with all kinds of crime and ignominies.[64] In fact, it was only in opposition to the Turks that Erasmus, a self-declared citizen of the world, considered himself a European.[65] Moreover, much praised for his apparently uncompromising rejection of war, Erasmus approved of war against the Turks. Whereas war among Christians was unquestionably unacceptable, war against the Turks was admissible on more than defensive grounds alone.[66] Erasmus, in a resigned mood, came to regard war as "the fatal malady of human nature." But if human nature was "quite unable to carry on without wars," why, he asked rhetorically, "is this evil passion not let loose upon the Turks?" If war in general seemed not "wholly avoidable," war against the Turks, he argued, "would be a lesser evil than the present unholy conflicts and clashes between Christians."[67] In his letters to the leading European rulers, Erasmus always urged concord among Christian princes and employment of their arms against the Turks.[68]

Erasmus's friend Thomas More had similar views. He considered the Turks a "shameful, superstitious sect," the "abominable sect" of Christ's "professed" "mortal enemies," representing forces of darkness and Belial.[69] Haunted by the Renaissance commonplace of "the bloody and cruell Turke,"[70] he wrote, "There falleth so continually before the eyen of our heart, a fearful imagination of this terrible thing: his mighty strength and power, his high malice and hatred, and his incomparable cruelty."[71] More saw this power as threatening "the whole corps of Christendom,"[72] and he joined the choir calling for peace and concord among Christians that alone would have allowed them to successfully fight the common enemy and defend God's name.[73]

With regard to the Turks, More rejected the validity of Christ's precept against violence, at least as he saw it interpreted by the Lutherans. The Lutherans maintained that Christ's "wyll and pleasure is / that we sholde not so moche as defende our selfe agaynst heretyques and infydels / were they paganes / turkes / or sarasyns. And moche lesse than sholde we fyght agaynst them and kyll them / but that we sholde perseuer in settyng forth his fayth agaynst myscreauntes and infydels / by such wayes as hym selfe began it."[74] In More's own view there was "no reason to loke that crysten pryncys sholde suffer the catholyke crysten people to be oppressed by Turkys / or by here-tykes worse than Turkys." To the contrary, "bothe nature / reason / and god-dys byheste byndeth / fyrste the prynce to the sauegarde of hys peple with the parell of hym selfe / as he taught Moyses to know hym selfe bounden to kyll Egypcyans in the defence of Hebrewe / and after he byndeth euery man to the helpe & defence of his good & harmles neyghbour / agaynst the malyce and cruelty of the wronge doer." Thus war against the Turks—"the batayle by whyche we defende the crysten countrees agaynste the Turkys"—was not only excusable: it was commendable.[75]

Praise of Erasmus and his friends, that they were "unsurpassed in the far-sightedness and maturity of their European vision,"[76] applies especially to the youngest among them, Juan Luis Vives. Vives saw Europe as suffering terrible damage because of incessant wars between Christian princes, of which the only result was Turkish military success.[77] Vives was obsessed with Muslims, and the only relation he could imagine with them was war.[78] If only the Christian princes would fight the Turks instead of each other, they would undoubtedly win. For Europeans were a superior race. Even dogs were fiercer in Europe than in Africa.[79] Vives's writings (especially *De Europae dissidiis et bello turcico*) were a reveille for Europe to unite against the Turk and to "rush with arms at the ready to destroy him."[80] Vives went beyond imagining a liberation of European nations from the Turkish yoke; he thought of conquest. Instead of fighting each other for the handful of soil they could wrest from one another, he argued, Europeans should march against the Turks as a united Christian army, crush their power, and take possession of the abundant land and wealth of Asia.

Speaking of conquest, the discovery and colonization of America was, to a large degree, conceived of in the framework of crusading imagination. In his own words, Columbus, the "bearer of Christ," sailed west after "the remaining Moorish kingdom on European soil" had been terminated. He was sent on his mission by the King and Queen of Spain—"Catholic Chris-tians and rulers devoted to the Holy Christian Faith and dedicated to its expansion and to combating the religion of Mahomet and all idolatries and heresies."[81] Columbus himself understood his "Indian enterprise," *empresa de las Indias*, as a step toward the recovery of Jerusalem.[82] His master plan was to reach India from the West, establish contacts with the pro-Christian Mongol grand khan, and encircle the Muslims, so that it would be easier to defeat them and liberate the Holy Land. The discovery of America, however, disclosed an earthly Paradise so rich that with its wealth, as Columbus was quick to figure out, it would be possible to finance an army of one hundred thousand infantrymen and ten thousand cavalrymen for the recovery of Jerusalem.[83] In his journal Columbus rejoiced at the thought that, with the newly discovered wealth, the king and queen of Spain were going to be able to make their "preparations to go to recover the Holy Sepulchre," and he reminded them of his request to them "that all the proceeds of this voyage of mine should be used for the conquest of Jerusalem."[84] It is telling that the Spaniards initially described the unfamiliar world and peoples they found beyond the Ocean with Arabic words. The Indians were regarded as a transatlantic variety of Moors.[85] The question of how the American natives were to be treated—as in the famous dispute between Las Casas and Sepúlveda—was decided on the grounds of whether or not they were like the Turks.

Las Casas and Sepúlveda shared a hostile view of the Muslims, but drew opposite conclusions from that common ground. Sepúlveda extended European attitudes toward the Turks to the dealings with the Indians, and used arguments for war against the Turks to justify war against the Indians.[86] Las Casas, in line with the theologians from Salamanca, became the great advocate of Indians' rights because he endeavored to prove that they were not Turks and should, consequently, have been treated differently than the Turks—that is, peacefully.[87] But his pro-Indian pacifism rested on his hatred of, and belliciosity against, the Turks, Moors, and Saracens. He did not spare invectives when talking of Muslims whose impiety was adverse to divine and natural law.[88] He used the Muslim name as invective, charging Sepúlveda with the desire to spread the faith with "Mohammedan method," that is, "with death and terror."[89] To condemn the *conquistadores*'s savagery in America, he described their doings as "worse than the assaults mounted by the Turk in his attempt to destroy Christendom" and Moorish barbarism.[90] But he was happy to authorize the use of methods he called Mohammedan against the Mohammedans themselves. For Las Casas, as well as for Sepúlveda, war against the Muslims was licit and just;[91] and so was conquest. Because the very term *conquest* was "tyrannical, Mohammedan, abusive, improper and infernal," Las Casas argued, conquest could be conducted only against "Moors from Africa, Turks, and heretics who seize our lands, persecute Christians and work for the destruction of our faith."[92] But, as to America, "there should be no talk of conquest, as if the Indians were African Moors or Turks, but only the preaching of the gospel of Christ 'with gentle and divine words.'"[93] The Spanish law of 1573 actually proscribed the word *conquest* (and replaced it with *pacification*), but the destruction of American Indians has endured, as has the obsession with the Turks.

Greater than these divisions in the sixteenth-century Europe about the methods of spreading the gospel of Christ among the Indians, however, were those concerning the gospel itself. But important as these religious differences (and their political implications and consequences) among Europeans in that "age of Reformation" may have been, they did not differ in their views of the Turks. To the Protestants and the Catholics alike the Turk represented sin, or evil, itself.[94] They were only divided on the question of who represented the "Turks" in Europe—that is, who were "our Christian Turks" as opposed to the "Mohammedan Turks"—the Protestants or the Catholics.[95] To be called a "Turk" by a Christian adversary was to be identified with the Antichrist and denounced as the enemy of Christ.

That the Reformation sent shock waves through Europe is a commonplace, but it did not shake European approaches to the "Turkish question." Against the background of some Catholic princes' negotiations and alliances with the Ottoman Empire during Luther's lifetime, the Lutherans who made no such alliances appear as old-timers.[96] But Luther questioned the papal power, condemned clerical participation in warfare, and rejected the idea of efficacy of good works in the individual's search for salvation. As such, he consequently objected to the crusade—war under the pope's command, in which clerics took part and individuals looked for salvation. Luther saw the Turkish military successes in Europe as divine punishment for Christians' sinful ways of life, and in his younger years argued against resistance to Turkish attacks. "To fight against the Turks," he wrote, "is to oppose the judgement God visits upon our iniquities through them."[97] Soon, however, Luther was to change his stance, and then he substituted war against the Turks (*Türkenkrieg*), conducted by lay princes, for the crusade, led by the pope and clerics. By the time the Turks held Vienna under siege, in 1529, Luther clearly declared his support of the *Türkenkrieg*—and accused the popes of having never seriously intended to fight the Turks.[98] Even though led by secular rulers, war against the Turks had a godly character, was a *gotseligen Krieg*.[99] The Protestants helped to secularize, yet not desacralize, war against the Turks. Holy war has survived the Reformation.

There is no doubt that Luther and his associates shared the hostility toward Islam so common among the Christians.[100] For Luther the Turks were servants of the devil and his instrument, a wild people under whom the Christian faith could not survive. Both Mohammed and the "Turkish emperor" were possessed by the devil, and their armies were the devil's own. The Turks' faith was scandalous, absurd, and filthy. The Qu'ran was a foul, shameful, and abominable book that distorted Christianity even while it praised Jesus and Mary. It taught a disorderly doctrine of worldly govern-ment as well and commanded the Turks to plunder and murder, to devour and destroy, ever further, everything around them. Unlike other powers that be, the Turkish *Regiment* was not a power ordained by God. *Mahmet*, the Prophet, was a son of the devil and the devil's apostle. The distinction between him and the pope was that *Mahmet* was the "rude devil" (*grobe Teuffel*) whereas the pope was the "subtle devil." The *Mahmetisten* who pro-fessed the lies of the Qu'ran did not deserve to be called human.[101]

Not all Protestants opposed the crusade. François de La Noue, a Breton Hugenot of some political weight, is a case in point. When he was captured by the Spaniards in 1580, he tried to persuade his captors to release him by proposing to fight the Turks in Hungary at his own expense.[102] As this wish to be released was not fulfilled, he wrote a crusading treatise, to prove that Christian princes could, if they only united, "chase the Turks out of Europe in four years."[103] His first priority was "the capture of Constantinople and the expulsion of the Turk from Europe."[104] There was nothing special about that, for the greater part of La Noue's contemporaries held similar views. But his crusading treatise has some marked traits. What characterizes it is an interesting mixture of "crusading commonplaces"[105] and (when the author is not swept away by his crusading fantasies and zeal) "realistic" political analysis.

La Noue continues the tradition of deploring discord among Christian princes and imploring Christian unity. But, beyond such commonplaces, he also presents a very down-to-earth assessment of the impediments to forming a "confederation" of European powers. First he moralistically contrasts an ideal time of old, when men were zealous for "just things" (or at least things that "appeared as such"), with the present, when man looks only after him-self. Most original, however, is his centering of analysis on the preservation of the state, which may represent a real difficulty for organizing a crusade. Security of the state (*la secureté de l'Estat*), he recognizes, may sometimes require making morally dubious decisions. Such was the French alliance with the Turks.[106] La Noue well understood that, in his own time, a crusade could be undertaken only by "kings & other potentates who have sovereign power over their peoples," but that it was complicated to make these sovereign princes ("les princes qui ne dependent que d'eux") accept the kind of obligations necessary for building the "confederation" of Christian powers needed for a crusade.[107] He therefore tried to convince the sovereigns that it was their duty as sovereigns to go to war against the Turks. For God appointed them for the safety of their subjects. As such, their duty was to stop the Turkish conquests that were bringing suffering and oppression to the Christian people. The worst thing the sovereigns could do was doing nothing, for doing nothing would allow the Turks, little by little, to eat up the Christians.[108]

The crusade, La Noue argued, was just, necessary, and—if well prepared—easy to accomplish. That it was more honorable and profitable to Christian princes than quarrels with their Christian neighbours was clear. And, at least to La Noue, it was clear that not even religious disputes should prevent the "voyage" (as he called the crusade) he had so carefully planned. Despite their religious disagreements, the Catholics and the Evangelical had "not ceased to be brothers, grafted on the same trunk which is Jesus Christ." As Christians all, however, they should have no fellowship whatsoever with the profane Mohammedans who worshipped an imaginary God who was, in actuality, a devil, and who polluted virtue and plundered the world. "It is against these enemies who are spoilers of our goods, butchers of our bodies, & poisoners of our souls, that we have to contest with our swords."[109]

With La Noue we have already entered the world of the new humanists, now inspired by the political realist Tacitus rather than by the moralist Cicero.[110] Like the Renaissance humanists before, these new humanist intellectuals did not begrudge spending time and energy to think about a common European military enterprise against the Turks. Justus Lipsius, a luminary of this new school of thought, was surprisingly conventional when it came to the "Turkish question." Europe was broken by incessant wars and civil strife, and needed—as he put it in his *De magnitudine Romana* (1598)—"one head" that would be an "effective force for religious unity, for the well-being of all its subjects, and for the struggle against the common enemy, the Turks."[111] In his old days the great humanist thought obsessively about making a crusade.[112] He was not alone. In the waning sixteenth century, as well as at the beginning of the seventeenth, appeals for European unity against the Turks were frequent and crusading plans more than a few.[113]

For men like Botero, Ammirato, and Campanella, leading figures of the second generation of the new humanists, Christian and European unity against the Turks remained a central concern.[114] Botero, for example, was clear that armed forces were of vital importance for defense and mainte- nance of the state, and regarded war as the best means for eliminating evil spirits and diverting people from dangerous thoughts. The question for him was only against whom arms could be legitimately used. Luckily, he stated, a Christian prince will always have a cause for war for there would always be enough Turks, Moors, and Saracens, against whom war would always be just, justified, and universally lawful.[115] His advice was to attack the Turks in their own land instead of sitting at home and waiting for them to come.[116] He had a realistic assesment of Ottoman military power, seeing it as a challenge:

> He who wishes to fight cannot claim that there is no public enemy against whom he may prove his valour: an enemy whose constant object is the oppression of Christianity, and whose might is such that to resist it, let alone overcome it, is to win far greater glory than can ever be achieved by bearing arms against Christians. We have the Turks at our gates and on our flanks: could there be juster or more honourable argument for war?[117]

Of all infidels the Muslims were in Botero's eyes the most alien to the Christian faith. They were enemies of Christianity and of the state as well.[118] For Botero the state was of central concern. This makes him a distinctively early modern thinker. But he looked back with nostalgia to the "heroic days" of the Crusades, when Christian princes united and assembled great armies to attack the Turks "with no other interest than the honour of God and the exaltation of the Church."[119] There was "no House in Christendom, no renown soldier, no nobleman of honor" who did not take part in that "holy enterprise." The Crusades did honor "not only to France, but to Europe, and the whole Christendom."[120]

At the other end of Europe, in England, Edwin Sandys and Francis Bacon were among those influenced by the new humanism, and they both pondered on war against the Turks. Their reflections upon this issue appear to have vacillated between the ideal of Christian/European unity (which had survived in the religiously split and politically divided post-Reformation Europe) and their particular loyalties and concerns in the *vita activa*.[121] Sandys's great desire was to see "Christendom re-united," and in his *Europae speculum* he systematically analyzed "what unity Christendom may hope for." For Sandys and his contemporaries, it was only against the background of the "Turkish threat" that such a union was imaginable. That threat, Sandys wrote, was "necessity, pressing to unity," since the growth of Turkish power left "no hope for Christendom to subsist, but in their inward Concord." Unity among Christian princes, he argued, was the only way to meet the Turks. The truism that "a foreign enemy is a reconciler of Brethren," acquired direct political relevance. Sandys considered the common danger of the Turks a possible inducement to Catholics and Protestants to unite. But much as he wanted it, he was also skeptical that such a union would be formed. He did not hesitate to blame the Roman Church for preventing that from happening. And much as he desired a reconciliation, he wanted first to bring the Catholics to their knees: the Roman Church should concede its defeat and the power of Spain was to be broken. Only then would Europe be freed from religious bickering and could turn against the Turks and defeat them.[122]

Sandys's book was first published in 1605 and burned later that year. King James VI and I disliked it because it ran counter to his policy of rapprochement with Spain and with the papacy,[123] which itself appears to have been embedded in James's hopes for a reunion of Christendom.[124] Already before his accession to the English throne the king had expressed his wish to bring together Christian sovereigns for united action against the Turk.[125] As king of England, he continued to contemplate the formation of a league of Christian princes against the infidel.[126] So did his advisers. When the marriage between Prince Charles and the Spanish infanta was being negotiated, Bacon—who was then James's minister—wrote of the impending agreement between England and Spain as the basis on which "will be erected a tribunal, or pretorian power, to decide the controversies, which may arise amongst the princes and estates of Christendom," and as a "beginning and seed . . . of a holy war against the Turk."[127] When relations between England and Spain became strained again seven years later, in 1624, Bacon decided that the differences between the two countries were irreconcilable and meditated upon a war with Spain instead.

As a writer, Bacon's assessment of holy war was not uniform either. In his history of Henry VII he gave a model Tacitist analysis of negotiations for launching a crusade between the pope and the English king. Henry appears, here, as a skilled statesman because he knew how to disentangle himself from the pending crusade. To the papal nuncio who came to enlist him for "this sacred enterprise," the king "made an answer rather solemn than serious." He declared that "no Prince on earth should be more forward and obedient both by his person and by all his possible forces and fortunes to enter into this sacred war than himself," but he did not commit himself to doing anything concrete, and yet not only preserved but increased his reputation.[128] This pretty cynical report (even if Bacon's literary invention) is to be seen in the context of Protestant critique of papal power: as distancing from holy war inasmuch as holy war was controlled by the pope. In the same year that he wrote the *History of the Reign of King Henry the Seventh*, 1622, Bacon penned a dialogue on holy war. Even though he had not completed the text he took care that it was translated into Latin and included among his *Opera moralia et civilia*, while the English fragment appeared in Bacon's posthumous *Certain miscellany works* in 1629. This little treatise testifies to Bacon's substantial interest in war against the Turks and, specifically, in arguments for and against holy war.[129]

The late sixteenth and early seventeenth centuries were also important for their contribution to historiography of the Crusades. The first great collection of sources for the history of the Crusades, the *Gesta Dei per Francos*, was published by French diplomat and humanist Jacques Bongars in 1611. The title page of Thomas Fuller's popular *History of the Holy War* iconographically represented the crusade as a common European undertaking. The author was critical of the papacy and thus of papally led crusades, and he did not consider the recovery of Palestine, even if desired, an urgent task for "princes of Europe" of his day. "There is a more needful work nearer hand," he pointed out, which was, "to resist the Turks' invasion in Europe."[130] That urgency called for an end to dissentions among Christian princes so that they might fight the "common foe."

Father Joseph incorporated St. Francis of Assisi into crusading history (with some reason, I would argue).[131] But this is not what Joseph, Richelieu's *éminence grise*, is remembered for. He was himself an "apostle of the crusade" and, as a Capuchin, believed that serving St. Francis meant working for the expulsion of the Turks from the whole of Europe (*ex universa Europa*) and the Holy Places, and laying the sectarians of Mohammed to grave.[132] Together with Charles de Gonzague, Duke of Nevers, he dedicated himself in the 1610s to organizing a universal crusade in which not only

European powers but also the adversaries of the Ottoman Empire from Asia and Africa were to take part.[133] The key to this enterprise lay, of course, in Europe, where peace had to be secured. Peace was the precondition for a crusade, and, at the same time, the crusade was an "excellent means" of channeling Christian military activities into a "great European movement against Islamism" and "maintaining Christendom in peace."[134] While soliciting the French king to undertake this "holy work," and persuading him to break his alliance with the Ottomans, Joseph promised all kinds of benefits and blessings that the liberation of Christians suffering under the Turkish yoke, as well as the good done for the "souls of Africa," would bring to the most Christian king. Most laudable in this "holy pursuit" (in the best tradition of the French kingship), however, would be the expected unification of Europe and "certainty and stability of peace among Christians." For, as Father Joseph expected, the "civil society of temporal arms," overcoming the most powerful enemy of Christendom, was going to appease hostility between the Catholics and Protestants and bring about a "great softening of the damaging harshness between those of the opposed religions bearing the Christian name."[135]

It is true that the Christian Militia—the military order Father Joseph and Duke of Nevers established in the preparations for the crusade—was, when it came to war, used against the Protestants. But, as a Father Joseph's biographer has warned, it would be wrong to dismiss this crusading project as chimerical.[136] Father Joseph was, after all, at the very center of French and European politics of the time. His ideas were shared by many. The "Turkish question" was of grave concern to many people all over Europe and discussed with real passion.[137] The best minds of Europe did not find it undignified to occupy themselves with the "Turkish threat" and war against the Turks. Leibniz was one of them.

Leibniz did not shun public affairs. He was a German imperial patriot and diplomat as well as a great philosopher. Striving for peace was a lifetime project for him. But when it came to the Turks, he thought about waging war against them with the ambition of a "staff officer."[138] His most ambitious plan for a crusade was a diplomatic failure. Wishing to divert French aggression from the Netherlands, obtain security for the German empire, and prevent war in Europe (the prospect of which he abhorred), Leibniz suggested to Louis XIV that he conquer Egypt. There was no other country that was of greater advantage to occupy. Its occupation would allow the French king to assume the title and prerogatives of emperor of the Orient and thus divide the world between himself and the House of Austria.[139] The conquest of Egypt was of great strategic importance, for it was there where the Ottoman Empire was most vulnerable. And the conquest was urgent, because by delivering a heavy blow to the Ottoman Empire it would block the reform of the empire that the sultan was about to undertake. The common good of Christendom and security of Europe required, Leibniz argued, that the reform of the Ottoman Empire be prevented and the Turks kept in their deep slumber of ignorance.[140] And whereas war within Europe was not only scandalous but also pointless, war against the barbarian infidels was, needless to say, just.[141]

The French king did not follow Leibniz's advice, but this is not a reason for dismissing Leibniz's argument. In his Egyptian project he employed ideas that he could find in a large body of Western writing on peace and war against the Turks and that were shared by his contemporaries as well.[142] And the themes he developed in this early work remained constant in Leibniz's later writings.[143] The only difference worth mentioning seems to be that, in his Egyptian project, Leibniz entrusted the leading role in fighting the Muslims to the most Christian king of France, whereas elsewhere he saw the emperor as "the born leader of Christians against the infidels."[144] But whatever his choice of commander, Leibniz considered Western Christian lands a unity, a unitary "Christian republic."[145] And integral to his striving for articulation, and realization, of the unity and peace of European peoples was war against the Turks.[146] Also, as a patriot, Leibniz thought about anti-Turkish wars. When he was worried about decline of martial spirit among Germans, he proposed the formation of a new Teutonic order to fight the *türcken* and other enemies. Ideally, war against the Turks should be permanent, unceasing warfare.[147] And as a European the old and resigned philosopher wrote to Saint-Pierre that a remedy for the evil of wars disturbing Europe might be "to help the Emperor to chase the Turks out of Europe."[148]

Only exceptionally were projects for European union not crusading plans as well. Penn and Bellers, for example, were such rare exceptions.[149] But even Penn pointed out that one of the advantages of a European Union would be "the great security it will be to Christians against the inroads of the Turk."[150] Abbé de Saint-Pierre, renowned as he may be as a great pacifist, was certainly not one of such benign "projectors."

D'Alembert, who eulogized Saint-Pierre as an "enemy of religious intolerance," mentioned that, as a "professed enemy of all the errors that debase and eat up the human race," this abbé "vowed a special aversion to the Mus-

lim religion." Saint-Pierre regarded Islam as "one of the greatest scourges of
the human race" and wanted to "extirpate Mohammedanism." The "acceleration of the annihilation of Mohammedanism" was "very much on his
mind."[151] D'Alembert's portrayal is fair. Saint-Pierre indeed believed that
Mahometisme had been declining in proportion to the strengthening of the
"universal reason" among the Mohammedans. All that was false, obscure,
absurd, and incomprehensible in Islam—a religion founded by a impostor,
deceiver, fanatic, and madman—was going to dissipate in the light of reason. The Muslims would be freed from the necessity of pilgrimages to
Mecca, daily prayers, circumcision, fasting during the Ramadan, and
washing. They would be liberated from the prohibition of eating pork
and drinking wine, and of their own religious intolerance (for which
Mohammedanism was especially blamed). As such, the Muslims would
become reasonable and, as *Mahometans rézonables*, could be tolerated.[152]
But until that time, said Saint-Pierre, Europeans had to get rid of the illusion
that "the Arabs are men like us"; consequently, "utterly ignorant" as they
were, they had to be put in their place.[153] We may see this imperative—
keeping the Mohammedans in their place—as Saint-Pierre's guideline for
solving the "Muslim question" in his plan for European unity and peace.

In the 1713 version of his peace project I have already mentioned above,
Saint-Pierre had half-heartedly rejected the idea of chasing the Turk out of
Europe as unpractical.[154] Four years later he returned to the question and
criticized himself. He admitted that he had been wrong to think it "impossible to chase the Turk out of Europe." Now, after he had "for some time meditated on this subject," he came to "believe that this thing is possible."[155] The
sole condition was the establishment of his European union, for "these
infidels made conquests in Europe only because the Christian princes were
jealous of each other and divided among themselves." The union, he
explained, was "an indissoluble League of all the Christian princes for their
mutual protection not only against the Turks but also against all other enemies of theirs." But behind his talk of defense was "an offensive League for
the extermination of the Turks." He was determined to demonstrate that
"this project to exterminate the Turks is less difficult than one would think."
His argument was rhetorics. What had ever been "more glorious and more
important to Christianity," he asked, "than to establish everlasting peace
among all the Christian princes, on the one hand, and to engage them, on
the other hand, to exterminate these infidels?"[156] Invoking the authority of
Henry IV—whose heartfelt wish (as Sully wrote in his *Grand Design*) had

been to "make a perpetual peace and chase the Turk out of Europe"[157]—Saint-Pierre proposed the formation of a European "Ligue totale" to carry out a general crusade.

A project for European union by one of Europe's greatest pacifists thus culminated in the conclusion that it was advantageous, facile, and glorious to Christian sovereigns to go to war to "chase the Turk out of Europe and even out of Asia and Africa."[158] Saint-Pierre's European union reveals itself, after hundreds of pages of torturous prose, as a device for "making the way to a universal crusade, incomparably more solid and better concerted than all the previous."[159] The great objective of the enlightened crusade was "the conquest of everything that the Turks possess in Europe and on the Mediterranean islands, in Asia and Africa."[160] Saint-Pierre thought of establishing "many new Christian sovereignties" on the ruins of the Turkish Empire,[161] and defined European union and peace as "the only means for making Europe and the European order [la police Europaine] reign in all the parts of the world."[162]

Saint-Pierre was often ridiculed in his time, but his popularity and influence were considerable. He was, in many ways, a man of his age, and his crusading project was neither eccentric nor anachronistic. The crusading spirit was not as alien to the age of reason as one might infer from Gibbon's remark that it was hard for the "cold philosophy of modern times" to share the fervor with which a "sinful and fanatic world" had responded to the preaching of the first crusade.[163] Crusade was now "projected," rather then preached, but crusading "projectors" were not confined to literary circles. Statesmen like Cardinal Alberoni, who was the Spanish prime minister, and Marquis d'Argenson, who was to become foreign minister to Louis XV, also contributed to the European crusading tradition.

Alberoni appealed to the "Interests" of the princes and states of Christendom—for "neither the Dictates of Humanity, nor the Duties of Religion" seemed cogent enough—to inspire them to undertake the "pious and salutary Work" of the conquest and partition of Turkey. He reminded them of the "History of the *Cruzades*" and pointed out that the weakness of the Turkish Empire made conquest "so practicable, that nothing is wanting to effect it, but a disinterested Union among *Christian* Powers."[164] Moved by a "fervent Desire of displaying the Banners of *Jesus Christ* in the Infidel World," Alberoni inveighed against the "unreasonable as well as unnatural" wars carried out by the princes of Europe against one another, "shedding Streams of *Christian* Blood" while "the inveterate and profess'd Enemies of Christianity" were "Masters of several large and flourishing Provinces, and Kingdoms, in *Europe* and *Africa*, and . . . Lords of, almost, all *Asia*."[165] As the antidote, Alberoni proposed an alliance of European powers, managed by a "perpetual Dyet" vested with the authority to "determine all Disputes and Controversies" among them "amicably" and which would take care to preserve the balance of power. Such a Union, establishing peace in Europe, was "the only Basis of all future Hopes and Expectations, and the only *Arcanum* that can pave the way to the conquest of the *Turkish* Empire in *Asia* and *Africa*."[166] The first objective of the just war against the Turks, who were of all the nations upon earth "the most finished Bigots, and Slaves to Superstition," who were "not posses'd of one Foot of Ground in the World that was not acquir'd by *Sacrilege* and *Imposture*, by *Violence*, *Treachery* and *Oppression*," and who had "usurp'd" all their possessions "contrary to all the Rights of Mankind," however, was to attack the Turks in Europe.[167]

D'Argenson—referring to Henry IV's, that is, Sully's *Grand Design* and praising Saint-Pierre as a "great genius in *politique*"[168]—thought about setting up a "European Tribunal" (as a means of instituting France as the "arbitre universel")[169] and launching a "true crusade" to be carried out as a common European enterprise pleasing to God and agreeable to the people. The intended objective of this "grand projet" was the conquest of Turkey, seen as "the first great European revolution."[170] This hoped for revolution was predicated on the unification of Europe. As with Saint-Pierre, d'Argenson's European unity was intimately tied to a vision of European expansion and domination of the world. D'Argenson had no doubts that—as "we shall step by step populate, discipline, Christianize, polish the entire habitable Earth"— "this will be of benefit for heaven and earth. This will be a grand and magnificent fruit of the establishment of the European Republic."[171]

In the second half of the eighteenth century an enlightened though rather obscure German, von Lilienfeld, was troubled by the lack of Europe's resolve to unite its forces in order to "chase the Turks out of Europe" and to "destroy the North African robbers."[172] Because the military enterprise he hoped for was based on the establishment of peace in Europe, he elaborated a plan to bring about "unity, peaceableness, and security" among Christian powers—excluding "barbarians."[173] He preemptively excluded *die Barbaren* because he was sure that they would reject the European peace. As enemies of peace, they would have to blame themselves for giving the "united military orders" the opportunity to attack them. Lilienfeld envisaged that these military orders—modeled on the old crusading orders and revived, in his head, to serve as shock troops of united, peaceful, and secure Europe—would "not only acquire rich booty but also cleanse the remaining non-Christian part of Europe from the Muslims and, if necessary, spread their conquests and retake from the Muslims also Cyprus and even the Promised Land."[174] Lilienfeld, just like Saint-Pierre, was convinced that the enlightened crusade would be more successful and effective than its historical precedents.

Other Germans cultivated similar, if somewhat less bloodthirsty, thoughts as their contemporary von Lilienfeld. Johann Gottfried Schindler, for example, a Silesian theologian, published a peace plan in 1788, in which he argued that a solution to the "Turkish question" was the *conditio sine qua non* for a peaceful and united Europe. Johann August Schlettwein, a leading German physiocrat, designed a "system of a lasting peace among European states" as well. He was willing to admit Turkey to this confraternity—under the condition, however, that Turkey submitted to Christian law. Should Turkey refuse, European states would partition Turkish lands among themselves.[175] In France, one among those who were, in the same period, making plans for the expulsion of the Turks from Europe was Simon Nicolas Henri Linguet, a notable lawyer and journalist.[176]

Today these men's names mean little. But others whose names we know well also expressed their animosity toward the Muslims and had ideas about European wars against the Turks. No less a figure than that very symbol of the Enlightenment, Voltaire, is an example. He wrote that the Turks were, along with the plague, the greatest curse on earth and wanted to annihilate them. "It does not suffice to humiliate them," he said, "they should be destroyed."[177] He deplored the fact that "the Christian powers, instead of destroying the common enemies, were engaged in bringing each other to ruin," and corresponded with the philosopher-king Frederick II about the hoped for pleasure of seeing "the Muslims driven out of Europe."[178] In a letter to Catherine II of Russia Voltaire confided himself in unequivocal terms: "Overcome the Turks, and I will die content." At the end of his life the great Enlightenment philosopher seems to have felt that his life was not really fulfilled, that there was more he could have done: "I wish," he wrote to the czarina, "I had at least been able to help you kill a few Turcs."[179]

In 1788, ten years after Voltaire's death and a year before the revolution, the French scholar and politician Volney tried to dissuade France from getting involved in the Russian-Turkish war. But Volney did not argue against anti-Turkish war as such. There are new tones in his work where he reflects on the process of universalization of civilization (radiating, of course, from Europe) and the gradual formation of a "great society" of humankind, and especially where he condemns the devastation of the world by the countries that called themselves civilized.[180] But the old anti-Muslim themes are here as well. Volney saw an impediment to the improvement of the human race in Asian despotism,[181] and he considered the Ottoman "barbarians" a plague, and a vicious one at that, because "with their stupid fanaticism they perpetuate the contagion by renewing its germes." The Turks had, of course, to be "chased out of Europe." But Volney expected that other powers than France would to do the job—defeat the Turks and invade Turkey. Russia had a big role to play here, and Volney was happy to imagine that Catherine II could become "the emperess of Constantinople and restorer of the Greek Empire," and that "other peoples" might establish themselves where the Turks had lived.[182]

The French Revolution, as Burke saw it, was a "violent breach of the community of Europe," threatening to "destroy all Europe."[183] But the revolution does not appear to have caused any drastic change in European attitude toward the Muslim world.[184] It was the European world shaped by the revolution that finally executed some very old ideas, like the conquest of Egypt, even if conceived, now, in terms of pronounced rivalries among colonial powers.[185] That conquest was a first major step in the process that, in about a century, brought three-quarters of the world Muslim population under European domination.[186] After the rivalries among European powers had already brought about a world war, a great historian of the Crusades was inspired to describe, in a book written for a large audience, French and English machinations in the Middle East as a replay of the old Crusades: in 1914 the "Franks" set foot in Syria again in order to, four years later, "deliver Tripoli, Beirut, and Tyre, the city of Raymond of Saint-Gilles, the city of John of Ibelin, the city of Philip de Montfort. As to Jerusalem, it was to be 'reoccupied' on December 9, 1917, by the descendants of King Richard under the command of Marshal Allenby."[187] Historiographically, such a view may not be irreproachable. But it shows how alive remained the crusading imagination even in the twentieth century. And not only the imaginative descriptions of a historian make the point: the last of crusading bulls issued by the popes to the kings of Spain expired only in 1940, when "there was no longer a Spanish king to receive another."[188]

Today, European diplomats are less than diplomatic when it comes to discussing Turkey's membership in the European Union.[189] Although

European politicians have been arguing for a multicultural Europe since the Nazis,[190] men who run European political business in our own times are perfectly clear that this multiculturalism is for Europeans' consumption only. Turkey, one of them explained, cannot be regarded as a candidate for becoming a EU member because "we are creating a European Union. This is a European project."[191] It is not surprising that it was while this "European project" was making progress that the talk of Crusades resurfaced in Europe — most clearly in the war against Bosnia. The term *crusade* was used by both the perpetrators of the genocide, when they tried to make sense of their actions to themselves (and to their Euro-American accomplices), and by those against whom this crime by humanity had been directed,[192] who were also struggling to understand what had befallen them.

Indeed, extravagant as the claims of Serb and Croatian masters of war — that they had designed and executed the war against Bosnia as Europeans, in the name of Europe, and for Europe[193] — may appear to be at first sight, they are accurate claims. The war against Bosnia was a European war par excellence. Much as this war tells us about Europe, understanding Europe is also key to understanding the war. There has been some awareness of this lately even in Europe, although this cognizance is usually expressed in rather perverted ways. Some Europeans have claimed, for example, that at stake in the Bosnian war was the fate of basic "European values." They saw those "values" negated by the brutality of the war. Some even warned in dramatic tones that Europe was dying in Bosnia. They were both right and wrong. Right, insofar as they connected Europe with the war. Wrong, because Europe was not an unhappy and unwilling victim of that war but rather an active party to it. Rather than dying in Bosnia, it helped to kill and cleanse away those whom Euro-ideologists (in unison with Serbian war propaganda) chose to call "Muslims." But these sad thoughts left untouched illusions about their own — European — community. Jean Baudrillard was a rare exception among European intellectuals when he clearly called, speaking as a European, the Serbs "ours" and as, "seen objectively, our collaborators in the ethnic cleansing of Europe."[194]

The Bosnians, too, had shared those illusions about Europe. They had seen themselves as standing for "European values" and had therefore believed "Europe" would defend them. They paid dearly for those illusions. But illusions finally faded away. Alija Isaković, a leading Bosnian writer, wrote:

We, Bosnians, are that which Europe ought to have been, that almost impossible humaneness among people, that which Europe calls international and universal, that which it describes with the word humanity and tolerance, regardless of what it understands by that. As such, we can be a dangerous model, we already are such a model, and as such the waves originating with us may reach from Ireland through Brittany and the Basque Lands to Corsica and Transylvania.

This is why Bosnia had to be "swept away before it is too late, just like Córdoba and Granada had been five hundred years ago, and 'humanized' like civilization of the Mayans and civilization of the Red-Skins had been." Linking the war against Bosnia with previous wars against Muslims in Europe, and seeing a continuum between the expulsion of the Muslims and Jews from Spain and the "ethnic cleansing" of Bosnia, Isaković expressed his and his country's disenchantment with Europe when he stated that "we, Bosniaks-Muslims, are not a European nation." The possibilities that the Bosnian Muslims faced during the war (and continue to face today under a peace settlement no less horrifying and more demoralizing than the war itself) was brutal and clear. As far as we Bosniaks are concerned, Isaković wrote, "there will be either no Europe and European spirit, or there will be no us."[195]

Notes

1. The term *Historia Futurorum* was used by Leibniz in his project for the conquest of Egypt, which I discuss later in the text. See *Synopsis meditationis*, in Leibniz, *Sämtliche Schriften*, series 4, vol. 1 (Berlin: Akademie der Wissenschaften der DDR, 1963), 225.
2. I have done this in Tomaž Mastnak, *Evropa: Med evolucijo in evtanazijo* (Ljubljana: Studia Humanitatis, 1998), chapter 3.
3. Throughout this text I tend to employ terms used for the Muslims by Christian and European writers I discuss. Thus the Muslims most often appear as Saracens, Turks, Mohammedans, infidels, pagans, and barbarians.
4. For a more detailed account, see Tomaž Mastnak, *Crusading Peace: Christendom, the Muslim World, and Western Political Order* (Berkeley: University of California Press, 2002), chapter 3. Cf. R. W. Southern, *Western Views of Islam in the Middle Ages* (Cambridge: Harvard University Press, 1962), 16; James Kritzeck, *Peter the Venerable and Islam* (Princeton: Princeton University Press, 1964), 15–16; N. Daniel, *The Arabs and Mediaeval Europe* (London: Longman;

Beirut: Librairie du Liban, 1975), chapter 1; Rainer Ch. Schwinges, *Kreuz-zugsideologie und Toleranz: Studien zu Wilhelm von Tyrus* (Stuttgart: Anton Hiersemann, 1977), 98; Ronald C. Finucane, *Soldiers of Faith: Crusaders and Moslems at War* (New York: St. Martin's, 1983), 147 ff.

5. See, for example, Southern, *Western Views of Islam*, especially 14–15; Kritzeck, *Peter the Venerable and Islam*; Marie Thérèse d'Alverny, "La connaissance de l'Islam en Occident du IXe au milieu du XIIe siècle," in *L'Occidente e l'Islam nell'alto medioevo*, Settimane di studio del Centro italiano di studi sull'alto medioevo 12 (Spoleto: Presso la sede del Centro, 1965); Daniel, *The Arabs and Mediaeval Europe*, 73; N. Daniel, *Islam and the West: The Making of an Image*, 2d ed. (Oxford: Oneworld, 1993); Dorothee Metlitzki, *The Matter of Araby in Medieval England* (New Haven: Yale University Press, 1977); Schwinges, *Kreuzzugsideologie und Toleranz*, 95–98; Alfons Becker, *Der Papst, die griechi-sche Christenheit und der Kreuzzug*, vol. 2, of *Papst Urban II, 1088–1099* (Stuttgart: Anton Hiersemann, 1988), 334, 361; Augustin Pavlović, "Introduc-tion," in Thomas Aquinas, *Razgovor s pravoslavnima i muslimanima; Protiv zabluda Grkâ; O razlozima vjere (protiv Saracena)* (Zagreb: Globus, 1992), 96.

6. I discuss this in Mastnak, *Crusading Peace*, chapter 3, where the relevant litera-ture is cited.

7. See especially P. Rousset, *Les origines et les charactères de la première croisade* (Neuchâtel: Baconnière, 1945), 17, 20–21, 151, 175.

8. Seymour Phillips, "The Outer World of the European Middle Ages," in S. B. Schwartz, ed., *Implicit Understandings: Observing, Reporting, and Reflecting on the Encounters Between Europeans and Other Peoples in the Early Modern Era* (Cambridge: Cambridge University Press, 1994), 54–55.

9. Maureen Purcell, *Papal Crusading Policy: The Chief Instruments of Papal Cru-sading Policy and Crusade to the Holy Land from the Final Loss of Jerusalem to the Fall of Acre, 1244–1291* (Leiden: Brill, 1975), 14–15. Moreover, the names used for the Muslims became the generic term for Christian enemies. See examples quoted in Carl Erdmann, "Endkaiserglaube und Kreuzzugsgedanke im 11. Jahrhundert," *Zeitschrift für Kirchengeschichte*, series 3, 51 (1932): 407; Purcell, *Papal Crusading Policy*, 15–16, note 19; Metlitzki, *The Matter of Araby in Medieval England*, 119–20, 126; Norman Housley, "Crusades Against Chris-tians: Their Origins and Early Development, c. 1000–1216," in P. W. Edbury, ed., *Crusade and Settlement* (Cardiff: University College Cardiff Press, 1985), 19.

10. See Raoul Manselli, "La res publica cristiana e l'Islam," in *L'Occidente e l'Is-lam nell'alto medioevo*, Settimane di studio del Centro italiano di studi sull'alto medioevo 12 (Spoleto: Presso la sede del centro, 1965), 136; Giulio Vismara, *Impium foedus: Le origini della "respublica christiana"* (Milan:Giuffrè, 1974), 13; Franco Cardini, "La guerra santa nella cristianità," in"*Militia Christi" e*

Crociata nei secoli XI–XIII, Miscellanea del Centro di studi medioevali (Milan: Vita e pensiero, 1992), 396.

11. I questioned the opinion that "Europe" functioned as a political concept in the Carolingian empire in Tomaž Mastnak, "Karolinška 'Evropa'? Prispevek k zgodovini evropske ideje," *Filozofski Vestnik* 21.1 (2000). "Europe," however, was used as a political concept by Greeks (and even by Romans)—to designate parts of the Balkans. As such, the ancient political concept of Europe has little to do with the political concept of Europe as we know it today. See Tomaž Mastnak, "Balkanska Evropa," *Revija 2000*, nos. 135–136 (2001).

12. Denys Hay, "Europe Revisited: 1979," *History of European Ideas* 1.1 (1980): 1; Manfred Fuhrmann, *Alexander von Roes: Ein Wegbereiter des Europagedankens?* (Heidelberg: Universitätsverlag C. Winter, 1994), 14. Further references for the history of the idea of Europe are cited in Mastnak, *Evropa*, chapter 2.

13. Werner Fritzmeyer, *Christenheit und Europa: Zur Geschichte des europäischen Gemeinschaftsgefühls von Dante bis Leibniz* (Munich and Berlin: Oldenbourg, 1931), 28; Denys Hay, *Europe: The Emergence of an Idea*, 2d ed. (Edinburgh: Edinburgh University Press, 1968), 72–73; Basileos Karageorgos, "Der Begriff Europa im Hoch- und Spätmittelalter," *Deutsches Arhiv für Erforschung des Mittelalters* 48.1 (1992): 144.

14. See, for example, Purcell, *Papal Crusading Policy*, 14; Francis E. Peters, *Jerusalem: The Holy City in the Eyes of Chroniclers, Visitors, Pilgrims, and Prophets from the Days of Ambarahm to the Beginnings of Modern Times* (Princeton: Princeton University Press, 1985), 251, 253; Hans Eberhard Mayer, *The Crusades*, trans. J. Gillingham, 2d ed. (Oxford: Oxford University Press, 1993), 5–6.

15. That is, contrary to the opinion that the "crusading message . . . could not be couched in European terms." M. E. Yapp, "Europe in the Turkish Mirror," *Past & Present*, no. 137 (1992), 138. See, for example, Piccolomini's understanding of war against the Turks as holy war, and his notion of the crusade, in Odoricus Raynaldus, *Annales ecclesiastici ab anno MCXXCVIII* (Lucca, 1753), 10:1a, 2b, and Aeneas Sylvius Piccolomini, *Die Geschichte Kaiser Friedrichs III.*, trans. Th. Ilgen (Leipzig: Dykschen Buchhandlung, 1889–1890), 2:103.

16. For these expressions, see Aeneas Sylvius Piccolomini, *Der Briefwechsel des Eneas Silvius Piccolomini*, ed. R. Wolkan, *Fontes rerum austriacarum*, vols. 61 (I/1), 62 (I/2), 67 (II), 68 (III) (Vienna: Holder, 1909–1918), 3:201, 212; B. Widmer, "Biographische Einleitung," in Aeneas Sylvius Piccolomini, *Papst Pius II.: Ausgewählte Texte aus seinen Schriften*, ed. B. Widmer (Basel: Benno Schwabe, 1960), 82.

17. Cf. Aeneas Sylvius Piccolomini, *Epistola ad Mahomatem II (Epistle To Mohammed II)*, ed. A. R. Baca (New York: Peter Lang, 1990), III, 23.

18. I cite evidence in Mastnak, *Evropa*, chapter 3.

19. Larry Wolff, *Inventing Eastern Europe: The Map of Civilization on the Mind of the Enlightenment* (Stanford: Standford University Press, 1994), discusses only the Enlightenment attitudes toward Eastern Europe, but the westerner's uncertainty about where in the east Europe ends has a longer history.

20. Abraham Ortelius, *Synonimia geographica* (Antwerp, 1578), 95; Louis Le Roy, *Oratio ad invictissimos potentissimosque principes Henricum II. Franc. & Philippum Hispan. Reges, de Pace et concordia nuper inter eos initia, & bello religionis Christianae hostibus inferendo* (Paris, 1559), 18. See Hay, *Europe*, chapter 6; John Hale, *The Civilization of Europe in the Renaissance* (New York: Atheneum, 1995), 5–7.

21. John Amos Comenius, *The Angel of Peace Sent to the Peace Ambassadors of England and the Netherlands in Breda, Whence it is intended for transmission to all the Christians in Europe and thereafter to all the nations throughout the world, that they should call a halt, cease to wage war, And make way for the Prince of Peace, Christ, who now desireth to announce peace to the nations*, ed. M. Safranek (New York: Pantheon, 1944 [1667]), 49.

22. Jonathan Swift, *The History of the Four Last Years of the Queen*, in H. Davis, ed., *The Prose Works of Jonathan Swift* (Oxford: Blackwell, 1951), 7:50, 54; cf. 131, 148; Jonathan Swift, *The Conduct of the Allies, and of the Late Ministry, in Beginning and Carrying on the Present War*, in H. Davis, ed., *The Prose Works of Jonathan Swift* (Oxford: Blackwell. 1951), 6:64; *An Enquiry Into the Behaviour of the Queen's Last Ministry*, in H. Davis, ed., *The Prose Works of Jonathan Swift* (Oxford: Blackwell, 1951), 8:167; cf. 188, 194.

23. Daniel Defoe, "Reasons Why This Nation Ought to Put a Speedy End to This Expensive War, &c.," in L. A. Curtis, ed., *The Versatile Defoe: An Anthology of Uncollected Writings by Daniel Defoe* (London: G. Prior, 1979), 111, 117. For a picturesque representation of European "balance," see A. Secord, ed., *Defoe's Review*, Facsimile Text Society (New York: Columbia University Press, 1938), 6:7 (April 19, 1709), facsimile book 14:26: "THE CHASE is *Exorbitant Power*; all the powers of *Europe* are the Hounds."

24. Henry St. John, Viscount Bolingbroke, *Letters on the Study and Use of History*, in vol. 2 of *The Works of Lord Bolingbroke* (London: Bohn, 1844), 250, 282. Cf. "A Plan for a General History of Europe," in vol. 2 of *The Works of Lord Bolingbroke*.

25. Bolingbroke, *Letters on the Study and Use of History*, 285, 293, 294, 297, 298, 300–303, 313.

26. Ibid., 298, 301, 328, 330, 331.

27. Charles Davenant, *Essays upon I. The Ballance of Power. II. The Right of Making War, Peace, & Alliances. III. Universal Monarchy*, etc. (London, 1701), 4, 87, 40.

28. Maximilien de Béthune, duc de Sully, *Memoirs of Maximilian de Bethune, Duke of Sully, Prime Minister to Henry the Great: Containing the History of the*

Life and Reign of that Monarch, And his Own Administration Under Him (London, 1757), 5:124.

29. Cf. note 51. A rare critical view of Sully's plan is to be found in Bolingbroke. See *Remarks on the History of England*, in vol. 1 of *The Works of Lord Bolingbroke*, 403; Bolingbroke, *Letters on the Study and Use of History*, 252.

30. Sully, *Memoirs*, 5:141, 143–144; cf. 3:368 ff.

31. See Edward W. Najam, "*Europe*: Richelieu's Blueprint for Unity and Peace," *Studies in Philology* 53.1 (1956).

32. William Penn, *An Essay Towards the Present and Future Peace of Europe by the Establishment of an European Diet, Parliament, or Estates*, in *The Peace of Europe, the Fruits of Solitude and Other Writings by William Penn* (London: Dent; New York: Dutton, 1916), 7–8.

33. Ibid., 13, 18, 21–22.

34. John Bellers, *Some Reasons for an European State, Proposed to the Powers of Europe, by an Universal Guarantee, and an Annual Congress, Senate, Dyet, or Parliament*, etc., in G. Clarke, ed., *John Bellers: His Life, Times and Writings* (London and New York: Routledge and Kegan Paul, 1987), 135. Whereas Bellers, a supporter of the Union of England and Scotland, wanted to divide Europe "into 100 Equal Cantons or Provinces" (140), Andrew Fletcher, perhaps the most articulate opponent of the "incorporating Union" of the two nations, proposed a division of Europe into ten parts—for different political reasons but with the same ideal end of preserving the "common Tranquility." Andrew Fletcher, *An Account of a Conversation Concerning a Right Regulation of Governments for the Common Good of Mankind*, etc. (Edinburgh, 1704), 61–64. Both authors referred to Sully's "Grand Design." For Fletcher's political reasons, see John Robertson, "An Elusive Sovereignty: The Course of the Union Debate in Scotland, 1698–1707," in J. Robertson, ed., *A Union for Empire: Political Thought and the British Union of 1707* (Cambridge: Cambridge University Press, 1995).

35. I discuss this project in detail in Tomaž Mastnak, "Abbé de Saint-Pierre: European Union and the Turk," *History of Political Thought* 19.4 (1998). A survey of other projects of this kind is to be found in Jacob ter Meulen, *Der Gedanke der internationalen Organisation in seiner Entwicklung 1300–1800* (The Hague: Nijhoff, 1917); Chr. Lange, *Histoire de la doctrine pacifique et de son influence sur le développement du droit international*, Académie de droit international, Recueil de cours 1926 (Paris: Hachette, 1927); Sylvester Hemleben, *Plans for World Peace Through Six Centuries* (Chicago: University of Chicago Press, 1943).

36. *Abrege du Projet de Paix Perpetuelle, Inventé par le Roi Henri le Grand, Aprouvé par la Reine Elisabeth, par la Roi Jaques son Succeseur, par les Republiques & par divers autres Potentats. Approprié à l'Etat présent des Affaires générales de l'Europe*, etc. (Rotterdam, 1729), 174–175.

37. Voltaire, *Le siècle de Louis XIV*, in R. Pomeau, ed., *Oeuvres historiques* (Paris: Gallimard, 1957), 620. Cf. M. E. Toze, *Der gegenwärtige Zustand von Europa, worin die natürliche und politische Verschaffenheit der Europäischen Reiche und Staaten aus bewährten Nachrichten beschreiben wird*, part 1 (Wismar: Bützow, 1767), 78, 144–145, who saw his contemporary European community as united not only through religion but also through European balance of power. Through that balance all European states had been linked together like a chain.

38. Edmund Burke, *Three Letters Addressed to a Member of the Present Parliament, on the Proposals for Peace with the Regicide Directory of France*, in Edmund Burke, *The Works* (London: Bohn, 1855), 5:214. Burke saw good reasons for calling "this *aggregate* of nations a commonwealth."

39. For a compelling representation of Europe as a historically formed society, "société des Peuples de l'Europe," see Rousseau, *Extrait du Projet de paix perpetuelle de Monsieur l'abbé de Saint-Pierre*, in B. Gagnebin and M. Raymond, eds., *Oeuvres complètes* (Paris: Gallimard, 1964), 3:565 ff. Cf. reflections on Montesquieu and the "question de l'Europe" in Simone Goyard-Fabre, *Montesquieu: La Nature, les Lois, la Liberté* (Paris: Presses universitaires de France, 1993), 232 ff.; generally, see Armando Saitta, *Dalla Res publica christiana agli Stati uniti di Europa: Sviluppo dell'idea pacifista in Francia nei secoli XVII–XIX* (Rome: Storia e letteratura, 1948), chapter 3; René Pomeau, *L'Europe des lumières: Cosmopolitisme et unité européenne au 18e siècle* (Paris: Stock, 1966); J. G. A. Pocock, "What Do We Mean by Europe?" *Wilson Quarterly* 21.1 (1997), 20 ff.

40. "A briefe and generall consideration of Europe," in Samuel Purchas, *Hakluytus Posthumus, or Purchas His Pilgrimes* (Glasgow: James MacLehose, 1905), 1:252.

41. Nothing was "more evident" than that civilizing was in the interest of English trade. But Defoe also pointed out that the interest of the *"Trade of Europe"* was higher than national interests, bringing riches to "every part of *Europe*"; if only pacific commerce would have prevailed, the wealth of African and American world "would center in *Europe.*" *A Plan of the English Commerce: Being a Compleat Prospect of the Trade of This Nation, As Well the Home Trade as the Foreign*, etc. (London, 1728), x; *A General History of Trade, & Especially Consider'd as it Respects the British Commerce, as well at Home, as to all Parts of the World*, etc. (London, 1713), 29–30.

42. Burke, *Three Letters*, 215.

43. See Novalis, *Die Christenheit oder Europa*, in H. and W. Kohlschmidt, eds., *Gesammelte Werke* (Gütersloh: Sigbert Mohn, 1967).

44. De Maistre, Conclusion to his *Du Pape*, calling Protestantism "le plus grand ennemie de l'Europe," in E. M. Cioran, ed., *Textes choisis* (Monaco: du Rocher, 1957), 109 ff.

45. Alexander von Humboldt (who, however, did not deny the existence of the "general interest of Europe"), cited in Andreas Osiander, *The States System of Europe, 1640–1990: Peacemaking and Conditions of International Stability* (Oxford: Clarendon, 1994), 182–183.

46. The *Moniteur universel*, Talleyrand's mouthpiece, July 1815, cited in Osiander, *The States System of Europe*, 172.

47. Cf. Hans Wehberg, *Ideen und Projekte betr. die Vereinigten Staaten von Europa in den letzten 100 Jahren* (Bremen: Donat & Temmen, 1984); Heikki Mikkeli, *Europe as an Idea and an Identity* (Houndmills: Macmillan, 1998), 69 ff.

48. *Convegno di scienze morali e storiche, 14–20 Novembre 1932-IX, Tema: L'Europa*, 2 vols. (Rome: Reale Accademia d'Italia, 1933), 1:14–15; cf. the coverage of the event by the *Nazionalsozialistische Monatshefte* 3.33 (1932).

49. A. Rosenberg, *Convegno di scienze morali e storiche* 1:110, 276; for a comprehensive survey, see P. Kluke, "Nationalsozialistische Europaideologie," *Vierteljahreshefte für Zeitgeschichte* 3 (1955).

50. The term *mystique of Europe* was used by Hugh Seton-Watson, "What Is Europe, Where Is Europe? From Mystique to Politique," the eleventh Martin Wight Lecture as delivered at the Royal Institute of International Affairs, April 23, 1985, *Encounter*, July-August 1985; and critically by J. G. A. Pocock, "Deconstructing Europe," *London Review of Books*, December 19, 1991.

51. Winston Churchill, *Europe Unite: Speeches 1947 and 1948* (Boston: Houghton Mifflin, 1950), 311.

52. Sully, *Memoirs*, 5: 120; on equilibrium, cf. 148.

53. Ibid., 167; cf. 126–127.

54. The term *l'Europe européenne* was used by Gonzague de Reynold, *Qu'est-ce que l'Europe?* vol. 1 of *La Formation de l'Europe* (Fribourg en Suisse: Librairie de l'Université, 1944), 55, to designate, of course, Western Europe.

55. Sully, *Memoirs*, 5:132, 134.

56. Ibid., 3:169.

57. Ibid., 5:134 ff., cf. 152.

58. Ibid., 135–136.

59. Ibid., 150.

60. See Dorothy Vaughan, *Europe and the Turk: A Pattern of Alliances, 1350–1700* (Liverpool: University Press, 1954); and references in Franklin Le Van Baumer, "England, the Turk, and the Common Corps of Christendom," *American Historical Review* 50 (1944): 26–27.

61. Cf. Baumer, "England, the Turk," 29.

62. Ibid., 27.

63. See T. G. Djuvara, *Cent projets de partage de la Turquie (1281–1913)* (Paris: Alcan, 1914).

64. Erasmus, *Vtilissima consvltatio de bello Tvrcis inferendo, et obiter ennaratvs Psalmvs XXVIII*, ed. A. G. Weiler, in series 5, vol. 3 of *Opera omnia Desiderii Erasmi Roterodami* (Amsterdam: North-Holland, 1986), 52; *Ep.* 2285, in P. S. Allen and H. M. Allen, eds., *Opvs epistolarvm Des. Erasmi Roterodami* (Oxford: Clarendon, 1934), 8:384.

65. See Marcel Bataillon, "Erasmo ¿europeo? (1467–1536)," in Marcel Bataillon, *Érasme et l'Espagne*, ed. Ch. Amiel (Geneva: Droz, 1991), 3:90 ff; L.-E. Halkin, "Erasme et l'Europe," in *Commémoration nationale d'Erasme: Actes* (Brussels: Centre interuniversitaire d'histoire de l'humanisme, 1970), 99; cf. Erasmus, *Vtilissima consvltatio*, 52–58.

66. "This is not to say that I absolutely oppose war against the Turks if they attack us." Erasmus, *Dulce bellum inexpertis*, omitted in J. W. Mackail, ed., *Erasmus Against War* (Boston: Merrymount, 1907), 57, cited in Robert P. Adams, *The Better Part of Valor: More, Erasmus, Colet, and Vives, on Humanism, War, and Peace, 1496–1535* (Seattle: University of Washington Press, 1962), 209; cf. Otto Herding, "Erasmus—Frieden und Krieg," in A. Buck, ed., *Erasmus und Europa* (Wiesbaden: Harrassowitz, 1988), 25.

67. Erasmus, *Qverela pacis*, ed. O. Herding in series 4, vol. 2 of *Opera omnia Desiderii Erasmi Roterodami*, (Amsterdam: North-Holland, 1977), 90; and see Erasmus, *Vtilissima consvltatio*.

68. Cf. Keneth H. Setton, "Lutheranism and the Turkish Peril," *Balkan Studies* 3 (1962), 155.

69. Thomas More, *A Dialogue of Comfort Against Tribulation*, ed.Th. Manley in *Selected Works of St. Thomas More,*(New Haven: Yale University Press, 1977), 4:196–198, 236. Cf. Thomas More, *Responsio ad Lutherum* ed. John M. Headley, in vol. 5, part 1 of *The Complete Works of St. Thomas More* (New Haven: Yale University Press, 1969), I,13, pp. 224/225.

70. C. A. Patrides, "'The Bloody and Cruell Turke': the Background of a Renaissance Commonplace," *Studies in the Renaissance* 10 (1963).

71. More, *A Dialogue of Comfort*, 6.

72. Ibid., 8, 40; cf. Baumer, "England, the Turk."

73. Cf. More, *A Dialogue of Comfort*, 40.

74. Thomas More, *A Dialogue Concerning Heresies* ed. Th. M. C. Lawler, G. Marc'Hadour, and R. C. Marins, in vol. 6, part 1, of *The Complete Works of St. Thomas More*, (New Haven: Yale University Press, 1981), I,1, 32; cf. IV,14, p. 411.

75. Ibid., IV,13, 407; IV,14, 414–415.

76. Carlos G. Noreña, *Juan Luis Vives* (The Hague: Nijhoff, 1970), 223; Adams, *The Better Part of Valor*, 264.

77. Juan Luis Vives, *Concordia y doscordia en el linaje humano (De concordia et discordia in humano genere)*, in L. Riber, ed., *Obras completas* (Madrid:

Aguilar, 1948), 2:75, and Juan Luis Vives, *De la insolidaridad de Europa y de la guerra contra el Turco (De Europae dissidiis et bello turcico)*, ibid., 2:43, 46, 50.

78. Vives, *De la insolidaridad de Europa*, 52; Rafael Gibert, "Lulio y Vives sobre la paz," in *La paix*, Receuils de la Société Jean Bodin (Brussels: Éditions de la librairie encyclopédique, 1961), 15:159; Noreña, *Juan Luis Vives*, 225, 226.

79. Vives, *De la insolidaridad de Europa*, 58.

80. Ibid., 50.

81. Columbus, *Journal*, prologue, in John Cummins, *The Voyage of Christopher Columbus: Columbus' Own Journal of Discovery Newly Restored and Translated* (London: Weidenfeld and Nicolson, 1992), 81.

82. See Abbas Hamdani, "Columbus and the Recovery of Jerusalem," *Journal of the American Oriental Society* 99.1 (1979).

83. Luis Weckmann, "The Middle Ages in the Conquest of America," *Speculum* 26 (1951), 132.

84. Columbus, *Journal*, 157.

85. See Cummins, *The Voyage of Christopher Columbus*, 207–208, note 6; cf. Weckmann, "The Middle Ages in the Conquest of America"; James Muldoon, *Popes, Lawyers, and Infidels: The Church and the Non-Christian World, 1250–1550* (Liverpool: Liverpool University Press, 1979), 136; Anthony Pagden, *European Encounters with the New World: From Renaissance to Romanticism* (New Haven: Yale University Press, 1993), 78–79.

86. Angel Losada, "The Controversy Between Sepúlveda and Las Casas in the Junta of Valladolid," in J. Friede and B. Keen, eds., *Bartolomé de Las Casas in History: Toward an Understanding of the Man and His Work* (DeKalb: Northern Illinois University Press, 1971), 301.

87. It was "fortunate for the Indians that Las Casas, along with Francisco de Vitoria and Domingo de Soto, emphasized the great distinction between wars against the Indians and those against the Moors and Turks." Lewis Hanke, *Aristotle and the American Indians: A Study in Race Prejudice in the Modern World* (London: Hollis and Carter, 1959), 107. I discuss the dispute and Las Casas's argument in greater detail in Tomaž Mastnak, "Fictions in Political Thought: Las Casas, Sepúlveda, the Indians, and the Turks," *Filozofski Vestnik* 15.2 (1994).

88. Cf. Las Casas, *Apologia*, in Juan Ginés de Sepúlveda and Fray Bartolomé de las Casas, *Apologia*, ed. A. Losada (Madrid: Editora Nacional, 1975), 222, 231, 353.

89. Ibid., 338, 342.

90. Las Casas, *A Short Account of the Destruction of the Indies*, ed. and tran. N. Griffin (Harmondsworth: Penguin, 1994), 43; cf. Pagden, "Introduction," ibid., xxxix.

91. Losada, "The Controversy Between Sepúlveda and Las Casas," 283, 293.

92. "Memorial de los remedios" (1542), cited in Pagden, *European Encounters with the New World*, 79.

93. Venancio D. Carro, "The Spanish Theological-Juridical Renaissance and the Ideology of Bartolomé de Las Casas," Friede and Keen, *Bartolomé de Las Casas in History*, 275.

94. Cf. Setton, "Lutheranism and the Turkish Peril," 147.

95. On the Christian and *Mahmetische* Turks, see Luther, *Verlegung des Alcoran Bruder Richardi*, in vol 53 of *D. Martin Luthers Werke: Kritische Gesamtausgabe* (Weimar: Bohlau 1920), 391.

96. Cf. Setton, "Lutheranism and the Turkish Peril," 164.

97. See Pope Leo X's bull *Exsurge domine*, which, in 1520, condemned "Martin Luther's errors," in C. Mirbt and K. Aland, eds., *Quellen zur Geschichte des Papsttums und des römischen Katholizismus*, 6th rev. ed. (Tübingen: Mohr [Siebeck], 1967), no. 789, p. 507; cf. Setton, "Lutheranism and the Turkish Peril," 142, for further references; and Harry Buchanan, "Luther and the Turks, 1519–1529," *Archiv für Reformationsgeschichte* 47.1 (1956), 142 ff.

98. Martin Luther, *Vom Kriege widder die Türcken*, in vol. 51 of *Kritische Gesamtausgabe* (Weimar: Böhlau, 1914), followed in the same year by the *Eine Heerpredigt widder den Türcken*, in vol. 30 of *Kritische Gesamtausgabe* (Weimar: Böhlau, 1909); for the accusation of the popes, see, for example, *Vom Kriege widder die Türcken*, 110.

99. Luther, *Vermanunge zum Gebet Wider den Türcken* in vol 30 of *Kritische Gesamtausgabe*, 620.

100. Setton, "Lutheranism and the Turkish Peril," 148, who also cites Melanchthon's words that "we must fight the Turks not only in defense of our liberty, laws, and the other refinements of civilization, but also for our religion, altars, and homes."

101. Luther, *Vom Kriege widder die Türcken*, 120–24; *Eine Heerpredigt widder den Türcken*, 161 ff., 173; Luther, *Vermanunge zum Gebet Wider den Türcken*, 617; Martin Luther, *Vorwort zu dem Libellus de ritu et moribus Turcorum* in vol 30 of *Kritische Gesamtausgabe*, 207; Luther, *Verlegung des Alcoran Bruder Richardi*, 276, 388–389, 394–395.

102. Ter Meulen, *Der Gedanke der internationalen Organisation*, 140.

103. François de La Noue, *Discours politiques et militaires*, ed. F. E. Sutcliffe (Geneva: Droz, 1967), discourse 22.

104. Michael J. Heath, *Crusading Commonplaces: La Noue, Lucinge, and Rhetoric Against the Turks* (Geneva: Droz, 1987), 32; cf. 9, that "almost every sixteenth-century writer had something to say on the subject." For a comprehensive treatment of the Turk in French intellectual history, see Clarence Dana Rouillard, *The Turk in French History, Thought, and Literature, 1520–1660* (Paris: Bovin, s.a. [1941]); Geoffroy Atkinson, *Les Nouveaux horizons de la Renaissance française* (Paris: Droz, 1935).

105. The term is used by Heath, *Crusading Commonplaces*, where one can find a more substantial discussion of La Noue.

106. La Noue, *Discours politiques et militaires*, 447–449; cf. discourse 21, where La Noue argues against alliances between Christain princes and the *mahumetistes*, the chief enemies of the Christian name, and hopes that the French king will not persist much longer "in friendship with these barbarians" but rather follow the steps of his predecessors devoted to "extirpation and destruction of the enemies of Christendom." Ibid., 435–436.

107. Ibid., 456, 515.

108. Ibid., 444, 490.

109. Ibid., 515–516.

110. Cf. Richard Tuck, *Philosophy and Government, 1572–1651* (Cambridge: Cambridge University Press, 1993).

111. Cited ibid., 62.

112. Antoine Coron, "Juste Lipse juge des pouvoirs politiques éuropéens à la lumière de sa correspondence," in *Théorie et pratique politiques à la Renaissance*, XVIIᵉ Colloque international de Tours (Paris: Vrin, 1977), 454.

113. See Tuck, *Philosophy and Government*, 62; Djuvara, *Cent projets de partage de la Turquie*; Baumer, "England, the Turk," 43 ff.; Theodor Kükelhaus, *Der Ursprung des Planes vom ewigen Frieden in den Memoiren des Herzogs von Sully* (Berlin: Speyer and Peters, 1893), 47 ff., 56 ff., 144 ff.; Gustave Fagniez, *Le Père Joseph et Richelieu (1577–1638)* (Paris: Hachette, 1894), 1: chapter 3; Iorga, "Un projet relatif à la conquête de Jérusalem, 1609," *Revue de l'Orient Latin* 2 (1894), 181; Kurt von Raumer, *Ewiger Friede: Friedensrufe und Friedenspläne seit der Renaissance* (Freiburg and Munich: Alber, 1953), 65 ff.

114. Cf. von Raumer, *Ewiger Friede*, 65–82; Anthony Pagden, *Spanish Imperialism and the Political Imagination: Studies in European and Spanish-American Social and Political Theory, 1513–1830* (New Haven: Yale University Press, 1990), 46–54.

115. Giovanni Botero, *Della Ragion di Stato Libri Dieci, Con Tre Libri delle Cause della Grandezza, e Magnificenza delle Città* (Venice, 1589), I,8, II,6, III,3, IX,2; *Della Ragion di Stato Libri Dieci, Con Tre Libri delle Cause della Grandezza, e Magnificenza delle Città* (Venice, 1606), X,9. On the omnipresence of a legitimate reason for war against the Turks, cf. Alberico Gentili, *De iure belli libri tres* (Oxford: Clarendon; London: H. Milford, 1933), I,12: Although no war is natural, as he argued, "it is almost natural for us to war with the Turks, just as it was for the Greeks to contend with the barbarians," because the Turks behave in such a way that "we constantly have a legitimate reason for war" against them.

116. Botero, *Della Ragion di Stato* (1589), VI,7.

117. Botero, *Della Ragion di Stato* (1606), X,9. I cite Waley's translation, P. J. and D. P. Waley, eds., *The Reason of State and The Greatness of Cities* (London: Routledge and Kegan Paul, 1956), 222.

118. Botero, *Della Ragion di Stato* (1589), V,3; cf. II,15–16.

119. Ibid., VIII,14; cf. Botero, *Della Ragion di Stato* (1606), X,9.

120. Giovanni Botero, *La prima parte de' Prencipi Christiani* (Turin, 1601), 6–7.

121. See Baumer, "England, the Turk"; Franklin Le Van Baumer, "The Church of England and the Common Corps of Christendom," *Journal of Modern History* 16.1 (1944); Franklin Le Van Baumer, "The Conception of Christendom in Renaissance England," *Journal of the History of Ideas* 4.2 (1945).

122. Edwin Sandys, *Europae Speculum: Or a View or Survey of the State of Religion in the Western Parts of the World* (London, 1673), 207 ff., 220. Cf. Baumer "The Church of England and the Common Corps of Christendom," 13; "The Conception of Christendom in Renaissance England," 139, 140; Tuck, *Philosophy and Government*, 117.

123. Tuck, *Philosophy and Government*, 117.

124. See W. B. Patterson, *King James VI and I and the Reunion of Christendom* (Cambridge: Cambridge University Press, 1997).

125. Baumer, "England, the Turk," 43–45; Patterson, *King James VI and I*, 29.

126. Baumer, "England, the Turk," 45; Patterson, *King James VI and I*, 34 ff.

127. Bacon's memorandum is attached to his letter to King James, March 23, 1617, in *The Works of Lord Bacon* (London: Bohn, 1846), 2:185.

128. Francis Bacon, *The History of the Reign of King Henry the Seventh*, ed. J. Weinberger (Ithaca: Cornell University Press, 1996), 177–178; cf. 95 ff. On Bacon's Tacitism, cf. Tuck, *Philosophy and Government*, 105 ff.

129. Francis Bacon, *An Advertisement Touching an Holy War*, in J. Spedding, R. L. Ellis and D. D. Heath, eds., *The Works of Francis Bacon*, vol. 7 (London, Longman, 1861); see "Editor's Preface," ibid., 5.

130. Thomas Fuller, *The Historie of the Holy Warre* (Cambridge, 1639); the citation is from a later edition, *The History of the Holy War* (London: William Pickering, 1840), 292. Cf. Laetitia Boehm, "'Gesta Dei per Francos'—oder 'Gesta Francorum'? Die Kreuzzüge als historiographisches Problem," *Saeculum* 8 (1957): 62–64; Franco Cardini, "Le crociate tra Illuminismo ed età napoleonica," in Franco Cardini, *Studi sulla storia e sull'idea di crociata* (Rome: Jouvence, 1993), 468–469; Christopher Tyerman, *The Invention of the Crusades* (Toronto: University of Toronto Press, 1998), 104 ff.

131 A verse in Father Joseph's Turciados IV,568, reads, for example: "Francia, Franciscus, fatalia nomina Turcis." Louis Dedouvres, *De Patris Josephi Turciados libris quinque* (Angers: Germain et G. Grassin, 1894), 35. Cf. Mastnak, *Crusading Peace*, chapter 4.3.

132. Louis Dedouvres, *Le Père Joseph de Paris, capucin, l'éminence grise* (Paris: Gabriel Beauchesne; Angers: S^{te} A^{me} des Éditions de l'Ouest, 1932), 1:356 ff., 457–459; Dedouvres, *De Patris Josephi Turciados*, 38.

133. A detailed description of the project in Fagniez, *Le Père Joseph et Richelieu*, 1: chapter 3; cf. Joseph's *Mémoire présenté au Roi* on his diplomatic mission to

Rome to discuss the crusading project with the pope and Italian princes, ibid., 2:467 ff.

134. Fagniez, *Le Père Joseph et Richelieu*, 1:140; and Joseph, *Mémoire présenté au Roi*, ibid., 2:467.

135. Joseph, *Mémoire présenté au Roi*, 468, 476–480.

136. Fagniez, *Le Père Joseph et Richelieu*, 1: 180–181.

137. Victor-L. Tapié, *France in the Age of Louis XIII and Richelieu*, trans. D. McLockie (Cambridge: Cambridge University Press, 1988), 111.

138. Ernst Benz, *Leibniz und Peter der Große*, cited in Paul Wiedeburg, *Der junge Leibniz: Das Reich und Europa. II. Teil: Paris* (Wiesbaden: Steiner, 1970), 3:202.

139. *Projet de conquête de l'Égypte*, in L. A. Foucher de Careil, ed., *Oeuvres de Leibniz* (Paris: 1859–1875), 5:7, 32, 57.

140. Ibid., 256–257.

141. In the concluding section of his project, proving the justice of the cause, Leibniz referred to Bacon's fragment on holy war. See Leibniz, *Justa dissertatio*, in Leibniz, *Sämtliche Schriften*, series 4, 1:379.

142. For Leibniz's contemporaries, cf. Foucher de Careil, "Introduction," in Leibniz, *Oeuvres de Leibniz*, 5:xxvi, xxviii; Wiedeburg, *Der junge Leibniz*, 1:403 ff., and on the tradition on which he drew, ibid., 378 ff. Leibniz, for example, wanted Louis XIV to accomplish Henry IV's (i.e., Sully's) "Grand Design." *Synopsis meditationis*, in Leibniz, *Sämtliche Schriften*, series 4, 1:227.

143. Patrick Riley, "Introduction," in Leibniz, *Political Writings*, ed. P. Riley, 2d ed. (Cambridge: Cambridge University Press, 1988), 34.

144. *Caesarinus Fürstenerius*, in Leibniz, *Political Writings*, 111.

145. Cf. Riley, "Introduction," 30 ff.; Hans-Peter Schneider, "Gottfried Wilhelm Leibniz," in M. Stolleis, *Staatsdenker im 17. und 18. Jahrhundert: Reichspublizistik, Politik, Naturrecht* (Frankfurt/Main: Metzner, 1977), 222–23; Wiedeburg, *Der junge Leibniz*, 1:430 ff.

146. Cf. Wiedeburg, *Der junge Leibniz*, 1:416, who speaks of a conceptual triad: league of nations—crusade—peace.

147. *Gedancken zum Entwurf der Teutschen Kriegsverfassung*, in Leibniz, *Sämtliche Schriften*, series 4, vol. 2 (Berlin: Akademie der Wissenschaften der DDR, 1983),579, 593.

148. Leibniz, letter to Saint-Pierre, February 7, 1715, in *Oeuvres de Leibniz*, 4:326. Wiedeburg, *Der junge Leibniz*, 4:478, sees close links between Leibniz's Egyptian project and his comments on Saint-Pierre.

149. Fletcher, whom I have mentioned in connection with Bellers (see note 34), was not such an exception. Whereas in his *Discorso delle cose di Spagna* he pointed out, as a reason for the decline of Spanish kingdom, the expulsion of the Jews and Moors, he recommended, as the first action to be undertaken by

the new king in order to obtain legitimacy and authority, a military expedition against the Moors of Barbary modeled on Ferdinand's capture of Granada; such a war against the infidels would gain him support of European states. Andrew Fletcher, *Discorso delle cose di Spagna: Scritto nel mese di Luglio 1698*, in *The Political Works of Andrew Fletcher, Esq.* (London, 1737), 183, 193, 232, 333 [= 233], 338 [= 238].

150. Penn, *An Essay Towards the Present and Future Peace of Europe*, 18.

151. D'Alembert, *Éloge de Saint-Pierre*, in vol. 3, part 1 of *Oeuvres de D'Alembert* (Paris, 1821), 261, 267, 278, 279.

152. "Aneantissement futur. Du Mahometisme & des autres Religions humaines par le progrèz continuel de la Rézon humaine universelle," Abbé de Saint-Pierre, *Pensées diverses, Ouvrajes de Politique [& de Morale]* (Rotterdam, 1733–41), 13:204–205, 210, 218, 219, 237; *Discours contre le Mahometisme*, in Abbé de Saint-Pierre, *Ouvrajes de Politique*, 5:121; cf. *Observasions Sur le progrèz continuël de la Raizon Universelle*, in Saint-Pierre, *Ouvrajes de Politique*, 11:282, 284.

153. Saint-Pierre, *Discours contre le Mahometisme*, 131.

154. Abbé de Saint-Pierre, *Projet pour rendre la paix perpétuelle en Europe* (Utrecht, 1713), 306–307. I cite this text from the edition prepared by S. Goyard-Fabre for "Corpus des oeuvres de philosophie en langue française" (Abbé de Saint-Pierre, *Projet pour rendre la Paix perpétuelle en Europe* [Paris: Fayard, 1986]), which also includes *Projet de traitè pour rendre la paix perpetuelle entre les souverains chretiens*, etc. (Utrecht 1717 [to which I refer as *Projet de traité*]). I discuss the project in greater detail in Mastnak, "Abbé de Saint-Pierre."

155. Saint-Pierre, *Projet de traité*, 549.

156. Ibid., 613.

157. Ibid., 677, 679.

158. Ibid., 689; cf. 690, where Saint-Pierre envisages that the same European army which was to chase the Turks out of Europe will easily chase them out of Egypt and a great part of Asia as well.

159. Ibid., 693. Cf. *Vue generale des efets merveilleux que produiroit nécessairement en Europe Le Nouveau plan de Gouvernement des Etats*, in Saint-Pierre, *Ouvrajes de Politique*, 6:326–327, where Saint-Pierre argued that, if a Union like the one he was projecting had been established among Christian princes at the time of Crusades, they would have cost much less in human lives and money, and Mohammedan and barbarian peoples would have, in Saint-Pierre's own days, been Christian and well ordered.

160. Saint-Pierre, *Projet de traité*, 690.

161. Saint-Pierre, *Suplement a l'Abrejé*, in Saint-Pierre, *Ouvrajes de Politique*, 2:69.

162. Saint-Pierre, *Abrejé du Projet*, in Saint-Pierre, *Ouvrajes de Politique*, 1:295.

163. Edward Gibbon, *The History of the Decline and Fall of the Roman Empire*, ed. D. Womersley (London: Penguin, 1995), chapter 58; for the Enlightenment histories of the Crusades, see Cardini, "Le crociate tra Illuminismo ed età napoleonica"; Tyerman, *The Invention of the Crusades*, 111 ff.

164. Giulio Alberoni, *Cardinal Alberoni's Scheme for Reducing the* Turkish *Empire to the Obedience of* Christian *Princes: And for a Partition of the Conquests. Together with a Scheme of a* Perpetual Dyet *for establishing the Publick Tranquility* (London, 1736), 1–4. The project was first published in French, in 1735, as *Système de paix générale dans la présente conjoncture.*

165. Ibid., 5, 10–11, 54.

166. Ibid., 40–41, 52–54.

167. Ibid., 6, 9, 51, 58.

168. Marquis d'Argenson, *Mémoires et journal inédit du marquis d'Argenson, Ministre des affaires étrangères sous Louis XV*, ed. M. le marquis d'Argenson (Paris, 1858), 5:259, 270.

169. Marquis d'Argenson, "Essai de l'Exercise du Tribunal Européen par la France seule. Pour la pacification universelle appliquée au tems courant", in d'Argenson, *Considérations sur le gouvernement ancien et présent de la France* (Amsterdam, 1765), 200.

170. D'Argenson, *Mémoires et journal*, 5: 384; Marquis d'Argenson, *Journal et mémoires du marquis d'Argenson*, ed. E. J. B. Rathery (Paris, 1859), 1:361–362.

171. D'Argenson, *Mémoires et journal*, 5:385.

172. Von Lilienfeld, *Neues Staats-Gebäude. In drey Büchern* (Leipzig, 1767), "Vorrede," n.p. Saint-Pierre, too, was concerned with the Mohammedan North African pirates. See Saint-Pierre, *Projet pour l'Extirpation des Corsaires de Barbarie* in vol. 2 of *Ouvrajes de Politique.*

173. Von Lilienfeld, *Neues Staats-Gebäude*, 265.

174. Ibid., 334.

175. See ter Meulen, *Der Gedanke der internationalen Organisation*, 298, 312.

176. See *Projet d'expulsion des Turcs de l'Europe et d'un nouvel équilibre politique*, reproduced in Djuvara, *Cent projets de partage de la Turquie*, 308–314; cf. François Charles-Roux, *L'Angleterre, l'isthme de Suez et l'Egypte au XVIIIᵉ siècle* (Paris, 1922), 161 ff.

177. Henry Meyer, *Voltaire on War and Peace*, Studies in Voltaire and the Eighteenth Century, 144 (Banbury: Voltaire Foundation, 1976), 49, 99.

178. Ibid., 82; and Frederick II to Voltaire, February 29, 1773, in *Correspondence*, ed. Th. Besterman (Geneva: Institut et musée Voltaire, 1953–65), 84:36.

179. Cited in Meyer, *Voltaire on War and Peace*, 49.

180. Volney, *Les Ruines ou Méditation sur les révolution des Empires*, in Volney, *Oeuvres*, Corpus des Oeuvres de philosophie en langue française (Paris: Fayard, 1989), 1:243–245, 248–249; Volney, *Considérations sur la guerre des*

Turks, en 1788, in *Oeuvres de C. F. Volney*, 2d ed. (Paris, 1825), 3:440. How much these reflections were indebted to Diderot and Raynal is not my subject here.

181. Volney, *Les Ruines*, 249. On *Oriental despotism*, a term finding a wide acceptance in the Enlightenment, cf. Franco Venturi, *Italy and the Enlightenment: Studies in a Cosmopolitan Century* (New York: New York University Press, 1972), 41 ff.; see also Alain Grosrichard, *Structures du sérail* (Paris: Seuil, 1979).

182. Volney, *Considérations*, 379, 397, 404, 440.

183. Burke, *Three Letters*, 215, 257.

184. I cannot discuss post-eighteenth-century European views of the "Orient" here, but see, for example, Edward W. Said, *Orientalism: Western Conceptions of the Orient* (New York: Pantheon, 1978); Albert Hourani, *Islam in European Thought* (Cambridge: Cambridge University Press, 1991); Maxime Rodinson, *Europe and the Mystique of Islam*, trans. R. Veinus (Seattle: University of Washington Press, 1991); Hichem Djaït, *Europe and Islam*, trans. P. Heinegg (Berkeley and Los Angeles: University of California Press, 1985); Thierry Hentsch, *Imagining the Middle East* (Montreal and New York: Black Rose, 1992). See also Michael A. Sells, *The Bridge Betrayed: Religion and Genocide in Bosnia* (Berkeley and Los Angeles: University of California Press, 1996), chapter 2, for the construction of Slavic Muslims as Christ killers by Serb nationalists and the idea of cleansing the Christian land of "Turkifiers"; and Muhsin Rizvić, *Bosanski muslimani u Andrićevu svijetu* (Sarajevo: Ljiljan, 1995), on the image of the Bosnian Muslims in the work of the Nobel Prize–winning novelist Ivo Andrić.

185. Cf. Charles-Roux, *L'Angleterre, l'isthme de Suez et l'Egypte*, chapter 16.

186. Cf. C. A. Nallino, "Il mondo musulmano in relazione con l'Europa," *Convegno di scienze morali e storiche* 1:434.

187. René Grousset, *L'épopée des Croisades* (Paris: Plon, 1939), 384–385.

188. Mayer, *The Crusades*, 287–288.

189. This text was written in 1997/1998.

190. Cf. A. Rosenberg, "Krisis und Neugeburt Europas," in *Convegno di scienze morali e storiche* 1:272 ff., who argued against the imposition of cultural/spiritual monism and for a "recognition without reservations of the vital diversity" of ways of life as the necessary condition for any imaginable unity of Europe: for a Europe "*vielgestaltig nach innen und einig nach aussen*." He applied the same principle of the inviolability of plurality of cultures to European relations with Asia and Africa: Europe should recognize "all existing cultures" and renounce any attempt to "impose the spiritual life of the white man on peoples of other races." This, of course, did not imply a renounciation of Europe's domination, *Herrschaft*, over Africa and Asia, which had to be ensured with a united European will. Ibid., 274–276, 283.

191. *New York Times International*, March 11, 1997; cf. March 27, 1997. I thank Mara Thomas for these references.

192. That what happened in Bosnia was not a series of "crimes against humanity" but rather a crime committed by humanity against the Bosnians is a point made by Ervin Hladnik Milharčić, who covered the war for the Ljubljana weekly *Mladina*.

193. Some examples are cited in Sells, *The Bridge Betrayed*, 113, 121–122.

194. "Naši Srbi," *Ljiljan* 4.132 (1995), July 26-August 2.

195. Alija Isaković, "Europa i mi," in Isaković, *Antologija zla* (Sarajevo and Ljubljana: Ljiljan, 1994), 344–345.

The Myth of Westernness in Medieval Literary Historiography

María Rosa Menocal

Leave to us, in Heaven's name, Pythaqoras, Plato and Aristotle,
and keep your Omar, your Alchabitius, your Aben Zoar, your Abenragel.
— Pico della Mirandola

Modern civilization's myriad pretensions to objectivity have
unfortunately tended to obscure the fact that much of our writing of history
is as much a myth-making activity as that of more primitive societies. We
often regard tribal histories or ancient myths that do not cloak themselves in
such pretensions as less objective than our own. We are prone to forget that
history is written by the victors and serves to ratify and glorify their ascendancy—and we forget how many tracks are covered in that process. The
writing of literary history, the close and often indispensable ancillary of general history, is preoccupied with the myths of our intellectual and artistic
heredity, and it, too, tells those stories we want to hear, chooses the most
illustrious parentage possible, and canonizes family trees that mesh with the
most cherished notions we hold about our parentage.

The most general, and in many ways the most influential and pervasive,
image or construct we have is that of ourselves and our culture, an entity we
have dubbed "Western," a clearly comparative title. Whether it is spoken or
unspoken, named or unnamed, we are governed by the notion that there is

a distinctive cultural history that can be characterized as Western, and that it is in distinctive, necessary, and fundamental opposition to non-Western culture and cultural history. Few of us, even less as laymen than as scholars, have conceived of developments or tackled specific problems in the literary and cultural history of western Europe assuming anything other than that this is an appropriate model.

While the value and accuracy of such a characterization for the modern (that is, usually the Renaissance and post-Renaissance) period is for others to decide, and while it has recently been the object of intense criticism,[1] its relevance for those whose scholarly domain is further back in time, namely Europe's medieval period, has been less carefully examined. In fact, the continued relatively routine acceptance of the clichéd East-West dichotomy for the medieval period is particularly noteworthy because medievalists have for some time been attempting to overthrow a series of other clichés and simplistic perceptions of the Middle Ages.

But this particular aspect of the myth of our past appears to be so fundamental that questioning it is not part of the various programs for the reorientation and revival of medieval studies, and its precepts continue to be part of the foundation of most studies, including many viewed as new, even revolutionary, in their approaches. What many consider to be the ravages of the new criticism have left at least this part of our old-fashioned notions intact.[2]

The irony is that while the Kiplingesque dichotomy, with its tacit presupposition of the superiority of West over East, had its grounding in the visible particularism of Europe and the irrefutable dominance of European empires over their colonies in more recent periods, the medieval situation has been characterized by many, with ample documentation, as something more resembling the reverse. A surprising number of historians of various fields, nationalities, and vested interests have described the relationship in the medieval world as one in which it was al-Andalus (as Muslim Spain was called by the Arabs) and its ancestry and progeny that were ascendant, and ultimately dominant, in the medieval period. It has been variously characterized as the age of Averroes, as an Oriental period of Western history, a period in which Western culture grew in the shadows of Arabic and Arabic-manipulated learning, the "European Awakening," with the prince, a speaker of Arabic, bestowing the kiss of delivery from centuries of deep sleep. For a considerable number of historians the "renaissance of the twelfth century" is a phrase that in part masks a revolution instigated and propagated by Andalusians and their cultural achievements.[3]

Remarkably little of the information and few of the hypotheses that have informed these views have passed into the realm of common knowledge, however. Even less so has this story—or its beginnings, the beginnings of a cultural history different from the one we are more used to nurturing—penetrated the ranks of the literary historians of medieval Europe.[4] The resistance to a consideration of this different story of our parentage, of a displacement of our conception of our fundamental cultural lineage, is quite deep-seated. The tenor of some of the responses to the suggestion that this Arab-centered vision might be a more viable historical reconstruction for the West has occasionally been reminiscent of the reactions once provoked by Darwin's suggestion (for so was the theory of evolution construed) that we were "descended from monkeys." It is time to scrutinize such responses more closely and critically than we have in the past.[5]

A preconceived and long-established, even canonized, image has a great impact on research on the literary and cultural history of a period. It would hardly be revolutionary to note that its import is enormous. We operate with a repository of assumptions, and knowledge based on those assumptions, that govern what concepts, propositions, and hypotheses we find tenable. The images we have of certain periods and cultures, the intellectual baggage we carry, is an inescapable determinant and shaper of what we are able to see in or imagine for those cultures or periods of time. Those images also determine what facts we include in our histories and what texts we canonize in our literary histories, although we then use those same facts and canons to justify and enhance the history they tell. The images and paradigms that thus govern or dictate our views, the parameters of our research, are not free of political and ideological factors or cultural prejudices, although the notion that there is such a thing as value-free, objective scholarship persists in many quarters to this day, particularly in literary scholarship.[6]

But the veil of supposed objectivity is not limited to the older, explicitly historicizing philological period of our literary studies. One of the effects of the advent and popularity of American new criticism, with its emphasis on the primacy of the "text itself" was to give greater vigor to that myth of the possibility of objectivity, the possibility of considering a text with very limited or no interference from external, and possibly distorting, considerations. There is some irony in the fact that while previous historically based literary studies may have explicitly tied texts to a cultural and historical paradigm that served to explicate the text, the new criticism in most instances succeeded merely in masking the effects that such an image had on the readings of the texts. While making believe that they had somehow miraculously been eliminated from the literary worldview of the scholar, the structuralist analysis of much literature, in fact, further cemented and canonized the historicocultural images and parameters that an earlier period of criticism had felt obliged to reestablish in each piece of scholarship.

At least in principle, the older procedure could lead to a questioning and criticism of the proffered cultural views and assumptions. There is little question, of course, of the benefits wrought by that shift in our perspective, of the value of many of the precepts of a supposedly purer and self-referential analysis of literary texts. It succeeded in restoring a notion of the special qualities of literature qua literature and corrected many of the deficiencies of previous scholarship.

But the silence of much of structuralism on issues such as the relevant sociohistorical background for a self-referential and supposedly purely synchronic analysis of a medieval text only ratified, for students as well as fellow scholars, the validity of the Europeanist diachrony and social milieu that clearly informed the semantic fields of such analysis.[7] Thus, the appearance of possible objectivity masked but did not eliminate the problem of a regnant ideological image in certain branches of literary historiography. Its dominance in literary criticism over the past thirty years has helped to preclude any direct examination of what images and paradigms we operate with and what their value and/or accuracy might be. Or it may be that it is merely coincidental that the effects of the shift away from a historical perspective in literary studies have been strongest in the precise period in which many historians and their textual discoveries (such as that of the *kharjas*) were suggesting that it was timely to revise our image of the past. In either case, the turning of the tide or the apparent end of a cycle makes it more critically acceptable to address the issue of our conceptual and imaginative paradigm of medieval history.

The notion that there are paradigms that govern both periods of history and bodies and periods of scholarship and that these paradigms undergo periodic revolutions has become so commonplace since the appearance of Thomas Kuhn's proposal as to make it redundant to quote Kuhn himself on the subject. It has become part of the common parlance of scholarly discourse in many areas to consider the nature and effects of such paradigms and, when they are perceived to exist, the shiftings of paradigms that signal major changes or revolutions of a "worldview" or an "image."

The paradigm that to such a great extent established our own notions of what constituted the Middle Ages was partially formed in the immediate postmedieval period, which viewed itself as a renaissance—a rebirth, if we accept the implications of the terminology—following that moribund period. The definitions of "self" and "other" that emerge during this period commonly regarded as primarily modern, both chronologically and for its formative influence, focus in great measure on the nature of its relationship with preceding periods, the classical and the medieval. It was in and through the Renaissance that the dominant position of the classical Greek and Latin worlds emerged. The concept of self, and ultimately of the Western self, would be strongly affected, in many cases completely dominated, by the emerging relationship between the modern and the classical worlds, a relationship viewed as ancestral. Out of this relationship there was derived, ultimately, the critical notion, which remains strong today, of the essential continuity and unity of Western civilization from the Greeks through fifteenth-century Italy, having survived the lull of the Dark Ages, and thence through the rest of Europe and European history. It is a notion of history formulated as much to deny the medieval past and its heritage as to establish a new and more worthy ancestry.[8]

But in this view of the world that preceded the Renaissance, the world from whose shadow it emerged, the paradigm of the Renaissance is necessarily paradoxical. A delicate balance must be maintained between sameness, in which the medievals were part of a continuum, and change, in which they were different and inferior. The depiction of the medieval world as a dark age during which the real knowledge and legitimate pursuits of Western man (those which had flourished and reached their zenith in Greece and Rome) were temporarily in hiatus, moribund, dormant, stifled, or nonexistent became so fundamental a part of the general perception of history that it is still operative in many spheres to this day. Although certain aspects of that paradigm, primarily the impression of a formidable primitivism due to the medieval world's divorce from the classical heritage, have been debunked (though only very recently), other vestiges of it are clearly part of the working assumptions of many scholars.[9]

Arguably, the notion clung to most tenaciously is a variation of what in Spanish literary historiography is succinctly called *estado latente*: despite the overt darkness and significant breaks in the continuity with classical ancestors, the medievals were still fundamentally, if covertly, Western. It may have been a relatively dormant period, but it was nonetheless a link with those whose accomplishments did more clearly define Western culture.

Several logical corollaries are implicit in this image of the Renaissance
and of how it is at once a period set apart from the medieval period, allied as
it was with the Greeks and Romans in their golden age, and a period that saw
the beginnings of modern western Europe. The first is the partial or complete omission of a recognition that the medieval world had included centers of learning and revival where men were conversant with the Greek heritage that was to be "rediscovered" in the Renaissance. Nor was it likely,
within the limits of this conceptual framework, that one would imagine that
one of the characteristics of the earlier, darker period could have been the
existence of a secular humanism in open struggle with the forces of dog-
matic faith. The admission of the existence of such phenomena would not
only have robbed the later period of its claims to being a renascence, at least
in any dramatic and absolute way, but it would also have deprived it (and us,
since in great measure we continue to cling to that particular historical
dialectic) of that clear-cut distinction between the two periods that is dominant in modern European historical mythology.

But the remainder of the myth, the crystallization of the concept of Europeanness and its ancestry, was largely spun out in the nineteenth century,
and it played a critical role at this moment of high-pitched awareness of the
particularity and superiority of Europe that came with the imperial and
colonial experience and the post-Romantic experience with the Orient. This
experience certainly helped sharpen the perception not only of European
community and continuity but also of its difference from others, or from the
Other. It was an Other (and the Arab world was one of its principal manifestations) that Europe was by its own standards bringing out of the darkness
and civilizing, at least as far as that was possible for those who were not European in the first place.

Thus was eliminated the possibility that the Middle Ages might be portrayed as a historical period in which a substantial part of culture and learning was based in a radically different foreign culture. To view an Arabic-
Islamic component, even in its European manifestations, as positive and
essential would have been unimaginable, and it would remain so as long as
the views and scholarship molded in that period continued to inform our
education. The proposition that the Arab world had played a critical role in
the making of the modern West, from the vantage point of the late nineteenth century and the better part of this century, is in clear and flagrant
contradiction of cultural ideology. It is unimaginable in the context of the
readily observable phenomenon that was institutionalized as an essential

element of European ideology and that has remained so in many instances to this day: cultural supremacy over the Arab world.

It is, consequently, altogether logical that part of the vision of the Middle Ages, that part that saw it as relatively backward, ignorant, and unenlightened, has by and large been eliminated, or at least substantially modified, while the structurally balancing notion of its fundamental sameness, its place in a largely unbroken continuum of what constitutes Westernness, is, if anything, more elaborately developed and more deeply entrenched. It is in the context of the nineteenth and twentieth centuries, the period during which modern philology (as it was once called) became an academic discipline and an intellectual field, that the major additions to the general cultural paradigms for the medieval period have emerged and been codified.

The earliest addition, which was clearly marked by the imprint of Romanticism, was the bringing into focus and prominence of the "primitive" European or folkloristic constituent elements of medieval culture, raising to a level of respectable analysis the inquiry into such things as the Celtic or Germanic influences on the culture and literature of the early Romance world. The other, not so much an innovation as a rigid codification of earlier notions about the "Age of Faith," is the elevation of scripture and scriptural exegesis as the most potent, usually the overwhelming, cultural component of the Middle Ages. In its most extreme form, this view of the power of Christian faith and its institutions is strong enough to completely eliminate most other possible cultural factors. The image was to attain its most exacting articulation in the scholarship of D. W. Robertson and the Robertsonians.[10]

The first of these major additions to or refinements of our notions of the nature of medieval culture highlights and enhances nonclassical but unmistakably European elements. It weaves the contributions of the cultural substratum into the story of the making of Europe and ratifies the legitimacy of that heritage as an integral part of the West. The second image, in turn, codifies Christianity, the triumphant religion of the West, as its dominant and shaping cultural force, an essential, rather than incidental, component of our cultural ancestry. Both the non-Roman substratum and the Christian superstratum are (not by accident, one might guess) elements peculiarly and characteristically European, essential ingredients in what sets the West apart from everywhere else.

While most individual medievalists have more complex and variegated views of the period on which they work than any of these simple paradigms, the paradigms are nonetheless there, and they are formative factors. To spell them out is to delimit and understand the parameters of the medieval cultural factors that are normally considered and that are normally accepted as reasonable. Thus if one's study is grounded in the pre-Latin substratum — its mythology, folklore, or literature — or if it relies on a close reading of the Latin sermons, the Church fathers, or the Latin "foundation," then it falls within those acceptable and canonized limits. It does not challenge the boundaries of the image of the medieval period but instead adds to the evidence for the validity of that image. Even more important, perhaps, a study that falls within the limits of those possible narratives of European history needs neither justification (as to why one would bring such texts or presumed sociocultural conditions to bear on the study) nor external, nontextual proof that the writer in question was specifically aware of the texts or other material adduced. Such studies need no apologies.

Within such contexts our paradigmatic views of the medieval period have not readily expanded to include the possibility of greater cultural polymorphism. Indeed, given the historical circumstances and cultural ambience of the formative period of our discipline, such a move would have been surprising and uncharacteristic. Nineteenth- and early twentieth-century medievalists could, without having radically to alter their view of themselves and their world, proceed to redefine the extent to which the medieval world was not as backward as it might previously have seemed to be. But a reappraisal of the role played by an essentially alien, Semitic world in the creation of the basic features of that same period would have involved dangerous and ultimately untenable modifications of the paradigms governing their view of themselves. While cultural ideology may often remain unarticulated — its very unconsciousness being one of its essential traits — it is no less powerful for being unspoken, and it would be naive to argue that the cultural unconscious does not play a formative role in any variety of cultural studies. An individual, even a scholar, can scarcely operate outside its bounds.[11]

The relative paucity of material wealth, the perceived cultural inferiority, and the demonstrable powerlessness of the Arab world in the period in which modern medieval scholarship was carefully delimiting its parameters could hardly have suggested or encouraged a dramatically different view of relations between East and West. Contemporary views generated by the relative positions of the two cultures — with one eclipsing and dominating, literally shaping, the other — could not have escaped being factors in the elaboration of an image of the Arab world, even in an earlier period, that could have been, at most, marginal in the formation of our own culture and civilization. It is fruitless and somewhat misguided to be sanctimonious about such matters, to judge or condemn others by moral and ethical standards that did not exist in their own universes. But it is equally misguided to ignore the fact that such ideologies have existed or to suppose that intellectual enterprises have remained unaffected by their tenets.

Within this context, then, how surprising can it be that, in the relatively short history of our discipline, not only has there been no addition to the medieval paradigm of an important Semitic or Arabic role but also that whatever intimations of such a role had survived from earlier periods or have been introduced more recently have largely been discarded or put aside.[12] The untenability of such a notion lies not so much in the difficulty of revising our view of an earlier period of history. In and of itself, that is relatively easy to do, and historical revisionism is one of the most popular of academic pastimes. The key to the unimaginability of this particular bit of revisionism is that it would have challenged and ultimately belied the regnant worldview, requiring the reversal of an ideologically conditioned sense of the communal Western self. It requires the ability not only to imagine but to accept as plausible and admissible an image of our own civilization, at one of its formative moments, as critically indebted to and dependent on a culture that was for some time generally regarded as inferior and, by some lights, as the quintessence of the foreign and the Other.

And yet, in the past one hundred and fifty years or so there have been numerous suggestions within the scholarly community that one of the critical components in the making of the Middle Ages was Arabic and/or Semitic. The critical literature exploring and detailing such views is in fact copious. But although a certain group of historians, and the odd literary historian, has stated or reiterated the view, or some aspect of it, that one or more basic features of our medieval world was directly or indirectly dependent on the medieval Arabic European world, such perspectives have never become part of the mainstream within the community of scholars who regularly deal with medieval European studies, particularly literary studies.[13] The Arabic component of our paradigmatic view of the Middle Ages has always remained incidental; it has never been systemic. It may perhaps account for a given, usually isolated, feature, but such a feature is literally a world apart from the cultural sets that are perceived to be integral to the general system of medieval European culture.[14]

The two closest approximations to a revision of such views, and what can only be described as their failure, are themselves indicative of the unflagging vitality of the paradigm. On the one hand, there has been a Europeanization, an adaptation and absorption into this paradigm, of the body of information that reveals that Arabic "translations," particularly in the eleventh and twelfth centuries, contributed decisively to the intellectual revival of Europe at that time.[15] The impulse and need to absorb this discovery that otherwise threatened the coherence of Western ideology as imposed on the Middle Ages, was dictated in great measure by the eminence of the European historian who first called the phenomenon to the attention of a wide audience of fellow Europeanists. The mode of its absorption into the existing matrices was suggested by the title of Charles Homer Haskins's own work, *The Renaissance of the Twelfth Century*. The association between this renaissance and the later and atavistically European renaissance was inescapable. In fact, the thrust of Haskins's argument could reasonably be construed as being that the dating of the European Renaissance was off by several centuries, that the European discovery or rediscovery of our ancestral and hereditary culture really began in the twelfth century, and that a general secular cultural revival of considerable proportions followed on its heels. But Haskins was aware of the fact that such translations were almost universally an essential feature of Arabic intellectual life in Europe at the time (both in Sicily and Spain); that many of the most influential "translations" were not at all translations from the Greek, as such, but rather translations of Arabic philosophical commentaries on Aristotle, who for some centuries had been one of the philosophical luminaries in the Arabic tradition; and that the propagation and reception of such texts was at least in some measure explicable only in terms of a deeper penetration and knowledge of Arabic intellectual life in Europe, and of its far greater prestige, than had previously been adduced.[16]

Another failure in introducing a paradigmatically meaningful Semitic component to the European view of its own medieval period is considerably more complex and perhaps more accurately described as a success, although one of very mixed blessings and benefits. The only image of the Middle Ages that regularly admits a shaping and globally influential role for Arabs and Jews is that cultivated and perpetuated by many Hispanists and Spaniards, both medievalists and more general historians and philosophers. This exception, as far as it goes, is undoubtedly due to the fact that the seven-century-long Arab "occupation" of large parts of the Iberian peninsula is a historical fact less easily dismissed and ignored by Spaniards than by other Europeans.[17] But, curiously enough, with a handful of very important exceptions, the nature of the molding influence and its effects on subsequent events and tendencies in Spanish culture and history as they are perceived by many generations of Spaniards and Hispanists is a derailing one. It was, in simplified form, a de-Europeanizing one at best and in most other cases a largely or overwhelmingly negative one.[18] The most popular vision is one that might be represented by citing the eminent historian Sánchez-Albornoz, whose views are succinct, if extreme: "Without Islam, who can guess what our destiny might have been? Without Islam, Spain would have followed the same paths as France, Germany and England; and to judge from what we have achieved over the centuries in spite of Islam, perhaps we would have marched at their head" (translation, Monroe 1970:257). While few other cultural or literary historians have been as vigorous and frank as he, it is difficult to dispute the prevalence and strength of some variety of this argument.[19] This and its many other companion pieces and like opinions reveal once more the firmness of the Europeanist view that the true Europe and Europeanness are not Arabic- or Jewish-influenced. What at first glance is a formative component is more accurately a deforming component in terms of the rest of Europe, the real Europe. In Sánchez-Albornoz's view (and that of numerous others), Spain's defects—its not being up to the standards of France, England, and Germany—are a result of the misfortune of having been de-Europeanized by Semitic influences. But is this really substantially different from the premise of those literary historians who appear to be writing the history of a country they present as fully a part of the Western tradition, one in which the existence of Muslims and Jews and their cultures might never be guessed by the innocent reader?[20] Do not both views express, in different styles, the same premises, that is, that Semiticized Spain is less than the rest of Europe and that Spain with those elements blotted out would be part of the European tradition? For other Europeanists, most of whom naturally enough take their cues on matters Hispanic from Hispanists, the result has often been that characterized by the notion of Spain's "cultural belatedness" vis-à-vis the rest of Europe.[21]

Even so, one must know that the question of the effect of the Arab sojourn in Spain is hardly a matter of vital importance to most medievalists. Sánchez-Albornoz's preoccupation with the subject is a result of his being a Spaniard, not the natural result of being a Hispanist or a medievalist. Most Hispanists and medievalists begin their study of medieval literature with the first texts in Romance and assume Latin, conceivably even Greek, to be the necessary classical languages to be learned. Hebrew and Arabic are normally considered superfluous. Even in the wake of the "discovery" of the Mozarabic *kharjas* nearly forty years ago, when a considerable number of Spanish medievalists actually teach these Romance refrains of classical Arabic and Hebrew poems, only a distinct minority of scholars and teachers read them or present them as part of the full poems (written in one or the other of the two classical Semitic languages) of which they are, in fact, a part.[22]

Knowledge of this body of poetry and the expected subsequent awareness of the world from which it came apparently has not affected the traditional canon of Romance literary history. There is no sign of the imminent appearance on required reading lists of Ibn Quzman, Judah Halevi, Moses ben Ezra, Maimonides, or Averroes. The signs abound that even in the period after the discovery of the *kharjas* which was once heralded as the beginning of a "new spring" for European lyric studies,[23] only a relative handful of the details of our story have been altered or expanded, few or none of its basic premises have been modified, and its vitality is hardly diminished. Anthologies of medieval European lyric can still be published with a paltry section entitled "Arabic and Other Nonmainstream Poetry," and it may be comprised solely of a fragment of Ibn Hazm's *Dove's Neck-Ring*, which would be as if in the section on Provençal lyric there were but a fragment of Andreas Capellanus's treatise.[24] Prominent cutting-edge journals in literary studies can still devote entire issues to the crossroads at which medieval literary studies find themselves and include not the slightest hint that one of the problems to be addressed is that of the cultural biases and boundaries that delimit the field itself, despite the many indications of the inadequacy of the canon and its parameters that have surfaced in the last forty years.[25] The crossroads, turning points, or moments of crisis that medieval literary studies have faced, and faced up to, in recent years have overwhelmingly been those concerning methods of literary criticism. The choice is most simply presented as being that between the formalist criticism of scholars such as Zumthor and the classicist criticism best exemplified by the still authoritative work of Curtius. What all this has increasingly boiled down to is the question of whether medieval literary studies, once the vanguard of the discipline of modern literary studies, will remain largely a bastion of old-fashioned, philological, historicizing study, which is increasingly removed from the critical and theoretical avant-garde. Either of the two possible answers to this question raises eyebrows and threatens those parties who have a vested interest in the dominance of one approach or another.

So far, neither answer has implied any necessary reevaluation of the very bases of our definition of the medieval period, its literature, or its salient cultural features and parameters. The compromise between the two extremes, stated both elegantly and succinctly by Poirion, is to see (and therefore presumably to analyze) the literary text as being "situated at the point of connection between the imaginary and the ideological."[26] The most reasonable critic, therefore, rejects both the dehistoricization of formalist criticism (and many of its progeny) and the devaluation of the essential literary or imaginative properties of texts, which is peculiar both to very traditional philological studies and to some contemporary new critical analysis.

But the most reasonable critic, of whatever critical stripe, might also wish to question and reevaluate his or her most basic concept of the fundamental historicocultural characteristics of the period, because such a concept ultimately affects in innumerable ways the results of the application of any method. The strength of the model or image with which we start out is paramount; at a minimum, it defines what is and is not possible, what a word or image that we "know" or "recognize" is likely to mean or not to mean. This is self-evident if the approach used is one of the several classicist variations, since at least one of the principal objectives of such a study is archaeological, to find and establish the historicocultural backdrop of the text at hand. This linguistic, literary, and cultural backdrop informs both the questions asked and the answers given. It determines the probable meaning and origin of a word in the twelfth century, a given author's presumed use of Aquinas or a Bernardine sermon, and the kind of assumptions we make about the relationships between a text and its society. But, as I noted earlier in this chapter, the impact of our model, this background, is scarcely less at the other end of the critical spectrum, in formalist studies.[27]

In both cases such premises are fundamental determinants, and yet, paradoxically, it seems they are also the premises we have least frequently questioned or examined. But, given the many studies that suggest that they may be inadequate, are these not rightly among those most deserving of scrutiny, justification, and validation? One knows, or believes it to be a fair assumption, that an eleventh-century word did not denote "airplane" or "tomato," or "relativity" in the Einsteinian sense of the word. But how have we determined, and is it a reasonable determination, that it is more or less likely that the word gazel used in Provençal could have meant what it did for speakers of Hispano-Arabic? How can we still be so certain of our assumption that the basic reading list for a budding medievalist should include Aquinas and Augustine but not Ibn Hazm or Avicenna? How revolutionary or revealing can the deconstruction of medieval texts be if the series of social and ideological mores or norms presumably being covertly subverted in such texts have themselves not been carefully scrutinized? The ideologically bound strictures and limits of our "common knowledge" and even "common sense" are not easily bypassed. As Stanley Fish has noted (in a discussion that was hardly concerned with the role of Arabs in medieval Europe):

> I argue that whatever account we have of a work or a period or of the entire canon is an account that is possible or intelligible only within the assumptions embodied in current professional practice. Rather than standing independently of our efforts, works, periods, and canons have the shape they do precisely because of our efforts, and therefore no act of literary criticism, no matter how minimally "descriptive" can be said to "bypass" the network that enables it.[28]

But even more engaging than the fact that our paradigms govern us *faute de mieux* should be the recognition that many of the most widely discussed critical problems of literary history and even theory, particularly as applied to medieval studies, dovetail well with an explicit exploration and reevaluation of the images we hold of the medieval period and the nature of the canon that derives from it directly or indirectly. It seems only logical that in the resurgent discussion of the dialectic of the sameness versus the alterity of the medieval period and its cultural relics, a discussion that tacitly recognizes the parallel and sometimes overlapping dialectic between self and other, we should more closely and explicitly reevaluate our assumptions and knowledge of the often hidden Other—the Arab, the Semite, the Averroes—who stands silently behind Aristotle in the thirteenth century. Perhaps more to the point, we might ask in this context whether he really was so silent in the thirteenth and fourteenth centuries or whether it is not instead our postrenascentist views and parlance of the period that have made him so, giving his place to others whose ancestry we find more illustrious and thus shielding ourselves from a recognition that strikes at the heart of certain beliefs about ourselves. And is the dialectic that governed the Middle Ages really or exclusively that between pagan and Christian, and between classical and modern, or is this, too, a legacy of the Renaissance view of that period and an ancillary to the colonial and postcolonial view of ourselves?

The theoretical questions of the nature of meaning, of whether it is created or received, and of the covert and self-subverting meanings of both literary and nonliterary texts, can obviously be carried out with no wider or more revolutionary a concept of the cultural and literary mores than those we already have, those explicitly canonized and triumphant in Western literary historiography. But should not the more revealing exploration of such questions be correlated with an investigation into the mores that were discarded or subsumed, damned explicitly or tacitly by the authorities of the time and the cleansing historians of later periods? Can we as medievalists afford to continue to believe that because an eleventh-century duke of Aquitaine was Christian and "European" his poetic lexicon was delimited by the official Christian and "European" ideologies of his time? Can we speak authoritatively about the repressions and subversions of his poetry if we begin by accepting as valid parameters for his universe what has emerged as legitimate and Catholic in subsequent periods of time? And are there not patent and often ironic gaps in discussions of the "anxiety of influence" that are informed only by possible influences that were and have been canonized?

Revisionism, in literary history as well as in other fields, is often unpopular. It can seem to involve the ritualized murder of cherished ancestry. This is the case no matter whether it is described in the oedipal terminology of Bloom, in the context of the notions of historical relativism and storytelling of White, or in terms that follow the concepts of discourse of Foucault.

But at this juncture it is important to clarify several issues that may make the particular literary-historical revision that I will suggest seem less dramatic and more reasonable. First, I am scarcely suggesting that the prevailing image and canon we have needs to be discarded in toto. In fact, I do not believe any segment of the canon need be discarded at all. Rather, my analysis of the ideological factors that have shaped our images leads me to believe that it is the existing canon and image that have unjustifiably discarded important figures and texts or have undervalued them or euphemized them to the point that they have lost much of the power and impact many believe they had for their contemporaries—and that in turn informed texts that we *have* canonized. The suggestion is not that Aquinas be removed or replaced. On the contrary, it is that we add the tradition of Averroes to it and perhaps then begin to see the extent to which Aquinas is a response to other, Averroean texts.

In other words, I believe that the selective process of history and literary history has, in the natural course of telling the story of the victors, deprived us of an appreciation of many critical subtexts and has in great measure eliminated or simplified and distorted beyond recognition many of the cultural forces that were catalytic in the medieval period. Thus the part of the image that I propose should be discarded is that part that has eliminated the possibility of seeing in the Andalusian world the impetus for change and that part that cannot imagine that a cultural force now seemingly alien to our own was once a part of its foundation.

My own casting of this period of cultural and literary history is itself selective, of course, and as much constrained to pick and choose facts and texts as any other. I have few delusions that it is any less a myth than those I am attempting to modify in the process, but I think it is a myth that has several advantages. The first is that it does not shy away from the concept of a mixed ancestry for western Europe that until recently has seemed largely unimaginable and insupportable. The second is that I believe that it enriches rather than impoverishes the recounting of the story we already work with, the readings of texts we have already agreed on. Thus my criticism of the existing myth is, as I have just noted, that it is insufficiently variegated to account for the medieval period and its considerably different historicopolitical circumstances and that it is too much shaped by cultural prejudices of an era in Western ideology that although just now in its death throes in some areas is still quite powerful in the realm of literary historiography. It can perhaps now be fruitfully discarded there as well.

Ten Years After: The Virtues of Exile

Finally, a foreign soil is proposed, since it, too, gives a man practice. All the world is a foreign soil to those who philosophize. . . . The man who finds his homeland sweet is still a tender beginner; he to whom every soil is as his native land is already strong; but he is perfect to whom the entire world is a foreign land.
— Hugh of St. Victor

The Arabic Role in Medieval Literary History first came out in 1987, almost exactly ten years ago as I write this, although it is a book that had its beginnings more than a decade before. I recount part of the story in the preface of the book itself, because it struck me at the time, as it still does, as emblematic: the story of a graduate student in medieval Romance languages more or less accidentally coming upon the Arabic verb *Taraba* in a first-year Arabic class, and figuring out, bit by bit, the very long story of the tortured scholarly quarrels over the etymology of Provençal *trobar*, and thus of the word *troubadour* as well as the entire cultural complex that word evokes. It is, of course, not just any word, nor any random one of the thousands of disputed etymologies in our languages. Instead it is the evocation of an unusually powerful set of cultural features that lies at the heart, as Nietzsche said, of the West's most profound and romantic notions of what it is, of its very essence. Even when we, as a culture, have pretty much forgotten what Provençal is, as we almost have, we retain a strong sense (as well we should) of the distinctiveness of that culture, and it is a vexing issue to deal with the "origins" — by which we really mean the "identity" — of that culture when it might appear that some significant and central aspect of it lies in a cultural complex that we are habituated, acculturated, to see as quintessentially "Other," in Said's vastly influential articulation of it.

Ten years later I believe more than ever that it is all about the question of identity and that the intellectual challenge is to have a working model, a language, of cultural identity that can account for the powerful hybridness of European cultural identity in its formative period. Ten years ago I saw the principal impediment to the development of such a vision as a rather crude, albeit powerful, prejudice "that Westerners — Europeans — have great difficulties in considering the possibility that they are in some way seriously indebted to the Arab world, or that the Arabs were central to the making of medieval Europe."[29] But during this past decade, in the American academic universe as well as in the wider world, the problem is subtly different, and perhaps more intractable: "identity" has become ever more narrowly and rigidly defined, and the point seems all too often to be not the dissolution of the dichotomous conceits of Self and Other (Christian and Muslim, European and Arab, and so forth) but its hardening. Edward Said's *Orientalism* (which appeared in 1978) radically altered the intellectual landscape in ways not only I but many others believed would help clarify how we think about cultures and their identities and alert us to the kind of prejudice vis-à-vis Arab culture I had seen as the principal culprit. But I believe many of its premises have instead been almost perversely understood and absorbed as arguments for a greater, rather than a lesser, degree of cultural and scholarly "purity."

As with many seminal insights in intellectual history (one thinks immediately of the "anxiety of influence" or the "structures of scientific revolutions"), Said's key concepts have suffered reductive simplification and, in my opinion, damaging misapplication, although it would be dangerous and unfair to necessarily attribute any of these views to Said himself. The brilliance of the original work lay in its setting out the ways in which disciplines are rooted principally in ideologies, in cultural constructs that define one culture's view of itself vis-à-vis another.[30] But among the many ironies that abound in the institutionalization of Said's analyses is that the thrust of the argument has become that any student (reader, interpreter, speaker) of another's language (literature, culture) is virtually by definition indulging in a species of "orientalism" and is per force treating the other as an "Other." The widespread acceptance of this sophistry dovetailed perfectly with what I perceive as the most damaging institutional development in literary and cultural studies: nationalization. This division into discrete national languages—of not just our departments but of our visions of cultures and our ways of reading literatures has become the sad hallmark of our times, and it has rendered the problem of understanding and appreciating complex cultural entities even more difficult, I think, than "mere" prejudice ever did. Our fractured visions are more fractured than they were ten and twenty years ago and are now overtly hostile to notions of cultural empires and seem to be mostly seeking to identify and champion the most discrete and least ambiguous "identities."

And it is, to say the least, ironic, that all this has happened at precisely the historical moment at which we should, if anything, see clearly the absurd premises and tragic consequences of these urges to so neatly define "identity." The recent tragedy of the destruction of the last iteration of the Ottoman Empire, the mutilation of Yugoslavia into "national" sectors, with its attendant denials (including genocidal ones) of religious and cultural tolerances and admixtures and kinships must be seen—although it rarely is—as a lamentable repetition of the end of the medieval era so powerfully marked by the year 1492. That year best represents not merely simple hatred of "others"—it is all too easy, and fundamentally false, to see it as the simple expulsion of "Jews" and the repression of "Islam" that will lead to the expulsion of "Arabs." What 1492 best represents (and I have written about this at some length in *Shards of Love*, a book I think of as a "sequel" to *The Arabic Role*)[31] is the utter fallacy of such reductive notions of identities, notions based on the false belief that there really are (or were) such essentially pure identities and that they should be "understood" as such: in political reality by the (often bloody) assertion of their sectors of dominance and in the intellectual realm by the elevation of such divisions as the principal paradigms and divisions of our expertise and interest. And whether the impetus and justification for these assertions of essentially uncontaminated identity come from "old-fashioned" prejudice or newly chic identity politics — from anti-semitism, in other words, or from the current practice of studying "Jewish" literature (or some diabolical combination of the two) — the results are disastrous and blinding.

They blind us to the fact that, at least in the history of "the West," which we are still writing, cultural achievements of transcendent value are rarely "pure." And that even when political realities "successfully" impose such divisions into clear-cut identities — when Spain in 1492 expels its Jews and in 1609 its Muslims, when Israel is defined as a Jewish state, when Yugoslavia is carved up as it has been — the "success" is dependent on the radical falsification of history, the denial of the fact that Jews had been Spaniards for a millennium and were native Arabic speakers, or the denial of the fact that Arabs may be Christian and speak Hebrew as a native tongue, or the denial of the fact that Europe today (not to speak of America) is peopled with Muslims who are originally of every conceivable ethnicity, some of them, indeed, originally and "authentically" as European as any Christian. The "success" of orthodoxies of all sorts must always be read against the far more complex and tragic truths that sometimes only literature reflects. When Cervantes publishes part 1 of the *Quixote*, in 1604, it is at a moment in Spanish history (called the *Siglo de Oro* or "Golden Age" by Hispanists) when Spain is theoretically the monolingual and religiously uniform modern nation, he begins that greatest of the novels of the European tradition by revealing that the book is actually a "translation." But even the lovely conceit of the translation, which at first sight we think is rather simply executed from "Arabic" to "Spanish" by a Morisco (what we call sixteenth-century Spaniards who clung to the Islamic faith of their ancestors even though most of them did not, in fact, know Arabic), is more complex than it appears. The subtler truth, which remains half veiled in that most subtle of literary texts, is that the "original" text is itself impossibly corrupt: it is no doubt an *aljamiado* text, written in the noble-but-soon-to-be-forgotten Arabic script, in a language that is the apocalyptic Spanish-laced-with-Arabic that was one of Spain's very real languages — even when its existence was officially forbidden — and then finally expelled in 1609. But exiles have a way of being the condition of literature—and past and future exiles lie at the very beginning and at the heart of the adventures of the wandering Don Quixote. And it is perhaps in the full embracing of the revelations and virtues of exile, and of the rejection of the nationalisms and other illusory orthodoxies of identity that have taken over literary and cultural studies in these last several decades, that we can read the past more truthfully.

The best work that has been done in the past decade, and that is likely to be done in the near future, on "Muslims" and "Arabic culture" in medieval (or, for that matter, modern) Europe, must be either implicitly or explicitly rooted in the rejection of the simplicities and isolations of its own categories and terms, in an appreciation of the profound ambivalences of such readily nameable identities and of the necessary interconnectedness with other (equally ambivalent) identities. Among the most important recent publications are a series of translations and reprintings of very old works that reflect and dwell on the complexities of religious-literary identities: the republication in post-Franco Spain of Miguel Asín Palacios' controversial masterpiece *La escatología musulmana en la Divina Comedia*, which first appeared in 1919, followed close on by its first translation into Italian, and translations, for the first time in both modern Spanish and modern Italian, of the Arabic *miraj* text that existed, in Dante's lifetime, in Latin and vernacular translation and, Asín posits, played a pivotal role in Dante's thinking and writing on the imaginative structure of the afterlife.[32]

The translations of this remarkable and central text, after some five hundred years of widespread inaccessibility, reveal the other virtue that must be cultivated, a virtue clearly championed by Hugh of St. Victor: translation of every sort and languages that explicitly speak intelligibly to others. And it is in this spirit (and in the rejection of the orthodoxies of national language departments that claim we can only know and read in "original" languages as well as the disciplinary orthodoxy that makes scholars write in languages that are only readable to the minuscule clan of which they are a part) that the other most important development in this decade has been the publication of translations of the multifaceted Hebrew poetry of al-Andalus. These volumes of translations, with invaluable introductions, as well as a limited number of important studies stand in stark (and rebuking) contrast to those of the Arabic-Romance *muwashshahat* with which they are inextricably linked.

While "*kharja* studies" became a wasteland of ever more specialized and unreadable technical minutiae, turned ever further inward and a prudish mockery of the original spirit of poetic and linguistic promiscuity that bred that exquisitely hybrid poetry, a handful of scholars and translators (Pagis, Scheindlin, Brann, Cole) who openly embraced the virtues of exile that permeate the culture of the Andalusian Jewish community have produced a growing body of work that is opened outward instead.[33] Among the benefits of these marvelously door-opening studies—and among the delicious ironies—is that the nonspecialist (which means anyone who has not done a decade's training as an Arabist) is far more likely to get a sense of the richness and openness of Arabic poetry and culture in al-Andalus from these volumes than from most of the work done by mainstream "Andalusianists" (Spaniards, Arabs, and Americans alike), who principally write out of that belated and purifying potion of "Arabism" that so distorts most aspects of European-Arab culture. Al-Andalus produced a culture so "corrupt," in all directions, that its literature even includes iterations as unexpected and complexly veiled as the *Divine Comedy*'s relationship to the *miraj* tradition or the varieties of "polymorphism" that are revealed in the poetries of Ibn 'Arabi or Ramon Llull or Judah Halevi.

Indeed, the other principal fine examples of criticism and scholarship recently published (or that I am aware are being written) are all, like that of Asín and those producing the infinite complexities of Sefarad's poetry, centered on the most corrupt and impure texts and guided by exilic principles: the studies and editions of Luce López Baralt, especially the book-length study of the thoroughly "Islamicized" and "Arabized" Catholic saint, San Juan de la Cruz, and her edition of the morisco "Kama Sutra español," L. Patrick Harvey's magnificent history of Islamic Spain between 1250 and 1500, which for the first time treats the fate of the Muslim populations of that period as a continuum, regardless of whether they lived in Christian states or Muslim states, as well as his forthcoming sequel, the history of the Moriscos themselves, and the study and edition that Consuelo López-Morillas has recently begun of the only complete Qur'an translated into Spanish, written in that same *aljamiado* that is the "authentic" original of the Quixote within no more than a few years of Cervantes's text.

In the destruction of the whole of the magnificent National Library and other major collections in Sarajevo several years ago, in 1992, it now appears one very significant book was rescued, the famous manuscript called the *Sarajevo Haggada*. A Haggada is of course a prayer book that is, appropriately, the collection of prayers to be said on Passover, on the eve of exodus, but despite its name this gorgeous and elaborately illuminated manuscript, considered the best of its kind anywhere in the world, and much treasured by Jews everywhere, is not "Sarajevan" at all, nor "merely" Jewish, but rather "Spanish." And what can "Spanish" possibly mean, what do I mean it to be that is so different from what it seems to be in most other uses of this and other "identity" tags? Made in Spain in the late thirteenth century, it is, to put it most reductively, one of the many reflections of a Jewish culture that flourished and had its Golden Age, the Golden Age, precisely because it adopted the virtues of exile and found its distinctly impure voice within an Arabic culture that was expansive and promiscuous and often exilic itself. It was thus altogether fitting that the precious object, the book that inscribes the story of the exile from Egypt, was carried out of Spain by members of the exiled Sephardic community in 1492: and remained, for the better part of the subsequent five hundred years, well-protected and cherished inside the Ottoman Empire, itself a remarkable example of the great good of empires, which learn how to absorb and tolerate and intermarry "identities," and which became, after 1492, the place of refuge of most Sephardic Jews and of many Andalusian Muslims. But the manuscript had to be rescued once again, during World War II, and it was when a Muslim curator in Sarajevo, attached as most Muslims are to the memory of Spain, saved that Spanish Haggada from Nazi butchers.

Surely, the morals of the story are perfectly clear: to understand the richness of our heritage we must be the guardians of the Haggada—the Muslim librarian who was not an Arab, of course, but who in saving the manuscript was fulfilling the best of the promises of Islamic Spain and Europe—and we must be the translators who reveal the exquisite ambivalence and sometimes painful conflict of identity of Judah Halevi, whose poetry is sung in so heavy an Arabic accent, and we must be the guardians and defenders of the interfaith marriage between the Christian girls who sang in corrupt Romance and the refined poets of the Arab courts, which is left inscribed, as a passionate and great love, in the *muwashshahat*. We must, in other words, reject the falsehoods of nations in our work, and reveal, with the exquisite Ibn 'Arabi, the virtues of what he more simply calls love. "My heart can take on any form," he tells us, and then he simply names those temples at which he prays, the temples that inhabit him: the gazelle's meadow, the monks' cloister, the Torah, the Ka'ba. These are the temples whose priests we need to be, if we are to understand what any of this history is about, and it is only in them that there can be any future understanding of the complex "identity" of Europe in the Middle Ages. And almost undoubtedly in its present and future as well.

Notes

1. See primarily Edward Said, *Orientalism: Western Conceptions of the Orient* (New York: Pantheon, 1978), and some of the extended criticism and further considerations engendered by his book. Three reviews are of particular interest: those of Lewis (1982), whose highly negative reaction reflects much of the response of the traditional "orientalist" academic community, Beard (1979), whose favorable reaction raises the question, among others, of the expansion of Said's model to other areas of academic scholarship, and Brombertt (1979), which is valuable because of its detachment from the orientalist scene and the issues of general academic interest it explores. See Bernard Lewis, review of *Orientalism*, by Edward Said, *New York Review of Books* 29.4 (June 1982): 49–56; Michael Beard, review of *Orientalism*, by Edward Said, *Diacritics* 9 (Winter 1979); and Victor Brombert, review of *Orientalism*, by Edward Said, *American Scholar* 48 (1979): 532–542. The salient points by Said relevant to my discussion (and, incidentally, those least contradicted, even by his staunchest critics) are found in the introduction (1–28) and can be summarized as follows: that the formation of the image of the West is contrapuntal to the formation of the image of the Orient, that the dominant discourse is one of superiority "reiterating European superiority over Oriental backwardness, usually overriding the possibility that a more independent, or more skeptical, thinker might have had different views on the matter" (7), that the distinction between "pure" and "political" knowledge is not an absolute and clear one and that the liberal consensus that knowledge is fundamentally apolitical "obscures the highly if obscurely organized political circumstances obtaining when knowledge is produced" (10), and that literary studies in particular have assiduously avoided discussion of the issue of political ideology shaping the structures of knowledge and generally "avoided the effort of seriously bridging the gap between the superstructural and the base levels in textual, historical scholarship" (13).

2. For two recent examples of collections of articles devoted to the pressing critical problems in medieval studies, see Morton W. Bloomfield, "Continuities and Discontinuities," *New Literary History* 10 (1979): 409–416, and *L'esprit créateur* 18 (1978) and 23 (1983).

3. George Makdisi includes both his own statement about the "European awakening" and pertinent quotes from some of his predecessors (Lombard and Dawson are among the most important). See George Makdisi, "The Scholastic Method in Medieval Education: An Inquiry Into Its Origins in Law and Theology," *Speculum* 49 (1974): 640–641. For this perspective on the history of medicine specifically, see George Sarton, *The Incubation of Western Culture in the Middle East* (Washington, D.C.: Library of Congress, 1951). From the point of view of the history of science in general, see Charles Homer Haskins, *Studies in*

the History of Medieval Science (Cambridge: Harvard University Press, 1924). Haskins's widely read and cited *Renaissance of the Twelfth Century* is also revealing. Roughly the last half of the book deals with aspects of that renaissance that were explicitly Arabic derived. In the area of the history of philosophy few have underestimated the importance of Averroes. Even Kristeller, who is primarily concerned with the Latin tradition, makes serious concessions to the importance of the Arabic tradition: "As is well known, the Aristotelianism of the Arabs, and especially that of Averroes, exercised a powerful influence upon the Jewish thought of the later Middle Ages . . . and strongly affected the philosophy of the Christian West." Paul Oscar Kristeller. *Renaissance Thought: The Classic, Scholastic, and Humanistic Strains* (New York: Harper, 1961), 28–29. He is nevertheless able to follow such an observation with this one: "If we want to understand the history of thought and learning in the Western Latin Middle Ages we must first of all realize that it had its foundations in Roman, not Greek, antiquity." Kristeller, *Renaissance Thought*, 29.

4. These generalizations about the attitudes among Romance medievalists are just that, generalizations, and they are hardly exempt from the enumeration of any number of exceptions. But even a cursory glance at the structures of our academic departments, the standard medieval canon, the sorts of courses that are (and are not) taught, requirements for degrees, general bibliographies, literary anthologies and literary histories, and so forth, will all confirm that as a rule such generalizations are accurate. It is curious that although there is widespread acceptance of the general indebtedness of the West to Arabic sciences and some branches of philosophy, this appears to be generally ignored when we construe the background of our literary history, although Latin-based developments in the sciences and philosophy—many of them dependent on the Arabic tradition—are almost invariably accounted for. Studies that recognize the centrality of the Arabic tradition in some other cultural sphere or its importance in terms of political history often proceed to discuss the literary problem as if those other instances of interaction were irrelevant. Thus Anthony Bonner notes both that there was substantial interaction between Provence and al-Andalus, and between Provence and the rest of the Arab world (because of the Crusades), and even that intellectual, cultural, and material developments in those areas far outstripped those of the rest of Europe. See Anthony Bonner, ed. and trans., *Songs of the Troubadours* (New York: Schocken, 1972).

Yet, not only does he then go on to discuss these new developments in Provence as if none of this had been the case, but the map he presents for the world of the Provençal troubadours cuts off at the Pyrenees—as graphic a representation as one can imagine of how irrelevant that world seems to be. Other explicitly contradictory analyses include Frank, which details the extent to which Arabic courtly poetry and song were a fact of everyday life at the court of

Alfonso 11, the rallying point of both Catalan and Provençal troubadours, but then says that, nevertheless, all of this in no way influenced that poetry, apparently assuming that such influence must be expressly and directly acknowledged in the poetic texts themselves, presumably in Arabic. See István Frank, "Les débuts de la poésie courtoise en Catalogne et le problème des origins lyriques," in *VIIe Congrés International de Linguistique Romane* (Barcelona: Abadía de San Cugat del Vallés, 1955). A comparable position is found in Umberto Rizzitano and Francesco Giuma, *Terra senza crociati* (Palermo: Flaccovio, 1967). Sutherland, a refutation of Denomy's work on the influence of Arabic thought on the troubadours, includes the comment that the influence was "diffuse" and thus is not to be found in the poetry, assuming, presumably, that poetic influence is not diffuse. See D. R. Sutherland, "The Language of the Troubadours and the Problem of Origins," *French Studies* 10 (1956): 199–215. Bezzola asserts that one cannot continue categorically to exclude the possibility of any Arabic influence on the first troubadours, and he then procceds to do just that through his lack of any further discussion of the influence that is in fact implicit in his presentation of the historical background of William IX Reto R. Bezzola, "Guillaume IX et les origins de l'amour courtois," *Romania* 66 (1940): 145–237.

In Van Cleve the chapter on the Italian lyric is presented as if no hint of Arabic culture, poetry, or song existed there, although that chapter immediately follows one on the intellectual life at the court, which he presents as completely Arabized. See Thomas Curtis Van Cleve, *The Emperor Frederick II of Hohenstaufen: Immutator Mundi* (Oxford: Oxford University Press, 1972). A distinction is made between poetry and other intellectual life that is difficult to reconcile with the unity of such traditions in virtually every other sphere of literary study, medieval or not. This split between the general historical background and literature is also reflected in the fact that while so much medieval literature elaborates or alludes to imaginary visions of the Arab world and characters—Saladin, for example—who are clearly identified as being a part of that world, relatively few of the critical discussions of these literary phenomena are concerned with either the extent to which they might reflect (and thus be understood in terms of) an influential view of that world and those people. See Gaston Paris, *La Littérature française au moyen âge (XIe au XIVe siècle)* (Paris: Librairie Hachette, 1895), for an early example that is not altogether outdated in its basic approach to the subject. Even studies on the French epic (so much of which is explicitly concerned with dealings with the Arab enemy) do not characteristically discuss the relationship with the Arab world as complex and problematic, nor do they regularly adopt any more sophisticated a view of the situation than that which is depicted at the surface level of the poems. Notable exceptions to this are Alvaro Galmés de Fuentes, *Épica árabe y épica castellana*

(Barcelona: Ariel, 1978), and "'Les nums d'Almace et cels de Durendal' (*Chanson de Roland*, v. 2143): Probable origen árabe del nombre de las dos famosas espadas," in *Studia Hispánica in Honorem R. Lapesa* (Madrid: Cátedra-Seminario Menéndez Pidal/Gredos) 1 (1972): 229–241. Even studies on *Aucassin and Nicolette*—a work clearly concerned with the question of dialogue, alterity, and juxtapositions and no less clearly allusive to the Arabic world conjured up by Aucassin's name and Nicolette's birth—can completely bypass the issue of the Arabic world in the *chante-fable*. For an example of the former, even in a critically sophisticated study, see William Calin, *The Epic Quest: Studies in Four Old French Chansons de Geste* (Baltimore: Johns Hopkins Press, 1966). For a recent example of the latter, see Eugene Vance, "*Aucassin et Nicolette* as a Medieval Comedy of Signification and Exchange," in Minnette Grunmann-Goudet and Robin F. Jones, eds., *The Nature of Medieval Narrative* (Lexington: French Forum, 1980).

5. The problem is perhaps best exemplified in cases where a scholar does comparative work and/or breaches the presumed demarcations of Arabic and European scholarship. One of the most noteworthy cases of this, an extreme case but far from a unique one, is certainly that of María Rosa Lida's work on the *Libro de buen amor* and its Semitic antecedents. See María Rosa Lida, "Notas para la interpretación, influencia, fuentes, y texto del *Libro de Buen Amor*," *Revista de Filología Hispánica* 2 (1940): 105–50; and "Nuevas notas para la interpretación del *Libro de Buen Amor*," *Nuevo Revista de Filología Hispánica* 13 (1959): 17–82. She was severely taken to task by the respected and influential Spanish historian Claudio Sánchez-Albornoz. See Claudio Sánchez-Albornoz, *Estudios polémicos* (Madrid: Espasa Calpe, 1979), 258-275. Although few other scholars are as vitriolic as he, this specific case is worth mentioning precisely because his attack on Lida's work makes explicit those attitudes that are in other cases covert, although no less powerful, and because it reflects certain premises that are characteristic of a considerable number of scholars working in an area that is not only marginalized but, it would seem, protective of its marginalization. Lida's work, according to Sánchez-Albornoz, is deficient because she is not an Arabist (a Spanish Arabist, it almost goes without saying) and consequently incapable a priori of sound knowledge of the Arabic and Hebrew texts she is discussing. Lida's impeccable scholarly credentials show just how exaggerated such a territorial attitude is, since it implies that this area is so special that others not of the same school and training have no business dealing with it at all and are incapable of working on it competently. Why is an otherwise competent scholar and reader of literary texts rendered incompetent when faced with a decent edition and/or translation of an Arabic or Hebrew text written and/or circulated in Spain or Sicily in the Middle Ages? And if we are working with deficient editions or translations, which is sometimes adduced, or if we

have incomplete knowledge of the historicocultural background of such texts, why is such a situation not remedied by those who in the same breath are staking this out as their territory? Such attitudes, coming as they often do from those concerned with Arabic studies, can only contribute in equal measure with the Europeanist's attitude of neglect perpetuating the isolation of the field.

But the criticism of Lida's work voiced by Sánchez-Albornoz goes a step further and in some measure sheds light on the nature of the other criticism he has made. He fails to comprehend her attempt to link the Hebrew (and thus Arabic) texts of medieval Spain with a Christian, truly "Spanish" text, which in his opinion can only be understood "dentro del cuadro de la literatura occidental." Sánchez-Albornoz, *Estudios polémicos*, 264. He sees her work, in fact, as the result of her "natural devoción . . . hacia los hombres y las empresas de su raza." Ibid., 259. This unmistakable allusion to her Jewish background is more than casual or incidental antisemitism, and that is why I have adduced it here. It is a reflection of the extent to which scholars who *do* work on the medieval European Semitic traditions, both Arabic and Hebrew, have been no more exempt from the prejudices of cultural ideology than the medievalist community as a whole. It would be fallacious to assume that those whose work is devoted to the study of those traditions necessarily have any more positive an attitude toward the object of their study than those who reflect the prejudices of our cultural ideology in their unwillingness to recognize the existence of those texts and cultural traditions in the first place. Most important, the reader should know that such attitudes are neither obsolete relics nor views restricted to Spaniards obsessed with the Semitic elements of their own past. The reader who glances at any of the issues years of the journal *Al-Andalus* (before its demise and rebirth as *Al-Qantara*), at Garcia Gómez's prologue to the second edition of *Las jarchas romances de la serie árabe*, or at his lecture on the occasion of the fiftieth anniversary of the Escuela de estudios Árabes de Madrid, can hardly come away with the impression that either acute territorialism or thinly veiled prejudice are things of the past in this field. Not only would one find there articles by a certain Angel Ramirez Calvente (whose identity is otherwise unknown, so this is probably a nom de plume) embodying a less-than-professional attack on Samuel Stern, who is Jewish, but also, from García Gómez himself, paterfamilias of Hispano-Arabic literary studies, invectives clearly directed at Monroe, who is dealt with as an *innominato*. Dismissals of those who are simply "norteamericanos," "anfibios," "pseudo-especialistas,"or "ajenos . . . a nuestra familia" stake out the boundary lines quite clearly—and they should serve as a warning that an attempt to cross them would not be welcome, or even tolerable.

The most recently published polemics between Jones and Hitchcock on one side and Armistead and Monroe on the other serve to show, among other things, the extent to which Jones rejects arguments made by Armistead and Monroe simply because neither are bonafide Arabists according to his definition of the term. For elaboration, see Alan Jones, "Romance Scansion and the Muwaššaḥāt: an Emperor's New Clothes?" *Journal of Arabic Literature* 11 (1980): 36–55; "Sunbeams from Cucumbers? An Arabist's Assessment of the State of Kharja Studies," *La Corónica* 10 (1981): 38–53; and "Eppure si muove," *La Corónica* 12 (1983): 45–70; Richard Hitchcock, "The Interpretation of Romance Words in Arabic Texts: Theory and Practice," *La Corónica* 13 (1984): 243–254; Samuel Armistead, "Speed or Bacon? Further Meditations on Professor Alan Jones's 'Sunbeam,'" *La Corónica* 10 (1982): 148–155; and "Pet Theories and Paper Tigers: Trouble with Kharjas," *La Corónica* 14 (1986): 55–70; Samuel Armistead and James Monroe, "Albas, Mammas, and Code-Switching in the Kharjas: A Reply to Keither Whinnom," *La Corónica* 11(1983): 174–207; and "Beached Whales and Roaring Mice: Additional Remarks on Hispano-Arabic Strophic Poetry," *La Corónica* 13 (1985): 206–242. Consequently Jones considers Armistead and Monroe incapable of comprehending why the *kharjas* can only be understood as part of the classical Arabic tradition (and by Arabic classicists). Leaving aside for the moment the substance of the argument, Jones's approach is reminiscent of the kind of argument Sánchez-Albornoz makes when Jones questions Armistead's competence in dealing with an Arabic text ("I have two problems," Jones states ["Eppure si muove," 51] "which Professor Armistead possibly does not share. . . . On principle I do not work on the Arabic texts on the basis of translations." (It is not difficult to understand, when reading Jones's works, that it all boils down to the belief that the lines that have been drawn between the Arabist's domain and the Romance scholar's domain are appropriate ones and that hybridization is unhealthy and produces bad scholarship (even, ironically, when one is dealing with clearly hybrid poetry.) Moreover, there is here an intellectual condescension that evokes memories of Sánchez-Albornoz's attitude toward Lida's "meddling." This is manifest in comments such as that cited above but even more so in Jones's adducing the authority of "most Arabs and Arabists" to back his views, *although his* principal cited sources for the view that the poetry is a part of the classical Arabic tradition exclusively could hardly be considered authoritative or up-to-date on the subject of Hispano-Arabic poetry. See Reynold Nicholson, *A Literary History of the Arabs* (Cambridge: Cambridge University Press, 1907), and Montgomery Watt with Pierre Cacchia, *A History of Islamic Spain* (Edinburgh: Edinburgh University Press, 1965). The latter devotes all of eight pages to the poetry of Spain but includes a paragraph-long rebuttal of the work of the major historian and critic of Andalusian poetry, Henri Pérès. The fact that Pérès and Monroe are the two scholars who have devoted the most attention specifically to Hispano-Arabic Andalusian poetry apparently counts for less than being a mainstream Arabist who has not altered his views by attempting to understand that poetry in terms of al-Andalus as a hybrid society and in the context of Romance as well as Arabic traditions. And Jones's condescension is such that, even in citing Watt and Cachia, he fails to cite their full opinions, as expressed in the concluding paragraph of those twelve pages: "So it was that in Spain, alone among Muslim lands, the vigorous spirit of the common people breached the wall of convention erected by the classicists." Watt and Cachia, *A History of Islamic Spain*, 121. For the two essential handbooks on the subject, see Henri Pérès, *La poésie andalouse en arabe classique au XIe siecle: Ses aspect généraux, ses principaux thémes et sa valeur documentaire* (Paris: Adrien-Maisonneuve, 1983), and James Monroe, *Islam and the Arabs in Spanish Scholarship (Sixteenth Century to the Present)* (Leyden: Brill, 1970).

   In a different sphere it is revealing to note that the most hostile attacks on Katherine Gittes's article on "The *Canterbury Tales* and the Arabic Frame Tradition" are by individuals who take her to task for incomplete and faulty knowledge when she speaks of the Arabic tradition. These letters are, in fact, primarily concerned with the accuracy of sources in *pre*-Arabic traditions, which Gittes has identified using the handful of sources accessible to a nonspecialist and that, in any case, as she points out, are not directly relevant to the fate of the narrative tradition within Europe. See Katherine Slater Gittes, "The Canterbury Tales and the Arabic Frame Tradition," *PMLA* 98 (1983): 237–51.

6. Since Aristotle, the notion that ideology affects all historical writing has been an important feature of the criticism of historiography and discussions of the inherent problems in distinguishing between history and poetry. For a recent exchange and discussion of the effect of ideology on literary studies and the effect it is currently having on the profession (though in general terms rather than on the medieval sphere specifically), see Edward Said, "Response to Stanley Fish," *Critical Inquiry* 10 (1983): 371–373; Stanley Fish, "Profession Despise Thyself: Fear and Self-Loathing in Literary Studies," *Critical Inquiry* 10 (1983); and Walter Jackson Bate, "To the Editor of Critical Inquiry," *Critical Inquiry* 10 (1983): 365–370. Other recent contributions to the subject are Edward Said, "Opponents, Audiences, Constitutencies, and Community," *Critical Inquiry* 9 (1982): 1–26; and especially Hayden White, *Metahistory: The Historical Imagination in Nineteenth-Century Europe* (Baltimore: Johns Hopkins University Press, 1982). White makes a series of observations that are particularly pertinent to our study: Hegel "was convinced . . . that you could learn a great deal, of both practical and theoretical worth, from the study of the study of history. And one of the things you learn from the study of the study of history is that such study is never innocent, ideologically or otherwise, whether launched from the political perspective of the Left, Right, or Center." See White, *Metahistory*, 137.

7. Ellis gives a succinct view of the application of structuralism to medieval stud-
    ies and maintains that the only difference is that of learning a different lan-
    guage, which is just like learning any foreign language (of which one need
    learn only the synchronic state and need not know any of its history). See John
    M. Ellis, "The Relevant Context of Literary Text," in John M. Ellis, *The Theory
    of Literary Criticism: A Logical Analysis* (Berkeley: University of California
    Press, 1974), 105–154. Two of the most striking and revealing cases of the pitfalls
    of this approach are found in Pierre Guiraud, "Les Structure étymologiques du
    'Trobar,'" *Poétique* 8 (1971): 417–424, and *Sémiologie de la séxualité: Essai de
    glosso-analyse* (Paris: Payot, 1978). Guiraud's first study of the etymological
    structures of *trobar* is explicitly synchronic, but the author is hardly free either
    from the problems of the enigmatic history of the word or, more significantly,
    from what diachronic studies of that history have told him. At a certain junc-
    ture he faces the fact that his synchronic analysis of what the word means is
    somewhat at odds with the range of possibilities provided by the diachronic
    studies he is aware of, and these exclude Ribera's proposal. In his reworking of
    this material in the later publication, Guiraud takes into account the possible
    Arabic etyma for Provençal *joi* and *jovens* in chapter 6. (This is Denomy's pro-
    posal, but clearly Guiraud is only familiar with Lazar's presentation of that
    material.) See Alexander Denomy, "*Jovens*: The Notion of Youth Among the
    Troubadours, Its Meaning and Source," *Mediaeval Studies* 11 (1949): 1–22, and
    Moshé Lazar, *Amour courtois et "Fin'amours" dans la littérature du XIIe siècle*
    (Paris: Librairie C. Klincksieck, 1964). However, still unfamiliar in 1978 with
    the suggested Arabic derivation of *trobar*, he is elusive about the problem of the
    apparent disjunction between synchronic and diachronic analyses, and, follow-
    ing on the heels of his presentation of the case of *jovens*, this seems all the more
    ironic. It is also a very explicit case of how illusory it is to attempt to separate the
    two areas of study so neatly. For further discussion of this general issue, see note
    26 below, and for different perspectives on the dehistoricization of medieval
    texts and studies of them, see Morton Bloomfield, "Continuities and Disconti-
    nuities," *New Literary History* 10 (1979): 409–416, and Stephen Nichols,
    "Deeper into History," *L'Ésprit Créateur* 23.1 (1983): 91–102. Hans Robert Jauss
    and William Alin tackle the problem from the perspective of the "otherness" of
    the medieval period and its dialectical relationship with the modern one. See
    Hans Robert Jauss, "The Alterity and Modernity of Medieval Literature," *New
    Literary History* 10 (1979): 181–227; and William Calin, "Singer's Voice and
    Audience Response: On the Originality of the Courtly Lyric, or How 'Other'
    was the Middle Ages and What Should We Do About It?" *L'Ésprit Créateur* 23.1
    (1983): 75–90.
8. It is revealing to take Petrarch, as many scholars do, as one of the first explicit
    advocates of such an analysis of history. His role as one of the first humanists

has been discussed by many, and his views on the primacy of classical studies, on the darkness of the Dark Ages, and on that entire constellation of notions are widely known and cited. It is revealing to note, and this is less often referred to, that such views were accompanied by quite virulent anti-Arabism. For a presentation and analysis of this phenomenon, see Francesco Gabrieli, "Petrarca e gli Arabi," *Al-Andalus* 42 (1977): 241–248. Hay is also helpful for understanding the relative modernity of our concept of what constitutes Europe. See Denys Hay, *Europe: The Emergence of an Idea* (Edinburgh: Edinburgh University Press, 1968).

9. The debunking of the myth of the darkness of the Middle Ages is certainly best exemplified by Haskins, but Pernoud indicates that many of those views have never been completely eradicated and why in her view they ought to be. See Régine Pernoud, *Pour en finir avec le moyen age* (Paris: Éditions du Seuil, 1977). Among general literary historians there is surprisingly often a notion of the primitivism of the medievals relative to the modern period, and prominent critics can still regard everything before the Renaissance as antediluvian. See Harold Bloom, *The Anxiety of Influence: A Theory of Poetry* (Oxford: Oxford University Press, 1973). Even among medievalists similar views are not unknown. Zumthor, to take one example, is able to characterize the period and its men as incapable of autobiographical writing. See Paul Zumthor, "Autobiographie au Moyen Age?" in Paul Zumthor, *Langue, text, énigme* (Paris: Seuil, 1975), 165–180. A recent nonacademic perspective on the surge of interest in medieval studies and what this implies for our general perceptions of the period is Cullen Murphy, "Nostalgia for the Dark Ages," *Atlantic* (May 1984): 12–16. See also Hans Robert Jauss, "The Alterity and Modernity of Medieval Literature," *New Literary History* 10 (1979): 181–227, and William Calin, "Singer's Voice and Audience Response: On the Originality of the Courtly Lyric, How 'Other' Was the Middle Ages and What Should WE DO About It?" *L'Ésprit Créateur* 23.1 (1983): 75–90.

10. For a succinct history and extensive bibliography of the development of these views as reflected in scholarship dealing with troubadour lyrics, see Roger Boase, *The Origin and Meaning of Courtly Love: A Critical Study of European Scholarship* (Manchester: Manchester University Press, 1976).

11. Prévost, inspired by Althusser, notes that people "use" ideology, but "sont également produits et mis en mouvement par l'idéologie, par ce qui fonctionne comme un veritable inconscient culturel." See Claude Prévost, "Littérature et idéologie: Propositions pour un réflexion théorique," *Nouvelle Critique* 57.238 (1972): 18. Evidence of the institutionalization of these general views surrounds us. General anthologies of European medieval literature do not, as a matter of course, include examples of literature written in Arabic or Hebrew, nor do they even, in many cases, acknowledge or discuss its existence as part of the general

historical background. Courses on medieval literature, with few exceptions, perform the same excision. Even the very definition of what is "Spanish" literature implicit in the structure of courses and histories and anthologies of the literature systematically excludes what was written in Arabic and Hebrew simultaneously with what was written in the Romance vernaculars. The definition of a Hispanist has rarely included knowledge of Islamic Spain from any but a rudimentary *fronterizo* point of view. In the often daunting inventory of languages deemed necessary tools for a medievalist, Arabic rarely figures. The respective bodies of literature are shelved in different sections of our libraries, are studied by different scholars, and are caught in different departments, even though in some cases they may come from the same place and time. A familiarity with the works of Dante, Boccaccio, and Petrarch is considered necessary for the truly competent French or Spanish medievalist, but even rudimentary information on the translations of Arabic and Hebrew works commissioned by Frederick II or of the Arabic poetry dedicated to his grandfather Roger is rare even in an Italian medievalist. Augustine and Aquinas are de rigueur, Averroes and Maimonides are obscure figures at best. To argue that there are and have been exceptions to such rules would hardly contradict the validity of this rudimentary outline of the general system. It is more telling that we are easily able to name the exceptions, whereas an enumeration of the instances of conformity to such norms would be a daunting task.

12. Curiously, much of the resistance to such a change in our appreciation of the Arabic role in medieval Europe comes from the area of Arabic studies as well, as indicated above in note 5. The only comprehensive and critical study of the historiography of Arabic Europe, undertaken by Monroe, confirms what even casual observation might well reveal: the conceptual schism between East and West (Arabic and Romance) has in turn resulted in the creation of fundamentally separate fields of inquiry, the setting up of a field that falls between two stools. See James Monroe, *Islam and the Arabs in Spanish Scholarship (Sixteenth Century to the Present)* (Leyden: Brill, 1970). No adequate equivalent of Monroe exists for Siculo-Arabic studies, but see Alessandro Bausani, "La tradizione arabo-islamica nella cultura europea," *Humanitas* 12 (1957): 809–828, reprinted in *I Problemi di Ulisse* 14 (1977): 9–20; Francesco Gabrieli, *La storiografia arabo-islamica in Italia* (Naples: Guida, 1957); and Aziz Ahmad, *A History of Islamic Sicily* (Edinburgh: Edinburgh University Press, 1975).

The study of Arabic culture as it existed in Europe is a poor and regularly neglected relation. While often there is a certain amount of lip service paid to the heights of the cultural glory of Córdoba, little recognition of the centrality of al-Andalus in the overall contours of Arabic history can be measured through institutional yardsticks. In fact, it is noteworthy that traditionally the scholars who have studied Arabic culture in Spain have been Spaniards, and those who have been students of Siculo-Arabic matters Italian. Further confirmation of how far from the orientalist mainstream this area of study and its scholars are may also be found where one might least expect it. Curiously enough, it is virtually completely ignored in Said's *Orientalism*. It is telling that in that wide-ranging and usually unsparing critical review of the discourse of Orientalism there is a virtually complete omission of both the phenomenon and the subsequent study of the history and culture of the Arabs in medieval Europe. One cannot but be struck by, and perhaps relieved at, this ignoring of the discourse of Orientalism when it has addressed the question of the Arab on European soil — let alone the further question of why scholarship in those instances has assumed that, despite seven hundred years there, the Arab never became European and even that the territory he occupied was thus not part of Europe for that period of time! There is clearly some irony in this, in that Said would have found even more convincing grist for his polemical mill in the annals of Spanish Arabism than he found in the writings of Arabists who worked in more traditional areas of Islamic studies, areas that do not address, for example, the question of how the Arabs actually de-Europeanized a group of otherwise legitimate Europeans under their control. There is further irony in the extent to which this reveals that even Said, critic par excellence of the orientalist discourse, is not altogether immune to what is certainly a part of that discourse — its segregation of Arabic or Arabized Europe. Part of the myth that he is attempting to demolish is ratified in his choice of texts and scholars, and his choice reflects the view that the real Europe is a Europe almost completely unaffected by hundreds of years of Arab domination, that the only real Orientalism, or Arabism, is that practiced solely by those who have always been the colonizers of the Arabs, not those who were transformed by Arabic colonization and who have had to come to grips with that fact in themselves. But even without going this far, without dissecting *Orientalism* from the same vantage point from which it dissects that field, one can certainly note that this most widely read and influential discussion of the marginalizing approach to the study of the Arabs outside Europe itself very much reflects the segregation of the study of European Arab culture and history and just how marginal the scholarship on the Arabs in medieval Europe really is.

13. Even traditional orientalists of the sort severely criticized in Said have noted the Orientalism of scholarship on the medieval period. See note 4 above. In Watt one finds a statement that might have been made by Said himself. "In this post-Freudian world men realize that the darkness ascribed to one's enemies is a projection of the darkness in oneself that is not fully admitted. In this way the distorted vision of Islam is to be regarded as a projection of the shadow-side of European man." W. Montgomery Watt, *The Influence of Islam on Medieval Europe*. (Edinburgh: Edinburgh University Press, 1972), 83. Daniel is the most

extensive exploration of the misconceptions of Europeans concerning Islam, and it is remarkable that many of his observations about the ignorance and prejudice that are part of this view are relevant not only for the medieval period. See N. Daniel, *Islam and the West: The Making of an Image* (Edinburgh: Edinburgh University Press, 1960). See also R. W. Southern, *Western Views of Islam in the Middle Ages* (Cambridge: Harvard University Press, 1962). A recent study of the Crusades concludes with the succinct observation that "modern Western European Christians seem in general to be as ignorant of the fundamentals of Islam as their twelfth-century predecessors." Ronald C. Finucane, *Soldiers of Faith: Crusaders amd Moslems at War* (New York: St. Martin's, 1983), 211. To fully realize how acceptable, even expected, much racial prejudice was until very recently, one need only read any of the social histories of the twentieth century or biographies of some of the individuals whose lives and views have spanned the period of vastly altered attitudes. It is enlightening, for example, to read of the matter-of-factness as well as the depth of anti-Indian and anti-Arab feelings among the British upper classes in Manchester's biography of Churchill. Or, on this side of the Atlantic, the overt racism and anti-Semitism that is considered unspeakable today but until recently was not only not shocking but expected of the educated classes are both described in some detail in Lash's biography of Eleanor Roosevelt.

14. Richard Hitchcock's *The "Kharjas": A Critical Biography* (London: Grant and Cutler, 1977) is a good indication of the studies dedicated to the *kharjas* alone, and a considerable number of those studies have discussed direct or ancillary questions of possible Arabic borrowings. Even more telling, perhaps, would be a glance at Cantarino, which includes a full bibliography of studies on Dante and on the possible influence of Arabic texts on the *Commedia*. Vicente Cantarino, "Dante and Islam: History and Analysis of a Controversy," in William de Sua and Gino Rizzo, eds., *A Dante Symposium in Commemoration of the Seven Hundredth Anniversary of the Poet's Birth (1265–1965)* (Chapel Hill: University of North Carolina Press, 1965).

One is struck both by the quantity of such studies (there are eighty-one entries in his bibliography) and by the fact that so very few of them are by mainstream Italianists. Cantarino himself notes that "Asín Palacios' theory, although rejected almost unanimously and without any qualifications by Dante critics, did not fail to leave a deep influence on subsequent research of *which, however, Dante scholars have not always been fully aware.*" Cantarino, "Dante and Islam," 182. Cantarino's survey of this scholarship and of the extent to which it has been ignored by Dante scholars led him to conclusions much like my own. In noting the impasse in the pseudodebate over Dante's indebtedness to Arabic sources, he concludes that it "shows rather to what extent the controversy has ceased to be a problem which can be restricted only to the study of Dante's sources. The controversy has become a problem to be solved only with a reinterpretation of our understanding of the European Middle Ages as a time in which Arabic and Jewish cultural elements as well are given the place they deserve as components of the so-called 'Western' tradition. In this light the 'influence' of a specific work on any particular author is only an episode." Ibid., 191.

15. The term *translation* is here used in quotation marks because, although it is the term normally used, it can be seriously misleading.

16. For examples of this Europeanist absorption of Haskins's work, see the following: R. W. Southern, *The Making of the Middle Ages* (New Haven: Yale University Press, 1953); Philippe Wolff, *The Awakening of Europe*, trans. Anne Carter (Baltimore: Penguin, 1968); and R. L. Benston, G. Constable, and Carol D. Lanham, eds., *Renaissance and Renewal in the Twelfth Century* (Cambridge: Harvard University Press, 1982). The centrality of the Arabic tradition is apparent even in studies that do not explicitly acknowledge it and that may seem to be saying something quite different. See note 3 above for Haskins's and Kristeller's indirect revelations. For explicit and detailed explorations of the centrality of Averroes, his own relationship with Aristotle, and the different translations available in Europe, see both Francis E. Peters, *Aristotle and the Arabs: The Aristotelian Tradition in Islam* (New York: New York University Press, 1968), and Richard Lemay, "Dans l'Espagne du XIIe siècle: Les Traductions de l'arabe au latin," *Annales: Economies, Sociétiés, Civilisations* 18 (1963): 639–665.

17. I use the term *occupation* in quotation marks partially because its accuracy is questionable when one is dealing with a seven-hundred-year period and most of all because the use of such terms is so often among the best indicators of current attitudes we have about the presence of Arabs in Europe. I can think of few other seven-hundred-year long "occupations," and it would seem that this usage, so often reflexive, is indicative of the general image of the entire phenomenon as something quite removed from Europe, a temporary (long but still transient) interlude. The terms *Western* and *Occidental*, to make another example, are often used as if they were geographical notions but at the same time in explicit juxtaposition to Islamic Spain without further explanation of how or why the Iberian peninsula comes to be relegated to the East. Clearly, geographical terminology has been reshaped by notions of cultural ideology in such cases. It is still more interesting to note that even studies specifically dedicated to exploring or demonstrating connections between the Arabic and Romance worlds often begin with the assumption of a fundamental separateness that must be "bridged." See, for example, the titles of many works, especially Henri Terrasse, *Islam d'Espagne, une rencontre de l'Orient et de l'Occident* (Paris: Plon, 1958), or Ramón Menéndez Pidal, *España, eslabón entre la*

Cristiandad y el Islam (Madrid: Espasa-Calpe, 1956), both among the best general sources of information on the admixture, rather than separation, of culture in medieval Spain. (Interestingly enough, it is the word for "bridge" in Arabic, *al-Qantara*, that was chosen as the name for the journal that has replaced *Al-Andalus*. See its first issue, in 1890, for a discussion.) Thus the name of a conference to explore the issue is "Islam and the Medieval West," with an intimation of the separateness of those two entities, and the title of the 1965 Spoleto conference, "L'Occidente e l'Islam nell'alto Medioevo" conveys a similar impression. No less so Makdisi's 1976 "Interaction between Islam and the West" or Jean Richard's 1966 "La Vogue de l'Orient dans la littérature occidentale du moyen age." Even Menéndcz Pidal's 1955 *Poesía Árabe y poesía europea*, one of the best essays on the subject of the close and vital interrelations between the two poetries, has a title that might well create a quite different impression: that the Arabic tradition (and he is, of course, speaking of the Andalusian one) is not European. The same notions impinge on concepts of nationality. As I note in several other places in *The Arabic Role in Medieval Literary History* (Philadelphia: University of Pennsylvania Press, 1987), the very use of the title *Spaniard* is implicitly defined in racial and religious terms. The Cid is a Spaniard, but Ibn Hazm and Maimonides are not; they are an Arab and a Jew respectively.

18. Monroe, who is both comprehensive and analytically acute, is undoubtedly the best source of the two closely related issues discussed here, covering both how the Arabs and Islam have been studied academically within the Spanish intellectual tradition and how the question of Spain's special character as a part of the European community has been shaped by Spaniards' views on the "Arab question." The now classic works on the latter issue are Américo Castro, *Semblanzas y estudios españoles* (Princeton: Ediciones Insula, 1956); Claudio Sánchez-Albornoz, *España, un enigma histórico* (Buenos Aires: Editorial Sudamericana, 1966); and Claudio Sánchez-Albornoz, *El Islam de España y el Occidente* (Madrid: Espasa Calpe, 1956). The polemic is far from dead, as Sánchez-Albornoz 1973 indicates. See Claudio Sánchez-Albornoz, *El drama de la formación de España y los españoles: Otra nueva aventure polémica* (Barcelona: EDHASA, 1973) . See also Thomas F. Glick, *Islamic and Christian Spain in the Early Middle Ages* (Princeton: Princeton University Press, 1979), the introduction to which includes a concise summary of the different views on the question. Glick begins his study by noting that "history seems scarcely distinguishable from myth" and goes on to note that, in the realm of dealing with the Spanish past, the problem is more than usually acute: "Long after the enemy was vanquished, the Jews expelled, and the Inquisition disbanded, the image of the 'Moor' remained as the quintessential stranger, an object to be feared." Glick, *Islamic and Christian Spain*, 3.

19. There are some views that are more explicitly negative on the Arabs than
    Sánchez-Albornoz's. Bertrand's comments verge on the unquotable and
    include observations that Arabs are "enemies of learning" and a "nullity as civi-
    lizing elements." Louis Bertrand and Charles Petrie, *The History of Spain* (New
    York: Macmillan, 1952). Those wishing to read as vitriolic an example as any of
    anti-Arab prejudice are referred to pp. 82–94 of the English translation.

20. It is important to remember here how closely related were the literary and
    philosophical traditions of Hebrew and Arabic in Spain. In many instances it is
    more accurate to recall them as a single reasonably coherent tradition with two
    different prestige languages than as two completely separate ones. Suffice it to
    recall that the *kharjas* that Stern deciphered were *kharjas* to Hebrew
    muwashshahas. For the close relationship between those poems in the two dif-
    ferent classical languages, see especially Samuel Miklos Stern, "The
    Muwashshahas of Abraham Ibn Ezra," in Frank. W. Pierce, ed., *Hispanic Stud-
    ies in Honour of I. González Llubera* (Oxford: Dolphin, 1959), and José María
    Millàs Vallicrosa, "Influencia de las poesía popular Hispanamusulmana en la
    poesía italiana," *Revista de Archivos Bibliotecas y Museos* 41 (1967). It is also
    helpful to recall the admixture of originally Hebrew and Arabic elements in
    prose narrative as well. See M. J. Lacarra, *Cuentística medieval en España: Los
    orígenes* (Saragossa: Departamento de Literatura Española, Universidad de
    Zaragoza, 1979). The melding of those traditions is evident in the text of the
    converso Petrus Alfonsi; see Eberhard Hermes, *The "Disciplina Clericalis" of
    Petrus Alfonsi* (Berkeley: University of California Press, 1970; repr. London:
    Routledge and Kegan Paul, 1977); M. J. Lacarra, ed. and trans., *Disciplina cler-
    icalis: Pedro Alfonso* (Saragossa: Guara Editorial, 1980); and Juan Vernet Ginés,
    La cultura hispanoárabe en Oriente y Occidente (Barcelona: Ariel, 1978) and
    Literatura árabe (Barcelona: Labor, 1972). Because of the prestige of Arabic as
    the language of letters and philosophy, Maimonides was perhaps the most note-
    worthy but far from the only Jewish writer to have used Arabic as his medium.
    For admixture in the textual history of the philosophical tradition, see Ralph
    Lerner, ed. and trans., *Averroes on Plato's Republic* (Ithaca: Cornell University
    Press, 1974), introduction.

21. Thus, when Curtius writes his brief observations on "Spain's Cultural 'Belated-
    ness'" (Ernst Curtius, *European Literature and the Latin Middle Ages*, Trans.
    Willard R. Trask [1953]: 541-543), he cites Sánchez-Albornoz in support of his
    views. The short piece by Curtius is worth reading in any case because it reveals
    much in its three pages about the sort of exclusionary and negative image some
    of the most important Romance medievalists have had of medieval Arabic cul-
    ture in Europe.

22. *Discovery,* too, is a misleading term. Stern's famous "discovery" of 1948 is much
    more accurately described as all "identification." The *kharjas* were not lost or

unknown—they even existed in published form. It was just that no one knew what they were. The Arabists and Hebraists who had worked on the *muwashshahas* of which they are a part had no idea of what they were, because, of course, they were studying Arabic or Hebrew literature, not Romance, and they did not imagine that the literature they were dealing with, despite its geographical provenance, had anything to do with Romance. Romance scholars, on the other hand, even those Hispanists working on medieval material, would have little if anything to do with material written in Arabic even within their own geographical and chronological sphere of interest, or even, as turned out to be the case here, with texts written in Romance but preserved in either Hebrew or Arabic transliteration and embedded in texts written in one of those two classical languages. The circumstances render Stern's identification and decipherment of these texts far more worthy of the greatest possible respect than any mere "discovery," any serendipitous stumbling on a lost manuscript, would have been. It was not accident or good fortune but rather his accurate understanding of the cultural situation in medieval Spain that made it possible, an understanding few scholars before him had had—or at least had applied. In addition, his success is best honored as a landmark, proof of the failure of our views of and approaches to the culture of al-Andalus, of medieval Spain, to accurately identify or deal with its literature. It is a failure that has not been overcome by Stern's discovery and that affects the study of the *kharjas* and other Hispano-Arabic poetry to this day. Instead, the achievement is popularly reduced to mere discovery, which many, if not most, Europeanists believe to be literally the case.

23. Dámaso Alonso, *De los siglos oscuros al de oro: Notas y artículos a través de 700 años de letras españolas* (Madrid: Editorial Gredos, 1958), in his essay "Un signo más para la poesía espanola," and Dámaso Alonso, *Primavera temprana de la litteratura europea: Lírica, épica, novela* (Madrid: Ediciones Guadarrama, 1961), in "Cancionillas 'de amigo' mozárabes: Primavera temprana de la lírica europea"; also, of course, the works of Ramon Menéndez Pidal, especially his "Origins of Spanish Literature Considered in Relation to the Origin of Romance Literature," *Cahiers d'Histoire Mondiale* 6 (1961).

24. Bernard O'Donoghue, ed., *The Courtly Love Tradition* (Manchester: Manchester University Press, 1982), is the most recent example, but it would be misleading to think that that editor is particularly negligent. In fact, this anthology is remarkable for having included anything Arabic at all, and O'Donoghue takes some pride in noting what a broadening of the usual range of texts this comprises. He is certainly justified in noting that even this is an improvement.

25. See citations in notes 2 and 7 above. See also Maria Corti, "Models and Antimodels in Medieval Culture," *New Literary History* 10 (1979), and Morton W. Bloomfield, "Continuities and Discontinuities," *New Literary History* 10 (1979).

In neither is there any hint that the Arabic cultural phenomenon might be an important example of an antimodel or that the question of alterity and sameness in the medieval period might be profitably reviewed, taking the Arab other and alterity as an informing concept.

26. Daniel Poirion, "Literary Meaning in the Middle Ages: From a Sociology of Genres to an Anthropology of Works," *New Literary History* 10 (1979): 406.

27. To understand and accept the Saussurian dichotomy between diachrony and synchrony as meaning that the two are absolutely separable rather than separable as different focuses of analysis is as fallacious in literary studies as it is in linguistics. For an extended and lucid discussion of this fallacy in linguistics, see Winfred Lehmann, "Saussure's Dichotomy Between Descriptive and Historical Linguistics," in W. P. Lehmann and Y. Malkeil, eds., *Directions for Historical Linguistics* (Austin: Texas University Press, 1968), 3–20. Many of the same kinds of problems explored here also come to light when concepts and terms are displaced from linguistics into literary studies.

28. Fish, "Profession Despise Thyself," 357.

29. María Rosa Menocal, *The Arabic Role in Medieval Literary History: A Forgotten Heritage* (Philadelphia: University of Pennsylvania Press), xiii (preface).

30. The huge proof text at hand for Said is of course *Orientalism*, a term that existed before as a more or less neutral designation of the study of the cultures of the Middle East, principally, but became, in the aftermath, a term so powerfully tainted by Said's often compelling denunciation of it as an instrument of imperial domination and a mode of reductive analysis of a whole culture that was diminishing rather than celebratory, it is scarcely usable any more except as a negative, an accusation. Many university departments, including what was the Department of Oriental Studies at the University of Pennsylvania, where I studied Arabic, have in fact changed their names as a result.

31. María Rosa Menocal, *Shards of Love: Exile and the Origins of the Lyric* (Durham: Duke University Press, 1994).

32. Miguel Asin Palacios, *Il Libro della scala di Maometto*, trans. Roberto Rossi Testa (Milan: SE, 1991), and Miguel Asín Palacios, *Libro de la escala de Mahoma*, trans. José Luis Oliver Domingo (Madrid: Siruela, 1996). For full bibliography and a history of the reprintings of the work of Asín Palacios, see my review article, "An Andalusianist's Last Sigh," *La Corónica* 24.2 (1996): 179-189.

33. For a full discussion of all these works see my review article "More Sighs" *La Corónica* 25 (1997): 1.

Islamophobia in France and the "Algerian Problem"

Neil MacMaster

International Islamic "fundamentalism" has, following the collapse of the USSR and the end of the cold war, come to be perceived as a major threat to the West. The Western military-industrial complex, it has been argued, structurally requires an external enemy and where one does not exist in the shape of communism, a replacement has to be found or invented.[1] Political analysis that interprets Islamic fundamentalism at the international level as a powerful but secretive global network, within which funds, arms, personnel, and ideologies circulate, is a key component of Islamophobic constructions. The myth of an Islamic "International" in many ways reproduces the classic antisemitic belief in a "cosmopolitan" Jewish conspiracy to gain global power through a centralized and unified network.[2] If Islamic fundamentalism is viewed as a coherent and interlocking phenomenon, this carries an attendant danger that Islamophobia may become essentialized rather than comprehended as a complex and multi-faceted phenomenon that can vary considerably from one specific sociopolitical and historical formation to another. At the level of the nation-state it might make sense to speak of Islamophobias in the plural, rather than in the singular. Public and governmental perceptions of Muslims are not the same in France as they are in Britain or the U.S. and elsewhere.[3]

The central concern of this chapter is not to look in any detail at the relationship between France and the external Islamic world in terms of military, strategic, and foreign policy considerations (the Gulf War, Libya, the Algerian crisis, etc.) but rather to examine Islamophobia as a phenomenon grounded in French perceptions of an *internal* threat, of Muslims as an "enemy within." The domestic reactions to Islam cannot, of course, be understood in isolation from the international context, but our aim is to show how Islamophobia is more a reflection of tensions within French society and politics than a reaction to any objective external threat.

When Did Contemporary Islamophobia Appear?

Before 1979 any debate on Islam in France was much the preserve of a few academic specialists like Bruno Etienne; as a topic it found very little mention in the national press.[4] A noticeable turning point came with the Iranian Revolution of 1979 and at the governmental level there were clear signs from 1982 of a growing anxiety about Islamic fundamentalism (*intégrisme*) and militant "Khomeinyism" beginning to penetrate mainland France. The French intelligence service began to build up a "dossier" on the activities of pro-Iranian students and activists in France, and this had a clear impact on government ministers, who soon demonstrated an exaggerated and ill-informed opinion of the threat to national security. Ministers, who claimed privileged access to police intelligence, played a key role—via dramatic public statements—in initiating a growing press campaign on the dangers of *intégrisme*. The prime minister, Pierre Mauroy, told the press in January 1983 that the wave of strikes among immigrant workers in the automobile industry "were stirred up by religious and political groups," an opinion elaborated by the minister of labor, Jean Auroux, in February.[5]

A bomb explosion at the Saint-Charles station in Marseilles (December 31, 1983) led to a climate of "psychosis" in which the local press presented the city as the capital of fanaticism.[6] In 1984 the minister of the interior and mayor of Marseilles, Gaston Defferre, claiming access to special information "in my capacity as minister of the interior," and implicitly therefore to a privileged position in the analysis of Islam, asserted that it was going through a dangerous mutation. Religious practice until then had been apolitical, "an excellent thing. . . . But, step by step, the fundamentalists got a foothold in the mosques, became the managers or the leaders, and began to make propaganda and to proselytise. This is dangerous because they can act as intermediaries when bombings are perpetrated."[7] In 1984 Defferre was already articulating one of the central components of French Islamophobia, which was to grow and deepen throughout the later 1980s and the 1990s in response to a sequence of terrorist assassinations and bombings. The fanatics did not constitute an isolated threat but would take root and find a support base in the wider Muslim community, in the classic Maoist style of the guerrilla as "fish in water." In time a widespread public perception would be generated in which all "Arabs" would be viewed as potential terrorists.[8]

An analysis of Defferre's political discourse reveals a second but equally important anti-Muslim theme, that of a willful refusal by "Arabs" to integrate or assimilate. He hinted at the fact that other immigrant groups, Italians, Spaniards, Poles, regardless of whether they were "Catholics, Protestants, Jews. or atheists," had assimilated, become naturalized, and now "occupy important positions, almost everywhere." But he intimated that Muslims were profoundly resistant to such processes. Algerians in particular reconstituted large extended family networks, "groupings often of several dozen people who, in addition, wear traditional clothing and live according to the customs of their country. They roast sheep in the yard, etc."[9] He made it clear that what was desired was that "they have a mode of dress and a style of living that is exactly the same as that of the French." The laws of Islam in the sphere of marriage, divorce, gender roles, and family life "are in contradiction with the rules of French law."[10] Here again Defferre articulated the second key element of French Islamophobia as it was to develop between 1984 and the 1990s—the idea that Muslims presented a fundamental danger to the "melting pot" ideology of France "one and indivisible."

The period 1982–1983 marked a crucial turning point in the emergence of Islamophobia, but it would be facile to ascribe this solely to ministerial responses to the Iranian Revolution. The discourse of Defferre can be read as a symptom rather than as a significant cause of a deeper and more fundamental shift in French society, a shift toward widespread and overt forms of racism. However, the specific construction of French Islamophobia needs to be understood against the background of French colonialism. Before looking in more detail at the factors that led to the racist "turning point" of 1980–1984, we need to make a brief excursion back in time to locate the colonial roots of an anti-Islamic prejudice that was grounded in bitter hostility toward North African immigrants, and to the Algerians in particular. Until the late 1970s prejudice was shown throughout French society and politics toward *les immigrés*, a term that was widely understood to refer to the Maghrebians or "Arabs."

During this period racism was rarely articulated in terms of hostility to Islam. However, as Islamophobia developed after 1979 it was profoundly shaped by the powerful and deep-rooted tradition of hostility toward "Arabs," and toward the Algerians in particular. The connection between the Algerian presence on French soil and a fanatical "fundamentalist terrorism" was powerfully reinforced by the Algerian crisis and the bombing campaigns of the 1990s. Yet the apparently new phenomenon of hostility toward expressions of Islam was in many ways a reformulation or revivification of a much older and entrenched prejudice.

The Colonial Roots of Anti-Algerian Racism

First-generation migrants from North Africa and their descendants (the *beur* generation) have during the 1980s and 1990s consistently been the object of more racist violence than any other ethnic minority group in France.[11] This pattern of targeting Maghrebian immigrants, particularly Algerians, is not a recent phenomenon but was already clearly established as early as the First World War, when three hundred thousand Algerian soldiers and workers were on French soil.[12] The process deepened during the interwar period when the massive rotation of migrant workers from the colony meant that some five hundred thousand Algerians, about one in five of all males of working age, had some experience of work in France.[13] Algerians constituted the largest non-European immigrant presence anywhere in Europe before 1945 and the great public controversy they aroused generated perceptions of colonial "barbarians" invading the very heart of empire. During the interwar period French industry was heavily reliant on immigrant labor from numerous sources, but surveys, like that in the Paris car industry in 1926, showed that Arabs were already placed at the bottom of a racial hierarchy and regarded as inferior to Italians, Poles, Spaniards, and all other nationalities.[14]

The systematic racialization of Algerians was primarily the work of European colonial elites in Algeria and of a well-organized lobby in metropolitan France that was keen to either halt or severely restrict and control migration. The basic anxiety of the lobby, constituted mainly of senior ex-Algerian administrators and police officials, was that the migrants could escape from the powerful authoritarian and oppressive controls of the colony, enforced under the Code de l'Indigénat, and in the much freer climate of metropolitan France come into contact with left-wing political movements, especially the Communist Party, with trade unions and the newly emergent nationalist movements like the Étoile-Nord-Africaine. The migrants, who rotated continually between Algeria and France, would then carry the dangerous germs of Communism and anti-imperialism back into every village and subvert the whole colonial order from within.[15]

In order to contain this threat, which turned out to be a very real one, the French authorities engaged in two strategies. First, although migration could not be completely halted, since Algerians had a right of entry as French subjects, a successful attempt was made to persuade public opinion and politicians that rigorous controls should be introduced by orchestrating a campaign that presented the immigrants as a threat to metropolitan society. A highly racialized stereotype of Algerians as criminals, primitive savages, rapists, transmitters of venereal disease and tuberculosis, was widely diffused through the press.[16]

Another factor that helped maintain a high level of official disquiet and hostility toward the Algerians, above that of any other immigrant minority, was their apparent resistance to integration into French society. What worried police chiefs and officials was that Algerians in France reconstituted "tribal" groupings in lodging houses and microghettoes that were impenetrable to surveillance. During the century of French conquest, spoliation, and devastation of Algerian society after 1830, the indigenous people had sought to protect themselves from the oppression of settlers and officials through a culture of resistance, which included a strategy of ruse, silence, and disinformation. Algerians in France reproduced these forms of resistance when confronted with officialdom and tended to live in small, impermeable enclaves.

However, other factors also worked against a "normal" process of gradual integration throughout the period 1918–1973. First, until the 1950s Algerians did not introduce their families. Since Algerian ports were only twenty-four hours away from Marseilles by ship, migrants tended to rotate constantly between French factories and their home village. Instead of integrating into the French working class, the Algerian maintained a primary identity as a peasant who constantly renewed his roots in the values, traditions, and preoccupations of his village society. Historians like Noiriel have argued that most immigrant groups, like the Italians and Spaniards, gradually assimilated into French society by participation in the central organizations of the working class—the trade union, the political party (primarily the PCF), sports clubs. and associations—as well as through the Catholic Church and the Republican school.[17] Such integrative organizations failed for the Algerians: the secularist PCF and CGTU union did not succeed in organizing among the immigrants who became much more drawn by the Étoile-Nord-Africaine which split away from the PCF and entered into bitter opposition to the Communists, who remained opposed to Algerian independence. The central concern of those Algerians who were politicized lay with the struggle for national independence and a future project in which all migrants would eventually return home from exile. The whole rationale of the migrants, down to 1962 and beyond, was founded on a project of return and this refusal to put down roots in France was emphasized by the policy of the ENA and successor nationalist organizations that opposed family migration.

The overall position of the Algerian community in France throughout the period 1918–1954 was then one in which it was the particular target of racial abuse and violence and, second, in which this was compounded by weak integration, relative isolation within the French working class, and French perceptions of radical and unchanging difference. This pattern of isolation was to gain a further radical impetus during the Algerian War of 1954–1962.

After 1945 the Algerians in Paris continued to be the target of large-scale police operations by the Brigade des agressions et violences (BAV), massive "sweeps" and arrests that then accelerated in 1955–1956 during the early stages of the Algerian War. Since the FLN established a sophisticated "countersociety" and network among the emigrants who raised enormous sums to finance the Algerian Liberation Army, French intelligence was particularly keen to penetrate and crush the organization. Maurice Papon, appointed Paris prefect of police in March 1958, introduced new and ruthless methods to counter the FLN, including the introduction of the North African units known as the harkis, which imported pschychological warfare and torture techniques from the colonial arena. In August 1958 the FLN opened a "second front" in France, a campaign of sabotage and assassination of police officers, in order to tie down military forces and to relieve pressure on the FLN in Algeria. This led to a phase of deepening state violence targeted at the Algerian community in general,[18] which culminated in the police massacre of a peaceful Algerian demonstration in central Paris on the night of October 17, 1961.[19] Metropolitan public opinion shifted from one of relative indifference toward both the war and the Algerian immigrants to one of deepening hostility during the phase of violence from 1958 to 1962.[20]

The Algerian War left a profound scar on French society and politics and has fuelled anti-Algerian racism down to the present day. The coming of

Algerian independence did not mark a rapid repatriation of migrants: on the contrary, the systematic uprooting of over three million peasants and their *regroupement* in military camps during the war, combined with the French sabotage of economic infrastructures in 1961–1962, led to a huge increase in emigration. The number of Algerians in France rocketed from 350,000 in 1962 to 845,000 in 1973. The acceleration in migration led to a heightened "visibility" among the French population and a sense of "invasion." This period of heightened tension was further deepened by the spatial proximity of the migrants, particularly in the Marseilles region, to the million refugees of European settler descent, known as the *pieds noirs*. In addition, some 2.3 million soldiers had seen action in Algeria, and many of them returned brutalized by actions against the civilian population and by the coarse racism of the platoon. Among them was Le Pen, the future leader of the Front National, who served as an intelligence officer in Algeria and was involved in torture.[21] It was among the *pieds noirs*, the ex-military, and the OAS that the fascist Ordre Nouveau and the Front National (FN) of Le Pen, founded in 1972, established a significant base. It is no coincidence that the FN has through the 1980s and 1990s developed its strongest electoral base in the Provence-Alpes-Côtes d'Azur region and that Le Pen scored 23.5 per cent in the first round of the 1995 presidential elections in greater Marseilles.[22]

The links between the *pieds noirs*, ex-army cadres, and extreme-right politics is well known; what has gone unnoticed is the extent to which colonial anti-Algerian attitudes have remained endemic, but concealed, within the highest echelons of the state and the senior management of private industry and business. Throughout the colonial period it was a standard practice of French ministries to circulate administrators, civil servants, police officers, urban planners, health officials, and other personnel between the metropolis and Algeria as part of a normal career pattern. Numerous ex-colonial functionaries were located after 1962 in sectors of central and local government where they played a key role in implementing policy toward Algerian immigrants. For example, Maurice Papon, former prefect of Constantine, continued—after the October massacre of 1961—to serve as prefect of police until 1967. Later he became the head of the aircraft corporation Sud-Aviation, national treasurer and deputy in the Gaullist UDF, and in April 1978 minister for the budget under Raymond Barre.[23]

During the period from 1962 to about 1980 Algerians continued, among all immigrant minorities in France, to be the particular target of both government and press hostility as well as of *quotidien* street-level acts of random abuse, assault, and murder. Between June and December 1973, for example, a wave of violence and killings swept through the south of France and up to fifty Algerians were murdered and three hundred wounded.[24] In response to the failure of the French government to protect its nationals, the newly independent Algerian state unilateraly halted all further labor migration to France.

The Racist "Turning Point," 1980–1984

The early 1980s saw a profound and deep level change in French society, one marked by the simultaneous resurgence of racial politics and by a redefinition of the "immigré /arab" as a Muslim.[25] The FN, founded in 1972, was able to make little impact on the French political system before the symbolic breakthrough in the Dreux by-election of 1983 and the dramatic success in the 1984 European elections when it gained 11 percent of the national vote. During the presidency of Giscard d'Estaing from 1974 to 1981 the government had deepened its anti-immigrant stance: all primary labor migration from outside Europe was halted in 1974, while various decrees and circulars tightened the screw on the minorities in France. But although Algerians continued to be the main target, the "immigrant problem" had still not become a central issue in electoral politics. During the 1973 legislative elections the FN mentioned immigration only once in its thirty-one-page programme, and Le Pen steered clear of the theme since he thought that it might damage the new party's image.[26] The severity of government anti-immigrant measures also meant that there was little to be gained by the FN in trying to use this as a mobilizing issue.

Some commentators have ascribed the rapid racialization of French politics after 1980 to the French Communist Party and, in particular, to the notorious Vitry affair of December 1980 when the mayor of the Parisian "red-belt" commune led a bulldozer attack on a hostel to prevent its occupation by immigrant workers. While the PCF at the local and national levels did begin to dabble in a dangerous way with anti-immigrant sentiment, the Communists were responding, as did the FN, to the growth of a powerful current of grassroots racism. While the FN was to succeed in channeling and mobilizing this groundswell in order to make a political breakthrough, it can be argued that it was in the early stage less a cause than a symptom of a deeper shift in French society. The best evidence for this fundamental hiatus has come from discourse analysis. Bonnafous, in a systematic analysis of

the French press between 1974 and 1984, has been able to demonstrate a process of growing homogeneity in media discourse by which the left/liberal
press began to be formulated in terms that were increasingly similar to those
of the right and far right. Across the press, regardless of politics, the immigrant was seen less and less in productive or class terms as a *travailleur* and
more and more in negative terms as an "immigrant" linked to the problems
of crime, drugs, and social disorder. Bonnafous places in 1979 the crucial
shift in balance toward a perception of the immigrant as a radically different
Other that presented a serious problem of integration into the "French
nation."[27] According to the economistic model put forward by Noiriel and
neo-Marxists like Stephen Castles, it might have been predicted that anti-
immigrant sentiment would deepen and coincide with the economic crisis
of 1973–1974.[28] France did impose controls on primary labor immigration in
1974. However, the fundamental shift in opinion was to come later and to
coincide with the realization that *les immigrés* were not going to return, but
were in France for good. The central issue was no longer one of "closing the
doors" but a profound disquiet toward those lodged permanently as an unassimilable foreign body within the Republican "universalist" order.[29]

The timing of this "racial turning" point in 1979–1980 is crucial to our
argument, since from that moment the whole debate on assimilability crystallized around the issues of Islam and the Muslim presence. As we have
seen, the statements made by Gaston Defferre and other ministers in 1982–
1984 linked the newly emergent Islamophobia to the Iranian revolution.[30]
However, this was only one small part of the story: Defferre had gone on to
raise the question of the nonassimilability of the Algerians who, he claimed,
refused to change their lifestyle and culture. The deeply entrenched French
animus toward Maghrebians, and Algerians in particular, was now given a
new dynamic. The 1970s equation "immigrant/worker = Arab = Algerian"
was slowly displaced through the 1980s by another interchangeable set of
terms, "Muslim = Arab = Algerian = Terrorist." This widening concern
over the "Islamic presence" within France can be in part explained by the
undoubted phenomenon of religious revivalism.

Islam and the Question of "Visibility"

Until the early 1980s there appears to have been singularly little public or
media interest or concern with Muslims living and working in France,

although they then numbered some 2.5 million, the largest group in any European state.[31] Why was this the case? Part of the answer to this lies in the area of "visibility" and what Gilles Kepel has termed "re-islamisation." Throughout the long period of migration from roughly 1910 until the 1970s North Africans, by far the largest Muslim grouping, maintained a modicum of religious practice and identity; worship and ritual in its various forms was largely carried out in private, inside lodgings or worker-hostels, inside factories, or within the backrooms of Algerian cafés. During the 1960s and 1970s, with family reunification, and movement into the huge council estates on the urban periphery, mosques were improvised in basements, garages, and council flats. Since these prayer rooms were not purpose built and had none of the external architectural symbolism of the traditional mosque (a minaret and dome, Islamic styling) they were largely unrecognizable, even to French inhabitants living within the same locality.

Between 1975 and 1986 the number of mosques and places of worship increased from 68 to 912, while the number of Islamic associations went from 60 to 635.[32] At the same time Muslims began to make a range of other demands—for a controlled supply of *halal* meat, Koranic schools, assertion of religious dress codes (*foulards*), the appointment of trained imams, the creation of cemetery space for Muslims, and the establishment of cultural centers. The creation of Muslim associations was greatly facilitated by the law of October 9, 1981, which allowed foreigners the right to establish registered associations under the law of 1901. The new dynamic mobilization and proactive stance of Muslims, especially after 1980, in the assertion of demands was an indication of the fact that Maghrebians, including older first-generation migrants, had come to accept that they were now settled in France for good. North Africans no longer accepted a position as postcolonial subjects, temporary sojourners, who could be denied equal rights and full citizenship. The construction of elaborate, purposely built mosques, of which the first was inaugurated at Mantes-la-Jolie in 1981, instead of "makeshift" prayer rooms, was a sign both of a newfound commitment to stay in France as well as a growing, confident assertion of religious identity and a refusal any longer to hide away in the private sphere.[33] Muslims were laying claim to legitimacy alongside the Catholic, Protestant, and Jewish faiths.

The new "visibility" of Muslims, which has been interpreted by some sociologists as an indicator of integration, was viewed by all major political parties and the general French public in quite opposite terms. The move of religious/cultural practices from the private into the public space, gave an impression of "invasion" and "aggressive" religious assertion by Muslims, whereas there was no significant change in the number of immigrants arriving from Muslim societies. This new "visibility" of Muslims was readily manipulated by the Front National for electoral purposes from 1982 onward.

The National Front and the Racialization of French Politics

The racial turning point of 1979–1980 soon became evident in the electoral breakthrough of the FN in 1983–1984. The FN moved rapidly during 1983–1984 from an insignificant party to a central and influential player that was able to break the hold of the so-called gang of four (the PCF, PS, UDF, and RPR) over the political system. In the European election of 1984 the FN gained over 11 percent of the national vote and sent ten deputies to the European parliament. Space does not allow a full analysis of the complex factors that led to this rapid growth in FN membership and electoral support.[34] Suffice it to say that the FN rise to influence was crucially linked to a platform of anti-immigrant measures and, second, that the growing public support for such policies led the other major parties, including the Socialists and the Gaullists, to swing to the right. Instead of placing a *cordon sanitaire* around the FN, and refusing to use racism as an electoral card, mainstream politics fell into the fatal trap of utilizing anti-immigrant rhetoric and policy statements to win support. As a consequence, racist and anti-immigrant sentiments achieved an unprecedented level of legitimation: for many millions of French people it was no longer felt to be shameful to make extreme and vile racist statements in public or as part of everyday "normal" discourse.

Although the political discourse of the FN centered on the issue of *les immigrés*, there were signs at an early stage of this being linked into the question of "Arabs/Muslims." This can be shown, for example, in relation to a crucial moment in the FN breakthrough at Dreux in 1983 when the extreme right won seats on the town council through an electoral pact with the RPR. This victory came as a result of a long and well-organized campaign by Le Pen's number two, Jean-Pierre Stirbois, to build up a strong base in the town. During this period (1981–1982) an anonymous, forged letter was widely diffused in Dreux, claiming to be from an Algerian to a friend in Algiers:

My Dear Mustapha. By the grace of all-powerful Allah we have become the lords and masters of Paris. . . . Come quickly, we expect you in large numbers, since Mitterrand has promised that we shall soon get the right to vote We kicked the French out of Algeria; why shouldn't we do the same here?[35]

The attack of the extreme right on Muslims and "Arabs" was increasingly expressed through the political discourse of the New Right. The FN astutely substituted a traditional biological racism with one based on cultural differ-ence and the right to defend French national "identity" and "heritage" from submersion by either immigrants or by "cosmopolitan" American/Jewish forces. The FN demand for "le droit à la différence," a slogan of the 1980s anti-racist and multiculturalist campaigns, was part of a deliberate hege-monic strategy to redefine or reconstruct identity in terms of an organic and populist nationalism. Unfortunately, the political left and antiracist organi-zations were slow to recognize and counter the threat from the New Right strategy.[36] In reality, cultural differentialism was a reformulated and dis-guised racism, and the FN position that French and Arab peoples shared the right to preserve their historic identity within their respective ancient "homeland" amounted in practice to an apartheid strategy in which Maghrebian Muslims would be "repatriated."

The Crisis of National Identity

During the 1980s the growth in anti-Islamic sentiment was not restricted to the extreme right (although the FN helped legitimate this racist dis-course) but was spread across the political spectrum, from the Communists to the Gaullist RPR. The surprising unanimity derived from the fact that all major parties shared the same political culture that derived from the ideol-ogy of Republican citizenship. The Jacobin tradition of France "one and indivisible," which had been constructed mainly under the Third Republic, was a pseudo-universalist ideology that emphasized the equality of all citi-zens within the state. In this scheme of things there could be no intermedi-ate bodies or poles of allegiance that might detract from the uniform rela-tionship between each individual citizen and the state. The historic process of state construction had involved the eradication of competing languages and identities (Breton, Basque, Corsican), and the introduction of universal primary education, following an identical, centralized curriculum, was viewed as the prime instrument for civic education and the welding of every individual into a shared national culture. The secularist "founding ideology" of French Republicanism is profoundly hostile to the kind of multicultural-ism and recognition of ethnic minority rights found in Britain and the United States.

By the mid 1980s French society was beginning to suffer from a deepen-ing sense of uncertainty and anxiety about national identity, a crisis that was rooted in a complex of factors: loss of sovereignty to the European Union, the invasion of Anglo-Saxon terminology into the French lan-guage, American "cultural imperialism," and other features of globaliza-tion.[37] However, the widespread feeling that the traditional French way of life, the very life force of cultural identity and community, was threatened became focused on the question of the Muslim presence. Islam, it was claimed, was profoundly opposed to Republican secular universalism and in its very essence was resistant to the "normal" processes of assimilation of immigrant minorities.

In 1987 Prime Minister Chirac established the Long Commission on nationality, the main intent of which was to erode the traditional French *jus soli* as the basis of citizenship and to undermine the position of the North African immigrants and their descendants. As Sami Nair commented, the lengthy debates in the commisssion were largely fixated on Muslims from the Maghreb—"Islam and the Arabs haunted the members of the Commis-sion."[38] Alain Touraine, a distinguished sociologist and member of the com-mission, expressed the standard position in relation to multiculturalism: "Nobody wants the Lebanization of France!"[39] Placed in the context of a dis-cussion of Algerians in France and the *beurs* generation, the reference to Lebanon, with all the resonances of bloody civil war, hostage taking, and Islamic fanaticism, carried a clear meaning. However, the whole isssue of the fundamentalist threat was to reach an extraordinary crescendo one year later.

1989: Islamophobia Comes of Age

Nineteen eighty-nine saw a remarkable conjuncture of events that led to a profound acceleration of French Islamophobia. The uprising in Algeria in October 1988 marked the first stage in the challenge to the military regime and the emergence of Islamic radicals onto the political stage. By 1989 the spreading influence of the FIS in Algeria was being viewed from France with some trepidation.[40] On February 14, 1989, Khomeini issued his *fatwah* against Salman Rushdie and on February 26 Muslim demonstrators marched through Paris chanting "Death to Rushdie!" In August 1989 the Gaullist mayor of Charvieu-Chavagneux near Lyons, fearing the invasion of "Islamic fundamentalists" into his commune, ordered a local Muslim prayer-room to be bulldozed, a dramatic symbol of growing local opposition to the establishment of mosques. In November the fall of the Berlin Wall symbolized for the whole world the collapse of European communism and opened the way for the "New World Order" that marked the end of the cold war and the redirection of Western military power away from the "Red Peril" to the "Green" threat of Islam—a realignment that was soon to find direct expression in the Gulf War. The year 1989 also marked the bicentenary cel-ebrations of the French Revolution, an occasion that led to conservative, revisionist attacks on the egalitarian Republican tradition and that brought to the surface anxieties relating to the ideological roots of French identity. But one event above all others crystallized the key issues of Islamophobia: the extraordinary national debate over the "headscarves affair."

In October 1989 three girls of North African descent were barred by the headmaster from a secondary school in Creil on the grounds that wearing a headscarf (*foulard*) was a provocative religious symbol in breach of *laicité* and the laws protecting the secular, nonreligious nature of state education.[41] The "affair" raised a whole complex of issues, but for many journalists and politicians, both of the left and the right, the young girls were being directly manipulated by bearded "fundamentalist" interests as a provocation, a plot by shadowy forces to challenge and subvert the foundations of secularism.

That the raging controversy over the integration and assimilation of eth-nic minorities should center on the state school was no accident. By 1989 specialists in the history of immigration were arguing that the successful integration of immigrants from Italy, Spain, Poland, and elsewhere between the late nineteenth century and the 1970s had been achieved through the institutions and associations of the French working class (the PCF, trade unions, sports clubs) and the Catholic Church. By the 1980s such bridges into French society were no longer functioning: in particular the North Africans and the second-generation *beurs* had become ghettoized in huge public housing estates where the collapse of PCF influence, mass unem-ployment, absence of trade union membership, and an atavistic Muslim opposition to Christianity had left an ideological void. Given this scenario, French politicians and intellectuals laid a particular emphasis on the

Republican school as the last remaining, but most powerful, institution for the systematic molding of all children, regardless of ethnic origins, into the universal values of the Republic.

In an open letter to the minister of education, Lionel Jospin, five leading Socialist intellectuals pleaded with him to uphold the ban on *le foulard islamique*. The appeal opened on an apocalyptic note in which the danger of Islamic fundamentalism was likened to that of Nazism: "Monsieur le Ministre, The future will tell if the year of the Bicentenary will have witnessed the Munich of the Republican school." The state had a duty to shield the girls from the oppressive patriarchal authority of fundamentalist fathers and brothers by protecting the school, as "a place of emancipation" in which they could "forget their community of origin" and hidebound tradition and be exposed to "reason," "the rights of man," and "the principle of the freedom of thought." "In our society the school is the only institution dedicated to the universal . . . This is why the destruction of the School will precipitate that of the Republic." By implication Islam represented the inverse of such values: opposed to reason, enlightenment and knowledge, intolerant, oppressive, antidemocratic, against the "rights of man," fanatical, and destructive of the Republic itself.[42]

The Algerian Crisis and the Islamic "Fifth Column"

During the 1990s Islamophobia was cranked up to fever pitch first by the events of the Gulf War and then by the deepening crisis in Algeria. Faced with a certain landslide victory by the FIS in the 1991 legislative elections, the Algerian government canceled the second round and installed a military junta (January 11, 1992) that was quietly buttressed by France as a bulwark against fundamentalism. After the FIS was outlawed in March 1992, it established a base in Europe. On November 9, 1993, Charles Pasqua, the hardline minister of the interior, ordered a massive police operation and arrest of FIS supporters, a move that confirmed in the public mind that "Islamic terrorist" networks inside France were both extensive and dangerous. From this moment the Groupes islamiques armés (GIA) extended its war to include France itself, through the assassination of French citizens in Algeria, the spectacular Airbus hijack of December 1994, and by a bombing campaign in Paris, most notably in the Metro in 1995–1996. It was in this context that the deeply rooted and racist hatred of "Arabs" and of Algerians in particular was given a new impetus and was turned to target the immigrant community.

Although the violent radicals offered a serious security threat, their numbers and support base in France remained minuscule, confined at most to a few hundred militants that were closely tracked by the French security. However, the French press, leading academic "experts," and politicians conspired to create a climate of opinion in which all Muslims and "Arabs" were viewed as fundamentalists and potential terrorists. During the last five years Islamophobia has shifted from a fear that Islamic revivalism is reinforcing ethnic identity and blocking assimilation into the Republican *cité*, to the view that the Muslim community as a whole is being won over to *intégrisme* and an "Islamo-terrorist international" that reaches from Iran, Afganistan, Palestine, and Algeria into the very core of French society. This nightmare and paranoid scenario has centered in particular on the position of disaffected minority youth in the *banlieue*, the huge public housing estates on the periphery of the major cities.

The riot of 1981 in the estate of Les Minguettes, a Lyons suburb, first drew national attention to the problem of ghettoization and social exclusion in the huge and dreary *grandes ensembles* that had been constructed during the 1960s and 1970s. In these zones minority youth, particularly the *beurs* of North African descent, faced high levels of unemployment and the effects of multiple deprivation and racist discrimination. Feeling trapped in the estates and deliberately segregated from mainstream French society, the youth vented their anomie and anger through drugs, crime, car theft "rodeos," and daily ritual conflict with local police forces. Throughout the 1980s government regarded the ghetto estates as one of the key problems facing French society, in part because their continuing existence presented the gravest concrete danger to the Republican model of universalism and assimilation. Academics and journalists constantly drew parallels between the frightening growth of ethnic enclaves and the United States and Britain, where multiculturalism and politicized minority interests, at war with each other over limited resources, offered the dystopia of a balkanized society.[43]

In 1981 the Socialists, in direct response to the riots, set up the Commission nationale pour le développement social des quartiers and from this followed a major programme of investment and renovation.[44] However, in spite of such intervention public opinion was shaken by further major riots throughout the 1990s, beginning with the violent disorders on the estate of Vaulx-en-Velin in 1990. The violence, alienation, and nonassimilation of minority youth became a central public concern, an issue symbolized by Mathieu Kassovitz's film *La Haine* (1995).

During the l990s Islamophobia reached new heights as journalists, academics, and politicians constructed a nightmare scenario in which the diabolic agents of international fundamentalism extended their networks and support base among the disaffected youth of the *banlieue*. This anxiety was already emerging with the headscarves affair of 1989, with the perception that young girls were being forced by shadowy agents of *intégrisme to* wear the veil. Tension was further heightened in January 1991 when France entered the Gulf War, and the media and politicians openly expressed fear of a youth intifada raging in the concrete jungles of suburban France. In reality a few isolated incidents of youthful bravado, the shouting of slogans and painting of wall graffiti in favour of Saddam Hussein, were eagerly read, in an atmosphere of deepening "moral panic," as signs of imminent revolt.[45]

Finally, all the worst fears of the Islamophobic current were confirmed by two events. On August 24, 1994, three men machine-gunned Spanish tourists in a hotel in Marrakech. The members of an extensive fundamentalist network were placed on trial in Morocco (January 1995) and France (December 1996), and this established that a large number of them had been recruited from big estates in Paris (La Courneuve), Orleans, Besancon, Carpentras, and Avignon and had received training in Pakistan and Afghanistan.[46] However, the most "exemplary" case of the delinquent "Arab" youth converted to Islam and then recruited as a fanatical terrorist was Khaled Kelkal. Kelkal, an Algerian-born youth from Vaulx-en-Velin—scene of the famous 1990 riot—was in September 1995 hunted down as France's number one terrorist and shot dead by the police. A German academic, Dietmar Loch, published in *Le Monde* the details of a long interview he had with Kelkal in 1992, in which the latter described a classic development from an embittered youth, angry at racism and exclusion and on a downward path of drug abuse, criminality, and self-destructive rage, through the discovery of Islam in jail and a conversion process that provided him with a sense of moral strength and identity.[47] Further proof of the deep penetration of "Islamic terrorism" into the bedrock of French society came in April 1996 with the police siege and death of five *islamogangsters* at Roubaix, among them Christophe Caze, a French convert.[48]

Such events seemed to provide irrefutable evidence of a very real and growing danger of Islamic fundamentalism taking root in French soil. In reality, as Farhad Khosrokhavar has shown, the number of Muslim converts who were recruited into the international networks of radical Islam was extremely small. Indeed, wherever Muslim youth organizations have been given a degree of recognition and support by local authorities this has tended to act as a bulwark against political fundamentalism.[49] However, an analysis of the press and of commentary by academic "authorities" on Islam reveals a process by which the activities of a highly unusual and relatively isolated minority were presented as a norm, as symptomatic of the Muslim community as a whole.

Islamophobia and the Press

The French press has played a major role in the dissemination of anti-Muslim stereotypes.[50] This can be shown through an examination of front-page covers and lead stories of national weekly magazines like *L'Express, Le Nouvel Observateur, Le Point,* and *L'Evenement du Jeudi.* The combined use of a striking headline, along with a visually powerful image or photo-graph, is a favored journalistic construction that aims to capture the eye of the public as it passes by the newsstand. Cover headings and photographs convey immediate and powerful meanings that may influence the way in which the following "small print" texts are read.[51] Two motifs are particu-larly common: first, covers that refer to the armed violence of Islamic "ter-rorists" and, second, those that use the image of veiled women. The special issue covers on terrorism deploy two kinds of images. The first utilize photo-graphs of "fundamentalists," frequently heavily armed and hooded, as in *Le Nouvel Observateur* issue "Investigation of the GIA. The men, the methods, the networks of Algerian Islamic terrorism."[52] The second construction shows the inverse, heavily armed French police or soldiers on patrol against the internal terrorist threat, as in *L'Express* issue "La France face au terror-isme," which positions two soldiers with automatic weapons below the Eiffel Tower.[53] The meanings here are clear enough: the contents elaborate, often with the aid of maps and diagrams, on the complex global, secret networks of international terrorism that reach from Iran, Afghanistan, Algeria, and Libya into the heart of French society.[54] The cumulative impact of such "inside investigations" on the French public has been to create an exagger-ated sense of insecurity, anxiety, and lurking, ever present danger.

However, by far the most widespread image that has reinforced anti-Muslim prejudice is that of heavily veiled women. Here the processes of deliberate construction, manipulation, and falsification become more evident. Among the 200,00 Muslim girls of school age in France today it has been estimated that between 0.25 and 1 percent wear the *foulard*.[55] However, the press in its cover reports on the *foulards* controversies of 1989 and 1994 invariably utilized photographs of girls or women not in headscarves but in full-length Iranian *chadors* or veils that left only the eyes visible. The wearing of a full veil is quite exceptional among Muslim women in France, yet editors have invariably selected images of maximum veiling, the style that carries the most negative connotations, to suggest that this is the norm, or may become so in a nightmare future in which France will be swamped by an alien presence. A *Figaro* special supplement on immigration (October 26, 1985) carried a cover with a bust of Marianne wrapped in a veil and the question "Will we still be French in thirty years time?" A *Nouvel Observateur* cover of 1986 used a fabricated studio image of a female model wearing a full veil in the red, white, and blue colors of the *tricolore*, alongside the heading "L'Islam en France."[56] Another fabricated studio photograph of a veiled woman was used by *L'Express* to make an explicit link to terrorism with the caption "Foulard. The Plot. How the Islamic Fundamentalists infiltrate France."[57] Repeatedly the veiled woman, her eyes just visible through a slit, is selected as the symbol or signifier for an entire social and religious order, the immigrant/Muslim community. There are multiple levels of meaning here: the maximum veil indicates a barbaric order in which women are the victims of patriarchal oppression, seclusion, and orientalist practices like child marriage and polygamy. The cultural distance between Muslims and French "civilization" is made as wide as possible so as to suggest the impossibility of integration and the danger presented to Republican values and universality. Veiling and concealment is also inherently sinister, as with masking in general, and lurking always behind the figure of the woman is the shadowy fundamentalist, the fanatical bomber who manipulates her.[58]

Islamophobia and the Republican "Experts"

Edward Said has explored the way in which Orientalism and Islamophobia has been constructed by "experts" who carry enormous influence through their ability to form government policy or to impact on public opinion via the media, specialist journals, think tanks, and official commissions.[59] In France the most prominent specialist in Islam and well-known media star is Gilles

Kepel, professor at the Institut d'études politiques and director of research at the CNRS, an Arabist with an outstanding academic record for his work on fundamentalism in Egypt and contemporary France.[60] In a review of *The Revenge of God* Hilton Obenzinger has noted how Kepel "unfortunately lapses into classic Orientalist chauvinism," particularly in his claim that "the rejection of even a chimerical notion of democracy is actually inherent in Islamic religious doctrine."[61] But Kepel has revealed his true colors as an "unreconstructed Jacobin" in his latest work, *Allah in the West*.

There has undoubtedly been a significant process of "reislamization" of French minority youth over the last decade. A major debate is now under-way in France between two schools of thought as to the underlying meaning of this phenomenon. One group regards Islamic revivalism as an extremely grave threat to Republican assimilation, while the opposing side views it as a positive and dynamic process of adaptation and modernization within the context of Western society. Kepel clearly belongs to the first camp. In his comparative treatment of Islamic movements in the U.S., Britain, and France, he choses to ignore the majority, the "thousand ways of being Muslim," to concentrate on the radical minority, "groups which are tempted to go to the limit."[62] In the body of the text this is rapidly overlooked, and the fundamentalists appear as the norm. Kepel's key obsession is "communal-ism" (*communautarisme*), an ideologically loaded term that is used to denote systematic ethnic community organization. In his one-sided and highly selective treatment of Muslim communalism in the United States and Britain, Kepel's purpose is to demonstrate the dangerous social and political fragmentation that follows from multiculturalism and to sound a warning of the mortal impact that similar policies would have for the Jacobin state, *laicité*, and citizenship.[63] Underpinning Kepel's work is a Republican assimilationist logic that fails to acknowledge that this inevitably involves a dominant power relationship and that the universal, far from being such, amounts to the "universality of France." In his concluding remarks on the "communalist challenge" offered by the reislamization of French minority youth, Kepel warns against the spread of radicalism, "as hundreds of thousands of 'little brothers' and 'little sisters' leave school and find the labor market . . . closed to them."[64]

However, in opposition to Kepel is a growing body of work, based on extensive research among Muslim youth in the estates of Marseilles, Dreux, Montfermeil, Sarcelles, Strasbourg, and elsewhere, that has arrived at quite different conclusions. In particular the books of Jocelyne Cesari and of

Farhad Khosrokhavar have, independently of each other, arrived at similar conclusions.[65] Although space does not allow me to do justice to this sophisticated body of research, a few points can be made. Cesari shows that at the local political level there has already been a significant de facto recognition of Muslim organizations: thus Kepel is still clinging on to a myth of Jacobin Republicanism that bears little relationship to the dynamism of grassroots change. Second, Muslim youth, far from returning to the traditional Islam of their parents or following the directives of foreign trained imams, ignorant of and hostile toward French society, are actively inventing new forms of religion that are individualistic, modernizing, and a means of adapting to a secular society. In a number of municipalities local politicians have encouraged Islamic associations and mosque construction since, far from endangering Republican unity, this has aided the process of youth integration and disarmed the potential for crime and violence or for *intégrisme*.

Recently this schism has crystallized in the controversy surrounding the Trocme Report. One of the great ironies of government policy, in view of the paranoia attached to external Islamic manipulation of the internal Muslim community, is that it has directly encouraged such foreign links. The secularist refusal to provide government funds to support Muslim religious foundations has driven Muslims to seek external aid from Saudi Arabia, the Gulf States, Pakistan, and elsewhere. Second, Charles Pasqua's attempt to make the Paris Mosque the central, official representative of Islam in France has gone along with Algerian governmental control of the institute.[66]

Modernizers have, however, sought to break such links through the creation of an indigenous and self-supporting French Islam. On November 20, 1996, Etienne Trocme published a report that recommended the establishment of a new Islamic studies center at Strasbourg University. The aim of the course was to foster a "home-grown" and modernizing Islam suited to the needs of the French Muslim community, an Islam *à la française* that would remove the dependency on conservative imams formed in and attached to the interests of foreign states. Kepel immediately went on the attack, claiming that the project was highly dangerous since it was not the function of the Republican university to "transmit a dogma of truth." The Trocme proposal was "an attack on *laicité*," and, as Iran and Egypt had shown, the university was "a preferred terrain for the Islamic fundamentalists."[67]

The constant play by Republican secularists on the threat of fundamentalism and communitarism is a dangerous game since it threatens to delegitimise and marginalize the forms of moderate Islam that are being promoted by those who wish to encourage integration.[68] What we may be seeing in France is a strange gap between current Islamophobia, whipped up by the racist FN or by secularist Socialists and specialists like Kepel, and a deeper level of change toward integration and adaptation. As Kapil aptly notes there is a "lag between the dominant ideology as vectored by politico-intellectual élites and the evolution of society at the grassroots. Intellectuals such as Kepel are simply behind the curve."[69] In this respect the recent contributions of Gilbert Granguillaume, Jocelyne Cesari, and others to the special issue of *Esprit* on "L'Islam d'Europe" provides a healthy sign of a growing awareness of the rich and positive diversity of an Islam in and of France.[70]

Notes

1. See Samuel Huntington's controversial "The Clash of Civilizations?" *Foreign Affairs* 72.3 (1993): 22–49; John L. Esposito, *The Islamic Threat: Myth or Reality?* 2d ed. (Oxford: Oxford University Press, 1995); Fred Halliday, *Islam and the Myth of Confrontation* (London: Tauris, 1995); Edward W. Said, *Covering Islam*, rev. ed. (London: Vintage 1997); Bobby Sayyid, A *Fundamental Fear: Eurocentrism and the Emergence of Islamism* (London: Zed, 1997).
2. See Norman Cohn, *Warrant for Genocide* (London: Serif, 1996).
3. For an insight into such national differences see Christopher T. Husbands, " 'They must obey our laws and customs!': Political Debate About Muslim Assimilability in Great Britain, France, and the Netherlands," in Alec G. Hargreaves and Jeremy Leaman, eds., *Racism, Ethnicity, and Politics in Contemporary Europe* (Aldershot: Elgar, 1995), 115–130. For Britain, in particular, see *Islamophobia, a Challenge for Us All: Report of the Runnymede Trust Commission on British Muslims and Islamophobia* (London: Runnymede Trust, 1997).
4. Simone Bonnafous, *L'Immigration prise aux mots* (Paris: Kime, 1991), 143–154, in a detailed computer analysis of terms employed by the French press between 1974 and 1984 shows an enormous statistical predominance of the word *immigrés*, a very small number of references to *arabes* and *musulmans*, and none to *islam* in any form.
5. Gilles Kepel, *Les banlieues de l'Islam* (Paris: Seuil, 1987), 250–254.
6. Jocelyne Cesari, *Etre musulman en France: Associations, militants et mosquées* (Paris: Karthala, 1994), 126.
7. *Les Temps Modernes* (March-May 1984): 1573.
8. Muslim immigrants were called "Arabs," a stereotype that carried Orientalist assumptions, when in reality many originated in non-Arab societies (Turks, Kabyles or Berbers, Pakistanis . . .).

310

NEIL MACMASTER

9. *Les Temps Modernes* (March-May 1984): 1567.

10. Ibid., 1568, 1574.

11. See the statistics of racist incidents registered by the Ministry of the Interior for 1990–91 in Commission Nationale Consultative des Droits de l'Homme, *1991: La Lutte contre le racisme et la xenophobie* (Paris: Documentation Française, 1992), 17–28; Fausto Giudice, *Arabacides: une chronique française, 1970–1991* (Paris: Découverte, 1992).

12. G. Meynier, L'*Algerie revelée* (Geneva: Droz, 1981).

13. N. Gomar, *L'Émigration algérienne en France* (Paris: Presses Modernes, 1931), 39.

14. A. Pairault, *L'Immigration organisée et l'emploi de la main-d'oeuvre étrangère en France* (Paris: Presses Universitaire de France, 1926), 189; R. Schor, *L'Opinion française et les étrangers en France, 1919–1939* (Paris: Publication de la Sorbonne, 1985).

15. For a detailed treatment see Neil MacMaster, *Colonial Migrants and Racism: Algerians in France, 1900–1962* (London: Macmillan, 1997).

16. N. MacMaster, "The Rue Fondary Murders of 1923 and the Origins of Anti-Arab Racism," in J. Windebank and R. Gunther, eds., *Violence and Conflict in the Politics and Society of Modern France* (Lampeter: Mellen, 1995), 149–160.

17. Gerard Noiriel, *Le creuset français: Histoire de l'immigration, XIXe–XXe siècles* (Paris: Seuil, 1988).

18. Ali Haroun, *La 7e wilaya: La guerre du FLN en France, 1954–1962* (Paris: Seuil, 1986).

19. J-L. Einaudi, *La bataille de Paris: 17 Octobre 1961* (Paris: Seuil, 1991). See also Jim House and Neil MacMaster, "*Une journée portée disparue*: The Paris Massacre of 1961 and Memory," in Kenneth Mouré and Martin S. Alexander, eds., *Crisis and Renewal in France, 1918–1962* (Oxford: Berghahn, 2002), 267–290.

20. C-R. Ageron, 'L'Opinion Française à travers les sondages' in J.-P. Rioux, ed., *La guerre d'Algérie et les français* (Paris: Fayard, 1990), 25–44.

21. Harvey G. Simmons, *The French National Front: The Extremist Challenge to Democracy* (Boulder, Colo.: Westview, 1996), 37–41.

22. On the implantation of the FN in Provence see V. Rogers, "The Front National in Provence-Alpes-Côtes d'Azur: A Case of Institutionalised Racism?" in M. Silverman, ed., *Race, Discourse, and Power in France* (Aldershot: Avebury, 1991), 84–97.

23. Einaudi, *La bataille de Paris*, 284.

24. Y. Castaut, "La flambée raciste de 1973 en France," *Revue Européenne des Migrations Internationales* 9.2 (1993): 61–73.

25. On the background to this shift see Alec G. Hargreaves, "Immigration, Ethnicity, and Political Orientations in France," in Brian Jenkins and Tony Chafer, eds., *France: From the Cold War to the New World Order* (London: Macmillan, 1996), 207–218.

26. Simmons, *The French National Front*, 159.

27. Bonnafous, *L'Immigration prise aux mots*, 269.

28. Noiriel, *Le creuset français*; Stephen Castles, *Here for Good: Western Europe's Ethnic Minorities* (London: Pluto, 1984).

29. A similar turning point was reached in Britain in 1968 when Enoch Powell, through his notorious speeches, shifted the debate from immigration controls to the "breeding power" of blacks and Asians and the threat to the traditional national culture. As with the FN, the solution to such an internal "fifth column" was "repatriation."

30. As a background here note that the American hostage crisis in Tehran had run right through 1980, until the negotiated release on January 20, 1981.

31. See S. Vertovec and C. Peach, *Islam in Europe: The Politics of Religion and Community* (Basingstoke: Macmillan, 1997), 14–18. Muslim numbers are notoriously difficult to calculate and most researchers rely on estimates derived from the numbers of immigrants and their descendants originating from Islamic societies.

32. Kepel, *Les Banlieues de l'Islam*, 227–234, for data and graphs.

33. On the local French opposition to the Mantes mosque during 1979–1980 see Mohamed H. Bekouchi, *Du bled à la ZUP: Problématique culturelle des immigrés dans l'agglomération mantaise* (Paris: L'Harmattan, 1984), 55–64.

34. There exists an enormous and growing body of research on the FN. Useful background information and bibliographies can be found in Jonathan Marcus, *The National Front and French Politics* (London: Macmillan, 1995) and Simmons, *The French National Front*. Particularly useful on the 1983–1984 breakthrough is Martin Schain, "Party Politics, the National Front, and the Construction of Political Legitimacy," in *West European Politics* 10 (April 1987): 229–252.

35. Françoise Gaspard, *Une petite ville en France* (Paris: Gallimard, 1990), 168.

36. On the cultural racism of the FN and the "New Right" see Pierre-André Taguieff, *La force du préjugé* (Paris: Découverte, 1987); Simmons, *The French National Front*, chapter 10; Douglas Johnson, "The New Right in France," in Luciano Cheles et al., eds., *The Far Right in Western and Eastern Europe*, 2d ed. (Harrow: Longman, 1995), 234–244; Gill Seidel, "Culture, Nation, and Race in the British and French New Right," in Ruth Levitas, ed., *The Ideology of the New Right* (Cambridge: Polity, 1986); Anne-Marie Duranton-Crabol, *Visages de la nouvelle droite: La GRECE et son histoire* (Paris: Presses de la fondation rationale des sciences politiques, 1988).

37. See Richard F. Kuisel, "The France We Have Lost: Social, Economic, and Cultural Discontinuities," in Gregory Flynn, ed., *Remaking the Hexagon: The New France in the New Europe* (Boulder: Westview, 1995), 31–48. Nonna Mayer, "Ethnocentrism and the *Front National* Vote in the 1988 French Presidential Election," in Hargreaves and Leaman, *Racism, Ethnicity, and Politics*

in *Contemporary Europe*, 96–109, shows that FN voters have an unusually high fear not only of immigrants and crime but of the world in general as an insecure and dangerous place.

38. Sami Naïr, "Où va la France?" *Le Monde* June 18, 1993, quoted in Christopher T. Husbands, "They must obey our laws and customs!" 121.

39. *Etre français aujourd'hui et demain: Rapport de la Commission de la nationalité* (Paris: Documentation Française, 1988), 1:408.

40. See for example the report of René Backmann and Farid Aïchoune, "Algérie: Quand les barbus mobilisent," *Le Nouvel Observateur*, October 19, 1989, 44–45.

41. On the affair see Antonio Perotti and France Thépaut, "L'affaire du foulard islamiques," *Migrations Société* 2.7 (January 1990): 61–82; Alec G. Hargreaves, *Immigration, "Race," and Ethnicity in Contemporary France* (London: Routledge, 1995), 125–131; François Gaspard and Farhad Khosrokhavar, *Le foulard et la république* (Paris: Découverte, 1995).

42. Elisabeth Badinter, Régis Debray, Alain Finkielkraut, Elisabeth de Fontenay, Catherine Kintzler, "Profs, ne capitulons pas!" *Le Nouvel Observateur*, November 2, 1989, 31–32.

43. There exists a huge literature on the problem estates, but note in particular François Dubet, *La galère: Jeunes en survie* (Paris: Fayard, 1987); Adzil Jazouli, *Les années banlieues* (Paris: Seuil, 1992); Wieviorka, *La France raciste* (Paris: Seuil, 1992); Pierre Bourdieu, *La misère du monde* (Paris: Seuil, 1993); Azouz Begag, *Espace et exclusion* (Paris: L'Harmattan, 1995).

44. See Anne Power, *Hovels to High Rise: State Housing in Europe Since 1850* (London: Routledge, 1993), 74–80; Hubert Dubedout, *Ensemble refaire la ville* (Paris: Documentation Française, 1983).

45. See Catherine Wihtol de Wenden, "Les beurs et la guerre" *Esprit*, no. 5 (1991): 102–107; Gilles Kepel, *Allah in the West* (Cambridge: Polity, 1997), 204–206.

46. On the network see Catherine Erhel and Renaud de La Baume, *Le procès d'un réseau islamiste* (Paris: Albin Michel, 1997).

47. *Le Monde*, October 7, 1995, pp. 10–11; Lahouair Addi, "Quoting an Arab," *Times Higher Education Supplement*, November 10, 1995: 18; Farhad Khosrokhavar, *L'islam des jeunes* (Paris: Flammarion, 1997), 247–257.

48. *Le Nouvel Observateur*, April 4, 1996, 37; August 15, 1996, 46–48.

49. Khosrokhavar, *L'islam des jeunes*, especially parts 3 and 4.

50. See Alain Battegay and Ahmed Boubeker, *Les Images Publiques de l'Immigration* (Paris: L'Harmattan, 1993); Husbands, " 'They must obey our laws and customs!' 123–126.

51. See Teun A. Van Dijk, *Racism and the Press* (London: Routledge, 1991), chapter 3, on the strategic and cognitive functions of the headline in activating the readers' relevant knowledge in memory and influencing the way in which the main text or "small print" is interpreted.

52. *Le Nouvel Observateur*, August 31, 1995. See, for another example, *Le Nouvel Observateur*, no.1641 (April 1996), special issue on "The New Fanatics," which includes an image of an armed Muslim and the caption "The Madmen of Allah."

53. *L'Express*, September 21, 1995.

54. See *L'Express*, May 30, 1996, which has a special issue cover of the bearded Djamel Zitouni, full-face as in a police identity photograph, and the caption "The Islamic fundamentalist who leads the war against France."

55. Gaspard and Khosrokhavar, *Le foulard et la république*, 29–30.

56. *Le Nouvel Observateur*, February 7, 1986.

57. *L'Express*, November 24, 1994. For some further examples see the covers of *Le Nouvel Observateur* for October 5, 1989, October 26, 1989, November 2, 1989, September 22, 1994, February 22, 1996, January 15, 1998.

58. For a fuller treatment of this issue see Neil MacMaster and Toni Lewis, "Orientalism: From Unveiling to Hyperveiling," *Journal of European Studies* 27 (1998): 121–135.

59. See Said, *Covering Islam*.

60. Gilles Kepel's main works are *The Prophet and Pharaoh: Muslim Extremism in Egypt* (London: Al Saqi, 1985); *Les banlieues de l'Islam*; *The Revenge of God: The Resurgence of Islam, Christianity, and Judaism in the Modern World* (Cambridge: Polity, 1993); and *Allah in the West: Islamic Movements in America and Europe* (Cambridge: Polity, 1997). For a biographical note by Dominique Dhombres see *Le Monde*, February 11, 1997.

61. Hilton Obenzinger review in *Middle East Report* (March-April 1995): 58.

62. Kepel, *Allah in the West*, 3.

63. For a trenchant critique of *Allah in the West* see Arun Kapil, "On Islam in the West and Muslims in France: Views from the Hexagon," *Third World Quarterly*, 18.2 (1977): 377–389.

64. Kepel, *Allah in the West*, 237.

65. Jocelyne Cesari, *Être musulman en France: Associations, militants et mosquées* (Paris: Karthala, 1994); Khosrokhavar, *L'islam des jeunes*.

66. Cesari, *Être musulman en France*, 138–139, 142.

67. *Le Monde*, December 3, 1996, 15; see the response by Sadek Sellam in *Le Monde*, January 13, 1997, 11; see also the *Times Higher Education Supplement*, December 20, 1996, 8.

68. Jim House, "Muslim Communities in France," in Gerd Nonneman et al., eds., *Muslim Communities in the New Europe* (Reading: Ithaca, 1996), 228.

69. Kapil, "On Islam in the West and Muslims in France," 389.

70. "L'Islam d'Europe," *Esprit*, no. 1 (1998), 5–135 (special issue).

The Nationalist Serbian Intellectuals and Islam: Defining and Eliminating a Muslim Community

Norman Cigar

Recent events in Bosnia-Herzegovina provide significant material for a case study on the impact that external images of Islam can have on Muslims as a community and as individuals.[1] Perhaps there was no more striking aspect in this process of creating images than the role that Serb intellectuals played as they exercised their craft of developing and disseminating knowledge and engaged in political activity. Their special position in society enabled the latter to serve as a guide to their fellow Serbs and, as this essay will seek to show, their impact has been felt strongly in creating images, forming attitudes, and crafting proposals for action against the Muslims of Bosnia, or Bosniaks, and ultimately in their major role in the creation of the policy of genocide.

In particular, these intellectuals have been instrumental in establishing and cementing an in-group/out-group dichotomy between the Muslims and the Serbs based on stereotypes, a factor which has been central to forming the environment and establishing legitimacy for much of the violence that occurred. In those cases where, as individuals, they have become part of the state machinery that has implemented policy, intellectuals have been direct agents of violence. But even when not the direct "cause" of what befell the Muslims of Bosnia, these intellectuals nevertheless have been intimately linked to what happened by setting the agenda, shaping public opinion, and legitimating state policies for "ethnic cleansing."

To be sure, with regard to the Muslims as well as to other war-related matters, there have been Serb intellectuals who have stood publicly against what they viewed as nationalist excesses and even racism—something that often required considerable courage in the charged atmosphere of the times.[2] Reactions against those who opposed violence and who were unwilling to join in attacks on the Muslims were often harsh, with frequent accusations of treason by fellow intellectuals or government officials.[3] Despite their moral stand, such voices—however distinguished—represented a minority view among intellectuals. The focus here, rather, will be on those "nationalist" intellectuals who represented the majority and who had a determining impact on policy. In part the influence of the latter was magnified by their alliance—at least in the early days—with the state and the Serbian Orthodox Church, which brought them exposure in the state-controlled media and political backing both in Serbia and in Serbian-controlled Bosnia. In particular the fact that no important Serbian institution, such as the Church or the major opposition political parties, took a critical stand against the anti-Islamic campaigns facilitated the work of those nationalist intellectuals who were the most hostile to the Muslim community. Although the Muslims were not the nationalist intellectuals' only target as the former Yugoslavia moved toward disintegration—and at times not even their main concern—once political energies focused on Bosnia the Muslims quickly became a dominant preoccupation for these intellectuals.

Defining Serbia's Nationalist Intellectuals

The unit of analysis here, the nationalist Serb intellectuals, is a subset (albeit a majority) of the "intellectuals" and, despite sharing a basic outlook, this too is an amorphous category. For the purposes of this study, Eva Etzioni-Halevy's working definition of intellectuals as "persons who are professionally engaged in the creation, elaboration, and dissemination of theoretical knowledge, ideas, and symbols" will be used.[4] As such, they are not a class or corporate body, but more an elite with considerable moral authority, "a group of people inordinately influential in shaping one or more areas of social life."[5] Traditionally, their power or impact on policy is not direct but, rather, they may influence policy decisions "by molding the climate of ideas and the general perspectives, or defining the general situation in whose framework policy decisions are made," although in this case many did enter the political arena directly.[6] While some bodies, such as the Serbian Academy of Arts and Sciences (SANU) or the Writers' Union of Serbia did speak on occasion as organizations and carried weight as such, nationalist Serb

intellectuals ordinarily exerted their influence as individuals, relying on
their personal academic or literary standing, or media and political connections, and thus provide, as individuals, the most appropriate unit of analysis
for this study. In some ways the categories for inclusion as intellectuals may
be arbitrary and vary from society to society and, in this case, "intellectuals"
will encompass such categories as academics (including orientalists—specialized scholars of Islam), writers, and artists, but not such professionals as
doctors, engineers, lawyers, journalists, or the clergy. The distinction at
times may be arbitrary, as in the case of senior clerics of the Serbian Orthodox Church or members of the military, many of whom have impressive
academic backgrounds and are scholars in their own right. However, the latter, working within separate and distinct hierarchies, reflect significantly distinct dynamics. Some medical doctors and psychiatrists who wrote on political and social matters, moreover, have been included. Membership in the
160-strong SANU was the ultimate peer recognition bestowed for intellectual achievement, but acceptance as an intellectual could also be granted to
lesser-ranking intellectuals by the state or by other institutions. Thus, orientalist scholar Miroljub Jevtić (a professor in Belgrade University's Political
Science Department) and writer Dragoš Kalajić, were recognized as worthy
to sit on the editorial board of *Vojno delo*, a journal published by the General Staff of the Yugoslav Army, while the Journalists' Union of Serbia
awarded its annual prize in 1995 to Dragoš Kalajić for his "patient and scholarly pointing out of all the traps of the New World Order." The scope here
will extend both to intellectuals in Serbia itself and in the Serb community
in neighboring republics of the former Yugoslavia.

The Intellectuals' Theoretical Underpinnings

In analytical terms the nationalist Serb intellectuals' participation in the
process of developing and spreading ideas and images about Islam and the
Muslims reflects elements of all three main forms in which racism traditionally has been embodied: the classical (expressed in terms of real or imagined
biological differences), the realistic group conflict theory (which focuses on
real or imagined threats posed by an out-group to individuals), and "symbolic racism" (a sociocultural approach based on the perceived transgression
of the in-group's traditional values).[7] These intellectuals have argued in
terms both of a combined perceived threat to the in-group (the Serbs) in

competition for scarce resources as well in terms of "abstract ideological symbols and symbolic behaviors" in an approach combining a discourse in both culture and Realpolitik.[8] In practical terms the classical biological and cultural approaches have often also intersected, with all three approaches containing elements of both biology and culture as discriminatory boundary markers, as the difference between these approaches was more one of emphasis varying over time or individual than one of essence.[9] In effect, for many nationalist Serb intellectuals *culture* or *mentality* became code words for an immutable, ascriptive, and communal inheritance with all of the permanent characteristics one would associate with biological traits and, at times, these intellectuals freely crossed the line into biologically based arguments when dealing with communal groupings. As writer Dragoš Kalajić asserted, local Muslims were only "an unconscious and spontaneous expression of pseudo-Arab culture" and the result of a "genetic predetermination and predisposition," claiming to see the influence of "a special gene of the Ottoman soldiery."[10] Likewise, speaking of the Bosniak Muslims, Bosnian Serb novelist Vojislav Lubarda established a link between the present and "some genetic characteristics which they have acquired over the centuries, that is habits which have become instincts."[11] Perhaps the most prominent proponent of a genetic explanation for the Muslims' alleged differences, deviant behavior, and inferiority was Biljana Plavšić, who eventually became leader of the Bosnian Serb entity and returned frequently to this theme, based on her training and work as a medical researcher.[12]

The Intellectuals and Political Engagement

Intellectuals have traditionally been held in high regard in Serbian society. In modern times Serb intellectuals have almost invariably been the originators and most consistent proponents of a Serbian national agenda designed to create a Greater Serbia. In that sense intellectuals have provided a thread of continuity, creating the vision and concrete programs in support of expansion, whether in the form of the nineteenth-century *Načertanije* (The Plan), Vasa Čubrilović's interwar plan to remove the Albanians from Kosovo, the World War II plan for a "Homogeneous Serbia," Čubrilović's postwar plan to expel the minorities from Yugoslavia, and, finally, SANU's controversial 1986 *Serbian Memorandum*.[13] Even during the Communist period intellectuals had increasingly set the tone for *civil* society in a system bounded largely by the state, which controlled the economy, media, cultural institutions, and the educational system, quite apart from its monopoly over the political environment. Only the intellectuals—and to an extent the Serbian Orthodox Church—had been able to carve a niche outside the official system, enjoying autonomy denied to most of their fellow citizens, and developed a reputation—not always deserved—of being dissidents. In actual fact, as was highlighted with the breakup of Yugoslavia, Serb intellectuals are a diverse lot, ranging along the entire ideological spectrum, from orthodox Communists to democrats to right-wing nationalists.

The focus here will be on intellectuals in their "intellectual" role, that is on how they developed, propagated, or legitimated their ideas—verbally or in their writings—rather than on their strictly political activity. However, one cannot always make a clear distinction between the intellectual and political arenas for, in many instances, major and minor nationalist intellectuals were very much involved directly in politics and often became significant political players in their own right, with their direct impact on policy implementation often far eclipsing their scholarly achievements. Among the best known in this category was the Montenegrin-born poet and psychiatrist Radovan Karadžić, who was to become the leader of Bosnia's Serbian Democratic Party and the Bosnian Serb entity's president, but there have been numerous others in the front ranks of everyday politics.[14] Mira Marković, Slobodan Milošević's wife and a university professor, notably, used her networks within academia to help forge an alliance between the intellectuals and her husband as he made a bid for political power and herself later became head of the orthodox Communist party, the Union of Communists-Movement for Yugoslavia (SK-PJ).[15] In addition, many other intellectuals across the political spectrum became at least second-tier players in the political system.[16] This dual role has often made the distinction between the categories of intellectuals and politicians hazy, but it also underlines the impact that intellectuals have had on influencing both the intellectual environment and concrete policies since the mid-1980s, whether by their scholarship or by direct participation in political life.[17]

Setting: The Out-group–In-group Environment

The shaping of Serb views about the Muslims has to be seen within a broader framework of out-group–in-group differentiation that began to assert itself by the early 1980s, following Tito's death. At that time nationalist Serb intellectuals, hoping to refashion Serbia's political system and expecting to play a greater role in society, became active in reinterpreting the sociopolitical situation in terms of communal relations, thereby reinforcing and even inventing stereotypes of the non-Serbs, including those relating to the Muslims.[18] Initially, works of fiction and discussions in narrow intellectual and church circles provided the principal mediums for the development of ideas about Islam and the local Muslim community. During this early phase writer Vuk Drašković, author of novels with Muslim-related themes such as *Sudija* [Judge] (1981), *Nož* [Knife] (1982), and *Molitva I* [Prayer 1] (1985), was perhaps the most popular and influential in disseminating what became widespread stereotypical profiles. For example, in his best-known, novel, *Nož*—reprinted seven times and now being made into a movie—World War II provides the background for presenting Muslims almost invariably as treacherous, cold-blooded murderers who betrayed their ethnic roots by converting centuries earlier to Islam, while the Serb characters all appear, in counterpoint, to be heroic and long-suffering.

This process of community stereotyping gathered force with the rise of Milošević within Serbia's League of Communists—as the ruling Serbian Communist Party was called—and his adoption of the nationalists' program in the late 1980s as part of a strategy to survive by developing a new base of legitimacy in order to avoid the fate of other Communist regimes throughout the Eastern bloc. As a result, the full weight of the government became engaged in this effort, giving rise to a systemic symbiosis with the nationalist intellectuals. Specifically, the revived goal of establishing a Greater Serbia—or "all Serbs in a single state"—as the proposed grand strategy raised the dilemma of how to manage with large non-Serb populations that were seen as an obstruction to success by their very presence. As a corollary the state promoted the cohesiveness of the in-group Serbs, both as a way to direct antigovernment discontent outward and to facilitate achieving the necessary territorial expansion enshrined as the national strategy. In some ways the intellectuals benefited from the fact that their ideas coincided with the interests of Serbia's political, military, and clerical leaders, since the ideas the nationalist intellectuals advanced often specifically legitimized the nationalist policies that they and other elites wanted to implement against the Muslims in pursuit of their concrete political objectives.

That intellectuals were asked so frequently by the Belgrade and Bosnian Serb authorities and state-controlled media to explain—and justify—to the public the government's official policy toward the Muslims, moreover, was a clear indication of the government's perception of the utility of such expert support and of the expectation that such cooperation would be readily forth-coming. Conversely, state support was a significant factor enhancing the impact of the nationalist intellectuals, as this enabled them to reach a wider audience through the media and public rallies than would otherwise have been the case. Typically, the Yugoslav Army weekly *Vojska* (Belgrade) endorsed Miroljub Jevtić's anti-Islamic tract *Islam i geopolitička logika* [Islam and Geopolitical Logic) and only regretted that it had not been avail-able sooner: "One is forced to conclude that a book has just been published whose information, education, and propaganda effect would have been total had it appeared, let us say, at least two years sooner. However, that does not reduce its substantive and historical value."[19]

The new wave of Serbian nationalism that emerged in the 1980s, to be sure, directed its attention toward all those communities that, by their physi-cal presence, were seen to stand in the way of the goal of a Greater Serbia and of what the Serb elites saw as their community's rightful place in the world. However, anti-Islamic antipathy carried with it a particular intensity, given the assumed obstacle the Muslim community represented to Serbian goals because of its size and location and the fact that its role was central in determining whether or not Bosnia-Herzegovina would be absorbed by Ser-bia. Although it was the Albanian community in Kosovo, most of which is also Muslim, that had been the principal target initially, the strong Islamic component of the discourse in Belgrade on the Albanian question also served to prepare the groundwork for the time when the primary focus of effort was to shift to the Muslims of Bosnia-Herzegovina. Significantly, at a meeting of Serb poets in 1988, a resolution was passed that expressed the threat in cultural terms, alleging that the "Albanian nationalists" in Kosovo "threaten to destroy everything that the human spirit has created over the centuries, everything that artistic hands have built, everything that repre-sents human civilization in that territory."[20]

Defining Islam and the Bosnian Muslims

At base what nationalist Serb intellectuals did was to define and interpret Islam from their own perspective as a religion, a culture, an ethnicity, a polit-ical agenda, or even as "genes," depending on their specific policy objec-

tives. The result was to establish or reinforce views about the Bosnian Muslims that were likely to evoke certain desired responses within the in-
group—the Serb community—and thereby fostered, and to a significant
degree created, the fatal salience of in-group–out-group images. Psychiatrist
and Serb nationalist leader Jovan Rašković especially, through his scholarly
writings and frequent public appearances, contributed to shaping such attitudes when he invested the communal group as a valid focus of attention
and repository of common characteristics. He thereby helped to systematize,
compartmentalize, and deindividualize the image of all those from the Muslim community. Rašković had inter alia, typecast the Muslims in psychiatric
terms as being burdened by "rectal frustrations" and, based on that, attributed negative traits to them. According to Rašković:

> I have determined that the Muslims have a fixation on the rectal phase
> . . . That is a personality which is prone to amass property, to rule as a
> boss, to judge people by their property and by how much money they
> have made, by their success in society, and so on. Also characteristic of
> this phase is a component of aggressiveness, fastidiousness, and clean-
> liness, which in its extreme form is manifested also when, in accor-
> dance with Muslim regulations and obligations, it is necessary to
> maintain the special hygiene of the lower intestine.[21]

His daughter Sanda Rašković, herself a psychiatrist, confirmed her late
father's conscious intent of using communal groups as his unit of analysis:
"He did not speak of Croats as individuals, or of Serbs as individuals, or of
Muslims as individuals. He spoke only of the behavior of groups throughout
history. . . . I understood him within that context, just as we Serbs have
always felt the need to be good, to be unifiers, and to forget the evil that has
been perpetrated against us."[22] Most Serb intellectuals cast Islam as the
polar negative—alien, backward, morally deficient, and aggressive—in
opposition to everything positive found in Serbian culture. The bleak portrayal of the Muslims that had begun in the 1980s was degraded even further
once actual fighting erupted in Bosnia in 1992 and has continued to a
significant degree in the same vein until the present. In many ways the treatment received by Islam and the Muslims at the hands of Serbia's nationalist
intellectuals has conformed very much to that common to traditional "Orientalism." At base, as Edward Said pointed out in his pioneering work on
the phenomenon, this is a remarkably stark and implications-laden division

into "them" and "us."[23] By encouraging the reification and isolation of the entire Muslim community at the hands of the intellectuals, any steps Belgrade might subsequently take against the Muslims in pursuit of its political goals would be more likely to acquire legitimacy and popular support. Even in criticizing Vojislav Šešelj for his positions when he was at odds with her husband, Mira Marković only compounded the problem by using negative stereotypes of her own, as she claimed that "no, Šešelj is not a Serb. He is a Turk, in the most primitive historical edition," calling him "this reincarnated Turk" as an insult.[24]

Muslims as a Moral Aberration

A key strand of the intellectuals' image creation focused on the idea that Muslims transgressed accepted values by belonging to an exotic and alien religion and culture. As a corollary the local Muslims—whom most Serb intellectuals usually called "Turks," thus allegedly had less legitimacy to live in Bosnia-Herzegovina than did the Serbs, despite the fact that, in reality, the Muslims are very much descendants of the autochtonous population, whether in Bosnia, the Sandžak, or Kosovo.[25]

In the late 1980s, typically, a Serbian scholar, Aleksandar Popović, then teaching in Paris, wrote a pamphlet published in Belgrade in order to, as he said, inform the "educated public" about Islam. He saw this as a difficult task because, or so he claimed, Islam is "a totalitarian system, one whose totalitarianism far exceeds that which a well-intentioned and uninformed Western mind could comprehend or imagine.[26] In general, such intellectuals were concerned with rejecting what they saw as the attempt by the Muslims in Bosnia to claim that they too were a European people, with one scholar calling such a notion, "naturally, a notorious absurdity."[27] Likewise, another Serbian scholar, Nada Todorov, purported to see the Muslims in Bosnia-Herzegovina as motivated by their "Islamic way of life, which has nothing in common with European civilization."[28] Allegedly, the focus of the Muslims' loyalties, based on religion, was abroad in the Middle East, not where they lived. As Bosnian Serb novelist Vojislav Lubarda, quoting from one of his own works, claimed of the Muslims, "They eat and defecate here, but they bow down for prayer over there."[29] Significantly, Milan Komnenić, later to become a high-ranking official in the Serb Renewal Movement, advised Muslim Albanians to choose Belgrade (which he equates to Europe) instead of the "Islamicized Orient."[30]

Conversely, nationalist Serb intellectuals have also been prone to make sweeping statements as to the unacknowledged or unconscious Serbian ethnicity of the Muslims (as well as of most of their other neighbors). Usually, nationalist Serb intellectuals insisted that the Muslims were really Serbs who had abandoned their original faith and identity, notwithstanding the absence of a scholarly basis for such a claim. Vuk Drašković, typically, insisted that "it is a historical fact that the vast majority of the Muslims are ethnically Serb . . . never having lost either the Serbian language nor many of their national traditions" and that in Bosnia "the vast majority of Muslims are of Serb ethnicity."[31] The Bosnian Muslims, thus, were deemed not to have a valid, enduring, identity of their own. Typically, SANU members spoke of their "artificial identity," while writer Momčilo Selić concluded that "it is painful to be in the Muslims' skins, because they do not know what they are."[32]

For historian Slavenko Terzić, the Muslims of Bosnia and the neighboring province of Sandžak, which Serbia had annexed in 1913, "are part of the Serbian people," while their "religious specificity" served as the basis for what he claims is a "separate ideology" invented by Austria, Germany, and the U.S. for political ends.[33] Equating power with natural right, philosopher Zoran Djindjić (subsequently president of the Democratic Party—Demokratska stranka—and premier of post-Milošević Serbia) claimed that the Muslims had no right to be a distinct people unless they had the power to enforce their claim. Otherwise, "if they do not have the power to do that, then surely they do not have a legitimate right either [to be a distinct people]."[34]

The nationalist Serb intellectuals' portrayal of the Muslims' putative identity, however, presented them with a dilemma. If their arguments about the Bosnian Muslims' origins were accepted, the question was how then to reconcile that with the alien image and ruthless policies that they were promoting toward the Muslim community. By and large, these intellectuals resolved the internal dissonance by maintaining that although the Muslims were indeed, or so they claimed, Serbs, they had betrayed their roots and were therefore morally deficient and treacherous, deserving of harsh treatment.[35] Indeed, the local Muslims were said to have at least an unconscious memory of their alleged roots and of their "betrayal," which was seen as an additional moral stigma beyond that common to all adherents of Islam, a misdeed that today was said to manifest itself in such characteristics as duplicity and hatred for everything Serbian. One writer, Dragoš Kalajić, even equated local Muslims to "transvestites" for having embraced Islam centuries earlier. Claiming that they had converted to Islam rather than resisting, he sneered that

> it is appropriate to point out that effeminacy and symbolic or actual homosexuality are not the only means by which to escape from a manly nature that is threatened with violence, terror or death. The Serbian experience shows that there are many other ways of avoiding duty and responsibility stemming from too onerous a fate, which history has imposed on the Serbs. Historically, the first and easiest path of avoidance from unavoidable fate was actually opened up by the Ottoman occupation ... [and] drove many Serbs along the road to treachery.[36]

The Muslims' supposed betrayal of their origins was a source of special opprobrium and was used to depict Muslims as morally inferior and as lacking a true identity.[37] Serb observers even passed judgement on the alleged lack of authenticity of the local Muslims' practice of Islam. For example, as Karadžić saw it, the Bosnians were not good Muslims because of the "strong Serbian element in their souls, in their thoughts and actions, and the Serbian national stamp. They are forced to overcome this by an aggressive and false Islam." In fact, Karadžić claimed to see an "internal struggle against the remains of Serbianness and Orthodoxy" within Bosnian Muslims and judged that "that is not authentic Islam and can never be, since it is not directed toward their God, but is rather directed above all against something [i.e., Serbianness and Orthodoxy]. Their identity is determined in negative terms."[38] Nationalist Serb intellectuals seemed particularly uncomfortable whenever Muslims failed to conform to the stereotypes embodied in the templates constructed for them. For example, one Serb writer was indignant that the Bosnian government had adopted the historic fleur-de-lis for its flag and coat of arms instead of some "Islamic" symbol, since that did not fit the portrayal of wanting to establish an Islamic state, and he accused the Muslims of pilfering a "Christian" symbol and of having no authentic identity of their own, holding that this showed their "appropriation of others' values as their own achievements." He concluded, "Beginning with the trademark of a people, which gave itself its name, the key characteristics of a [Muslim] nation do not exist. More exactly, not a single one exists. The fleur-de-lis, as the symbol of Izetbegović's fictive state, assuredly is not the most felicitous pictorial solution of the false Muslim picture of independence and self-confidence."[39]

Islam as Inferior and Immoral

Not only was Islam alien, but it was also portrayed as morally deficient and backward. Much as European orientalists of an earlier era had done, their Serbian counterparts taxed Islam with being retrograde and the root cause of a threat to "modern civilization," both in general terms and, specifically, to Serbia. For some, a moral inferiority inherent in Islam itself was the problem. Writer Momčilo Selić, for example, held that "when we speak of Islam, that is not a religion at all, as it cannot in any way stand up to a comparison with Christianity in theological, philosophical, or any other terms. This is a cartoon version of Christianity, and anyone who accepted it was either corrupt or stupid. . . . Western experts agree with this."[40] For Miroljub Jevtić, Islam supposedly mandates the banning of tourism, sports, and going to cafés where alcohol is served, thus inevitably leading to xenophobia and to "one hundred percent segregation."[41] Any accusation that could serve to denigrate Islam and isolate the Muslims seemed fair game. Professor Nada Todorov, for example, claimed that "in Islamic teaching, no woman has a soul, but instead serves only to satisfy a man's needs and to serve him."[42] Local Muslims were said to be particularly reprehensible. Dragoš Kalajić, for example, emphasized that local Muslims, in particular, allegedly exhibit a long list of inherited character flaws, such as propensity to theft, a lack of ethics, laziness, authoritarianism, a "neoprimitive lust for power," and even discomfort with wearing European clothing. Local Muslims, he continued, are supposedly incapable of ruling themselves, since, like their "desert ancestors," they will only use "nomadic-robber means." When in power, local Muslims, according to Kalajić, will plunder, "not in the least showing any of the shame that is characteristic for a European in a similar situation." Moreover, "simply put, the pseudo-Arab is not capable of understanding the essence of one of the basic traits of the European, namely the institution of the uniqueness of personal freedom that is fundamentally above any collectivity."[43]

As was true about most non-Serb nations in the former Yugoslavia, the Muslims were depicted as transitory flotsam and jetsam who were unable to set up a state of their own and therefore doomed to disappear. For example, historian Milorad Ekmečić held that "the American formula that an independent state be created on the basis of a fictitious Bosniak [Muslim] nation is also impossible."[44] The Serbs, on the other hand, were seen as the naturally dominant group embodying all the positive elements.[45] At the same time, however, nationalist Serb intellectuals portrayed their own people as maligned, cheated, and threatened, and reproached others as unwilling to recognize the Serbs' "rightful position."

For Radovan Karadžić, Islam in Bosnia was especially debased.[46] Karadžić, in fact, promoted a stark moral duality between Serbs and Muslims, casting the alleged differences in cultural terms. In a speech delivered in Trebinie in 1995, he drew a parallel with Homer's differentiation between Asiatic collectivism and European individualism to explain events in Bosnia:

> Already the difference we were discussing that today characterizes the clash of civilizations in the Balkans as well was laid out there perfectly. In contrast to the Muslim, who cannot imagine a life outside his collective community [kolektiv] and who was born for collectivism, the Serb is a [distinct] personality, a persona, an owner, independent and sovereign.[47]

The significant number of intellectuals who joined the Bosnian Serb leadership was itself used as further proof of the cultural superiority of the Serbs over the local Muslims. As Miroslav Toholj argued, "The Serbs in Bosnia have the greatest concentration of academic training within their political leadership. . . . Is this the 'uncivilized band of crazies,' which is attacking 'the poor civilized Muslims,' among whom, incidentally 50 percent lack the most elementary level of literacy?"[48]

Islam and the Muslims as the Threat

Related to the alleged exoticism and inferiority of Islam was what would become a key element of the nationalist Serb intellectuals' message, namely, that the Muslims represented an imminent and dangerous threat to the Serbs as individuals and as a community. As such, these intellectuals sought to alert their countrymen of the potential danger by focusing on this facet of the situation and by suggesting policies to counter what they claimed was a conspiracy by the Muslims against the Serbs.

Some made theoretical distinctions between "genuine" Islam and what they termed "fundamentalists" or "fanatics" to show their good faith and lack of prejudice. Thus, writer Gojko Djogo urged that "we must liberate the Neretva Valley and the enclaves in Eastern Bosnia not from the Muslims but from the madmen infected by the Asiatic plague who hold a knife at our back."[49] In practice such distinctions had little meaning, as nationalist Serb intellectuals automatically equated virtually all Muslims with religious and political extremism. Although clearly not all Muslims in Bosnia-Herzegovina were religiously observant (including many who have been members of the Communist Party), Serb intellectuals stretched their definition of "fundamentalism" to cover a wide area. By broadening the term, they could put any political activity whatsoever involving Muslims, or even simple ethnicity, under this rubric. Miroljub Jevtić, for example, spoke of "secular Islamic fundamentalism" and "Communist Islam," which could encompass anyone and everyone who is in any way a Muslim, as valid targets for censure.[50] For Vojislav Šešelj, even Hamdija Požderac, a secular Muslim politician who had been part of the former Communist leadership, fit in this category, despite the fact that he was married to a Serb and had given his children Serbian names.[51] Others, such as poet Ljubomir Zuković, argued more openly that all Muslims were inevitably the same:

The Turkish convert must act as a Turk
And keep company with loathsome Satan.
It is our very great illusion
That there is any difference between them:
Every Bosnian *balija* [pejorative term for Muslim]
Dreams the same dream as Alija [Izetbegović].[52]

To a great extent the very essence of Islam was interpreted as an immutable and undifferentiated abstraction that in and of itself supposedly constituted a threat. Muslims were portrayed as inherently violent, and many intellectuals held that the explanation was to be found in Islam itself and in its culture. Novelist Vojislav Lubarda, for example, argued that "the fundamentalists" were "bloodthirsty" and responsible for "today's many brutal crimes against Serb noncombatants—butchering women and children, gouging out eyes, flaying skin from living people, and so on." Lubarda also justified a harsh policy toward Muslims by stressing that they allegedly only understood force, as in his 1993 statement: "Let me mention just two per-

sonal characteristics that are true of the majority of Muslims: when faced by
that which is stronger (such as a stronger man or a stronger force), they
become as docile as lambs and submissive beyond words. However, their
nature changes as soon as they sense that they are the stronger ones and that
power is in their hands, whereupon they become insatiably ruthless."[53]
Miroljub Jevtić's interpretation of why the Muslims were supposedly so
ready to kill others also focused on their religious upbringing. Writing in the
press in late 1993, he explained:

> Islam clearly prescribes that its faithful must bring a victim to Allah.
> That animal victim is a ram, which is slaughtered ritually, so that its
> blood gushes out all over. If the members of the Islamic civilization
> become used from their childhood to seeing how a lamb—which is
> everyone's favorite animal—is slaughtered, then it is clear that a per-
> son who partakes in the Islamic worldview becomes easily accustomed
> to the shedding of blood in a very brutal fashion. It is not a great step to
> go from killing animals to killing human beings.[54]

What is more, nationalist Serb intellectuals as a matter of course claimed
that hostility to the Serbs, to Western culture, and to Christianity were
already preprogrammed by the Muslims' culture, history, and religion.
Often, the present was seen as a mechanical extrapolation of the past, based
on a literal reading of the Qur'an and a linear application of past Islamic history to today's society. A tendentious interpretation of the Qur'an, in particular, was often used as proof of Muslim aggressiveness and antipathy toward
all non-Muslims. At a conference in 1993, ironically focused on religious tolerance, Darko Tanasković proposed, based on his interpretation of early
Islamic texts, that for Islam "permanent peace with members of other religions is impossible." Islam's "permanent war restricts the parameters of tolerance," he added.[55]

As a result, conflict was seen as unavoidable, for "every Muslim feels closer
today to a shaykh in Saudi Arabia than to a Serb from his neighborhood. To
such people we must say, 'You wanted war, and now you have it.'"[56] Already by
the 1980s nationalist Serb intellectuals purported to see a conscious and systematic conspiracy to subvert and destroy Serbia and the Serbian Orthodox
religion. For example, according to Miroljub Jevtić, "the assumption is completely mistaken that the Republika Srpska could have a Muslim minority on
its territory that would not constitute a threat to the latter."[57]

Islam was depicted as an international monolith and an aggressive faith, political program, and community that are the same around the world. As part of their scheme, Muslims worldwide were alleged to be acting in collusion in a conspiracy against the West and, in particular, against the Serbs. Culprits abroad, ranging from nameless Islamic forces to specific actors such as Saudi Arabia, supposedly aided and abetted the local Muslims. Turkey, in particular, was accused of wanting to revive the Ottoman Empire, while Islam and Pan-Turkism were often treated as the same phenomenon for greater effect. In practical terms, nationalist Serb intellectuals sought to link the Muslims of Bosnia-Herzegovina with an undifferentiated homogeneous Islam worldwide. They lumped together all conflicts in which Muslims were involved—whether in the Philippines, Azerbaidzhan, or Kashmir—and stressed that it was a seamless phenomenon of which Bosnia-Herzegovina was an integral link.

Beyond that, the nationalist intellectuals sought to portray the Serbs' "Muslim problem" as part of a broader, unified, Muslim threat applicable to the entire West, and they saw as their mission to warn what they claimed was an unsuspecting West. In an apparent attempt to win over the sympathies and support of the West, as well as perhaps to give the Serbs a feeling of undertaking, unselfishly, a noble mission on behalf of a wider world, the local Islamic threat was often portrayed as a prelude to a new invasion of Europe and the destruction of Western civilization as a whole. Radovan Karadžić, for example, warned that "they [i.e., the Muslims] have dark schemes, wishing to make Bosnia a springboard for Islamic penetration in Europe. This is as plain as a pikestaff."[58]

For his part, Vojin Dabić, professor of contemporary history at Belgrade University, pointed to the Muslim communities in Great Britain, Italy, and France, countries that are in his view "flooded" and "suffocated" by Muslims, and sought to gain the Western countries' sympathy, since, as he argued, Serbia was only trying to deal with the same problem.[59] In fact, another scholar, Radoslav Stojanović, a professor at Belgrade University's Law School and a member of the executive council of one of the opposition parties (the Serbian Democratic Party—Srpska Demokratska Stranka), was especially optimistic about the convergence of Serbian and Western interests toward the Muslims. He believed that the West's real priority in becoming active in Bosnia-Herzegovina was to stop "Islamic fundamentalism," and he therefore fretted that the Serbs, by not understanding this, had missed their chance to carve out an even larger Serbian zone of control, allegedly with at least the passive consent of the West. He regretted that, "unfortunately, the Serbian government in both Bosnia and Serbia was unable to comprehend one thing: that the West was far more interested in preventing the creation of a Muslim state in Bosnia than in preventing the creation even of a Greater Serbia." This, as he saw it, was true because even a Greater Serbia would not threaten Europe, "Whereas a Muslim state in the Balkans, that is in Europe, could become the stronghold of the most extreme Islamic fundamentalism, and a state to which money would flow from the most extreme Islamic countries. Such a state could do horrible things in Europe."[60] Yet, by an "Islamic" state what these intellectuals meant was not one ruled by a government inspired by political Islam or headed by Islamists, which is a changeable variable dependant on specific circumstances, but simply a state in which the majority of the population would be Muslims, as in contemporary Albania, which is an ascriptive constant. That is, simply being Muslim by birth, irrespective of political orientation, was in itself an inadmissible threat, and sufficient justification for condemnation and suppression.

Ultimately, many of these intellectuals cast themselves in the role of protecting Europe from Islam and viewed their mission as a noble one on behalf of Western civilization. As Dragoš Kalajić contended, unless something was done, mass migrations would result in every other European being Muslim within a decade: "From the preceding, it is also clear that the Serbs in Bosnia-Herzegovina, by defending its freedom from Islamic threats are also defending Europe and the Europeans."[61] For Radovan Karadžić, indeed, the Serbs were "a formidable bulwark against Asiatic darkness."[62] In this context nationalist Serb intellectuals often portrayed events in Bosnia-Herzegovina as nothing less than "a war of civilizations," as Momo Kapor called it, adding that the anti-Islamic stand "is a question of preserving civilization and culture."[63]

The theme of defending Europe and European civilization was not new, of course, as this had been a standard element of Nazi Germany's propaganda, which cast Germany as Europe's champion against the "Mongol hordes," "the Eastern way of life," and "Atlantic capitalism," considered to be the enemies of "all that was sacred and traditional in Europe."[64] Paradoxically, however, many Serb intellectuals had their own vision of a notional "West" they were to protect, and for them it did not equate to the actual "corrupted" West. Writer Miroslav Toholj, for example, concluded that "they will never again be able to convince us of the supposedly elevated cultural values of the West. The high political kitsch and the love of pornography there annul any possibility of conceiving elevated cultural values."[65] Nevertheless, many were optimistic that Europe would approve of Serb policy, and looked to sympathetic quarters such as the xenophobic Jean-Marie Le Pen in France for inspiration and support.[66] Even Professor Dragan Veselinov (head of Serbia's liberal Popular Peasant Party—Narodna seljačka stranka) assumed that Europe saw "the Muslims supported by Turkey" as a greater evil than nationalist governments in Belgrade or Zagreb, since that would represent "their [i.e., the Turks'] return from the Bosphorus to Vienna."[67]

Karadžić himself assessed that although the Serbs might be criticized for their actions, in the end "the West will be grateful to us one day because we decided to defend Christian values and culture."[68] The publication of Samuel P. Huntington's tract on the clash of civilizations in 1993 came as a windfall for nationalist Serb intellectuals, who could now claim scholarly respectability for their views. Not surprisingly, henceforth many routinely sought to establish a link with his ideas and Huntington became a frequently quoted authority in this context.

Proposing Solutions

In conjunction with their definition and shaping of the "problem," nationalist Serb intellectuals also proposed their "solution" as a reasonable consequence and extension of their ideas. Based on their analysis and portrayal of the Muslims, the solutions proposed by these Serb intellectuals were predictably harsh and involved symbolic and physical separation or elimination. Karadžić and others, typically, stressed frequently that Serbs and Muslims were so diametrically different that the Serbs could not live with the latter. As he saw it, "We simply could not exist in a community with the Muslims and Croats. . . . Distancing ourselves and setting up borders with the Muslims and Croats is our priority political and strategic goal."[69] Likewise, according to Dobrica Ćosić: "It is no longer possible to expect people there [i.e., in Bosnia] to live together again. Let us not force them to do something they are unable to do."[70]

Paradoxically, conversion was proposed as a solution for at least some Muslims. Historian and SANU member Veselin Djuretić, proposed conversion and assimilation with the Serbs as the solution to what he saw as the divide between the "Christian West" and the "Muhammedan East, or Balkan fundamentalism, 'Bosnjakism'." According to Djuretić, "This [divide] will quiet down if the Muslims reintegrate themselves on a complementary ethnolinguistic and cultural-historical basis. They know very well what that basis is."[71]

However, only some Muslims were seen as redeemable and suitable to be brought into the Serbian fold, while most Muslims were considered to be beyond the pale. According to Radovan Karadžić, however, some Muslims reputedly had "a collective memory" of their roots and, depending on whether a Serb or Muslim cultural element was predominant in their personal internal orientation, could be converted to Orthodoxy and be a Serb. As he argued:

> When it is a question of the Serbs of the Islamic faith, there was always a great divide that determined whether they were to be more Muslim or more Serb. Those in whom the religious element predominated, and orientation toward Islam's fundamentals, were lost forever to the Serbian nation. Those, on the other hand, whose national consciousness was greater than the Islamic past of their families felt themselves to be Serbs in the national sense. They did not have an Orthodox spirituality, but they had an Orthodox struggle with God; they had some ingredients, a sensing and collective memory that was carried along within their family. However, it must be noted that only great minds could reach that level of development to become Serbs while also having the Islamic past of their families.[72]

In many ways Muslims were seen as an unnatural and temporary category, whose alleged internal identity and spiritual confusion could only be solved by their abandonment of Islam. According to Radovan Karadžić, for example,

> It is clear that the means of salvation for the Serbs of Muslim faith is to return to Orthodoxy. I say that with full consciousness. I know that not everyone is capable of that and that it is not easy, but I also know that it is only by that means that the duality in their personality can be overcome, and the fact that they temporarily . . . belonged to another religion . . . does not mean that they do not contain a lot that is Serbian, Christian, and Orthodox. . . . Therefore, I believe that the Ser-

bian nation as a whole will recover completely [only] when the majority or all of the—in a national sense—Serbs of the Islamic faith are healed in their souls and enter into the fullness of their personality.[73]

Even so, there were doubts about the loyalty of potential converts.[74]

The more realistic solution proposed seemed to be one of separation and conflict. The depiction by Dobrica Ćosić—which had much in common with views expressed by other intellectuals—of the threat posed by "militant Islam" and "a Muslim jihad" seemed to lead logically to his conclusion that the Serbs "were forced into a terrible defensive war."[75] As poet Milan Pantović saw it:

> They would turn our cross into a crescent,
> They would turn our priests into imams,
> And would turn our faith into Islam.
> So, to preserve ourselves, the cross, and our name-day feast,
> We must act thus: fight fire with fire.[76]

Speaking of the Muslims, writer Momo Kapor also saw violence as the only solution, claiming that "those opponents, as you know, are hardly admirers of James Joyce and have not graduated from Oxford or Cambridge but, rather, are a wild, psychopathic, bloodthirsty element, with whom one can only discuss with weapons and in no other way."[77] Vuk Drašković, for his part, had long agitated in the 1980s to make expulsions and violence against non-Serbs acceptable:

> All Shiptars who, beginning with April 6, 1941, up to now, have settled in Kosmet [which he estimated without any basis at four hundred thouand] or anywhere else in Serbia, as foreign citizens, unquestionably, should be returned to Albania. Their numerous descendants born in Serbia should be treated the same way. . . . Anyone who in any way has worked for Tirana's occupation plan for an Albania stretching to Kopaonika and the Morava must lose his Serbian and Yugoslav citizenship and be expelled to Albania.[78]

In such an atmosphere, it was perhaps not surprising that many other intellectuals were also willing to propose harsh measures to deal with what they portrayed as the Muslim threat, although this uprooting of people might be alluded to with euphemisms such as "population exchanges" or, as Miloš Knežević, fellow of the Belgrade Institute of Geo-Political Studies, suggested the "voluntary resettlement of populations" following a partition of Bosnia between Serbia and Croatia.[79]

Poet Danilo Gavrilović also celebrated and encouraged such a violent solution:

> The Turkish hordes have begun to run,
> An unyielding encirclement is tightening around them.
> Although UNPROFOR is helping them,
> Their outlook is bleak.
> They [the Serbs] will continue to chase the Turks,
> Why should they be in Serbian territory?
> One day we will say to all:
> Serbian land belongs to the Serbs.[80]

Some Serb scholars even looked for inspiration on how to deal with the Muslims to Petar Njegoš, the stridently anti-Muslim nineteenth-century Orthodox bishop and ruler of Montenegro, whose writings extolled and justified the violent eradication of all traces of a Muslim presence in that land.[81]

The Impact of the Nationalist Intellectuals

Ultimately, this study suggests that all three strands of racism—classical, realistic group conflict theory, and symbolic—may coexist in a single movement and have a mutually reinforcing effect. Appeals to biological characteristics, the need to protect against physical threats to a community and its individual members, and allusions to the infringement of cultural values can all be used simultaneously as the basis for defining, isolating, and assailing another community. To be sure, in today's world arguments cast transparently on the basis of race are unpopular, and most nationalist Serb intellectuals felt compelled to make their case in other, more palatable, terms of culture and self-protection. However, such arguments, even when phrased in the more genteel idiom of "culture," nevertheless connote all the immutability, inevitability, and potentially devastating impact conceded to classical arguments based overtly on race. In the end what is fundamental is the ultimate effect of such a process of discrimination, more so than the specific methods used to argue in its support.

The experience in the Serbian community also illustrates how great an impact intellectuals can have. To a great extent it was the intellectuals who crafted the basic national agenda focused on the establishment of a Greater Serbia and the strategy for how to deal with impediments to that objective, in this case specifically the Muslim community. While the actual implementation of the agenda would be controlled by the state, as one would expect in an authoritarian system, the intellectuals continued their activity by not only mobilizing support within the general public and the elites but also by making the implementation of policy more effective. Specifically, thanks to their standing as academics and molders of public opinion, the nationalist Serbian intellectuals provided the key conceptual armature for the emerging nationalist ideology as applied to the Muslims. In particular, by creating the appropriate sociocultural arguments and symbols, in other words an intellectual justification and the trappings of respectability, the intellectuals provided policy makers with the legitimacy to pursue concrete political objectives at whatever level of violence the latter thought necessary. They thereby enhanced the overarching nationalist ideology's credibility and the likelihood that it would gain the Serbian public's support.[82]

Conversely, had there been a challenge from these intellectuals, based on their specialized knowledge and ability to articulate ideas, this would have revealed the shortcomings and immorality of such policies and would have made it more difficult for the Serb authorities to justify and continue their initial strategy of confrontation with the Muslims. However, rather than using their recognized position to counter the process of victimization, the nationalist intellectuals instead lent their credibility to reify, isolate, and condemn the Muslim community, making anti-Muslim acts intellectually acceptable. The use of stereotypes—whether cast in terms of scholarship or of raw emotions—not only served to mobilize the Serbs but helped to lump Muslims into a common category as dangerous, alien, and implacable enemies against whom it was legally and morally acceptable, and even mandatory, to use any means available.[83] In a very real sense the nationalist intellectuals contributed to the delegitimization of the very existence of the Muslims as a community and as individual human beings, acting as accessories to the ethnic cleansing that occurred. Negative categorizing, such as was common in these intellectuals' discourse, can have a devastating effect by dehumanizing the target group and can contribute to the killing of those seen as members of an undifferentiated collection of undesirables.[84]

By 1993, as Milošević sought to dampen nationalist influence in order to consolidate gains made up until then—and to stabilize his own domestic position—hardline rhetoric toward the Muslims lost its practical utility, and its most outspoken proponents saw their prominence in the state-controlled media in Serbia decline, while war weariness also led to diminished public interest. Those who wished to express hardline opinions on this issue, however, found a more welcoming atmosphere from the Bosnian Serb authorities and the media they controlled.[85] However, Belgrade's revived confrontational policies in Kosovo (where most of the Albanians are Muslim) gave nationalist Serb intellectuals a renewed role, even though most viewed Milošević as an unreliable ally. All in all, the Serb intellectuals' attitudes and recent behavior do not augur well for the future. Although many intellectuals have muted their earlier public rhetoric, others reprised their earlier arguments about Islam for use in Kosovo. Without a basic reconsideration of values and goals, even Milošević's departure from power might not lead to a major change in attitudes toward Muslims, at least among these intellectuals, some of whom—such as pragmatist Zoran Djindjićor traditionalist nationalist Vojislav Koštunica or extremist Vojislav Šešelj—will vie to become the nation's new leaders.[86]

Notes

1. Among the best analyses of recent events in Bosnia-Herzegovina are Mark Almond, *Europe's Backyard War: The War in the Balkans* (Reading: Mandarin, 1994); Christopher Bennett, *Yugoslavia's Bloody Collapse* (New York: New York University Press, 1995); Ed Vulliamy, *Seasons in Hell: Understanding Bosnia's War* (London: Simon and Schuster, 1994); and Rabia Ali and Lawrence Lifschultz., eds., *Why Bosnia?* (Stony Creek, Conn.: Pamphleteer's, 1993). The author would like to thank Igor Primorac for his helpful ideas on an early draft of this study.

2. Though it would not be possible to list all those Serb intellectuals who refused to go along with the hostile approach toward the Muslims, special mention should go to poet Vladimir Srebrov (who spent several years in a Bosnian Serb prison for his opposition to such policies) as well as the individuals grouped in the Belgrade Circle of Intellectuals, founded in January 1992, some of whose writings were published in a special issue of *Les Temps Modernes* (Paris) as "Les

intellectuels et la guerre: Les opposants de Belgrade" (Summer 1994). Others, such as Vuk Drašković, were also to retreat from some of their earlier, more strident positions.

3. General Ratko Mladić, for example, accused dissident intellectuals of not being patriots. Interview by Jovan Janjić, "Otpor paklenom planu" [Opposition to the devilish plan], June 18, 1993, in Jovan Janjić, *Srpski odgovor*, 3d ed. (Novi Sad: Matica Srpska, 1995), 78–79. Poet Rajko Petro Nogo, for his part, lashed out against such dissidents: "We have here, in the middle of our capital city, worthy recent converts to Islam [*poturčenjani novovjerci*]. Put together two [Muslim] crescents and you get the Belgrade Civic Circle." Interview by Jovan Janjić, "Osudjeni na pamćenje" [Condemned to remember), June 18, 1993, in Janjić, *Srpski odgovor*, 170. SANU member Ljuba Tadić, similarly, accused such intellectuals of "self-hate" and of being "the Serbian quisling phenomenon." Interviews with Ljuba Tadić by Milan Nikolić, "Intelektualci u zaklonu" (Intellectuals in a shelter], *Intervju* (Belgrade) (September 16–30, 1994): 10, and "Srpski kvislinški fenomen" [The Serbian quisling phenomenon], *Interviu* (November 11, 1994): 7.

4. Eva Etzioni-Halevy, *The Knowledge Elite and the Failure of Prophecy* (London: George Allen and Unwin, 1985), 9.

5. Ibid., 15.

6. Ibid., 26.

7. On realistic group conflict theory the classic work is Robert A. LeVine and Donald T. Campbell, *Ethnocentrism: Theories of Conflict, Ethnic Attitudes, and Group Behavior* (New York: Wiley, 1972). On symbolic racism see John B. McConahay and Joseph C. Hough, Jr., "Symbolic Racism," *Journal of Social Issues* 32.2 (1976): 23–45; David R. Kinder and David O. Sears, "Prejudice and Politics: Symbolic Racism Versus Racial Threats to the Good Life," *Journal of Personality and Social Psychology* 40.3 (1981): 414–431; Paul M. Sniderman, "The New Racism," *American Journal of Political Science* 35.2 (May 1991): 423–447; and Louk Hagendoorn, "Ethnic Categorization and Outgroup Exclusion: Cultural Values and Social Stereotypes in the Construction of Ethnic Hierarchies," *Ethnic and Racial Studies* (January 1993): 26–51.

8. For this description of symbolic racism, McConahay and Hough, "Symbolic Racism," 23.

9. For example, even what was perhaps the epitome of classical biological racism, Nazi ideology, contained at the same time a pronounced cultural tinge. As Raul Hillberg has pointed out, although the Nazis used the term *racial* to define "Aryans" and "non-Aryans," what was key was the cultural marker of the religion of the individual's ancestors. See Raul Hillberg, *The Destruction of the Jews* (New York: New Viewpoints, 1973), 45 and 52. This stands out especially starkly in the Nazis' tortuous efforts to determine whether the "German" or

"Jewish" cultural element was dominant in mixed offspring (the *Mischlinge*) in order to classify an individual. Ibid., 47–53.

10. Dragoš Kalajić, "Kvazi Arapi protiv Evropljana" [The pseudo-Arabs against the Europeans), *Duga* (Belgrade), September 13–19, 1987, 14–15.

11. Interview with Vojislav Lubarda by Jovan Janjić, "Bespuća tamnog vilajeta" [The pathless ways of the dark province], June 18, 1993, in Janjić, *Srpski odgovor*.

12. See quotes from Biljana Plavšić's interviews to that effect in the article by Belgrade University sociologist Slobodan Inić, "Biljana Plavšić: Geneticist in the Service of a Great Crime," *Bosnia Report* (London) (June-August 1997), 8–9. Conversely, the Serbs were portrayed as genetically and culturally superior. For example, novelist and political leader Vuk Drašković, in a speech on December 1991, claimed that "within this Yugoslav area, biologically we (the Serbs) are the strongest nation and have the strongest historical roots." Speech of December 8, 1991, "Ovde je njiva—tamo je saksija" [The field is here, the flowerpot is there], *Srpska reč* (Belgrade), December 23, 1991, 13. For his part, Marko Mladenović, professor at the Belgrade University Law School, was to posit that "we [i.e., the Serbs] are, by genetic preselection, a strong people . . . there are indications that we are a root nation (*pranarod*), [and that] we gave birth to other peoples." Interview by Vesna Malisić, "Svi Srbi u jednoj legendi" [All Serbs in a single legend], *Duga*, May 28–June 10, 1994, 5.

13. For an insightful overview of Serb intellectuals and nationalism over the years, see Igor Primoratz, "The Moral Responsibility of Intellectuals: The Case of Serbia," *Res Publica* 11.2 (1997): 11–14.

14. Among these are writer and university professor VojislavŠešelj, the leader of the Serbian Radical Party and of its Chetnik militia, Shakespearean scholar Nikola Koljević, who became the Bosnian Serbs' vice president, writer Miroslav Toholj, who was the Bosnian Serbs' minister of information, psychiatrist Jovan Rašković, leader of the Serb nationalists in Croatia, writer Dobrica Ćosić, who for a time became president of the rump Yugoslavia, novelist Vuk Drašković, the leader of the Serbian Renewal Movement (Srpski pokret obnove—SPO) and of its Serbian Guard militia, film director Dragoslav Bokan, who was commander of the White Eagles militia, and SANU members Antonije Isaković, Kosta Mihajlović, and Mihajlo Marković, who helped Milošević transform the League of Communists of Serbia into the Socialist Party of Serbia, with the latter becoming a vice president in the new party and one of Milošević's key advisers until 1995.

15. According to Slobodan Milošević's biographer Slavoljub Djukić, the intellectuals courted Milošević, whom they saw as a potentially willing partner and tool to implement their program. By the summer of 1988, in turn, Milošević had become more sympathetic to the nationalist intellectuals, as he toyed with

a new means to mobilize support and gain legitimacy while he consolidated power when the traditional legitimacy of Communism eroded. Slavoljub Djukić, *Kako se dogodio vodja* [How the leader came to be] (Belgrade: Filip Visnjić, 1992), 272–273. Djukić identifies Milošević's wife Mira Marković—a party activist at Belgrade University—as key in establishing Milošević's linkages with professors at the university. Ibid., 77–78.

16. Still other intellectuals were appointed to administrative positions in the government, such as the orientalist Darko Tanasković, who became ambassador to Turkey in 1995; he was motivated, as he said, by his "wish to serve the state," quoted in Zdenka Aćin, "Aladinova filološka lampa naše orijentalistike" (The philological Aladdin's lamp of our orientalism], *Duga* February 4–17, 1995, 26. For Radovan Karadžić's wife, Ljiljana, herself also a psychiatrist and involved in political life, the fact that so many Serb intellectuals took part in politics was a source of pride: "Journalists and politicians would be surprised if they knew how many within the leadership of the Republika Srpska have finished university or are university professors and have doctorates. " Interview with Ljiljana Karadžić by Dragomir Simović, "Spas u milosrdju" [Salvation in good works], *Javnost* (Pale), September 12, 1996, 13.

17. Typically, asked whether, as the newly elected president of the Writers' Union of Serbia, he would remain in politics, poet and political party figure Slobodan Rakitić noted that he would, since "we live in a time when everyone is involved in politics. "Ostajem u politici" [I am remaining in politics], *Vreme* (Belgrade), December 26, 1994, 33. Writer and SANU member Antonije Isaković, likewise, explained his political involvement thus: "In difficult times, it is normal for even a writer to become politically engaged. . . . What made me decide were my patriotic feelings." Interview with Antonije Isaković by Jelena Jovović, "Miran zločin u Dejtonu" [Peaceful crime in Dayton], *NIN* (Belgrade), February 9, 1996. 39. The high degree of political engagement on the part of so many leading Serb intellectuals lends weight to those who have criticized the paradigm of the intellectual as "a politically autonomous critic pursuing knowledge for its own sake." See Clyde W. Barrow, "Intellectuals in Contemporary Social Theory: A Radical Critique," *Sociological Inquiry* 57.4 (Fall 1987): 415–427.

18. On the functions served by such a differentiation process and its impact on communities, see Johan M. G. van der Dennen, "Ethnocentrism and In-Group/Out-Group Differentiation," in Vernon Reynolds, Vincent Falger, and Ian Vine, eds., *The Sociobiology of Ethnocentrism; Evolutionary Dimensions of Xenophobia, Discrimination, Racism, and Nationalism* (Athens: University of Georgia Press, 1987), 1–47.

19. Review by B. Dj. "Islam i geopolitika" [Islam and geopolitics], *Vojska*, May 4, 1995, 23. Jevtić, significantly, also was a regular contributor to *Javnost*, the Bosnian Serb authorities' official magazine.

20. Reported in Janko Vujinović, "Pesnici, mi vas slušamo" [Poets, we are listening to you], *Duga*, October 29–November 11, 1988, 72. One of the most insightful interpretations of Serb attitudes about Kosovo is provided by Olga Zirojević, "Kosovo u kolektivnom Pamćenju" [Kosovo in collective memory], in Nebojša Popov, ed., *Srpska strana rata* [The Serbian side of the war] (Belgrade: BIGZ, 1996), 201–231.

21. Jovan Rašković, *Luda Zemlja* [Crazy land] (Belgrade: Akvarijus, 1990), 105 and 129. Rašković gave many interviews in the media in which he reiterated the same views.

22. Interview with Sanda Rašković by Borislav Soleša, "Nisu shvatili mog oca Jovana Raškovića" [They did not understand my father Jovan Rašković], *Duga*, October 12–25, 1996, 27.

23. Edward W. Said, *Orientalism* (New York: Vintage, 1979). As another scholar has categorized it, the thrust is to create "the mirror image of the paradigmatic Occident, and thus a repository of negativity, both as abstract negativity and as particular negatives with respect to things Occidental." Aziz Al-Azmeh, "The Articulation of Orientalism," *Arab Studies Quarterly* (Fall 1991): 386–387. As Said has pointed out elsewhere, this sort of Orientalism is not an objective exercise of scholarship, much less an interchange with the population studied, but rather an uncompromising affirmation of dominance guided by political motives. As he assessed, "Now this, I submit, is neither science, nor knowledge, nor understanding: it is a statement of power and a claim for absolute authority. It is constituted out of racism, and it is made comparatively acceptable to an audience prepared in advance to listen to its muscular truths." Edward W. Said, "Orientalism Reconsidered," *Race and Class* (Autumn 1985): 8.

24. Mira Marković, "Nada i . . . sećanje na sreću" [Hope and . . . memories of happiness], *Duga*, July 23–August 5, 1994, 10–11.

25. Miroljub Jevtić, for example, claimed that "a Turkish mentality (*duh*) has remained." "Panturcizam i njegova uloga u jugoslovenskoj krizi" [Pan-Turkism and its role in the Yugoslav crisis], *Vojno delo* (January-April 1994): 10. Paradoxically, some leading Serb nationalists themselves have Islamic family names, as is the case with intellectuals Radovan Karadžić, Dobrica Ćosić, Antonije Isaković, Slavenko Terzić, and Dragoš Kalajić.

26. Aleksandar Popović, *Jugoslovenski muslimani* [The Yugoslav Muslims] (Belgrade: Akvarijus, 1990), 5.

27. Interview with Darko Tanasković by Aleksandra Tomić, "Evropa nece izbeći demografski džihad" [Europe will not escape the demographic jihad], *Vojska*, September 23, 1993, 10.

28. Interview with Nada Todorov by (Colonel) Nikola Ostojić, "Genocidne poruke iz 1001 noći" [The genocidical messages from *The Thousand and One Nights*], *Vojska*, April 8, 1993, 20.

29. Interview with Lubarda by Janjić, "Bespuća tamnog vilajeta" [The pathless ways of the dark province], 123. Miroljub Jevtić claimed that the local Muslims "love Turkey more than their own homeland." "Panturcizam i njegova uloga u jugoslovenskoj krizi" [Pan-Turkism and its role in the Yugoslav crisis], *Vojno delo* (January-April 1994): 10. Poet Ljubomir Zuković described Bosnian Muslims thus: "My soul will be in Asia, While the rest I cannot hide, Will belong to heathen Europe, Until the time that Islam also overruns it." "Nema više turkovanja" [There is no more behaving like Turks], in *Za krst časni i slobodu zlatnu* [For the noble cross and dear freedom] (Sarajevo: Institute for Textbooks and Educational Materials of the Republika Srpska, 1994), 263. This is a poetry anthology used in Bosnian Serb schools. Likewise, Vuk Drašković told an American audience that Alija Izetbegović "opens his umbrella in Sarajevo if somebody informs him that it's raining in Teheran," *Charlie Rose Show*, PBS-TV, April 7, 1997.

30. Speech at Writers' Union of Serbia on April 26, 1988, printed in Milan Komnenić, *Kosovski polom* [Kosovo rupture] (Šabac: Glas Crkve, 1988), 55.

31. Respectively, interview with Vuk Drašković in *Politica exterior* (Madrid), December 1987, and at a speech at a literary soirée in Belgrade, September 11, 1988, "Svi nabukodonosori roda srpskoga" [All the Nebuchadnezzars of the Serbian stock], reprinted in *Koekude Srbijo* [Quo Vadis, Serbia?] (Belgrade: Nova Knjiga, 1990), 36 and 86. More recently, Drašković asked rhetorically, "Whose is Bosnia-Herzegovina? . . . Historically, all of Bosnia-Herzegovina is Serbian. Today's Muslims are former Serbs, the Bosnian Croats are former Serbs who changed their religion." He was critical of Bosnia's partition specifically because that would create an Islamic state "in the middle of Serbian ethnic space." Interview with Vuk Drašković by Slobodan Savić, "I dalje za Veliku Srbiju" [Still in favor of Greater Serbia], *Intervju*, July 21, 1995, 12. Likewise, historian Mile Nedeljković devoted most of his monograph to arguing that Bosnia-Herzegovina had always been Serbian and Orthodox and that the Muslims were therefore merely apostate Serbs. Mile Nedeljković, *Krst i polumesec* [The cross and the crescent] (Belgrade: Politika, 1993). Another historian, Veselin Djuretić, claimed that 99 percent of the Bosnian Muslims were really Serbs. Interview by Momir Djoković, "Vatikanski polip" [Vatican polyp] *Spona* (Frankfurt), August 19, 1993, 10. Vojislav Šešelj also concurred, interview by Dragan Stavljanin, "Sa dr Šešeljem tri godine nakon Sarajevskog procesa" [With Dr. Šešelj three years after the Sarajevo trial] 1987, reprinted in Vojislav Šešelj, *Osvajanje slobode* [Achieving freedom] (Belgrade: NIGP ABC Glas, 1991), 172–173.

32. Respectively, interview with Milorad Ekmečić by D. B., "Podele nam mogu doći glave" [Divisions can cost us our heads], *Intervju*, December 23, 1994, 13; and Selić quoted in Goran Cogić, "Ljiljani od laži vezeni" [Fleurs-de-lis

embroidered with lies], *Oslobodjenje* (Sarajevo, Serb ed.), January 6, 1995, 91. For more scholarly analyses of the historical development of the Muslim community, see Noel Malcolm, *Bosnia: A Short History* (London: Macmillan, 1987); Vatro Murvar, *Nation and Religion in Central Europe and the Western Balkans: The Muslims in Bosnia, Hercegovina, and Sandžak: A Sociological Analysis* (Brookfield: University of Wisconsin, 1989); Robert J. Donia and John V. A. Fine, Jr., *Bosnia and Hercegovina: A Tradition Betrayed* (New York: Columbia University Press, 1994); and Mark Pinson, ed., *The Muslims of Bosnia-Herzegovina* (Cambridge: Harvard University Press, 1994).

33. Interview with Slavenko Terzić by Ljiljana Begenišević, "Bosnjaštvo—uvezen projekat" [Bosniakism—an imported project], *Javnost*, December 13, 1997, 9.

34. Interview with Zoran Djindjić by Karen Thurnau on Radio Deutsche Welle, reprinted as "Miloševića nema tko svrgnuti" [There is no one to overthrow Milošević], *Danas* (Zagreb), September 21, 1993), 45.

35. Typically, painter Milić od Mačve claimed that "the Bosnian Muslims's language . . . is Serbian, but that means nothing, since their heart is Muslim." Quoted in Ilija Žurovac, "Pravoslavlje pre slovenstva" [Orthodoxy above Slavism], *Evropske Novosti* (Frankfurt), March 15, 1994, 2. *Evropske Novosti is* the European edition of the pro-government Belgrade daily *Večernje Novosti*, initially published in Germany to bypass the international sanctions on Serbia.

36. Dragoš Kalajić, "Srbi i transvestiti" [The Serbs and transvestites], *Duga*, May 27–June 9, 1995, 80. Darko Tanasković summed up his indictment with a well-worn criticism of local converts to Islam, even of those whose ancestors might have converted centuries ago: "A convert to Islam, it is well-known, is worse than a Turk (that is, a nonlocal Muslim)." Darko Tanasković, "Turci brane Sarajevo" [The Turks are defending Sarajevo], *Epoha* (Belgrade), January 7, 1992, 21. *Epoha* was published by Serbia's ruling Socialist Party of Serbia.

37. Thus, according to Dragoš Kalajić, "However, judging by everything in the conscience of the Muslims of Serb origin, the memory of flight from the Serbian spiritual community has endured for centuries, giving rise to a sentiment of moral inferiority and envy that is manifested as hate for everything Serbian." "Srbi i transvestiti," 80.

38. Interview with Radovan Karadžić, published in *Svetigora* as "Vodja kakav nam treba" [The type of leader we need], and republished as "Radovan Karadžić: Šta mi sapuće Sveti Duh" [Radovan Karadžić: What the Holy Ghost whispers to me], in *Svet* (Belgrade), September 1, 1995, 8.

39. Cogić, "Ljiljani od laži vezeni" [Fleurs-de-lis embroidered with lies], 91. Belgrade writer Momčilo Selić, likewise, stressed that the fleur-de-lis symbol is "very clearly a Western European symbol." Ibid.

40. Momčilo Selić quoted in Cogić, "Ljiljani od laži vezeni" [Fleurs-de-lis embroidered with lies], 91.

41. Miroljub Jevtić, "Rezervisti Alahove vojske" [The reservists of Allah's army], *Duga*, December 9–12, 1989, 21. He asked rhetorically, "If you cannot eat, drink, be buried in the same cemetery or marry a neighbor of another faith, what then can you do?"

42. Interview with Todorov, *Vojska*, April 8, 1993, 21, 43. Dragoš Kalajić, "Kvazi Arapi protiv Evropljana" [The pseudo-Arabs against the Europeans), 14.

43. Vuk Drašković, likewise, claimed that "in Kosovo and Metohija, the Sharià-based practice of the harem is carried out. Greater Albania loves children and some Shiptars have fifty of them!" Letter, dated June 18, 1987, from Drašković to the Albanian writer Ismail Kadare; *Odgovori* [Responses], (Belgrade: Prosveta, 1987), 128.

44. Interview with Milorad Ekmečić by D. B., "Podele nam mogu doći glave" [Divisions can cost us our heads], *Intervju*, December 23, 1994, 13. Writer Momo Kapor, speaking of the Muslims and Croats, likewise noted that "the Serbs, as the oldest nation, were bothered by the adolescent uproar by the others, who had not fulfilled their history and their state. The latter had a complex vis-à-vis the Serbs." Interview by Tamara Nikčević, "Izgradiću novo Sarajevo" [I will build a new Sarajevo], *Intervju*, October 13, 1995, 18. Historian Vasilije Krestić also spoke disparagingly of Tito's alleged creation of "heretofore nonexistent nations." Quoted in Zoran Marković, "Drugi Kongres srpskih intelektualaca: Srpsko pitanje danas" [The Serb intellectuals' second congress: The Serbian question today], *Duga*, April 30–May 13, 1994, 85.

45. In fact, for Dragoš Kalajić, "It is well known that in the ruins of Yugoslavia the Serbs are the only people who have the talent, energy, experience, and tradition to build a state." "Džamahirijom protiv Evrope" [With a Jamahiriyya against Europe], *Duga*, March 15–28, 1992, 15.
    In a January 1989 meeting of Serbia's leading intellectuals held in Belgrade, one speaker allowed with some condescension that "it is not easy (for others) to live alongside a people [i.e., the Serbs] that liberated itself, [a people] that has a history of its own. Envy of this is very much a human emotion. There is also something called a lack of gratitude that exists between peoples [when] a debt is both psychologically and morally burdensome. . . . What Serbia did for others, which she is forced to talk about herself [because no one else will], did not arouse gratitude, but stimulated other types of feelings instead." Quoted in Jevrem Damjanović, "Ko mrzi Srbe; Razbijena zavera ćutanje" [Who hates the Serbs: The conspiracy of silence is broken], *Ilustrovana Politika* (Belgrade), January 17, 1989: 15. In one case, when the Yugoslav Army's weekly asked a professor of psychology at Belgrade University to analyze the reason why others allegedly hated the Serbs, he replied that "looking, in general, at other peoples, one notices the Croats' and the Muslims' inferiority." Interview with Dr. Jovan Marić by Snežan Djokić, "Plovidba do ostrova zdrava" (Sailing toward the

344

island of health), *Vojska*, October 21, 1993, 16. Already in the late 1980s Serb intellectuals were investing the political friction with Slovenia with racial over-tones, accusing the Slovenes of seeing themselves as "Aryans" in relation to the victimized Serbs. On the development of the Serbs' self-image, see Zoran M. Marković, "Nacija—žrtva osveta" [The nation—victim and revenge], in Popov, *Srpska strana rata*, 637–684; and Norman Cigar, *Genocide in Bosnia; The Politics of "Ethnic Cleansing"* (College Station: Texas A&M University Press, 1995), 73–80.

46. Interview with Radovan Karadžić, published in *Svetigora*, republished in *Svet*, September 1, 1995, 8.

47. He further compared the Muslims unfavorably to the Serbs: "The Muslim villages are all crowded in disorder, wall to wall, house to house, while Serbian villages are very open, widely spread out. . . . Every householder wants to be absolutely free." Radovan Karadžić quoted in Dragoš Kalajić, "Priznanje Republike Srpske" [Recognition of the Republika Srpska], *Duga*, September 16–29, 1995, 84.

48. Interview with Miroslav Toholj by Slavica Jovović, "Rasprodaja naše nesreće" [The sale of our misfortune], *Intervju*, February 2, 1996, 13.

49. Interview with Gojko Djogo by Jovan Janjić, "Srbijica, Srbija, Serbija" [Serbia, Serbija], June 18, 1993, in Janjić, *Srpski odgovor*, 153. Dragoš Kalajić even claimed that the Serbs, by their actions, were protecting "many Muslims who do not want to become mediums for Islamism and want to preserve the virtues and values of their Slavic being." "Usamljeni kao Nemci" [Isolated like the Germans], *Duga*, February 1–14, 1992, 35. In Kosovo a similar artificial distinction has been made between "honorable Albanians" and the rest of the Albanian population.

50. Jevtić, "Rezervisti Alahove vojske" [The reservists of Allah's Army], 20 and 22.

51. Interview with Vojislav Šešelj, "Kad Vuka hapse to je demokratija, kad mene hapse to je diktatura" [When they arrest Vuk, that is democracy, when they arrest me, that is dictatorship], *Srpska reč*, January 15, 1996, 19. Šešelj characterized Požderac's actions as just "a front."

52. Zuković, "Nema više turkovanja" [There is no more behaving like Turks], in *Za krst cašni i slobodu zlatnu* [For the noble cross and dear freedom], 264.

53. Respectively, interview with Lubarda by Janjić, "Bespuća tamnog vilajeta" [The pathless ways of the dark province], 123; and Vojislav Lubarda, writing in *Javnost*, quoted in "Ljudi i vreme" [People and time], *Vreme*, December 13, 1993, 57.

54. Miroljub Jevtić in *Javnost*, quoted in "Ljudi i vreme" [People and time], *Vreme*, November 15, 1993, 55. Likewise, to explain this alleged propensity for violence, Darko Tanasković also blamed "the tone of the Qur'an," for it was said to be "openly authoritarian, uncompromising, and menacing." Interview with Darko

Tanasković by Aleksandra Tomić, "Evropa nće izbeći demografski džihad" [Europe will not avoid the demographic jihad], *Vojska*, September 23, 1993, 8.

55. Reported by Andjelka Cvijić, "Ekumenizam—problem epohe" (Ecumenism—the issue of this era], *Spona*, December 2, 1993, 14. According to Jevtić, Islam by its nature allegedly "excludes every other outlook on the world and seeks for itself a monopoly of the scene. That is why it is dangerous for all modern societies." Jevtić, "Rezervisti Alahove vojske" [The reservists of Allah's army], 20. Vuk Drašković, likewise, in a speech about the Albanians asked rhetorically: "How can we prevent their [i.e., the Albanians] intolerant, Islamic, destructive, and anticivilization indoctrination?" Speech to the Writers' Union of Serbia, March 4, 1989, "O srpskom nacionalnom programu" [On the Serbian national program], *Koekude Srbijo* [Quo Vadis, Serbia?], 111.

56. Professor Novica Vojinović, speaking at the Serb Intellectuals' Second Congress, quoted in Marković, "Drugi Kongres Srpskih Intelektualaca: Srpsko pitanje danas" [The Serb intellectuals' second congress: The Serbian question today], 86.

57. Miroljub Jevtić, "Kuran—etnička metla" [The Qur'an—an ethnic broom], *Javnost*, August 19, 1995, 31. Marko Mladenović, a professor at the Belgrade University Law School, spoke of the threat of the "the dream of four million Muslims originally from the Balkans, who are waiting to return." Quoted in Vesna Mališić, "Svi Srbi u jednoj legendi" [All the Serbs in a single legend], *Duga*, May 28–June 10, 1994, 5.

58. Radovan Karadžić, "Commentary," *Washington Times*, June 12, 1994, B4. Dragoš Kalajić warned that the U.S. itself would soon fall apart along ethnic-racial groupings, one of whose fault lines was being created by "a much greater wave of Islamization of the Blacks." "Afrikanizaciia Amerike" [The Africanization of America], written September 26, 1992, reprinted in Dragoš Kalajić, *Američko zlo* [The American evil], 2d ed. (Belgrade: BIGZ, 1994), 194. Kalajić also claimed that "the Serbian people are again defending Europe, as was true six centuries ago. . . . Today, the Serbian people are defending Europe from the hostility of the Atlantic forces and from the hegemonistic ambitions of the latter's Turkish vassal." "Let belog orla" [Flight of the white eagle], *Duga*, June 10–23, 1995, 92.

59. Interview with Vojin Dabić, "Polumesec muči Zapad" [The crescent worries the West], *Evropske Novosti*, April 14, 1993, 18. Extending the net widely, Vojin Dabić saw not only the Muslims in Bosnia-Herzegovina but also those in the Sandžak, the Albanians in Kosovo, and the Turkish minorities in Bulgaria and Greece as "a danger for Europe, since Islam cannot accept that religion is separate from the state. They [i.e., the Muslims] subscribe to a bizarre symbiosis of religion and state, and of religion and nation." Radovan Karadžić, likewise, told a Russian audience that "I must say that we found ourselves face to face with

the first threat of Islamic fundamentalism in Europe. This was the first, but not the last. The Europeans are going to have headaches from what happened in Bosnia." Interview by Sergey Sidorov, "Est I sily, kotorym nevygodna stabil'nost' na Balkanakh" [There are powers who are not happy with stability in the Balkans], *Krasnaya Zvezda* (Moscow), June 21, 1994, 3. According to Dragoš Kalajić, "It is necessary to undertake a broad political, diplomatic, and propaganda action throughout the European Union, to warn of the threat that menaces Europe, European and Christian culture, civilization, and tradition from the project to create an Islamic jamahiriyya." "Džamajirijom protiv Evrope" [With a jamahiriyya against Europe], *Duga*, March 15–28, 1992, 18.

60. Interview with Radoslav Stojanović by Momir Djoković, "Povratak vrednostima Srbije" [A return to Serbia's values], *Spona*, June 10, 1993, 15.

61. Dragoš Kalajić, "Usamljeni kao Nemci" [Isolated like the Germans], 35.

62. Radovan Karadžić speech in Knin, Belgrade TANJUG, July 19, 1993, in *Foreign Broadcast Information Service, Eastern Europe (FBIS-EEU-93-138)*, July 21, 1993, 41.

63. Interview with Momo Kapor by Jovan Janjić, "Bosna—zemlja izabrana" [Bosnia—chosen land], June 18, 1993, in Janjić, *Srpski odgovor*, 180 and 189. Darko Tanasković, also took this stand, "Islam i rat" [Islam and war], *Vojska* (April 1994): 10. Likewise, Radovan Karadžić noted in a speech in Trebinje in 1995: "This is very much a war between civilizations, a war between implacable opposites," quoted in Dragoš Kalajić, "Priznanje Republike Srpske" [Recognition of the Republika Srpska], *Duga*, September 15–28, 1995, 84.

64. See David Welch, *The Third Reich: Politics and Propaganda* (London and New York: Routledge, 1993), 103, 112. Also see Omer Bartov, *Hitler's Army* (New York and Oxford: Oxford University Press, 1991), 35, 152–153, 169, and 176–177; Z. A. B. Zeman, *Nazi Propaganda*, 2d ed. (London: Oxford University Press, 1965), 158–170; and Robert E. Herzstein, *The War Hitler Won: The Most Infamous Propaganda Campaign in History* (New York: Putnam's, 1978), 363–364. Typically, the wartime SS periodical *Signal* stressed this theme, with articles having such titles as "Europe's Shield: Concerning the Spiritual Foundations of the German Army Tradition," by Major Doctor Wilhelm Ehmer, in S. L. Mayer, ed., *Signal: Hitler's Wartime Picture Magazine* (London: Bison, 1976); or "We, the Europeans" by Giselher Wirsing, in S. L. Mayer, *Signal: The Years of Retreat, 1943–1944* (Englewood Cliffs, N.J.: Prentice-Hall, 1979). Also in this vein, orders from the Wehrmacht's headquarters in 1941 to German forces on the Eastern front read: "The essential aim of the campaign against the Jewish-Bolshevist system is the complete crushing of its means of power and the extermination of Asiatic influence in the European cultural region." Reprinted in Lucy S. Davidowicz, *A Holocaust Reader* (New York: Behrman House, 1976), 70–71.

65. Interview with Miroslav Toholj by Slavica Jovović, "Rasprodaja naše nesreće" [The sale of our misfortune], *Intervju*, February 2, 1996, 12. SANU member Ljubomir Tadić also had "great reservations about the democratic nature of that Western democracy, which in many ways has become depraved and denatured." Interview with Ljubomir Tadić by Predrag Popović, "Najlakše je da mi za sve budemo krivi [It is easiest for us to be guilty for everything], *Intervju*, February 24, 1995, 52. SANU president Aleksandar Despić spoke of Europe showing its face of "hate, mutual killing, and arrogance and aggression" toward the Serbs; interview with Aleksandar Despić by Tatjana Njezić, "Constanta humana," *NIN*, January 5, 1996, 40. As painter Milić od Mačve summed it up, "The West is spiritually dead." "Ocrnjeni beli andjeo" [Blackened white angel), *NIN*, June 2, 1995, 59. For Dragoš Kalajić, Serbian nationalism was an alternative to "the nihilism of the West in agony . . . the monstrous, usurious, poisonous civilization of the West," "Priznanje Republike Srpske" [Recognition of the Republika Srpska], *Duga*, September 16–29, 1995, 83. This theme was constant in his collected works, such as *Americko zlo* [American evil] and *Izdana Evropa* [Europe betrayed] (Belgrade: Jugoslavijapublik, 1994).

66. It was reportedly Le Pen who suggested to film director Dragoslav Bokan — commander of the White Eagles militia, which was linked by international organizations with numerous war crimes — that the Serbs portray their conflict as a struggle against an "anti-Christian coalition" and "fundamentalism." Interview with Bokan by Dada Vujasinović, "Firer mekog srca" [Fuehrer with a soft heart], *Duga*, March 29–April 11, 1992, 47. On the mutual support between Šešelj and Le Pen, see the interview with Vojislav Šešelj by Dragan Bujosević, "Srbi vole Le Pena" [The Serbs love Le Pen], *NIN*, November 8, 1996, 18. As Dragoš Kalajić saw it, "The absolutely positive reaction by the European Community and European political opinion vis-à-vis the recent military coup in Algeria offers excellent arguments that all resolute means available be used to prevent the creation of an Islamic jamahiriyya on European territory. . . . If, from the position of European interests, it is more welcome even in Africa to violate ruthlessly democratic principles than to set up an Islamic order, the same political realism can be applied in Europe, and especially in Europe, which is subject to the same threat." "Džamahirijom protiv Evrope" [With a jamahiriyya against Europe], *Duga*, March 15–28, 1992, 18. Slavenko Terzić, director of SANU's History Institute, also was convinced that "the Western world . . . does not want a greater penetration of the Muslim factor into Europe" and would therefore support the integration of Bosnia's Muslims into Croatia. Interview with Slavenko Terzić by Radmila Popović, "Odnarodjavanje Muslimana nije završeno" [The denationalization of the Muslims has not been completed], *Duga*, February 4–17, 1995, 32.

67. Interview by Aleksandar Cvetković, "Dovodimo i vola" [We will bring even an ox], *Srpska reč* (Belgrade), June 7, 1993, 17.

68. Interview in *Pogledi* (Kragujevac, Serbia), November 12, 1993, in *FBIS-EEU-93-228*, November 30, 1993, 41. In a similar vein, writer Miroslav Toholj, who was the minister of information for the Bosnian Serb entity, posited that "Europe could not have had a more convenient method to rid itself of the Muslims than to recognize the latter's state: they will all perish down to the last one in pursuit of that narcotic dream." Interview with Miroslav Toholj by Jovan Janjić, "Tri malo duža prsta" [Three somewhat longer fingers], *NIN*, March 10, 1995, 38.

69. Radovan Karadžić quoted in Dragoš Kalajić, "Priznanje Republike Srpske" [Recognition of the Republika Srpska], *Duga*, September 16–29, 1995: 84. In making this point, he often used metaphors of opposites: "A multicultural society, in our case, is like mixing the unmixable, oil and water." Radovan Karadžić quoted in Kalajić, ibid., 84. Elsewhere, he claimed that "one can never put a dog and a cat in the same cage. "Interview with Karadžić by Kai Herman, "Nebeska Prestonica" [Heavenly capital], *Intervju*, September 14–30, 1994, 23; also, interview with Karadžić by Yelena Kalyadina, "Nobody Is Paying President Karadžić, Not Even Wages," *Komsomolskaya Pravda (Moscow)*, May 17, 1995, in *FBIS-EEU-95-097*, May 19, 1995: 9.

70. Interview by Richard Swartz, *Svenska Dageblat* (Stockholm), December 16, 1992, in *FBIS-EEU-92-246*, December 22, 1992, 48. Biljana Plavšić, a biologist who became a leading member of the Bosnian Serb hierarchy, and in 1996 took over from Karadžić, also held that "at present, the only solution I see is to create ethnically clean territories for the three ethnic groups." Interview by Richard Schneider, "We Should Exchange Sarajevo for Another Town," *Kurier* (Vienna), June 26, 1993, in *FBIS-EEU-93-122*, June 28, 1993, 27. Historian Milan Protić, similarly, noted that "the greatest crime is to allow the three peoples to live together [in Bosnia]." Interview with Milan Protić by Milan Nikolić, "Intelektualci u zaklonu" [Intellectuals in a shelter], *Intervju*, September 16–30, 1994, 11. Using circular reasoning, Šešelj concluded that "we could not live together with them [i.e., the Muslims]; the best proof of that is the fact that the Muslims were expelled from here and the mosques demolished." Interview with Vojislav Šešelj, "Kad Vuka hapse to je demokratija, kad mene hapse to je diktatura," *Srpska reč*, January 15, 1996, 19.

71. Interview with Veselin Djuretić, "Srbi se u ovom ratu nisu svetili" [The Serbs in this war did not sacrifice themselves], *Telegraf International*, March 26, 1996, 14.

72. Interview with Radovan Karadžić, published in *Svetigora*, republished in *Svet*, September 1, 1995, 7. Historian Veselin Djuretić was confident that the Muslims would convert: "Remember this. A time will come when the light of our lighthouse will also become the historic reference point for the Mohammedan naturalized Serbs and for the Croatian naturalized Serb Catholics. Beneath a

thin clerical layer of their consciousness, the great Serbian Kunta Kinte is laying low." Interview with Veselin Djuretić by Srboljub Vrbić, "Gde stanuje Krajina" [Where is the Krajina residing?], *Javnost*, August 17, 1995, 15.

73. Interview with Radovan Karadžić, published in *Svetigora*, reprinted in *Svet*,
September 1, 1995, 8. In an analogous approach the Nazis engaged in a search
for "racially valuable elements" among the conquered populations, whose
ancestors were said to have once been German or who were "suitable for Ger-
manization." The stated goal was that of "bringing the related peoples back into
the Germanic family," and the emphasis was on Germanizing the upper
classes, such as "the Polish leader types" and "the better educated Czech
classes." Three percent among the Czechs, for example, qualified for Class A,
the "racially good and fit for assimilation." Later, due to labor needs, plans were
made to Germanize four hundred to five hundred thousand Ukrainian women,
portraying this as a move to "retrieve those of German blood." Ihor Kamenet-
sky, *Secret Nazi Plans for Eastern Europe; A Study of Lebensraum Policies* (New
York: Bookman, 1961), 82–102; and Clarissa Henry and Marc Hillel, *Of Pure
Blood*, trans. Eric Mossbacher (New York: McGraw Hill, 1975), 148–177.

74. This applied even to Jovan Zametica, who had become a hardline personal
adviser to Karadžić. As Radislav Vukić, a medical doctor and the first president
of Karadžić's Serbian Democratic Party (SDS) for the Bosnian Krajina,
ironized: "And, Karadžić's adviser is a certain Jovan Zametica, the well-know
Muslim Omer Zametica from Banja Luka. He was baptized here to be Jovan,
but is someone like that going to advise him [i.e., Karadžić]?" Interview with
Radislav Vukić by Branko Perić, "Za knjaza jabuka" [For the prince of apples],
NIN, March 17, 1995, 29. Dragoš Kalajić likewise questioned Zametica's sin-
cerity, noting that "doubts are completely understandable at a time of massive
betrayal of the Serbian people, when the adherence by a Muslim son to the
Serbian side is a very exceptional event." Dragoš Kalajić, "Sladak život u Sara-
jevu" [Sweet life in Sarajevo], *Duga*, December 10–23, 1994, 33. Zametica (first
name originally Omer) was born of Muslim and Slovak parentage; after changing his name to John, he studied in Britain, then changed his name again to
Jovan, and went to Bosnia as an international election monitor in 1993 and
stayed on to work for Karadžić.

75. Dobrica Ćosić's speech to SANU, "Srbija izmedju preporoda i katastrofe" [Ser-
bia between a rebirth and catastrophe], *Politika* (Belgrade) June 16, 1992, 7.
Indeed, he believed that "the religious character of antagonism between the
Bosnia-Herzegovina Muslims and the Orthodox Serbs is even more pro-
nounced and total than the Catholic-Orthodox antagonism." Interview with
Dobrica Ćosić in the Italian newspaper *Avanti*, February 3, 1992, reprinted in
Dobrica Ćosić, *Srpsko pitanje; demokratsko pitanje* [The Serbian question: The
democratic question] (Belgrade: Politika, 1992), 230.

76. Milan Pantović, "Na ljutu ranu—ljutu travu" [Fight fire with fire], *Srpska vojska* (Sarajevo, Serbian side), August 25, 1995, 50. *Srpska vojska* was the Bosnian Serb army's official publication.

77. Interview by Janjić, "Bosna—zemlja izabrana" [Bosnia—chosen land], June 18, 1993, in Janjić, *Srpski odgovor*, 189.

78. Vuk Drašković, speech at literary soirée in Zrenjanin, April 2, 1989, "Kako voditi i dobiti boi na Kosovu" [How to fight and win the battle in Kosovo], reprinted in *Koekude Srbijo* [Quo Vadis, Serbia?], 124 and 126.

79. Interview with Miloš Knežević, "Savez sa Amerikom-fiks-ideja" (An alliance with America—an obsession], *Javnost*, October 18, 1997, 11. Dobrica Ćosić had suggested already in 1991 "planned exchanges of population"; according to him, these "are very difficult and very painful, but better than living in hate and mutual killing—[and] are possible." Interview with Dobrica Ćosić, "Istorijska prekretnica za srpski narod" (A historic turning point for the Serbian people), *Politika*, July 26, 1991, 2. Radovan Karadžić, likewise, urged that "if it is necessary, [then] carry out an exchange of territory and an exchange of populations." He gave as examples to follow the cases of the Greeks and Turks and the partition of India; interview with Karadžić by M. Durić, "Karadžić: Sporazum Srba i Hrvata vodi miru" [Karadžić: An agreement between the Serbs and the Croats leads to peace], *Politika*, December 30, 1992, 8. Also, according to Šešelj, "First, I did not support any ethnic cleansing. As far as the SRS (Serbian Radical Party) is concerned, we were only in favor of a civilized exchange of populations," interview with Vojislav Šešelj by Ljilja Jorgovanović, "Branili smo Muslimane od Arkana!" [We protected the Muslims from Arkan], *Srpska reč*, September 11, 1995, 41. Miroljub Jevtić concluded that "every exchange of population from free Serbian territory with those that are still under Muslim occupation can be seen only as legitimate self-defense." Miroljub Jevtić, "Kuran—etnicka metla" [The Qur'an—an ethnic broom], *Javnost*, August 19, 1995, 31. Writer Milan Stojan Protić, also referring to the population exchanges between Greece and Turkey, concluded that "had we established the precedent of a voluntary resettlement of populations, everything would have looked different. . . . Today any discussion about free resettlement of populations is completely acceptable." Interview with Milan Stojan Protić by Mirjana Bobić-Mojsilović, "Staka za sakatu dušu" [A crutch for a crippled soul], *Duga*, May 28–June 10, 1994, 24.

80. Danilo Gavrilović, "Srbi brane otadžbinu svoju" [The Serbs are defending their fatherland], *Za krst cašni i slobodu zlatnu* [For the noble cross and dear freedom], 148.

81. At an academic gathering in 1993 celebrating Njegoš's birth, Serb scholars praised him for having been a "great poet and humanist philosopher. " One of them, Dragutin Vukotić, citing what he viewed as a permanent conflict between "East and West, [between] the cross and the crescent," concluded that "we must adhere to Njegoš' views today too, since they are relevant and not

made obsolete by time. The analogies are very apparent, and applying these assessments by Njegoš to our times is unavoidable." Cited in "Da čovjek bude čovjek" [In order for a man to be a man], *Spona*, October 7, 1993, 22.

82. As sociologist Leo Kuper stresses, for the occurrence of genocide the development of an ideology is especially significant, insofar as a guide and justification are needed: "At least when operating collectively, they [i.e., the perpetrators of genocide] need an ideology to legitimate their behaviour, for without it they would have to see themselves and one another as what they really are—common thieves and murderers." Leo Kuper, *Genocide: Its Political Use in the Twentieth Century* (New Haven: Yale University Press, 1981), 84.

83. As Gordon W. Allport stressed in his pioneering work, the function of stereotypes—which he defined as "an exaggerated belief associated with a category"—"is to justify (rationalize) our conduct in relation to that category." *The Nature of Prejudice* (Garden City, NY: Doubleday, 1958), 187. Such an external definition of another group inherently implies an exercise in power, Richard Jenkins, "Rethinking Ethnicity: Identity, Categorization, and Power," *Ethnic and Racial Studies* (April 1994): 197–223.

84. As an expert on genocide, Herbert C. Kelman, notes perceptively: "Sanctioned massacres become possible to the extent that we deprive fellow human beings of identity and community. Thus when a group of people is defined entirely in terms of a category to which they belong, and when this category is excluded from the human family, then the moral restraints against killing them are more readily overcome. " Herbert C. Kelman, "Violence Without Moral Restraint: Reflections on the Dehumanization of Victims and Victimizers," *Journal of Social Issues* 29.4 (1973): 49. Also see van der Dennen, "Ethnocentrism and In-Group/Out-Group Differentiation," 29–30.

85. *Javnost*, for example, listed many of the intellectuals that feature in this study as "patriots." Milovan Simić, "Nije polemika, već replika" [It is not a polemic but, rather, a rebuttal], *Javnost*, August 17, 199, 8. Subsequently, in response to changing political conditions, however, the Bosnian Serb entity also began to limit access to more extreme views on Islam in the state-controlled media. Orientalist scholar Miroljub Jevtić complained, "To be honest, I have to say that there are those within the leadership of the Republika Srpska who informed me that they do not like 'my Muslim line' and that in their view I am too radical." Interview by Srboljub Vrbić, "Islam kao sudbina" [Islam as destiny], *Javnost*, December 14, 1996, 10.

86. Zoran Djindjić, for example, noted that the "the Albanians by culture, language, and way of life are an element in our life that is hard to integrate, and that would be hard to integrate in any Western civilization. . . . That is an objective problem: the confrontation of two ways of life, of two civilizations." Interview by Gordana Janicijević, "Ispraviću krivu Drinu" [I will straighten out the crooked Drina], *Duga*, September 3–16, 1994, 31.

Christ Killer, Kremlin, Contagion

Michael A. Sells

In the summer of July of 1995 the United Nations civil and military authorities in Bosnia refused to authorize air strikes to protect the U.N.-declared "safe area" of Srebrenica as the forces of Serb general Ratko Mladić closed in on the enclave. In front of UN soldiers Mladić's men separated the thousands of captive Muslim civilians into two groups. Women, elderly men, and boys were placed in one group, older teenage boys and men in a second. Serb soldiers and militiamen began torturing and killing captives within the sight and earshot of UN officials. Approximately seventy-five hundred boys and men were then led away for extermination. In the ensuing days they were killed, disposed of in mass graves throughout eastern Bosnia. Many surviving women and children were sexually abused. The town's mosques were dynamited, as were mosques throughout the territory occupied by Serb nationalists.

Srebrenica came to symbolize Western policy in Bosnia-Herzegovina. For three years UN military and civil officials ignored or minimized the systematic nature of the "ethnic cleansing." Officials at both the U.S. State Department and UN repressed early reports on concentration camps and killing centers. A language of "all sides are guilty," "these people are killing one another," and "civil war" was used to equate victim and perpetrator and to deny any moral responsibility for forceful action to stop the atrocities. With the media largely limited to covering the siege of Sarajevo, the international public rarely saw the more systematic mass killings and organized atrocities taking place in the countryside. What was euphemistically called ethnic cleansing—and has now been recognized by the UN International Criminal Tribunal for the Former Yugoslavia as genocide—took place during a Western-enforced arms embargo that affected primarily the vulnerable Muslims of Bosnia and a simultaneous Western refusal to use UN or NATO forces to stop the mass killing. European and North American officials, from British foreign minister Douglas Hurd to U.S. general Colin Powell warned repeatedly that the Serb forces carrying out the atrocities were the same, in terms of courage and resistance to outside force, as the Yugoslav partisans of World War II. The result over three years was consistent: in each town and village taken by Serb and Croat nationalists, the Muslim populations would be singled out for persecution, detention, torture, rape, mass killing, and cultural annihilation.[1]

The Srebrenica massacre finally goaded the UN into authorizing NATO air strikes against the Serb military. Within a few weeks the Serb army siege of Sarajevo had collapsed and Serb forces, hailed by General Powell and others as nearly invincible, were routed by a Croatian and Bosnian counteroffensive. As the Serb army, which had been so powerful while attacking civilian populations, was on the verge of complete defeat, NATO nations then forced Bosnian and Croat forces to halt their advance. The Dayton peace agreement was signed in November of the same year.

The UN general secretary has since issued a self-critical report on its betrayal of Srebrenica. The report acknowledges persistent, systemic UN failure, over three years, to recognize what the Serb militant nationalists were doing and stop it. One item merits full citation.[2]

496. The failure to fully comprehend the extent of the Serb war aims may explain in part why the Secretariat and the Peacekeeping Mission did not react more quickly and decisively when the Serbs initiated their attack on Srebrenica. In fact, rather than attempting to mobilize the international community to support the enclave's defence, we gave the Security Council the impression that the situation was under control, and many of us believed that to be the case. The day before Srebrenica fell we reported that the Serbs were not attacking when they were. We reported that the Bosniacs had fired on an UNPROFOR blocking position when it was the Serbs. We failed to mention urgent requests for air power. In some instances in which incomplete and inaccurate information was given to the Council, this can be attributed to problems

with reporting from the field. In other instances, however, the reporting may have been illustrative of a more general tendency to assume that the parties were equally responsible for the transgressions that occurred.

At one point the report raises what it calls the foremost question concerning the betrayal of Srebrenica: "How can this have been allowed to happen?" (par. 469). That question leads beyond a review of UN peacekeeping procedures toward wider issues of ideology. Why would many Bosnian Serbs and Croats, at the urging of leaders in Serbia and Croatia, turn so quickly against their former neighbors and colleagues? How could Western policy makers have ignored the intentions of Serb military and paramilitary forces that had been openly proclaimed and clearly manifested in a three-year pattern of organized atrocity?[3] How was it possible to equate victims with perpetrators for years, in the face of clear evidence of the persecution? And why were Western powers adamant in ignoring the genocide convention of 1948 requiring them, as signatories, to prevent genocide or stop it when it occurs?

It may be madness to turn on one's neighbors, colleagues, and friends with the intent to exterminate them. It may be madness for forces that could stop such a crime to acquiescence in it, with willful determination, for three long years. But there is an interior logic to such madness. That interior logic begins with the myth of age-old antagonisms: Muslims and Christians in Bosnia have been killing one another for centuries we are told. It is not only that there have been tragic conflicts in the past in Bosnia but that the root of those conflicts are inscribed into the fabric of the culture: the conflict is inevitable, and it would be a form of cultural imperialism for anyone to interfere with it. Serb and Croat militants turned this myth of age-old antagonisms into an ideology to motivate and justify their attempt to create religiously pure and homogenous Orthodox Serb and Croat Catholic states. A wider circle of writers from outside the Balkans, writing for a different audience, have advanced their own version of essential Balkan incompatibilities. The ideology of conflict built upon the myth of age-old hatreds contains within it a robust logic and a complex set of mutually reinforcing historical assumptions that lead to an ineluctable conclusion. Once the presumed age-old Balkan antagonisms were established as received wisdom, the tenacious three-year acquiescence in the ethnic cleansing was guaranteed.

Islam as "Christ Killer"

The central text for the contemporary Serb religious nationalism manifested at Srebrenica was in fact composed during the nineteenth century. At
that time Serb nationalists reimagined the story of Prince Lazar, the Serb
prince killed in the 1389 Battle of Kosovo, transforming it into a Christ story.
They portrayed Prince Lazar as a Christ figure, at a Last Supper before the
battle and surrounded by twelve knight-disciples, one of whom was a traitor.
Lazar's death at the hands of the Ottoman army was the death of Serbia.
Lazar's passion was the Serbian Golgotha. Both Turks and Muslim Slavs
were (and are) responsible for the death of the Christ-prince Lazar.

The implications of the story were set out most powerfully in 1857 by
Bishop Petar Njegoš, in his most famous work, *The Mountain Wreath*.[4] The
work depicts not the battle of Kosovo itself but a later event known as the
extermination of the Turkifiers (*istraga poturice*), believed to have taken
place in eighteenth-century Montenegro. The extermination of the Slavic
Muslims of Montenegro is glorified as the great act that will allow the resurrection of the Serb people.

The drama opens with a decision of the Montenegrin Serb bishops and
nobles to honor the feast day of Pentecost by cleansing the nation of non-
Christians. Serb prince-bishop Danilo summons the Islamic leaders to his
court and offers them one last chance to convert, explaining that they can
convert by water (baptism) or by blood. The Muslim elders propose to
resolve the strife through a "godparent" *(Kum)* ceremony, the Montenegrin
ritual traditionally used for resolution of blood feuds. In such a ceremony
the chiefs of two warring clans each adopt the son of the other as a godson.
When Serb elders reply that the Kum ceremony requires baptism as part of
the adoption ceremony, the Muslims respond by suggesting an interreligious ceremony; Christian children would be baptized and Muslim children would have a ritual tonsure—the nearest Islamic equivalent to baptism.

The Serb elders reject the suggestion, cursing the Muslims as Turkifiers,
race traitors, and defilers of the cross. The epithet "Turkifiers" *(poturice)*
implies that, by converting to Islam, Slavic Muslims had transformed themselves ethnically or racially into an alien people. *The Mountain Wreath* cul-
minates with a graphic depiction of the Christmas-day slaughter of these
Slavic Muslims of Montenegro—men, women, and children—and the
annihilation of their homes, mosques, and other monuments. The Serb warriors are then given the sacrament of communion, without prior confession.

In traditional Montenegrin Christianity, killing (including killing in war) was ritually polluting and required confession. In this case, however, the extermination of the Turkifiers was viewed as an inherently sanctifying act; no confession was needed.

A choral interlude in *The Mountain Wreath* becomes a turning in the decision to proceed with the destruction of the Muslims. The chorus laments the "accursed supper of Kosovo," chants the praises of the knight, Milos Obilić, who killed the Ottoman sultan to avenge Lazar, and curses the memory of Vuk Branković, the knight who betrayed Lazar. The curse of Vuk Branković becomes simultaneously the curse of all those who do not fight the Turks and thus imitate Branković's betrayal. The Slavic Muslims have themselves become Turk by adopting Islam and thus are, by nature, traitors to the Serb people. God is angry with Serbia because its leaders have refusing to act forcefully against the Turkifiers.[5]

The Lazar story was at the center of the revival of Serb nationalism in the 1980s. Violent confrontations broke out between the majority Albanian and minority Serb populations in Kosovo, where Lazar had perished. The Serbian Orthodox church claimed that Albanians, the majority of whom are Muslim, were attempting to "ethnically cleanse" Serbs from the region and were carrying out organized rape against Serb women and organized annihilation of Serb monuments. By 1986 Serb Orthodox clerics were claiming that Serbs were suffering genocide in Kosovo. Human rights reports showed something quite different: interethnic tension, fights between Serb and Albanian young men, a higher Albanian birthrate, and Serbian emigration for a variety of economic and cultural reasons. Religious nationalists labeled Albanian women "breeding machines" engaged in a "dirty demographic war."[6] Orthodox bishops in Serbia urged Serb women to bear more children as part of the effort to defend Serb civilization.

At the same time, the Serb nationalist intellectuals and politicians were manipulating historical memory. During World War II most Serbs had lost family to Croat nationalist groups known as Ustashe that had been allied with Nazi Germany. In the later 1980s Serb victims of Ustashe atrocities were disinterred in emotional ceremonies organized by Serb clergy. Because such ceremonies had been repressed during the Tito era, the disinterments, when they finally occurred, carried the power of the return of the repressed. Serb religious nationalists manipulated the ceremonies to portray all contemporary Croats and Bosnian Muslims as identical to the Ustashe of World War II and as peoples genocidal by nature.

The emotionally charged environment of the late 1980s gave immense significance to the events of June 28, 1989, the six-hundredth anniversary of the battle of Kosovo. Reenactments of the battle of Kosovo were staged both before and on Lazar's commemoration day, known as the feast day of Vidovdan. In an extraordinary ritual, the relics of Lazar were transported throughout the area claimed by religious nationalists as the Greater Serbia and arrived in time for Vidovdan at the Gracanica monastery to be ceremonially unveiled, allegedly for the first time in history. On that occasion Slobodan Milošević mounted the podium on the Kosovo battlefield, only a short distance from Gracanica, and stood before a crowd estimated at more than a million. As he spoke of battles of the past and battles to come, Milošević was framed on the podium among key symbols of Serbian religious nationalism. Behind him, at the back of the stage, was the primary symbol, a huge cross formed of four Cs (the "s" sound in Cyrillic) that stand for the slogan "Only unity saves the Serb." Pictures of Milošević's were held up in the crowd alongside those of Lazar.[7]

In a passion play reenactment of the death of a martyr, time collapses. The audience ceases to play the role of mere spectator (as actors who play the villains in passion plays are fully aware, knowing to exit the stage immediately after killing the hero, to avoid being pummeled by the audience). Boundaries between the primordial event and the representation, between actor and audience, melt. The crowd begins to become the participants in the primordial event—in this case the killing of the Christ-prince Lazar. Through the dramaturgy and the prior marshalling of symbols, Serb nationalists harnessed the time collapse and directed it against Muslims, who were branded traitors and put in the role of Christ killers. Sacred space and sacred time were brought together. The primordial event, the Serbian Golgotha, was combined with the alleged current threat (the fabricated genocide against Serbs by Albanians) and the all-too-real recent crimes (the atrocities suffered by Serbs during the Ustashe persecutions). The alleged threat by Albanians to Serb monasteries and the heritage of medieval Serbia, the "Serb Jerusalem," was continually evoked as well. All these strands of myth, memory, and historical recollection were intensified through the prism of Njegoš's *Mountain Wreath*, the central text of Serb religious nationalism. Those caught up in the mass psychology that culminated at Vidovdan in 1989 were ready to turn on their neighbors and see, not the human beings they knew, but the phantasms of a historical mythology. In the collapse of time there is only one timeless moment in which Serbia is forever martyred at the hands of the Turk and, most cruelly, the traitor Vuk Branković who was used as a sign of the Mulsim Slav in its midst.

In the decade preceding the assault on Bosnia, the Serb Orthodox Church played a key role in reviving the most militant version of the Kosovo ideology, in using it to create a mass psychology of fear and revenge, and in legitimating the most extreme Serbian militia and military leaders as defenders of Europe against the "Turks." Official organs of the Serb Orthodox Church served to disseminate the anti-Muslim polemic. Later, bishops and priests supported and gave legitimacy to war-criminals such as Arkan, the architect of the "ethnic cleansing" campaign in Bosnia. In return Arkan supplied bodyguards for the bishops. Priests blessed the "ethnic cleansing" squads before and after their attacks. After the cleansing of the area of its Muslim inhabitants, Serb clergy presided over ritual celebrations, including dedications of new churches and monasteries on or near the sites of destroyed mosques. The Serb bishops also worked to convince Serbs and the wider world that the "ethnic cleansing" never occurred. They reacted to the revelations of the Omarska and Trnopolje concentration camps by "taking full moral responsibility" and "in the name of God's truth" declaring that "such camps neither exist nor ever existed in the territory of the Serbian Republic of Bosnia-Herzegovina."[8] The official Orthodox Christianity represented by the bishops blended into religious nationalism. Militia leaders recited the verses of Njegoš in celebration of the extermination of the Turkifiers before going into battle. They were blessed by Orthodox priests before and after their attacks. After cleansing a town or village of Muslims, they were awarded medals named after the heroes of the Lazar story. They renamed the villages and the streets and other sites within them after heroes of the battle of Kosovo, Serb saints, and figures from the works of Njegoš.

Yugoslav Nobel laureate Ivo Andrić had played a central role in adapting the ideology of Njegoš to the twentieth-century context. According to Andrić, Njegoš's view that Muslim converts were traitors and cowards was not only the view of Njegoš but the view of "the people."[9] If "the people" held such a view, a view of a timeless chasm between Muslim and Christian, then clearly Bosnian Muslims could never be considered part of the people. Andrić took the notion of conversion as transformation of nationality (Njegoš's Turkification) and mixed it with twentieth-century racial theory; conversion was a transformation from the Slavic race to the Turkic race. I have used the term *Christoslavism* to designate the belief that Slavs are

Christian by nature and that conversion from Christianity is both a race-betrayal and race-transformation. Andrić's version of Christoslavism was disseminated through his historical novels, such as *The Bridge on the Drina*, a novel popular among both Croatian and Serbian religious nationalists and still used today throughout much of the Western world to give an "authentic" introduction to Balkan history and society.[10]

Njegoš wrote during the period of the Serb revolution against Ottoman rule. It would be anachronistic to project back upon the author the intentions of later religious nationalists. Yet it is vital to understand the role Njegoš's writings played in the explosion of radical Serb nationalism at the end of the twentieth century. Those writings had been read continuously since their composition. They had been memorized by Gavrilo Princip, who ignited World War I by assassinating the Austrian archduke Ferdinand on Vidovdan of 1914. They were read during the Tito period as literature, but their anti-Muslim ideological element, though left unspoken, was not forgotten. They helped form a popular imagination that, given the right historical circumstances, could bring them into the present and read them as national scripture. The break-up of the former Yugoslavia and the political manipulations of Serb politicians and intellectuals provided the right circumstances. And within a couple years after the 1989 Vidovdan commemoration, those manipulating Serb historical mythology had helped created a mass psychology that they could no longer control.

For those impassioned spectators at the Vidovdan commemoration, Muslim and Christian are indeed age-old antagonists. In *The Mountain Wreath* this antagonism is not only old, it is primordial, inscribed within the essence of Serb Orthodox Christianity and Islam: the Serb nation can never be healed until the poison of Islam is removed from its body politic. Once violence had been instigated and Serb soldiers and militias had spilled blood, the die was cast; there was nothing Slavic Muslims could do, say, or be that could redeem their existence in Bosnia in the eyes of Serb nationalists. In *The Mountain Wreath* the final temptation of Bishop Danilo was a gesture of peace and fraternity offered by Slavic Muslims. He could carry out his heroic act only when he realized that behind the smiling faces of the Turkifiers were the traitors who betrayed Lazar and would do so again. This revived and intensified nineteenth-century version of the clash of civilizations was passed on to the non-Serb world through a variety of writings, including the works of Bat Ye'or and Robert Kaplan.

Islam as Jihad and Dhimmitude

The writings of Giselle Litmann, who writes under the pseudonym of Bat Ye'or ("Daughter of the Nile"), were championed by Protestant theologian Jacques Ellul, who authored prefaces to her books. In two books, *The Dhimmi: Jews and Christians under Islam* and *The Decline of Eastern Christianity Under Islam: from Jihad to Dhimmitude*, Ellul and Bat Ye'or portray Islam—always and everywhere—as an unchanging force of aggressive violence (jihad) and parasitic, enslaving absorption (*dhimmitude*).[11] Although Bat Ye'or claims to be writing a history of Jewish and Christian peoples under Islamic rule, she concludes with a totalizing claim about the nature of Islam and its relationship to all non-Muslim peoples granted *dhimmi* status under Islamic governance, which would include Jews, Christians, and other "peoples of the book":

> The oblivion which surrounds the dhimmi past is not accidental; it reflects the abolition of dhimmi history. The annihilation of a community transfers its cultural heritage—civilization, arts, and sciences—to the dominating group. Cultural imperialism accompanies territorial imperialism; culture, monopolized by the authorities, becomes an additional instrument of domination and alienation. In fact, the umma claims a monopoly of culture: the dhimmis' languages are banned, relegated to the liturgy; their monuments, testimony to their civilizations' greatness, are destroyed or Islamized.[12]

These categorical judgments are buttressed with an elaborate scholarly apparatus that might seem quite impressive to those not familiar with Islamic history and with how much has been left out of the picture or falsified. The golden age of Hebrew poetry serves as one example of such falsification. Up through the period of late antiquity Hebrew poetry was confined to religious and liturgical contexts. It was only in the medieval Islamicate civilization that Jewish poets, in close cultural interaction with Arabic culture and poetic traditions, created the golden age of Hebrew secular poetry—in Andalus, foremost, but also in other areas of the Islamicate world, such as Egypt and Yemen.[13] Although Jews in neighboring Christian-ruled territories made impressive cultural and literary achievements (in Kabbala mysticism, for example), they lacked the kind of secular poetic tradition their Jewish near neighbors had created under Islamic rule. Not only did

Islam not relegate Hebrew to liturgical purposes and not forbid Jews from creating a secular poetry, it was Islam-governed Andalus that provided the conditions for the major premodern sustained manifestation—and a stunning manifestation it was—of Hebrew secular poetry.[14]

Bat Ye'or does similar violence to the history of the Balkans. Under Ottoman rule South Slavs developed a major poetic tradition, both epic and lyric, a tradition that Catholics, Muslims, and Serb Orthodox shared. In the nineteenth century one version of this language became the self-conscious basis for Serbian national identity. Bat Ye'or's own earlier admission that Serbian became the "official language of the Turkish chancellery for affairs related to the Balkan peninsula"[15] does nothing to slow her rush to the categorical claim that under Islam the languages of dhimmi peoples were banned or confined to the liturgy.[16]

Bat Ye'or's claim that the *umma*, or Islamic polity, abolishes the history of Jews and Christians turns out to be less a description of an objective reality than a kind of self-reflection. If the history of Jews and Christians has been abolished under Islam, it is under the peculiar version of Islam presented by Bat Ye'or, where, indeed, the cultural achievements of Jews and Christians have been either expurgated or—insofar as they are mentioned at all—dismissed as treasonous collaboration with a slave master.[17] The result is an erasure of all cultural achievements of non-Muslims in Bat Ye'or's version of history in which Non-Muslims exist only as victims, deprived of all culture and meaning, or as treasonous collaborators in the annihilation of their own people.

Islam developed its cultural ambience and civilizational treasures, Bat Ye'or claims, "in the midst of conquered peoples, feeding off their vigor and on the dying, bloodless body of dhimmitude."[18] This portrayal of Islam as cultural vampire is based in part upon an ignorance of nomadic societies that Bat Ye'or identifies with savagery and barbarism. She cannot entertain the possibility that the Arabs of Arabia could have had any culture at all; by definition, then, they had to be parasites on the cultures of those they conquered.[19]

Bat Ye'or's negation of the cultural achievements of non-Muslims under Islamic governance is exemplified by implicit denial of the existence of the Serbian monasteries in Kosovo and throughout much of the former Yugoslavia. In the same way, Serbian nationalists, who extol the beauty and majesty of the Serbian art of Kosovo, who follow the ritual transportation of Prince Lazar's relics from monastery to monastery, who catalogue the hundreds of

architectural masterworks and priceless frescoes and icons that were built in
pre-Ottoman times and survived five hundred years of Ottoman rule, will
maintain, tenaciously, that the Ottomans annihilated or Islamicized all non-
Islamic sacral and artistic heritage.[20] This conflicted rage reached the level of
mob pathology through the demonstrations in Serbia from 1987–1991, the rise
to power of Slobodan Milošević, and the subsequent genocide in Bosnia. In
Bosnia Serb nationalists, motivated in part by fabricated claims of Muslim
annihilation of Serb sacral heritage, waged a campaign of organized destruction against all Islamic monuments, including mosques, Sufi shrines,
libraries, museums, tombs, and Ottoman-style secular architecture. When
challenged on their portrayal of Ottoman rule as absolute evil, Serbian
nationalists find in Bat Ye'or's writings a non-Serb, academic validation.[21]

Bat Ye'or depicts the Ottoman *devşirme* (conscription of young boys into
the Janissary corps) as another essentialized aspect of Islamic polity, which
she claims (echoing Serb nationalist polemic) "steals the blood of subject
peoples." No people should be expected to look back fondly at the abuses of
their former colonizer, and Serbs have every justification for feeling resentment at the years of humiliation and domination symbolized most powerfully in the forced conscription (and conversion) of Serb boys. Yet in her
portrayal of *devşirme* as the evil and eternal essence of Islam she fails to note
that Ottomans, however flawed in this regard, were infinitely more tolerant
of religious diversity than the rulers of Christian Europe who quickly eradicated the Muslim minorities in Spain and much of the Balkans.[22] One of
the few authorities Bat Ye'or cites on the evil of the *devşirme* system and its
globalizing quality in Islam is the early twentieth-century Serb nationalist
Jovan Cvijić.[23] *Devşirme* elicits from Bat Ye'or not an analysis of the institution in history and in relation to Islam as religion and as polity, nor a condemnation of specific practices and specific abuses in the past, but generalizations about the timelessly evil essence of Islam.[24]

Serbian religious nationalists cite in defense of their goal of destroying
Bosnian Muslims a 1994 interview in which Bat Ye'or announces that
Bosnia is a "spearhead" for the Islamicization of Europe. In the interview,
Bat Ye'or even suggests that the independent Bosnia will serve as a staging
ground for this attack on Europe by providing Muslim immigrants with
European passports received in Bosnia.[25] The accusation is particularly
forced given the fact that most Muslims come to Europe for employment
and even a successful Bosnia would hardly offer the employment opportunities offered by Germany and France in the past few decades. Bat Ye'or's

polemic against Islam has moved full circle, as supporters of contemporary Serb nationalists cite her as a scholarship authority, while she bases her observation upon the writings of an earlier Serb religious nationalist who worked for a greater Serbia.

Whereas Bat Ye'or poses her metaphysics of Islam as history, her collaborator Jacques Ellul writes from the position of Christian superiority over other religions, Islam in particular. Ellul claims that Islam (as opposed to his own tradition) treats women unfairly and is, unlike Christianity, "essentially violent!" (exclamation Ellul's). Ellul finds a quote from an almost unknown fourteenth-century misogynist Islamic theologian about the alleged lack of souls in women and, like Bat Ye'or, makes an immediate extrapolation from a particular example to generalization about the nature of Islam.[26] (Ellul at this point is seemingly oblivious to similar statements found throughout the works of St. Augustine, the most influential figure of the western Christian tradition.)

The moral polemic is founded upon an implicit comparison of Islamic polity to Christian polity, particularly to the polity of European Christianity. Thus the alleged dhimmi-jihad nature of Islam is said to be impervious to Western, Christian values (human rights, democracy, tolerance, and peace). Bat Ye'or, in rejecting analogies between dhimmi communities in Islam and Islamic minorities in Europe, alleges that the Muslims in Europe are "voluntary, economic immigrants" and that the "religious minorities of Christendom have never represented the remnants of national majorities.[27] The claim is doubly dubious. First, European Muslim communities such as Slavic Muslims are defined out of existence, since they are obviously not economic immigrants or even immigrants at all. Second, Bat Ye'or accepts the myth of purity of origin that would postulate Christianity as an indigenous religion throughout Europe, the Americas, Australia, and other parts of Christendom. Along with Slavic Muslims, American Indians and Australian Aborigines are also defined out of existence. As for those areas in Christendom where there really are no "indigenous, formerly majority populations, reduced by persecution and exile to a minority status," the reason for the absence is that the earlier populations were so thoroughly annihilated, converted, or forcibly assimilated that they no longer exist as communities that could be subjected to minority status. Bat Ye'or's claims erase the fact that pre-Christian pagans were killed or converted by force in the early Middle Ages (without the relative luxury of any analogous status to that of dhimmis), that any trace of religious dissidence during the High Middle Ages and

Renaissance was effaced by the Inquisition and witch burnings, that the descendants of Muslims, the Moriscos, were "ethnically cleansed" in 1609, that the Jewish community of Spain was expelled in 1492, and that European Jews were subjected to repeated persecution ending in the Holocaust. By obscuring the existence of pre-Christian and other old, non-Christian communities in Europe as well as the reason for their disappearance in other areas of Europe, Bat Ye'or constructs an invidious comparison between the allegedly humane Europe of Christian and Enlightenment values and the ever present persecution within Islam. Whenever the possibility is raised of actually comparing circumstances of non-Christians in Europe to non-Muslims under Islamic governance in a careful, thoughtful manner, Bat Ye'or forecloses such comparison.[28]

While Bat Ye'or claims to write history, Ellul writes a theology of history:

> It will probably be said that every religion in its expanding phase carries the risks of war, that history records hundreds of religious wars and it is now a commonplace to make this connection. But it is, in fact, "passion"—it concerns mainly a fact which it would be easy to demonstrate does not correspond to the fundamental message of the religion. This disjuncture is obvious for Christianity. In Islam, however, *jihad* is a religious obligation. It forms part of the duties that the believer must fulfill; it is Islam's *normal* path to expansion.[29] (emphasis Ellul's)

Christianity's superiority to Islam rests in Ellul's proposition that religious violence in Islam is a duty, whereas religious war and persecution in Christianity has only been a matter of passion. Passion, precisely. Passion is a defining moment in Christian theology. Passion is reenacted in the calendar, in the Mass, in the art. The manipulation and abuse of the passion of Jesus was a guiding motif for the original persecutions of the Jews, often stirred up directly in connection with the Passion Play. Passion was the dynamis of the six hundredth Vidovdan anniversary at Kosovo that set the stage for the assault on Bosnia's Muslims. The passion of Lazar is the central construct behind the proposition that Serbs can never live with Muslims and that the Serb nation will not be resurrected until the Christ killers and race traitors are exterminated.[30]

Miroljub Jevtić, one of Belgrade's academic specialists on the question of Muslims, stated at the beginning of the genocide in Bosnia that Slavic Muslims of today bear the blood on their hands for the death of Serbs martyred in fight against the Ottoman Turks. Such a statement is rooted in the Kosovo passion and the Christoslavic notion of conversion as race betrayal and race transformation. A more recent statement by Jevtić is rooted in the same globalized "history" of Islam that is presented by Serbian religious militants and by Bat Ye'or. The Serb nationalist academic and "expert" can gaze at the Serbian monasteries, art, and culture that survived five hundred years of Ottoman rule, draw inspiration from them, and then speak as if those same monuments do not and can not exist, that by the very definition of Ottoman rule they must have been "destroyed or Islamized." Jevtić meditates upon the evil essence of Islam and upon the premise—woven throughout the works of Ellul and Bat Ye'or, that, unlike Christianity, Islam is unchanging and unchangeable; that even when it appears to change it quickly reverts to its essence of aggressive violence and enslavement.[31] He meditates upon the killing of the Christ-prince Lazar, the racial transformation that supposedly occurs when a Slav converts to Islam (Turkification), and he brings together passion and historical postulate to conclude:

> If you want to destroy a Turk, you must destroy his every part. If you do not do this, you risk that he moves about like a whole Turk, that is the whole of Bosnia, and becomes dangerous like the whole of Bosnia. Acting strategically, the designers—that is the leaders of the Federal Republic of Yugoslavia—did not know this, and the leaders of the Republika Srpska, having followed the advice from Belgrade, made a strategic mistake that is difficult to correct. The only remedy would be to completely destroy each "part of the Turk's body."[32]

If Ellul and Bat Ye'or's thesis is correct, if Islam is an unchanging force of aggression and enslavement, if any appearance of tolerance, democracy, or multireligious compatibility is by nature ephemeral and will lead to an inevitable reversion to the unchanging Islamic core nature, then Jevtić's conclusion is ineluctable and the totalizing violence he advocates against his Slavić Muslim neighbors is not only justified, it is required.

The influence of Jacques Ellul and Bat Ye'or has extended beyond Serbian nationalists and their sympathizers in French-speaking Europe to North America. Their writings have become central to what might be called the "Global Persecution of Christians Awareness Movement," an attempt by the religious right in the U.S. to make the protection of Christians and

Christian evangelization around the world a congressionally mandated
aspect of U.S. foreign policy.[33] Through such efforts the Christian Awareness Movement works assiduously to supplement the traditional anti-Com-
munist ideology of the religious right with an equally developed anti-Muslim position.[34] Bat Ye'or has also been championed by the influential U.S.
Institute on Religion and Public Life, one of the organizations that has
helped gain her a major voice in the U.S. Congress.[35]

In the writings of Bat Ye'or and Jacques Ellul the parallel between the
two "evil empires" is made explicit. Not only is Islam a global threat to Western civilization, it has already begun to create the "Dhimmitude of the
West."[36] Through unargued assertions that, while Christianity has changed,
Islam has not changed and cannot change, Bat Ye'or creates a vision of Islam
as an evil, infiltrating force that, even if it seems capable of evolution, will
revert to its innate character of jihad and dhimmitude. Bat Ye'or and Ellul
offer one and only possibility for change: Islam can change, they write, as
Soviet communism changed at the end of the cold war—that is, by ceasing
to exist. [37]

Islam as Contagion

In the spring of 1993 the Clinton administration abandoned its previously
pledged commitment to resist ethnic cleansing and genocide in Bosnia.[38]
The change occurred after the president, first lady, and chairman of the
Joint Chiefs of Staffs read Robert Kaplan's *Balkan Ghosts*, a work that portrayed the Balkans as a world of irrational hatreds and of peoples fated, by
genetics or history, or some murky combination of the two, to incessant wars
and atrocities.[39] From a commitment to protecting the innocent from genocidal attack, the administration shifted to a position that nothing could be
done until the various parties in the region stop "killing one another," slid-
ing back into the same moral equivalence and stereotypes that had marked
the earlier Bush administration's disastrous refusal to confront the 1992
assault on Bosnia.

Bat Ye'or and Jacques Ellul are ideologues. They have a single paradigm
of the unchanging essence of Islam and follow it consistently. Robert Kaplan
is a journalist-traveler whose writings reflect the sources and inspiration he
has most recently encountered; though all his writings are united around the
authorial concern over virility. In a book on the Afghan war Kaplan is not

unsympathetic to what he takes to be Islam. Indeed, like the traveler-adventurers he admires and on whom he bases his self-portrayal, he is attracted to what he thinks he finds. Thus, he begins with the standard generalization: "Women are oppressed throughout the Islamic world." After characterizing Pathan Islamic culture as one that can be summed up by the misogynist proverb "Women have no noses. They will eat shit,"[40] Kaplan opens a two-hundred-page romance, with himself as a major character, emulating the Pathan fighters, growing a beard, reveling in what he finds to be their manly virtue, bonding with them, and emulating their contempt for the other, allegedly less virile ethnic groups in the area.

In *The Arabists* Kaplan singles out, as the island of virility in a sea of State Department impotence, an embassy official who poses as a Muslim, imitating Richard Burton, and sneaks into the Ka'ba, Islam's most sacred space, or *haram*. Kaplan entitles the chapter on this State Department modern-day Richard Burton "Indiana Jones."[41] In the popular Indiana Jones adventurer films the protagonist starts out as a mild-mannered, bespectacled scholar in University of Chicago, wood-paneled academia. He abandons academia, gets outfitted in the latest version of "Banana Republic" colonial-style khakis, and sets off to penetrating the darkness of the third world, seeking treasure and finding it, armed with a whip to keep at bay both snakes and the swarming chaos of the non-Western world.[42]

The adventures of Indiana Jones—white man savior with a whip—were criticized by some for their depiction of non-Western peoples (Middle Eastern and South Asian) as mindless savages. The saving grace of Indiana Jones for many is filmmaker Stephen Spielberg's ironic refusal to take the films' stereotypes seriously. Modeled after earlier action serials that had been part of American war propaganda, the films appeared from 1981–1989, roughly the Reagan era of "evil empire" cold-war confrontation and post-hostage-crisis tension. They both revel in and parody the classic American adventurer fantasy.

Kaplan knows no irony. He implies that if only there had been more people in the State Department like his hero Ka'ba-penetrating hero, Saddam Hussein would have been deterred from invading Kuwait. And while Spielberg's Indiana Jones discovers the power of the Biblical ark of the covenant hidden within a maze of Middle Eastern cultures, Kaplan's State Department hero, after all his dissimulation and his deception of his Islamic hosts, finds nothing in Mecca aside from some preachers preaching at a "low intellectual level." He might have listened more carefully to what they were preaching; the low intellectual level of Wahhabi fanaticism has not prevented it from playing a major role in the radicalization of anti-Western militancy in Islam. To understand the signficance of the recent domination of Mecca and Medina by Wahhabi ideology requires something other than the ability to dissemble as a Muslim and penetrate the intimate chambers of the Islamic *haram*. Ultimately, Kaplan's hero is a rather limp version of Indiana Jones, acting out of what he perceives is a sense of mission, ignoring essential clues, discovering little, and enjoying it less.

While the Kaplan of *The Arabists* is fixated on questions of impotence and virility, the Kaplan of *Balkan Ghosts* is obsessed with Islam as Ottoman despotism, rot, filth, disease—themes taken directly and transparently from the writings of Rebecca West and Joseph Brodsky. This obsession intersects tragically with the stereotypes of Serbian nationalists and of Ellul and Bat Ye'or. In the case of Brodsky it can be called "Balkanism," the notion that Islam infected the Balkans through Ottoman rule in such a way as to make it impossible for its people to live together, establish any kind of functioning society, or even basic human decency. Balkanism is at the core of the "age-old antagonisms" cliché used by Western governments as an excuse for acquiescence in the genocide in Bosnia, criticized by 1992 presidential candidate Bill Clinton, used by Clinton himself after the *Balkan Ghosts* readings, and then formally renounced by the Clinton administration after the Srebrenica massacre.

"I hate the corpses of empires. They stink as nothing else."[43] It is fitting that *Balkan Ghosts* begins the book with a quote from that traveler-adventurer Rebecca West who presented a vivid depiction of the Balkans filtered through a perspective she took from the Serb nationalists she favored. West portrays the Balkans as the region of age-old tribal killers, conditioned by history and Ottoman oriental despotism to perpetual slaughter.[44]

Kaplan adopts as his own motto the following remark by West: "The Turks ruined the Balkans, with a ruin so great that it is has not been repaired. . . . There is a lot of emotion loose about the Balkans which has lost its legitimate employment now that the Turks have been expelled."[45] West writes of loose emotion but she and Kaplan after her accept without question the premise and condition of such emotion, the claim that "the Turks ruined the Balkans." Kaplan then supplements and updates West's vision with that of Russian émigré poet Joseph Brodsky. Kaplan writes:

If like the Russian Nobel laureate Joseph Brodsky you view the Communist Empire as the twentieth-century equivalent of the Ottoman Turkish Empire, with the historical compass line of decrepit, Eastern despotism traveling north from Istanbul (formerly Constantinople) to Moscow—from the Sultan's Topkapi Palace to the Kremlin—then Dame Rebecca had already capsulized the situation in Serbia, in the rest of former Yugoslavia, and in the other Balkan states for the 1990's. Now that Communism has fallen and the Soviets have been expelled, *there is a lot of emotion loose about the Balkans which has lost its legitimate employment.* (emphasis Kaplan's)[46]

Therefore, Kaplan explains, "Without the cultural and economic limbo of half a millennium of Turkish rule, Communism might not have been established here [in Serbia] so easily."[47] Brodsky's earlier vision of Communism as the reincarnation of Ottoman oriental despotism was popularized in a *New Yorker* essay entitled "Reflections (Byzantium)": "As for ideas, in what way does the late M. Suslov, or whoever is now scraping the ideological dish, differ from the Grand Mufti? What distinguishes the General Secretary from the Padishah—or, indeed, from the emperor? . . . What distinguishes the Politburo from the Great Divan? And isn't it only one step from a divan to an ottoman?"[48] In Brodsky's case the thesis of a common Eastern (Asiatic-Muslim-communist) despotism rises out of his poetic meditations on the barbarism of Islam. "Reflections" consists of a series of observations: that castration is the soul of the East, that East lacks rationality, order, principles of rhythm, and respect for the individual that marks "our civilization." Brodsky's forty-six reflections are made up of passages like the following:

> The delirium and horror of the East. The dusty catastrophe of Asia. Green only on the banner of the Prophet. Nothing grows here except mustaches. A black-eyed, overgrown-with-stubble-before-supper part of the world. Bonfire embers doused with urine. That smell! A mixture of foul tobacco and sweaty soap and the underthings wrapped around loins like another turban.[49]

Kaplan echoes Brodsky's metaphors and horror of pollution in his description of the Albanian Muslim population of Kosovo. Elevators in the capital Prishtina remind him of a toilet stall. The hotel room "smelled of the previous occupant—unfiltered cigarettes and hair tonic." The carpet was "bile green," although later he assures us, "Green was one color you never saw in Prishtina,"[50] a characterization that echoes Brodsky ("Green only on the banner of the Prophet"). While Brodsky's imaginative gaze focuses upon "the underthings wrapped around loins like another turban," Kaplan's gaze fixes on Albanian young men "who wore threadbare pants held up by safety pins in places where zippers should have been."[51] The Tito-era prefabricated apartments in Prishtina remind Kaplan of vomit.[52]

The problem here is not confined to slavish literary imitation. Kaplan not only echoes Brodsky's metaphors, obsessions, and artful polemic but also then adopts, wholesale, Brodsky's attribution of East European despotism to Islam. Not until he traveled to Prishtina, Kaplan writes, did he "fully grasp the extent of the crime committed by Tito and the other sultans going all the way back to Murad."[53] The areas of Prishtina he describes, built largely after World War II, represent not only the communist regime that constructed them but the Ottoman progenitor of that regime: "Prishtina seems a regurgitation not only of the Turkish past, but of the Turkish present too."[54] Later Kaplan refers to the Turkish border town of Adrianople as the "Europe's forgotten rear door."[55]

The derivative nature of Kaplan's book did not prevent it from being aggressively marketed and from becoming an influence on U.S. policy in Bosnia. Major booksellers tended to make a minishrine to *Balkan Ghosts*, singling it out on the shelf for special display. Kaplan was sought out as for what the press considered his expertise on the Balkans. In an op-ed piece in the *New York Times*, Kaplan repeated his central stereotype: "Those European countries with Ottoman legacies close to the Middle East have had an extremely difficult time adjusting to a free society."[56] No specific legacies were mentioned in the op-ed and no evidence was given.

Toward the end of "Reflections (Byzantium)," Brodsky admits that he has not bothered meeting or talking to the people of Istanbul he has just dehumanized in his writing. But then, in a final move, he attributes his dehumanizing stance to the fact that he is also a product of the East: "Who knows? Perhaps my attitude toward people has in its own right a whiff of the East about it, too."[57] In Christian theology, both Catholic and Orthodox, Brodsky's final reflection is a form of false confession: the deed is confessed, but moral responsibility and moral agency is rejected. Or the only responsibility lies with that part of him he detests and projects onto Stalinists, Muslims, Turks, and Asiatics who lack any individuality but are all duplicates (the original meaning of a stereotype) of the same figure.

Brodsky is more self-consciously aware of what he is doing and thus able to couch it in a guise of pseudo-irony, shielding himself from responsibility through the "perhaps" or with the fiction that opens the essay, that he does-n't really mean what he writes: "I suggest that what follows be treated with a due measure of skepticism, if not with total disbelief."[58] After the disclaimer, however, he reasserts his intent and concedes "nothing in quality to the sub-ject [the East, the Turk, Islam] under scrutiny"—that is, he is joking but he means what he says.

Neither Brodsky nor Kaplan ever allows the object of their nausea, the human residents of Istanbul or Prishtina, to speak. Neither tests the idea that, were he to speak to some of them, he might fight them less revolting, and perhaps even human. Both superimpose the East of the geopolitical cold war upon the East of orientializing fantasy.

Obsession and the Bosnian Genocide

In *The Anatomy of Prejudice* Elisabeth Young-Bruehl offers a history and critique of social-scientific theories of prejudice, a discussion of the work of victims of prejudice outside of and contrary to social-scientific discourse. She divides prejudice into three character types or ideologies of desire. The obsessional type is characterized by an ideology of filth and cleansing and is classically illustrated by modern antisemitism. The hysterical type is charac-terized by fear of impotence and castration and by the prejudice of color formed within slavery and its subsequent effects on American society. The narcissistic type is typified by sexism, homophobia, and the constricted soci-eties they reflect and help construct.

While Young-Bruehl emphasizes that these three types are commonly intermixed, her definition of the obsessional prejudice is the type that binds together the three examples of Islamophobic discourse discussed:

The obsessional prejudices feature conspiracies of demonic enemies everywhere, omnipresent pollutants, filthy people, which the obses-sionally prejudiced feel compelled to eliminate—wash away, flush away, fumigate, demolish. The obsessionally prejudiced attribute to their victims a special capacity for commercial or economic conspir-acy and diabolical behind-the-scenes cleverness, and they both envy this capacity and, acting imitatively, turn the fruits of this cleverness (particularly in the domain of technology) on their victims. They imagine the conspirators as having the capacity to penetrate them, get into their bowels and their privacies.[59]

Each of the three texts above fits Young-Bruehl's characterization. Bishop Njegoš portrays Slavic Muslims as those who defile Montenegro and transmogrify into Turks, while still remaining indistinguishable in language, physical type, and culture from their Christian neighbors; they are, therefore, a continual pollution of the body politic and the Serbian nation that must be "cleansed" before the Serbian nation and its Christ-prince can be resurrected. Even the attempts at reconciliation and the sympathetic aspects of the Slavic Muslims are nothing more than a final temptation, a final effort to inject the poison of Turkification into the purity of Serbian people (and, in the later, World War II discourse of Ivo Andrić, race). Modern Serbian clerics and intellectual bring together Christoslavic notions of Turkification, the charge that Muslims have on their hands the blood of the Christ-prince Lazar, and the claim that Serb militias are protecting Europe from the infiltration and conspiracy of fundamentalist Islam.

Ellul and Bat Ye'or present as history a mythology and metaphysics of Islam. Islam is—essentially and always—nothing more than jihad (aggressive penetration) and dhimmitude (parasitic absorption). They write of the "Dhimmitude of the West," the infiltration into the West by the corrupting despotism of Islam through immigration, and they make explicit analogies between Islam and the former Soviet threat. They warn not only of the external threat of Islam but also of the more insidious invasion of the body of Western, Christian, Enlightenment, and democratic values, an invasion represented by the Muslim immigrant.

Kaplan draws on both West and Brodsky to present the Balkans as fatally polluted and constantly infiltrated by the rotting Oriental despotism of the Turk and to present anxiety about the "rear door" of Europe. Anxiety over the rear door of Europe ties back into the conflictual definitions of Europe. As Croat and Serb nationalists were competing to carve up Bosnia in the 1990s, Croat nationalists repeatedly accused Serbs of being contaminated from their contacts with Turks and with Islam, of being Balkanized by such contact, and thus of being incapable of assimilation into Europe. Part of the viciousness of Serb nationalists in their attempt to cleanse themselves of Bosnian Muslims was grounded in the same insecurity; if one feels the infection is within, the desperation of the effort to cleanse it away leads to progressively more extreme measures.[60] As Young-Bruehl writes of the bearers of the obsessional ideology, "They imagine the conspirators as having the capacity to penetrate them, get into their bowels and their privacies."

Serb militants refer to Bosnian Muslims as "Balije," a term believed to be related to the word *bala*, for "mucus" or "spit"—a term that is, according to Bosnian Muslim survivors of ethnic cleansing, "spit out" at them. As Mary Douglas has suggested, the appearance of bodily, interior fluids on the outside (menses, saliva, semen) are classic sources of anxiety about boundaries and occasions for ritual purification.[61] With the collapse of the communist Yugoslavia, the Slavic Muslim, the Turk within, began to appear on the outside surface of the body politic.

Another common term used against Bosnian Muslim women within the rape-camps at Foča was "Turkish whores." The epithet is bound up with the harem fantasy: the accusation (far-fetched given the social realities of Bosnian Islam but deadly in its effectiveness) that Bosnian Muslims had a plot to put Serb women in harems—an accusation that became a signal to militias to begin coordinated actions of organized rape by Serb militiamen against Bosnian Muslim women.[62] As Young-Bruehl writes, "The obsessionally prejudiced attribute to their victims a special capacity for commercial or economic conspiracy and diabolical behind-the-scenes cleverness, and they both envy this capacity and, acting imitatively, turn the fruits of this cleverness (particularly in the domain of technology) on their victims." In this case the "technology" is the alleged biological genocide—both the classical "bloodletting" of the Bat Ye'or and Ivo Andrić version of the Ottoman devşirme, by which Serbian blood and souls would be "drained" into the alien Islamic world, but also the alleged genocidal conspiracy by Slavic and Albanian Muslims to destroy Serbia through their high-birth rate. By turning the tables through organized rape, Slavic Muslim women ("breeding machines") are impregnated with "Serb seed" and rendered unfit for procreation within a Mediterranean society that blames the victim of rape and forecloses her future possibilities for marriage and motherhood.

The harem obsession is directly related to the metaphors of "ethnic cleansing" or "purification." The word *harem* in Arabic means a sacred space, a space to which access is strictly limited and which requires purification before entering. The *harem* par excellence is the precinct around the Ka'ba in Mecca, which is open only to Muslims under certain conditions—and during the Hajj under condition of *ihram*: the ritual preparation (in dress, prayers, ablutions, fastings, abstention from sex) for entering

the sacred place. There are other sacred spaces in the Islamic world in addition to the Ka'ba. Medina and Jerusalem are considered the second and
third *harems*. The prayer niche *(mihrab)* of every mosque points in the direction *(qibla)* of the *harem* in Mecca and orients the worshipper toward that
space. Unsurprisingly, worshippers are expected to ritually purify themselves
before praying in the direction of Mecca. In the West and in Serbian and
Croatian nationalist literature, the term *harem* is almost universally associated with the women's quarter, particularly as it has been known and fanta-
sized through images of Ottoman and other Eastern "harems."[63] For the
militias operating throughout Bosnia, the dynamiting of the mosques was
followed by redynamiting, bulldozing, and, in some cases, hiding rubble. An
estimated one thousand mosques of Bosnia-Herzegovina in Croat- and Serb-
controlled areas—mosques that had in many cases stood side-by-side with
Christian churches for five centuries of interreligious civilization—were
methodically destroyed in less than three years of rule by militant Christian
religious nationalists.[64] These acts occurred simultaneously with organized
rapes. For the Christoslavic nationalist the desecration of the mosques and
the despoiling of Muslim women were related by a logic that made one the
concomitant of the other.

When the ethnically or religiously other is portrayed as filth, the portrayal
helps guide a logic of atrocity, the attempt to systematically reduce the other
to filth. Prosecutors from the ICTY summarized the conditions of the Keraterm camp in Prijedor as consisting of constant beatings, torture, rape, and
killings. In addition, the camp commanders took special sadism in the matter of hygiene. Prisoners would be beaten on their way to and from the toilet.
Their food would be placed near overflowing toilets. In some cases they
would be given only a few seconds a day to leave their overcrowded cells,
with a choice to spend those seconds eating their single ration or using the
toilet. The Muslim victims confined to the Safe Haven Srebrenica were kept
for years in insufficient hygienic conditions, a factor leading to the
identification of Dutch UN soldiers with the Serb soldiers whom they considered cleaner.[65]

All three discourses discussed here contain elements of obsessional ideology. In all three Islam is seen as real evil empire behind the broken communist system—as, in the words of Kaplan repeating Brodsky, "the poison of
eastern despotism and decline, seeping from Byzantium, to the Sultan's
Palace, to the Kremlin."[66] The audiences for each overlapped, but were centered differently. Njegoš as refigured in post–cold war Serb nationalism was

memorized and recited by the Serbian militias who triumphantly posted his verses on the Internet as Bosnian towns were cleansed of their Muslim inhabitants. Ivo Andrić's modernized version of Njegoš continues to be cited by reporters and taught throughout U.S. high schools and colleges as the most authentic Balkan version of Bosnian history. The works of Bat Ye'or and Jacques Ellul have become the centerpiece for the Islamophobic wing of the Global Awareness of Persecution of Christians movement, which calls for Christians to stand up against the global enemies of communism and Islam. Kaplan's model, Brodsky's "Reflections," appealed to that section of the cultural elite that dresses up its prejudice and xenophobia as art and literature. Kaplan's *Balkan Ghosts* disseminated the stereotypes that were limited to specific audiences (Serbs, political and religious circles, and the culture elite) to a wider general readership in the West, one that included congressmen, cabinet members, generals, and the president, all of whom conjured the ghosts of age-old hatred and incompatibility to construct a rationale for acquiescence in the killing.

When, after the Srebrenica massacre, NATO finally intervened, what it found was something less romantic than embattled Christian soldiers under perennial attack from the perennial enemy Islam. Behind the mask of civilizational clash, evil empire, and Muslim contamination it found the common tragedy of human history: victims who, contrary to expectations, had done nothing to deserve their fate and had threatened nobody. And perpetrators building their identity through a vain attempt to reject an other who was, in fact, a part of themselves.

Notes

1. See the extensive documentation at the Balkan War Crimes Web site: http://www.haverford.edu/relg/sells/reports.html. Among the documents are the reports of the UN special rapporteur on human rights, eight detailed U.S. State Department reports, and the indictments, rulings, and sentencings of the International Criminal Tribunal on War Crimes in the Former Yugoslavia (ICTY).

2. From the *Report of the Secretary General Pursued to Security Council Resolution 53/35 (1998): Srebrenica Report, paragraph 496*. The full report can be found at http://www.haverford.edu/relg/sells/reports/Unsrebrenicareport.htm. The following paragraphs are also essential:

495. Nonetheless, the key issue—politically, strategically and morally—underlying the security of the "safe areas" was the essential nature of "ethnic cleansing." As part of the larger ambition for a "greater Serbia," the Serbs set out to occupy the territory of the enclaves; they wanted the territory for themselves. The civilian inhabitants of the enclaves were not the incidental victims of the attackers; their death or removal was the very purpose of the attacks upon them. The tactic of employing savage terror, primarily mass killings, rapes and brutalization of civilians, to expel populations was used to the greatest extent in Bosnia and Herzegovina, where it acquired the now-infamous euphemism of "ethnic cleansing". The Bosnian Muslim civilian population thus became the principal victim of brutally aggressive military and para-military Serb operations to depopulate coveted territories in order to allow them to be repopulated by Serbs.

467. The tragedy that took place following the fall of Srebrenica is shocking for two reasons. It is shocking, first and foremost, for the magnitude of the crimes committed. Not since the horrors of World War II had Europe witnessed massacres on this scale. The mortal remains of close to 2,500 men and boys have been found on the surface, in mass grave sites and in secondary burial sites. Several thousand more men are still missing, and there is every reason to believe that additional burial sites, many of which have been probed but not exhumed, will reveal the bodies of thousands more men and boys. The great majority of those who were killed were not killed in combat: the exhumed bodies of the victims show large numbers had their hands bound, or were blindfolded, or were shot in the back or the back of the head. Numerous eyewitness accounts, now well corroborated by forensic evidence, attest to scenes of mass slaughter of unarmed victims.

468. The fall of Srebrenica is also shocking because the enclaves inhabitants believed that the authority of the United Nations Security Council, the presence of UNPROFOR peacekeepers, and the might of NATO air power would ensure their safety. Instead, the Serb forces ignored the Security Council, pushed aside the UNPROFOR troops, and assessed correctly that air power would not be used to stop them. They overran the safe area of Srebrenica with ease, and then proceeded to depopulate the territory within 48 hours. Their leaders then engaged in high-level negotiations with representatives of the international community while their forces on the ground executed and buried thousands of men and boys within a matter of days.One need only add that this refusal to recognize the Serb nationalist aims was one made in the face of three years of massive and consistent atrocities by Serb forces and open statements by Serb nationalist leaders.

The UN report also discusses the actions of the Dutchbat (Dutch UN Battalion) in Srebrenica in helping the Serb army select victims for extermination and refusing to report the atrocities. It does not detail the racism in the Dutchbat batallion, the Dutchbat senior officer drinking a toast with Mladić after he gave Srebrenica over to Mladić's killers, Dutchbat soldiers running over fleeing civilians in the armored vehicles, and the destruction of key evidence that was turned over to Dutch authorities.

For the full account of the Srebrenica massacre, see David Rohde, *Endgame: The Betrayal and Fall of Srebrenica, Europe's Worst Massacre Since World War II* (New York: Farrar, Straus and Giroux, 1997).

3. On June 9, 1995, General Bertrand Janvier, General Rupert Smith, and Special Representative to the Secretary General (SRSG) Yasushi Akashi met in Split, Croatia. This meeting in effect sealed the fate of Srebrenica and led directly to the betrayal of the Safe Haven. During the meeting Janvier and Akashi opposed Smith's argument on behalf of protecting the enclave with air-strikes. In the face of a consistent three-year pattern of organized killings of Muslims, Janvier stated the following:16. The Serbs need two things: international recognition, and a softening of the blockade of the Drina. I hope that these conditions will be met quickly, given the urgent situation. I think the Serbs are aware of how favorable the situation is to them—I don't think that they want to go to an extreme crisis. On the contrary. they want to modify their behavior, be good interlocutors. It is for this that we must speak to them—not negotiate, but to show them how important it is to have a normal attitude. From the "Transcript of the June 9, 1995 Meeting at Split: Akashi (SRSG), Janvier, and Smith." The complete transcript is available at http://www.haverford.edu/relg/sells/srebrenica/splitjune9.html

4. Bishop Petar II Petrović (Njegoš), *The Mountain Wreath (Gorski vijenac)*, trans. and ed. Vasa Mihailovich (Irvine, Ca: Schlacks Jr., 1986). This edition contains facing Serbian and English versions of the work.

5. Njegoš, *The Mountain Wreath*, verses 200–290.

6. See Marko Mladenović, "Counter-Revolution in Kosovo, Demographic Policy and Family Planning," in A. Vukadinović, ed.,, *Kosovo 1389–1989: Special Edition of the Serbian Literary Quarterly on the Occasion of Six Hundred Years Since the Battle of Kosovo* (Belgrade), *Serbian Literary Quarterly* (1989), 141–150, 141.

7. For a detailed account of the role of the Lazar story and the Vidovdan commemoration of 1989 in the motivation and justification of atrocities against Bosnian Muslims, see Michael Sells, *The Bridge Betrayed: Religion and Genocide in Bosnia* (Berkeley: University of California Press, 1996), chapters 2–4.

8. The Church's government body, the Holy Episcopal Synod, stated: "In the name of God's truth and on the testimony from our brother bishops from

Bosnia-Herzegovina and from other trustworthy witnesses, we declare, taking full moral responsibility, that such camps neither have existed nor exist in the Serbian Republic of Bosnia-Herzegovina." See "The Extraordinary Session of the Holy Episcopal Synod of the Serbian Orthodox Church in Response to the False Accusations Against the Serbian People in Bosnia-Herzegovina," *Pravoslavni misionar* (June 1992), 250–251, cited by Norman Cigar, *Genocide in Bosnia: the Policy of "Ethnic Cleansing" in Eastern Europe* (College Station: Texas A&M University Press, 1995), 89; See also the "Memorandum of the Holy Episcopal Synod's Session of May 14–20, 1992," *Pravoslavlje*, June 1, 1992, 2, in Cigar, *Genocide in Bosnia*, 78.

9. Ivo Andrić, *The Development of Spiritual Life in Bosnia Under the Influence of Turkish Rule* (Chapel Hill: Duke University Press, 1990), 20. This is the translation of Andrić's doctoral dissertation, presented to the dean of the Faculty of Philosophy at Karl Franz University in Graz, Austria on May 14, 1924, under the title *Die Entwicklung des geistigen Lebens in Bosnien unter der Einwirkung der türkischen Herrschaft*.

10. Ivo Andrić, *The Bridge on the Drina*, translated from the Serbo-Croat by Lovett F. Edwards (New York: Macmillan, 1959; Chicago: University of Chicago Press, 1977) from *Na Drini cuprija*, 1942. For an analysis of the Christoslavic symbolism of *The Bridge on the Drina*, see Sells, *The Bridge Betrayed*, 45–50. For a discussion of the role played by Andrić's story "A Letter from 1920" in the Bosnian genocide, see Ivan Lovrenović, *Bosnia: A Cultural History* (New York: New York University Press, 2001), 214–228. Lovrenović writes (221): "Nothing has changed in the 'reception' of Andrić's story since the time when it was written, long ago in 1938. In the oral culture of Bosnia-Herzegovina it usually continues to be treated as 'that letter in which Andrić said that Bosnia was a land of hatred'. Only the circumstances have changed, widening the circle of users. Thus, we saw the European negotiations (Lord Owen and others), having been given a short course of literary criticism by the Koljević-Karadžić circle, waving the letter to prove that the Bosnian apocalypse was inevitable, indeed almost deserved."

11. Bat Ye'or, *The Dhimmi: Jews and Christians Under Islam* (Madison: Farleigh Dickinson University Press, 1985), trans. David Maisel, Paul Fenton, and David Littman, with a preface by Jacques Ellul, first published as *Le Dhimmi: Profil de l'opprimé en Orient et en Afrique du Nord depuis la conquête arabe* (Paris: Anthropos, 1980). Bat Ye'or, *The Decline of Eastern Christianity Under Islam: From Jihad to Dhimmitude, Seventh-Twentieth Century*, with a foreword by Jacques Ellul, trans. Mirian Kochan and David Littman (Madison: Farleigh Dickinson University Press, 1996), first published as *Les Chrétientés d'orient entre Jihâd et Dhimmitude. VIIe–XXe siècle* (Paris: Cerf, 1991).

12. Bat Ye'or, *The Decline of Eastern Christianity*, 239.

13. For two important recent studies, see Ross Brann, *The Compunctious Poet: Cultural Ambiguity and Hebrew Poetry in Muslim Spain* (Baltimore: Johns Hopkins University Press, 1991), and Raymond Scheindlin, *Wine, Women, and Death: Medieval Hebrew Poems on the Good Life* (Philadelphia: Jewish Publication Society, 1986).

14. See María Rosa Menocal, *Ornament of the World: How Muslims, Christians, and Jews Created a Culture of Tolerance in Medieval Spain* (Boston: Little, Brown, 2001). See also the articles by Ross Brann, Raymond Scheindlin, Tova Rosen, and Rina Drory in María Rosa Menocal, Raymond Scheindlin, and Michael Sells, *The Cambridge History of Arabic Literature* (Cambridge University Press, 2000).

15. Bat Ye'or, *The Decline of Eastern Christianity*, 133–134.

16. In the literature of Serbian religious nationalism this contradiction is continually apparent. For example, in discussing the period of the Serbian-Ottoman Mehmed Pasha Sokolović, who reestablished the Serbian patriarchate, Dimitrije Bogdanović first describes how the Ottoman-authorized, Janissary-organized reestablishment of the Serbian Orthodox patriarchate was key to the linking of Serbs together as a nation [part A below], and then, without missing a beat, makes the generalized claim that the effects of Ottoman rule were "absolutely negative" [part B]: "[A] The reestablished Serb Patriarchate (1557) not only played in linking up the Serbs scattered over the Balkans and even the Pannonian plain, it was also instrumental in organizing Serbian resistance against the Turks, especially in Kosovo. By the end of the 17th century this region had reopened its former religious centers, and Serbian power to resist grew apace. The Serbs were in a desperate position under the Turks. [B] The effect of Turkish government and forced conversions to Islam, as Ivo Andrić wrote in his doctoral dissertation, was 'absolutely negative.'" Vukadinović, *Kosovo*, 147.

17. Thus, to follow the single example of Jewish secular poetry of the golden age, the literary achievements of Ibn Gabirol, Moses Ibn Ezra, Samuel the Nagid, Solomon ibn Ezra, and Judah Halevi are ignored—in writings that claim to be a tribute to the culture of non-Islamic peoples under Islamic rule.

18. Bat Ye'or, *The Decline of Eastern Christianity*, 128. For other examples of Islam as the "blood-sucking" religion, see 115 ("blood tribute," "regular blood letting") and 265 ("drained of their blood and spirit").

19. Bat Ye'or, *The Decline of Eastern Christianity*, 128. For one other example of Bat Ye'or's contempt for nomadic peoples, see Bat Ye'or, *The Decline of Eastern Christianity*, 136, where she speaks of the "contrast between nomadic wretchedness with its cultural poverty on the one hand and, on the other, the prodigious material and cultural wealth, arts, sciences, and literature of the most prestigious civilizations, Judeo-Christian and Persian." Similarly, Bat Ye'or assumes

throughout her works that nomadic Turks, like the Bedouin Arabs, are essentially devoid of culture. For the Arabian poetic tradition, see Michael Sells, *Desert Tracings: Six Classic Arabian Odes by 'Alqama, Shanfara, Labid, 'Antara, al-A'sha, and Dhu al-Rumma* (Middletown: Wesleyan University Press, 1989). For the history of dismissal of Arabic culture, in the context of poetry, see Michael Sells, "The *Qasida* and the West: Self-Reflective Stereotype and Critical Encounter, *Al-'Arabiyya* 20 (1987): 307–357.

20. William Dorich, president of SAVA (Serbian American Voters Association), and the SAVA publications are a classic example. Thus the Serbian glorious heritage of Kosovo is sumptuously illustrated and depicted in *Kosovo*, compiled and produced by William Dorich, edited by Basil W. R. Jenkins (Alhambra, Cal.: Kosovo Charity Fund '92, Serbian Orthodox diocese of Western America, 1992). At the same time, SAVA has produced a volume of virulent anti-Islamic writings, filled with presentations and stereotypes of Islam and Ottoman culture: SAVA, *The Suppressed Serbian Voice and the Free Press in America*, 2d ed. (Los Angeles: SAVA, 1994), published on Vidovdan.

21. Ivo Andrić is a classic example of the Serbian nationalist view that Ottoman rule was "absolutely negative." In his doctoral dissertation, *The Development of Spiritual Life in Bosnia Under the Influence of Turkish Rule* (Chapel Hill: Duke University Press, 1990), 23–38, after meditating on how the Oriental race of Turks hindered Serbian development, Andrić cites instances of difficulties Jews and Christians had in applying to build or rebuild synagogues and churches in Bosnia. Yet clearly those synagogues and churches were built and rebuilt and maintained. They were part of the extraordinary multireligious heritage of Bosnia that was destroyed from 1992 to 1995, not by Muslims but by Croatian and Serbian religious nationalist militias.

The case of Žitomišlići offers an illustration. See András Riedlmayer, "On the History, Significance, and Destruction of the Žitomišlići Monastery Complex, at the Community of Bosnia Foundation home page, at the Žitomišlići click on: http://www. haverford.edu/relg/sells/reports.html.

The construction was authorized by the Ottomans in 1566. After offering a short history of the origins of the monastery, András Riedlmayer makes the following comment:

> In short, while the founder of the monastery was a pious member of the Orthodox Church (and certainly not a Muslim), he and his family were part of the local Ottoman establishment. Far from being powerless subjects groaning under the "Turkish yoke" and biding their time for the distant day of liberation (as goes the nationalist historical myth), these were people integrated into a culture and society where religious boundaries did not necessarily constitute an impermeable barrier. The Hrabren family were able to amass wealth, hold official positions, serve the Sultan in

military and administrative capacities . . . at the same time that they were patrons of an important Orthodox religious foundation. Zitomišlići in its heyday (16th-18th c.) was not only an impressive work of religious art and architecture, but also a leading center of the Orthodox religious and cultural tradition in this region.

The monastery lasted through the Ottoman period. It was damaged by Croatian religious nationalists in World War II and destroyed by Croatian religious nationalists in 1993, as Serb religious nationalists were destroying all mosques and Croatian churches in territories under their control.

22. Bat Ye'or also ignores the fact that Muslims were also subject to the *devşirme*, and ignores her own earlier admission that a Janissary from the *devşirme* system, Mehmed Pasha Sokolović reestablished the Serbian patriarchy, and that this system—though unacceptable by any contemporary standards of human rights—could and did contribute to the survival of some indigenous religious communities.

23. Bat Ye'or, *The Decline of Eastern Christianity*, 258–259. Jovan Cvijić, *La Peninsule Balkanique: Géographie Humaine* (Paris: Armand Colin, 1918).

24. Bat Ye'or protests that she is only combating historicism and bringing ethics back into the writing of history. Bat Ye'or, *The Decline of Eastern Christianity*, 259. The problem, however, is not that she condemns a specific practice (devşirme, or the conditions of dhimmi communities) at a particular period in Islamic history, but that she essentializes the practices. Thus, it is correct, as Bat Ye'or states, that we can and must take a moral position on "the cruelty of enslavement, the fanaticism of medieval laws, all the barbarity that the modern conscience today condemns." But to resist moral relativity is one thing; to essentialize, to state that enslavement or inquisition or the Holocaust is the eternal essence of Christianity, for example, would be as dangerous and as arrogant as Bat Ye'or's claim that dhimmitude is the eternal essence of Islam. In addition, if one covers an entire civilization with the blanket charge of being aggressively violent and parasitic, then it becomes impossible to credibly criticize any particular crime, since all acts by the targeted civilization would be considered equally evil.

Elsewhere, Bat Ye'or traced the human rights abuses in the Sudan ruled by dictator General Omar Beshir to the Ottoman practice of *devşirme*. Bat Ye'or, *The Decline of Eastern Christianity*, 259–260. No strand of evidence was offered to link such practices to *devşirme* Horrific abductions and enslavements have taken place just across the Sudanese border. The group carrying out these abuses, with the support of the self-styled Islamic government of Omar Beshir, is the Lord's Liberation Army which, through enslaving, torturing, sexually abusing, and killing thousands of adolescent boys and girls, claims it is creating a society based upon the biblical ten commandments. As reported on National

Public Radio, August 1, 1997. These regional practices, carried out by those of Muslim and Christian affiliation, are clearly related to localized contexts.

25. Paul Gienewski's interview with Bat Ye'or, "The Return of Islam to Europe," *Midstream: A National Jewish Monthly* (March 1994), 16ff. The piece was cited by Serbian nationalists on the *New York Times* Bosnia Web forum, http://www.nytimes.com/comment/, under the title "The Islamicization of Europe."

26. Jacques Ellul, *The Betrayal of the West* (New York: Seabury Press, 1978), 16, trans. Matthew J. O'Connell, *Trahison de l'Occident.* The Islamic misogynist that Ellul uses to characterize all of Islam is Qurban Said. In this book Ellul's attack on Islam comes after his virulent attack on the World Council of Churches for the effort it was supporting at the time the book was written to end apartheid in South Africa.

27. Bat Ye'or, *The Decline of Eastern Christianity,* 257.

28. Ibid., 242–265. In their overarching assumption of the exclusively Western heritage of values of equality and respect for those of differing religions, Bat Ye'or and Ellul show special blindness on the moral ramifications of the Holocaust, the complicity or acquiescence in it by large portions of Western Christendom, and the continual refusal by much of the Christian world to confront it in an authentic way. To give one example, former French president Francois Mitterand protected and admired René Bousquet, the Vichy police official in charge of sending Jews to death camps. After Mitterand admitted in his memoirs the full extent of his collaboration with the Nazis, his popularity in France rose. For an important recent article on the silence of the Catholic Church on the problem of the Holocaust, see James Carroll, "The Silence," *New Yorker,* April 7, 1997, 52–68.

29. Jacques Ellul, "Foreword," Bat Ye'or, *The Decline of Eastern Christianity,* 18–19.

30. The placing of Christianity over Islam, with the suggestion that violence motivated by passion is superior to that motivated by duty, is yet another example of the claim of by extreme Christian apologists that Christianity offers the superior way of spirit over law. Ellul's claims of moral superiority are echoed by apologists for the Serbian and Croatian annihilation of Bosnian Muslim cultural heritage and peoples. We are all guilty, Serb religious nationalists argue (original sin), but crimes by Christians are done out of passion, against the teachings of their religion, while those by Muslims are done out of duty, in accordance with the teachings of their religion.

31. Ellul, "Foreword," 29: "The Christian concept of God or of Jesus Christ is no longer the same for Christians today as it was in the Middle Ages, and one can multiply examples. But precisely what seems to me interesting and striking about Islam, one of its peculiarities, is the fixity of its concepts." Cf. Jacques

Ellul, "Foreword," *The Decline of Eastern Christianity*, 21. "But whatever the evolution, it must never be forgotten that it can only be superficial because doctrine and conduct are based upon a religious foundation: even if this may seem to be weakened or modified, nevertheless what I have elsewhere called the 'persistence of religiousness' remains unchanged. In other words, even if the rites, structures, and customs are all that continue to exist of a once-strong religion — today, seemingly neglected — these visible survivals only need a spark for everything immediately to revive, sometimes violently."

32. Dr. Miroljub Jevtić, professor at Belgrade University, *Vreme*, November 21, 1994.

33. The groups lobbying for such congressional hearings claim that Christians are being persecuted at a rate unprecedented in history, that Christians are being persecuted in a manner far greater than any other religion, that the persecution of Christians now is the equivalent to the persecution of Jews in the Holocaust. The movement is led by evangelical Christian organizations such as Voice of the Martyrs, Campus Crusade for Christ, the Southern Baptist Convention, the National Association of Evangelicals, World Evangelical Fellowship, Christian Solidarity International, along with right-wing lobbying groups such as the Christian Coalition, Freedom House, the Family Research Council, and Empower American. Individuals of prominence within this movement include Nina Shea, Baroness Cox, Charles Colson (the former Watergate criminal turned evangelist), and two militant Jewish writers: A. M. Rosenthal and Michael Horowitz. Among the more influential literature, in addition to the works of Bat Ye'or and Jacques Ellul, are Paul Marshall, with Lela Gilbert, *Their Blood Cries Out: The Worldwide Tragedy of Modern Christians Who Are Dying for Their Faith*, introduction by Michael Horowitz (Dallas: Word, 1997), and Nina Shea, *In the Lion's Den: A Shocking Account of Persecution and Martyrdom of Christians Today and How We Should Respond*, foreword by Chuck Colson (Nashville: Broadman and Holman, 1997).

34. The two central chapters of Shea's *In the Lion's Den*, for example, are "Persecution in Islamic Countries," and "Persecution in Communist Countries." Shea, *In the Lion's Den*, 26–56 and 57–84.

   See also Bat Ye'or, "Past is Prologue: The Challenge of Islamism Today," U.S. Congressional Briefing, Human Rights Caucus, "The Persecution of Christians Worldwide," Tuesday, April 29, 1997, 2:00–4:00 p.m. While Bat Ye'or pleads in her statement that the Global Awareness movement should not become anti-Islamic, the statement incorporates the same essentialist stereotypes about Islam as her books. The years 1996–1997 saw a resurgence of Christian Awareness events in the U.S. Congress, with hearings, resolutions, briefings, and acts. See also "Persecution of Christians Worldwide," Hearing Before the Subcommittee on International Operations and Human Rights of the Committee on International Relations, House of Representatives, 104th Congress, February 15, 1996.

35. Bat Ye'or's characterizations were taken up with enthusiasm by Father Richard John Neuhaus in his column in *First Things: The Journal of the Institute of Religion and Public Life*. See the article entitled "Approaching the Century of Religion," in the Neuhaus's section entitled *First Things* (October 1997): 75–93, available online at http://www.firstthings.com/ftissues/ft9710/public.html. Neuhaus was particularly impressed with Bat Ye'or's characterization of Islamic civilizations as parasitic, living off of the blood of captive civilizations. See Bat Ye'or, *The Decline of Eastern Christianity*, 115, 128 (where Islamic civilization is characterized as "feeding off their [the subject peoples'] vigor and on the dying, bloodless body of dhimmitude"), and 165. Neuhaus also championed Bat Ye'or's characterization of Islam as based on the absolute division between the House of Islam and the House of War and, not unsurprisingly, explains that the same characterization was given by "that intrepid scholar Bernard Lewis." He also asserts that the nature of Islam as jihad as formulated by Bat Ye'or can be seen in Bosnia.

36. Ellul, "Foreword," Bat Ye'or, *The Decline of Eastern Christianity*, 20; Bat Ye'or, *The Decline of Eastern Christianity*, 217–220.

37. Ibid., 21; Ibid., 220.

38. Elizabeth Drew, *On the Edge: The Clinton Presidency* (New York: Simon and Schuster, 1994), 157–163.

39. Robert Kaplan, *Balkan Ghosts: A Journey Through History* (New York: St. Martin's, 1993).

40. Robert Kaplan, *Soldiers of God: With Islamic Warriors in Afghanistan and Pakistan* (New York: Random House, 2001), 49.

41. Robert Kaplan, *The Arabists: TheRomance of an American Elite* (New York: Free, 1993).

42. The films were produced by George Lucas and Stephen Spielberg, and directed by Stephen Spielberg, with actor Harrison Ford playing Indiana Jones: George Lucas and Stephen Spielberg, *Raiders of the Lost Ark*, Paramount, 1981; *Indiana Jones and the Temple of Doom* (Paramount, 1984); and *Indiana Jones and the Last Crusade* (Paramount, 1989).

43. Rebecca West as quoted by Robert Kaplan, frontpiece to the prologue, *Balkan Ghosts*, xiv. Rebecca West, *The Black Lamb and the Gray Falcon* (New York: Viking, 1941). For an excellent analysis of the influence of Rebecca West on Western reporting of the Bosnia tragedy, see Brian Hall, "Rebecca West's War," *New Yorker*, April 15, 1996, 74–83.

44. Journalists and commentators on the Balkans have made West, along with Ivo Andrić, a foundational source on Bosnian culture, history, and religion. In *The Black Lamb and the Gray Falcon* she assumes the Serbian nationalist view of

history as well as the ambivalence common within Serbian religious mythology. The gray falcon in the title refers to the falcon that came as Elijah to Prince Lazar and offered him the choice of the kingdom of heaven or the earthly kingdom. Lazar, following the example of Jesus during his temptation in the desert, chooses the heavenly kingdom and is defeated in battle, leading to the five-hundred-year Ottomans' rule.

Serb religious nationalists cite Lazar as the example of Serbian Orthodox pacifism and cite Christian pacifism as the reason the superiority of Christianity over Islam. Yet this glorification of the martyrdom of Lazar brings ambivalence: the more Lazar's pacific response is emphasized, the deeper the desire for revenge. Thus extreme Serb nationalism can advocate the most ruthless violence under the guise of a defense of Christianity that is superior because of the pacifist response shown by the victim at Golgotha and, later, at the Serb Golgotha. The dual version can be seen in the two major characters celebrated in Lazar commemorations: Lazar, the holy symbol of the choice of the heavenly kingdom, and Milos Obilić, Lazar's knight who avenges the fallen Christ-prince by killing the sultan Murad, thus becoming the role model par excellence for Serbian religious nationalists. After Serbian militias carried out their ethnic cleansing, the most violent and effective leaders of the cleansing operations were given "Miloš Obilić" medals of heroism, in ceremonies marked by both civic and religious pomp and circumstance.

45. He describes a Serbian portrait of John the Baptist as showing the "oriental strength" that is the key to Serbian history. Kaplan, *Balkan Ghosts*, 30. In describing a painting of the medieval Serbian king Milutin, who built many of the great monasteries, Kaplan writes that "virility dripped from Milutin's gold-encrusted sleeves." After interviewing a Serbian nun in Kosovo, he relates with obvious assent her complaint that had it not been for the Ottoman Turks the Serbs would have been "greater than the Italians." The tragedy is that the Serb nun had no cause to feel inferior to the Italians in the first place, given the extraordinary richness of classical Serbian culture.

   West, quoted ibid, 32.

46. Ibid.

47. Ibid, 35.

48. Joseph Brodsky, "Reflections (Byzantium)," *New Yorker*, October 28, 1985, 73–74, reflection 39.

49. Ibid., 47, reflection 9. Here is quote from reflection 33:

> How familiar it all, including the slaughter, is! All these turbans and beards, that uniform for heads possessed by one idea only—massacre . . . totally indistinguishable from one another! and perhaps "massacre" precisely because all are so much alike that there is no way to detect a loss. "I massacre, therefore I exist."

Then there is this from Brodsky's number 24:

> We are castrating a bastard, so that when he grows up there will be no
> extra claim to the throne. That, indeed, is the Eastern attitude toward
> things—toward the human body in particular—and whatever era or
> milennium it is is irrelevant. So it is hardly suprising that the Roman
> Church turned its nose away from Byzantium.

    Brodsky seemed unaware that castrati were a prized aesthetic attraction in
the Vatican choir until the last century.

50. Kaplan, *Balkan Ghosts*, 42.
51. Ibid., 41
52. Ibid., 48.
53. Ibid., 41.
54. Ibid., 41.
55. Ibid., 283.
56. Robert Kaplan, "Limited Options in Serbia," *New York Times*, January 14, 1997, A15.
57. Brodsky, "Reflections," 78, reflection 43.

> Presumably, it would have made sense to make friends with someone, get
> into contact, look at the life of the place from the inside, instead of dis-
> missing the local population as an alien crowd, instead of regarding peo-
> ple as so much psychological dust in one's eyes.
>   Who knows? Perhaps my attitude toward people has in its own right a
> whiff of the East about it, too.

58. Ibid, 39, reflection 1.
59. Elisabeth Young-Bruehl, *The Anatomy of Prejudice* (Cambridge: Harvard University Press, 1996), 33–34.
60. Tomaž Mastnak writes of this fear, particularly as it relates to the question of Turkey's acceptance into the European Union: "The question of whether to affiliate the countries we today call Eastern Europe to his united and peaceful Europe, raised the quandary of Europe's eastern border. To this question that still besets 'European Europeans' and would-be-Europeans in our own times, Sully gave the following answer: 'The peoples living in those lands were partly idolaters and partly schismatics, and belonged 'to Asia at least as much as to Europe' Almost barbarous, they and their 'infidel princes who refuse to con-form to any of the Christian doctrines of religion' were to be forced entirely out of Europe. Any contact with the Turks and Tartars, even fighting wars against them, rendered Poles, Prussians, Livonians, Muscovites and Transylvanians 'in some manner foreign in regard to those of the Western part of Europe.' See Mastnak, "Europe and the Muslims," this volume.

61. Mary Douglas, *Purity and Danger: An Analysis of Concepts of Pollution and Taboo* (New York: Praeger, 1966).

62. See Sells, *The Bridge Betrayed*, 21–24, 172–173.

63. The interdicted sacrality of the Ka'ba precinct and the interdicted sacrality of the woman are challenges to the Serb religious nationalist, the French Christian apologist and missionary, and the American writer-adventurer. The repeated efforts to penetrate the harem can lead to a polarization where each effort to penetrate the harem results in the countereffort to protect it more securely. Kaplan cites his own conversations with Central Asian women who are veiled and reveals that as they were speaking he was obsessed with how they looked under their veils. He also cites an Iranian who states that the extreme form of the chador is just a reaction to Western threats against Islam and will disappear as soon as the Iranian-West polarization is reduced. See Kaplan, *The Ends of the Earth*, 225–226, 229. Women are placed at the center of conflict between men. Farzaneh Milani has written of how both forced unveiling (by the two Shah regimes) and forced veiling in Iran (by the regimes of mullas) have made women the object of an inverse-obverse related form of violence; for a woman accustomed to complete covering, forced veiling and forced removal of the chador are equally violent. Concepts of privacy and nakedness are culturally relative; for an Iranian woman in the period of the first Shah, forced removal of the chador in public could be the equivalent of a woman being stripped naked and forced to walk down a public street in the West. Throughout her work Milani offers an alternative to the exploitation of women in East-West polemics over the veiling. See Farzaneh Milani, *Veils and Words: The Emerging Voices of Iranian Women Writers* (Syracuse: Syracuse University Press, 1992).

Serb nationalists have attacked the victims of rape in Bosnia by demanding an exact number count to prove allegations, now overwhelmingly established, of organized rape. The few women who have publicly spoken have been subjected to savage attack. The vast majority remain silent, marginalized within their Mediterranean society that views rape as a shame and responsibility of the victim. In many cases the rape victims, alienated from community, family, and sense of future, have been made to disappear. Meanwhile, the new Serb nationalist mayors of the towns of Foča and Zvornik, when asked why all the mosques had been destroyed, replied that there "never were any mosques" in their towns. There are blank spaces throughout Bosnia-Herzegovina, areas blasted free of memory. Yet the programmatic nature of the mosque destructions has been far more difficult to conceal than the rapes; mosque destruction served as a key sign and clue that other organized atrocities were taking place out of view.

64. For documentation and analysis of the cultural annihilation in Bosnia, see András Riedlmayer, *Killing Memory: Bosnia's Cultural Heritage and Its*

Destruction (Philadelphia and Haverford: Community of Bosnia Foundation, 1994), András Riedlmayer, "From the Ashes: The Past and Future of Bosnia's Cultural Heritage," in Maya Shatzmiller, ed., *Islam and Bosnia* (Montreal: McGill-Queen's University Press, 2002), 98–135, and András Riedlmayer, "Convivencia Under Fire: Genocide and Book Burning in Bosnia," in Jonathan Rose, ed., *The Holocaust and the Book: Destruction and Preservation* (Amherst: University of Massachusetts Press, 2001), 266–291.

65. See the indictments and transcripts for the International Criminal Tribunal trials of the commandants and guards of the Keraterm and Omarska concentration camps. The tribunal documentation is corroborated by reports of the U.S. State Department, the U.N. special rapporteur, and numerous accounts of survivors. For all these reports and indictments, see http://www.haverford.edu/relf/sells/reports.html.

66. Kaplan, *Balkan Ghosts*, 286.

Contributors

Norman Cigar, who is on the faculty of the U.S. Marine Corps Command and Staff College and a senior associate with the Public International Law and Policy Group, has written extensively on the Balkans and has consulted for the International Criminal Tribunal for the former Yugoslavia at the Hague.

Mujeeb R. Khan is a doctoral candidate in political philosophy at the University of Chicago. He is a past recipient of a Fulbright Scholarship. He has written extensively on the war in Bosnia-Herzegovina.

Neil MacMaster, senior lecturer in European Politics at the University of East Anglia (UK), is the author of *Colonial Migrants and Racism: Algerians in France, 1900–62* and *Racism in Europe 1870–2000*. He is currently completing a coauthored book, *Paris Massacre: Papon, Algeria and Post-Colonial memories* for Oxford University Press.

Tomaž Mastnak is a senior research scientist at the Institute of Philosophy at the Center of Scientific Research, Slovene Academy of Arts and Sciences. He has been a visiting scholar at King's College, University of Cambridge and Harvard's Center for European Studies. He has recently completed a major study on European Union identity formation.

María Rosa Menocal is director of the Whitney Humanities Center at Yale University and has been writing for many years on the complexities of medieval culture. Most recently she coedited *The Cambridge History of Arabic Literature: Al-Andalus* with Raymond Scheindlin and Michael Sells (Cambridge, 2000) and she is the author of *The Ornament of the World: How Muslims, Jews, and Christians Created a Culture of Tolerance in Medieval Spain* (Little, Brown, 2002).

Fatema Mernissi is a professor of sociology at the University of Mohammed V in Rabat, Morocco. An Islamic feminist whose books have been published in twenty-six countries, she is the best-selling author of *Dreams of Trespass, Tales of a Harem Girlhood, The Veil and the Male Elite,* and *Beyond the Veil.*

Roy P. Mottahedeh is Gurney Professor of Islamic History and chair, Committee on Islamic Studies at Harvard University. He is the author of *The Mantle of the Prophet, Religion and Politics in Iran,* as well as numerous contributions to books, journals, and newspapers.

Rob Nixon is Rachel Carson Professor of English at the University of Wisconsin–Madison. He is the author of *London Calling: V.S. Naipaul, Postcolonial Mandarin; Homelands, Harlem,* and *Hollywood: South African Culture and the World Beyond,* and *Dreambirds.* He is the recipient of a Guggenheim and is a frequent contributor to the *New York Times.* His work has appeared in the *New Yorker,* the *Nation,* the *Village Voice,* the *Atlantic,* the *London Review of Books,* and elsewhere.

Emran Qureshi is an independent scholar and freelance journalist. His articles and reviews have appeared in the *Los Angeles Times,* the *Toronto Globe and Mail,* the *Washington Post,* and the *Guardian Weekly.* He resides in Ottawa, where he is working on his next book, a study of Islam and human rights.

Edward W. Said is University Professor of English and Comparative Literature at Columbia University. He is the author of more than twenty books, including *Orientalism, Culture and Imperialism, Power, Politics, and Culture,* and, most recently, *Parallels and Paradoxes.* His books have been published in thirty-six languages.

Michael A. Sells is Emily Judson Baugh and John Marshall Gest Professor of Comparative Religions at Haverford College. He is the author of *The Bridge Betrayed: Religion and Genocide in Bosnia* and six other books on Arabic poetry, mystical language, and the Qur'an. He is currently working on a new book, *Jihad and Crusade,* that offers a critique of religiously motivated violence in both the Islamic and Western context.

John Trumpbour is the research director for the Labor and Worklife Program at Harvard Law School. He is the author of *Selling Hollywood to the World: U.S. and European Struggles for Mastery of the Global Film Industry, 1920–1950,* which won the Allan Nevins Prize for Literary Excellence in History from the Society of American Historians. He is also the editor of *The Dividing Rhine: Politics and Society in Contemporary France and Germany* and *How Harvard Rules: Reason in the Service of Empire.* He and Elaine Bernard recently wrote a history of Latinos and the U.S. labor movement for the collection *Latinos Remaking America.*

Index

Abderazik, Ali: *Al-Islām wa Usūl al-Hukm* (Islam and the Foundations of Power), 66n16

Abiola, Mashood, 135

Abkhazians, 135

Abrahamic religions: defined against one another, 4; violently intolerant, 31n6

Aćin, Zdenka, 339n16

Achebe, Chinua, 154

Adab, 33n11

Adams, Henry, 77

Adonis, 76

Adrianople, 370

Afghanistan: dangers of Wahhabi influence, 16–17; war fought between the West and the Soviet Union, 6

African Americans: neoconservative view of assimilation, 112; reversals in the depictions of, 77

Afrocentrism, 75

"Age of Faith," 255

Ahmad, Eqbal, 166–67; on effects of colonialism and modernization on traditional Muslim order, 163; on Naipaul's ideology of conversion, 19–20; political ideas, vii–viii; in regard to U.S. support for the Afghani mujahidin, 17

Airbus hijacking, 302

Ajami, Fouad, 92

Akashi, Yasushi, 377n3

Al-ahmad, Jalal, 161

Al Ahram Weekly, 59

Al-Andalus, 274n5, 285n22; Arabic poetry, 269; centrality of to Arabic history, 280n12; dominance in medieval world, 250; Hebrew poetry, 268, 360–61; Hispano-Arabic poetry, 274n5, 285n22;

Islamicate civilization in, 22; richness of culture, 269

Al-Andalus (Al-Qantara), 274n5

Al-Anfal, genocide campaign against Kurds, 13

Al Azmeh, Aziz: *Secularism in Modern Arab Life*, 57–58; *Thought (al' ilmaniya)*, 57–58

Albanians: artificial distinction between "honorable" and others, 344n49; confrontations with Serbs, 356; in Kosovo, 345n59; nationalism, 34n20; perceived as dangerous, 345n55; perceived as unassimilable, 351n86; as primarily Muslim, 330, 336; Serbian plan to remove from Kosovo, 317

Alberoni, Cardinal Giulio, 227–28

Alcalay, Ammiel, 34n17

Alfonso II, 272n4

Algeria, 23; assassination of French citizens in, 302; crisis in, and the Islamic "fifth column," 302–5; independence, 79, 294; question of nationality, 79; uprising, 300; War of 1954–1962, 293–94

Algerian Liberation Army, 293

Algerians: guest workers, 23; largest non-European immigrant presence in Europe before 1945, 291; struggle for national independence, 293

Algerians in France: and assimilation, 290; ghettoization and social exclusion, 303; increase in after 1962, 294; resistance to integration into French society, 292–93; target of large-scale police operations in Paris, 293; during World War I, 291

Aljamiado text, 267

Allport, Gordon W., 351n83